THE ANNUAL OF THE TYPE DIRECTORS CLUB

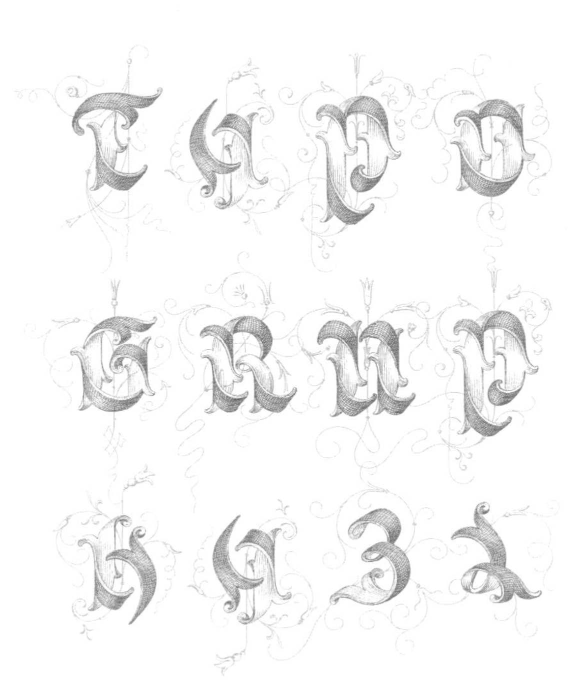

HARPER
DESIGN
An Imprint of HarperCollinsPublishers

MIKE PARKER & ERIK SPIEKERMANN

Mike Parker received the TDC Medal on April 6, 2011, at the Type Directors Club office.

MIKE PARKER

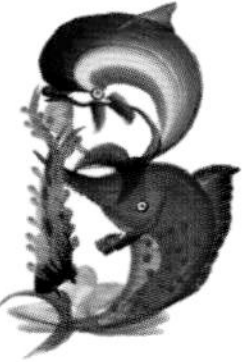ritish by birth, but American thereafter, Parker is a prominent figure in the development of the type industry from hot metal through photocomposition to digital, and he played a major part in turning type design and technology into a digital medium. As Director of Typography for Mergenthaler Linotype, he managed the production of more than a thousand typefaces. In 1981, he and Matthew Carter co-founded Bitstream, the first all-digital type company. In 2000, Parker joined David Berlow and Roger Black at the Font Bureau as a consultant, type historian, and type designer.

Born in London in 1929, Parker has degrees in architecture and graphic design from Yale. After receiving his MFA in 1956, he was selected to spend eighteen months cataloguing the extraordinary collection of punches, matrixes, and molds at the Plantin Moretus Museum in Antwerp, Belgium. This is a comprehensive collection of the sixteenth century type founders' artifacts. The Museum remains virtually unchanged to this day and, as Parker describes it, "The Plantin Museum is the biggest physical manifestation of history anywhere, of any time. Everything is real."

Jackson Burke at Mergenthaler Linotype believed that this experience might be valuable in preparing type libraries for photocomposition machines. As Director of Typography, Parker managed the expansion of the Linotype library from a collection of 150 American hot metal designs for text-setting to an inclusive library of nearly 1,500 international digital designs, including complete series of Hebrew and Greek scripts, for full page setting. This was made possible through Parker's organization of shared typeface development among the five separate companies in the Linotype Group worldwide. Parker was responsible for bringing in internationally known designers such as Matthew Carter, Adrian Frutiger, and Hermann Zapf. The result was a library that became the standard of the industry.

In 1981 he left Linotype with Matthew Carter to found Bitstream in Cambridge, Massachusetts, the first font company based purely on digital technology. While revenues from the sale of typesetting equipment were dwindling in the 1980s, they recognized a business opportunity in the design and sale of type itself, due to the changing technologies that allowed type to be independent of equipment. Bitstream developed a library of digital type that could be licensed for use by anyone. He went on to found The Company (la Societe Anonyme) in 1987, and Pages Software in 1990. Pages developed a word processor on the NeXT platform that provided the writer with powerful graphic support for readership online or on paper. Pages was in the beta stage of development when the Next Computer and the NextStep platform were discontinued in 1995. Upon the closing of Pages Software in 1995, Parker licensed the Pages patent to Design Intelligence in Seattle and joined the company as an in-house consultant. In 2000, Design Intelligence was bought by Microsoft. The same year, Parker joined Roger Black and David Berlow in their co-founded company, the Font Bureau, as a consultant, type historian, and type designer.

In 1994, Parker published evidence that the design of Times New Roman, credited to Stanley Morison in 1931, was based on William Starling Burgess's 1904 drawings for Lanston Monotype Foundry. In 2009, Parker released "Starling," a roman font with a matching italic series.

SCULPTURE GARDEN

BLACK

HOURS DEBATING THE ORIGIN OF CONTEXT

ROMAN

Bronze Rhinoceros

ITALIC

Imposing herd of 1,602 wildebeests

BOLD

Realism

ULTRA

I Could Swear I Heard Hoofbeats

BOOK ITALIC

Minimalist Ostrich

HEAVY

She awoke briefly during the endless oration

BOOK

DRY ACADEMICIANS

BOLD

Shall we examine these 45 cultural assumptions?

BOLD ITALIC

Lecture Hall

ULTRA ITALIC

Skeptical Feline Scholar

BOLD SMALL CAPS

POUNCED

BOOK

In 1904 William Starling Burgess, Boston racing sailor, designed his second type. Six years later, now the Wright Brothers' partner, Starling quit type, returning the drawings to Monotype. Frank Pierpont collected the nameless roman for British Monotype, passing it to Stanley Morison in 1932 for the *London Times.* Mike Parker found the original superior, and prepared this Starling series for Font Bureau, who found it to be "the right stuff"; FB 2009

12 STYLES: BOOK, ROMAN, BOLD, HEAVY, BLACK, AND ULTRA; ALL WITH ITALICS AND INCLUDING SMALL CAPS

ERIK SPIEKERMANN

Erik Spiekermann received the TDC Medal on June 6, 2011, at the Cooper Union in New York City.

Born in Stadthagen, Germany, in 1947, Spiekermann studied art history at Berlin's Free University, funding himself by running a hot metal printing press in the basement of his house. Between 1972 and 1979 he was a freelance graphic designer in London, and then returned to Berlin and founded MetaDesign with two partners. MetaDesign, which became Germany's largest design firm, combined clean information design with complex corporate design systems for clients including BVG (Berlin Transit), Düsseldorf Airport, Audi, Volkswagen, and Heidelberg Printing. In 1989 Spiekermann and his wife, Joan, and Neville Brody started FontShop, the first mail-order distributor for digital fonts. FSI FontShop International followed, which now publishes the FontFont range of typefaces. In 2001 Spiekermann left MetaDesign and started UDN | United Designers Networks, with offices in Berlin, London, and San Francisco. UDN became SpiekermannPartners in 2007, and in 2009 was renamed Edenspiekermann.

Spiekermann has designed both commercially available and proprietary typefaces as part of corporate design programs. His faces include ITC Officina Sans (1990), ITC Officina Serif (1990), FF Meta (1991–1998), FF Govan (2001), FF Info (2000), FF Unit (2003), and FF Meta Serif (with Christian Schwartz and Kris Sowersby, 2007).

Spiekermann wrote *Rhyme & Reason: A Typographic Novel* in 1987 and co-authored *Stop Stealing Sheep & Find Out How Type Works* with E. M. Ginger in 1993.

Spiekermann is Honorary Professor at the University of the Arts in Bremen and has served on the Boards of ATypI and the German Design Council. He is Past President of the ISTD (International Society of Typographic Designers), and the IIID (International Institute for Information Design).

In 2003 Spiekermann received the Gerrit Noordzij Award from the Royal Academy in The Hague. In 2006 the Art Center College of Design in Pasadena, California, awarded him an Honorary Doctorate for his contribution to design. In the same year his family of typefaces for Deutsche Bahn (German Railways), designed with Christian Schwartz, received a Gold Medal at the German Federal Design Prize, the highest such award in Germany. In 2007 Spiekermann was named to the European Design Hall of Fame and was declared Honorary Royal Designer for Industry by the RSA (Royal Society for the encouragement of Arts, Manufactures and Commerce) in London. In 2009 he was named Ambassador for the European Year of Creativity and Innovation by the European Union, and in 2011 he was recognized with the German Design Award for Lifetime Achievement.

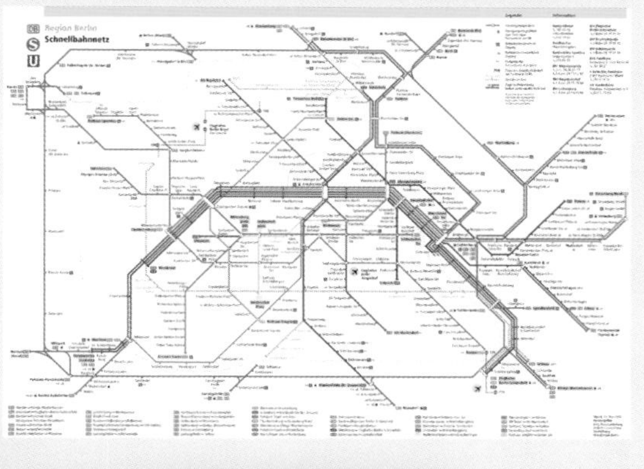

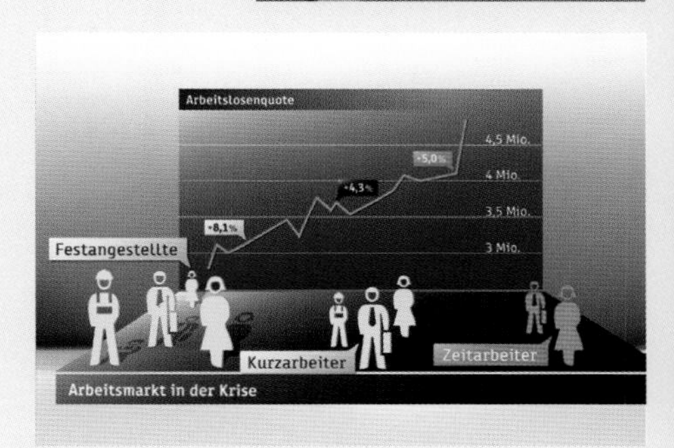

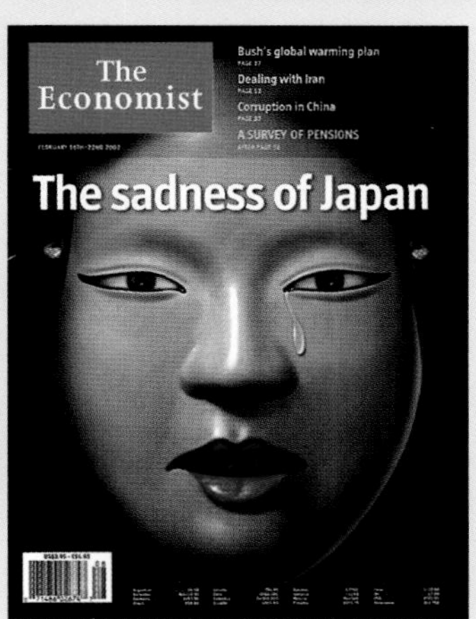

CREDITS Clockwise from top left

AUDI My team at MetaDesign redesigned the Audi brand between 1994 and 1997. **BOOKS** Some of the books I wrote and designed. **BERLINTRANSIT DIAGRAM** When the two halves of Berlin were re-united in 1990, the diagram for the newly combined transit system was a major factor in bringing people back together. **DÜSSELDORF INFOSIGN** We designed the passenger information system for Düsseldorf Airport using a specially designed typeface, FF Info. **ECONOMIST COVER** I redesigned *The Economist* in 2001. It hasn't been changed since. **TV TYPE** We designed the typeface and lots of icons for Germany's public TV channel, ZDF **FONTBOOK** I have designed and edited this book since it first appeared in 1991. **FF META HOUSENUMBERS** Made in cast aluminum for Design Within Reach.

CHAIRMAN'S STATEMENT

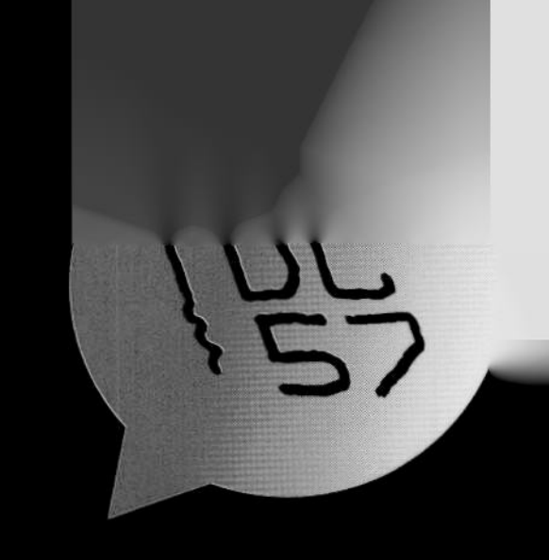

"It stinks!"

"Too much good work being done, all around . . . and not by me!"

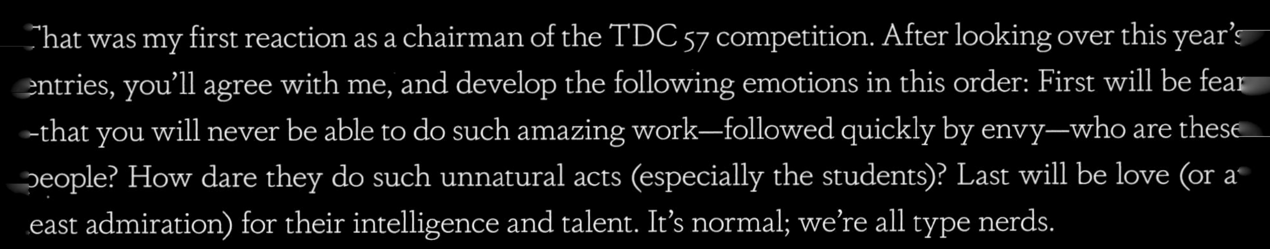

That was my first reaction as a chairman of the TDC 57 competition. After looking over this year's entries, you'll agree with me, and develop the following emotions in this order: First will be fear—that you will never be able to do such amazing work—followed quickly by envy—who are these people? How dare they do such unnatural acts (especially the students)? Last will be love (or at least admiration) for their intelligence and talent. It's normal; we're all type nerds.

The TDC 57 entries were especially tough on our judges—Art Chantry, Arem Duplessis, Fons Hickmann, Mario Hugo, Jason Kernevich (Heads of State), Angela Voulangas, and Bruce Willen (Post Typography). While I knew of their incredible work, I had never met most of them personally. Unlike other competitions where the judges were "too cool" to express any emotion or find outstanding examples of typographic excellence, this was not the case this year. They were a very vocal group and extremely passionate about type (we had to hose them down a couple of times).

There were three changes in this year's competition. First, we introduced a "Best in Show" category (or what we call "The King {or Queen} of Type"). A beautiful poster by veteran Niklaus Troxler won the crown, with the combination of stunning lettering and expressive sensibility. He was awarded a beautiful trophy designed by Graham Clifford at our annual ceremony in NYC this past summer. The second change was the introduction of the "Unpublished" category. It revealed a trove of unseen work done for ungrateful clients, as well as personal projects by designers who relish burning the midnight oil.

The third change was going paperless on our "call for entries." We were all nervous that we were going to be lost and forgotten in everyone's "junk" e-mail folder. Happily, that was not the case. Matteo Bologna (who designed this beautiful tome) created the campaign of "type nerds" that very successfully grabbed the attention of our type community. My thanks to him for his wise counsel, fathomless talent, and effervescent good nature. I would also like to thank Carol Wahler for her invaluable work. The TDC operation is extremely complex, and she single-handedly coordinates it all so masterfully.

In other trends, the TDC is becoming more and more global. This year, we had entries from 30 countries, and winners from 17 of them. We saw a decrease in entries in categories like Annual Reports and Brochures, and an increase in Books and Digital Media (perhaps due to the fragility of the world economy or just better taste in the quality of the reading material).

After all that the only words of wisdom that I can share are "go forth and kern ... "

COMM
UNIC
ATION
DESIG
N

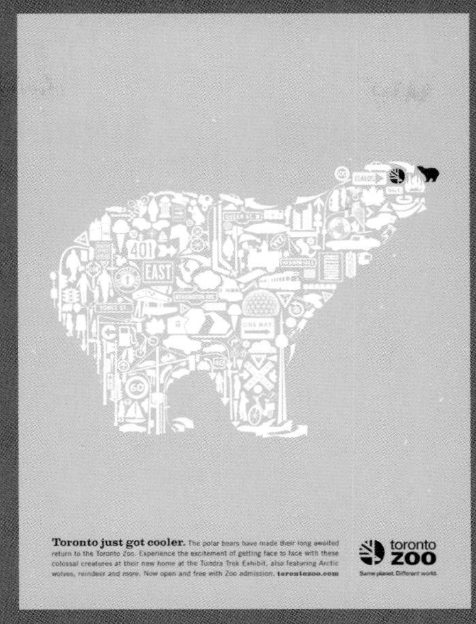

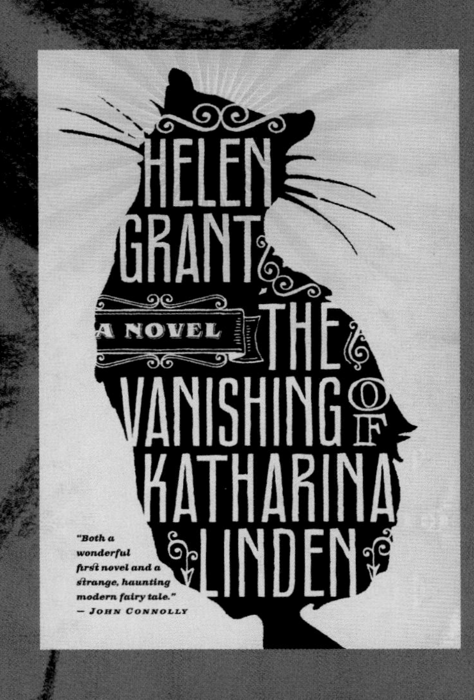

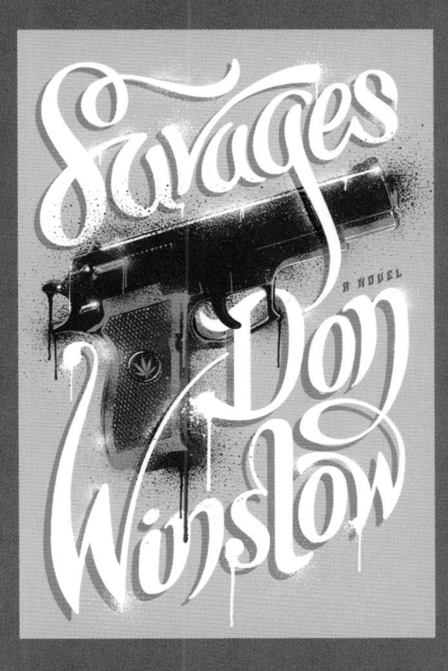

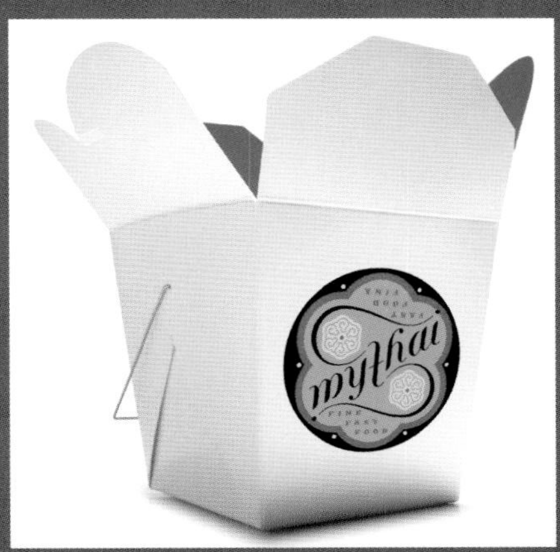

TDC 57 CHAIR

ROBERTO DE VICQ DE CUMPTICH

Roberto de Vicq de Cumptich is currently principal at his own design firm in NYC specializing in publications, restaurant design, and branding. He speaks frequently on typography and type design. He is also the author of several books featuring his own work. His most recent book, *To All Men of Letters and People of Substance*, was selected as one of the AIGA's 50 best books of 2008. He has received numerous awards from the Art Directors Club, AIGA, D&AD, *Communication Arts, Eye, Graphis, How, Print,* and Type Directors Club, and two Webby Awards. He is on the board of the Type Directors Club, and was the chairman for the TDC competition of 2011.

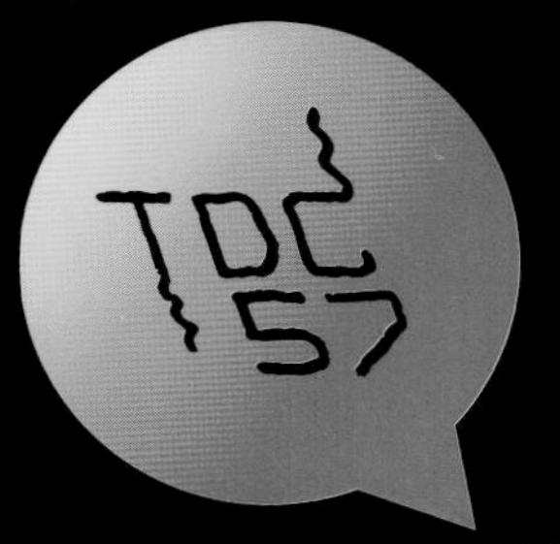

BEST IN SHOW

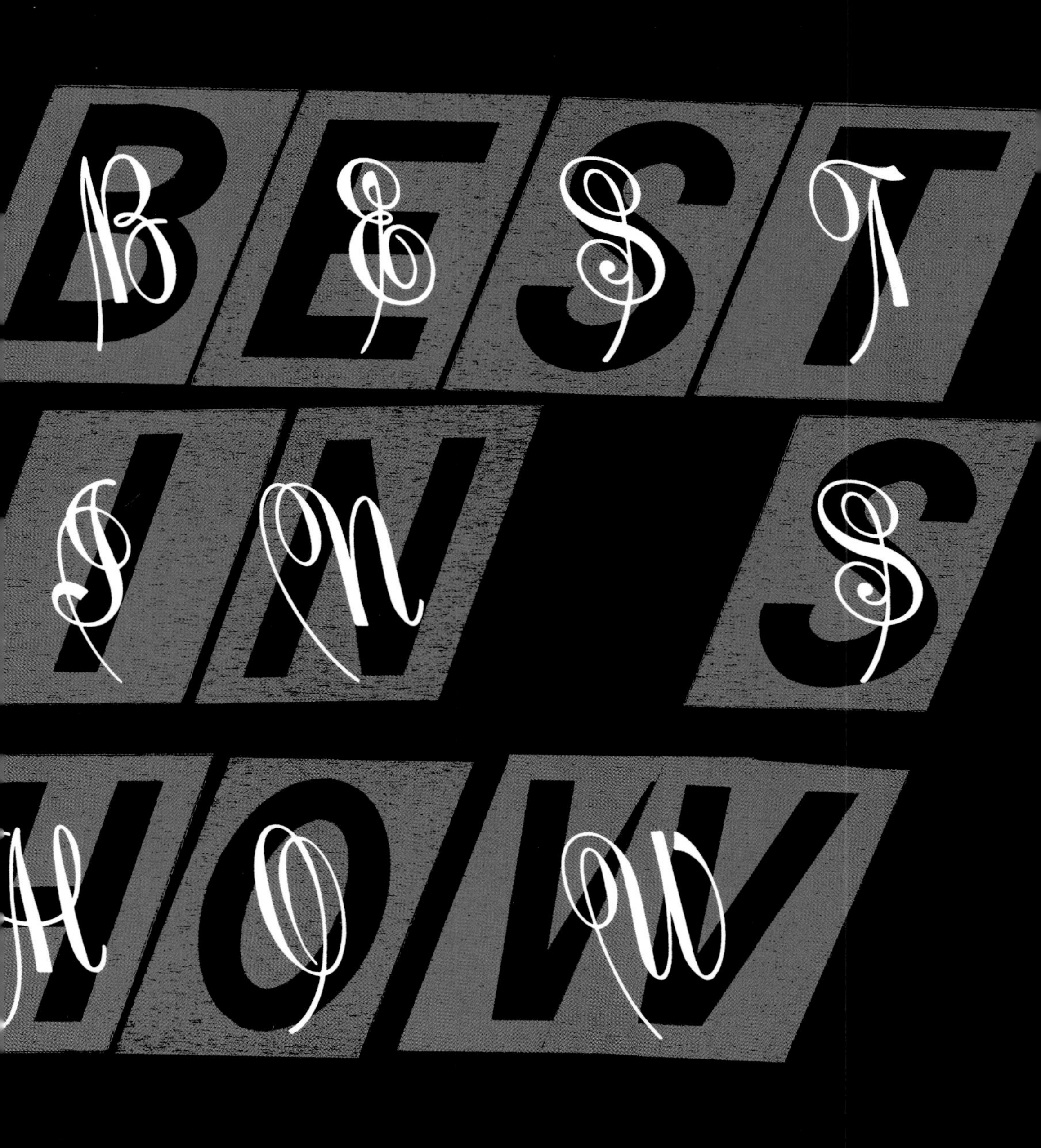
BEST
IN S
HOW

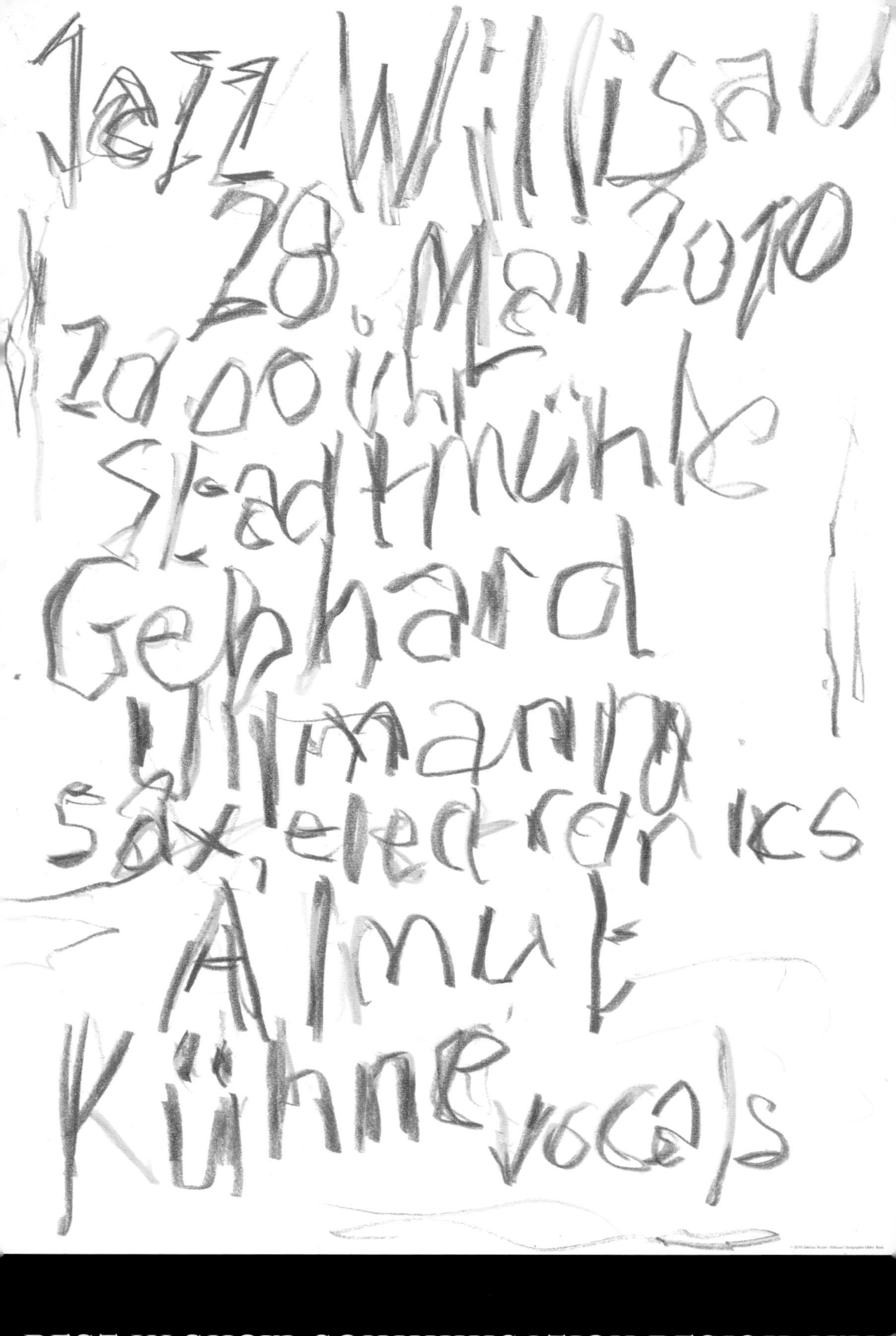

er BEST IN SHOW, COMMUNICATION DESIGN AWA

Niklaus Troxler, *Willisau, Switzerland* LETTERING Niklaus Troxler, DESIGN OFFICE Niklaus Troxler Design, CLIENT Jazz in Willisau

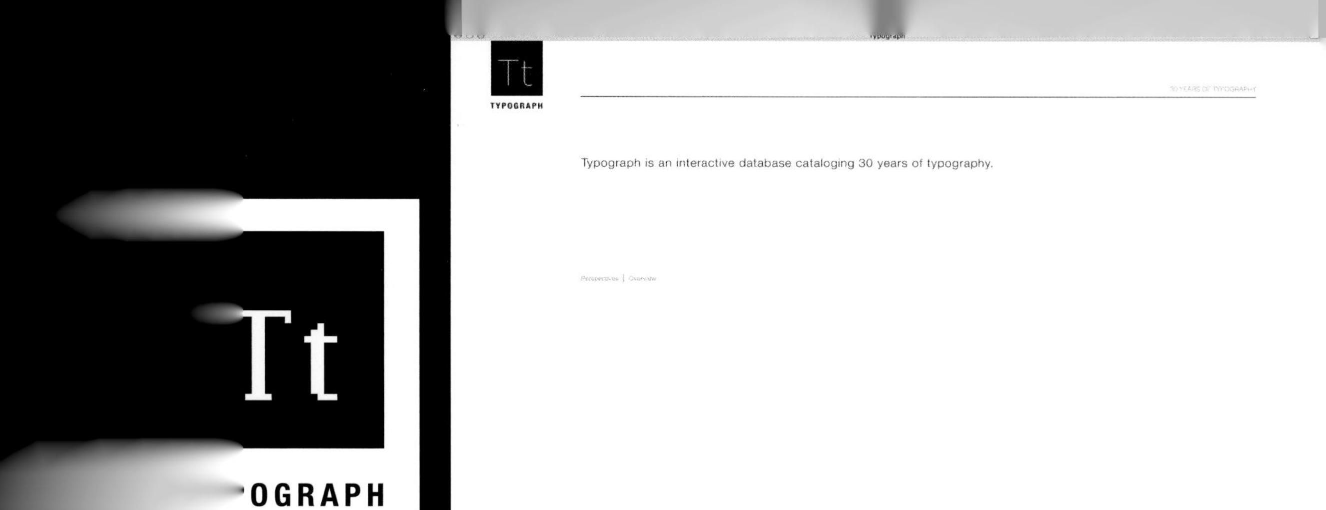

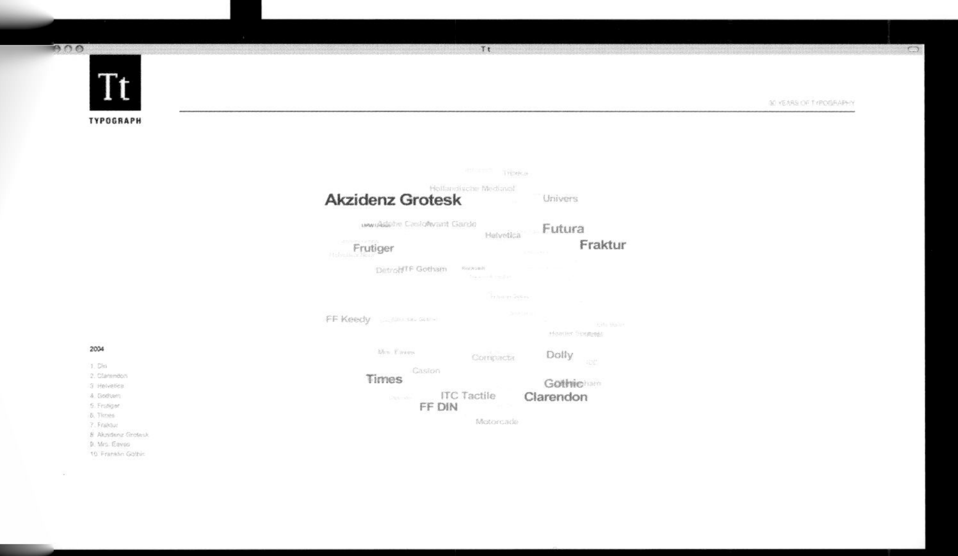

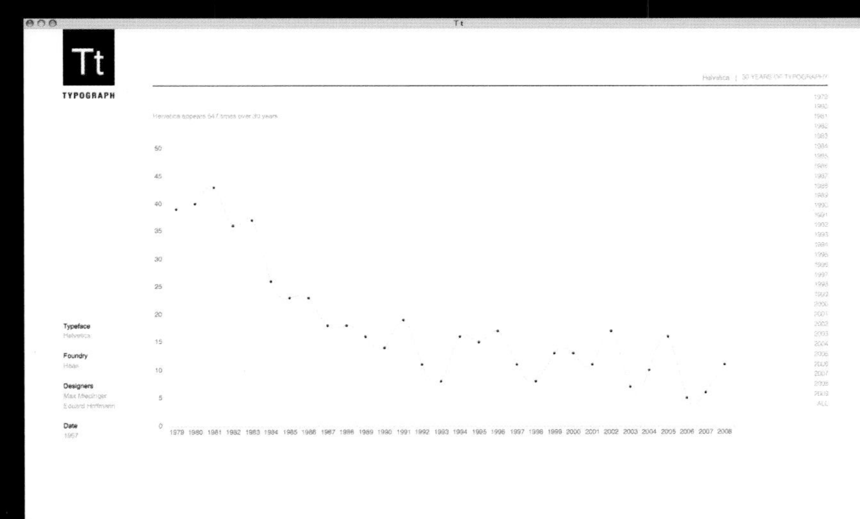

ST IN SHOW, STUDENT DESIGN AWARD Student Projec

Niko Skourtis *New York* California College of the Arts *San Francisco* Dennis Crowe and Michael Vanderby

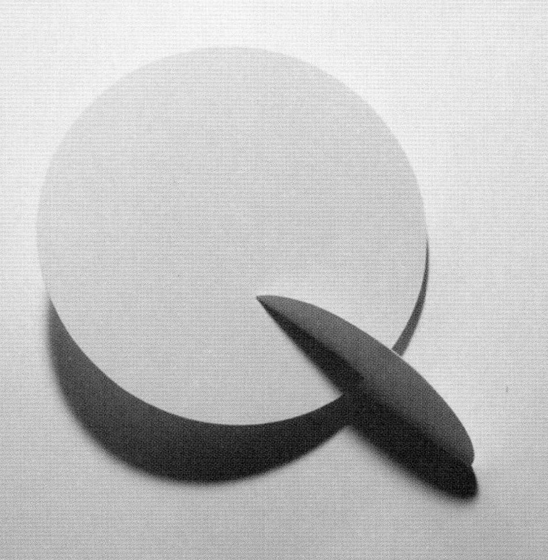

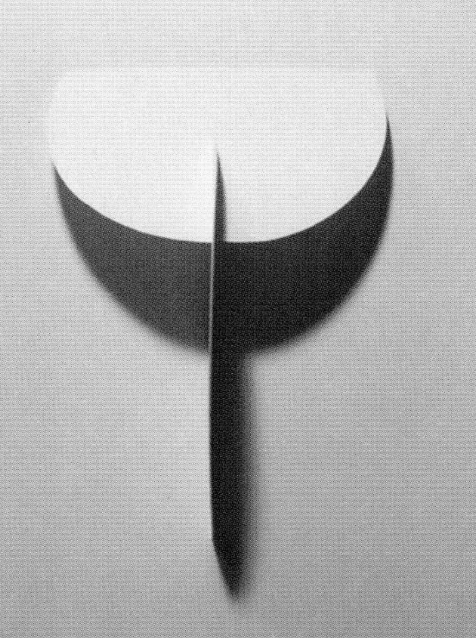

NATIONAL
MUSEUM
OF QATAR

OPENING FALL 2013

Student Project **SECOND PLACE, STUDENT DESIGN AWARD**

Min Hee Lee, *Ridgewood, New Jersey* University of Pennsylvania Etta Siegel

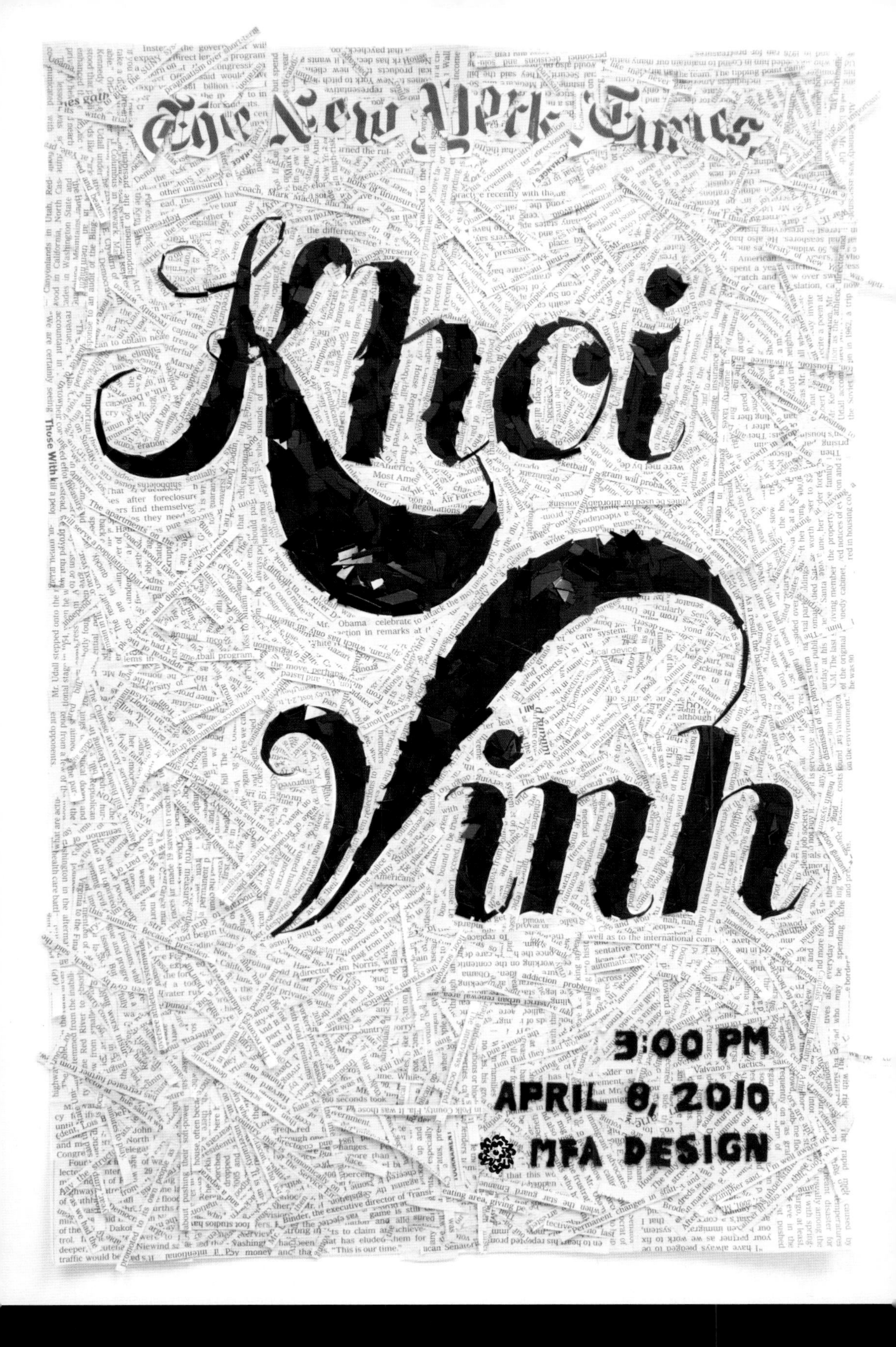

THIRD PLACE, STUDENT DESIGN AWARD Student Projec

DESIGN Cristina Vasquez, *New York* SCHOOL School of Visual Arts, *New York* INSTRUCTOR Steven Helle

JUDGES, JUDGES' CHOICES, AND DESIGNERS' STATEMENTS

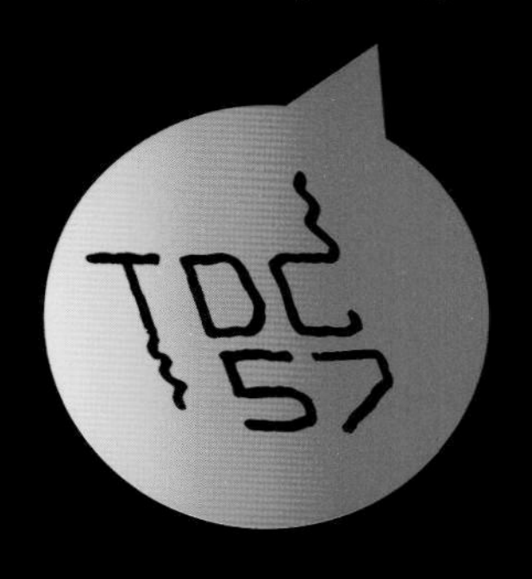

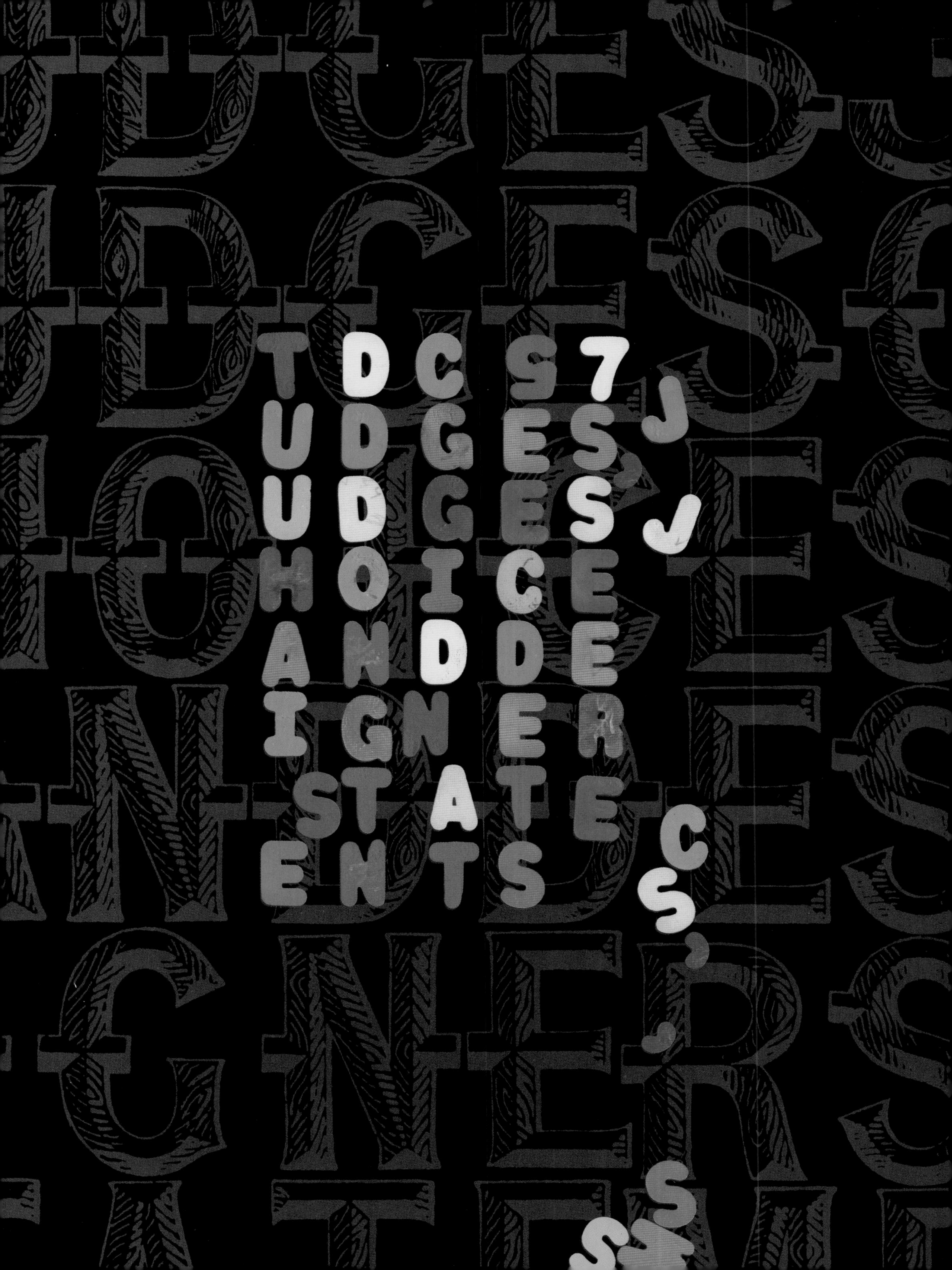

T D C 5 7
U D G E S' J
U D G E S J
H O I C E
A N D D E
I G N E R
S T A T E
E N T S C S'
S S

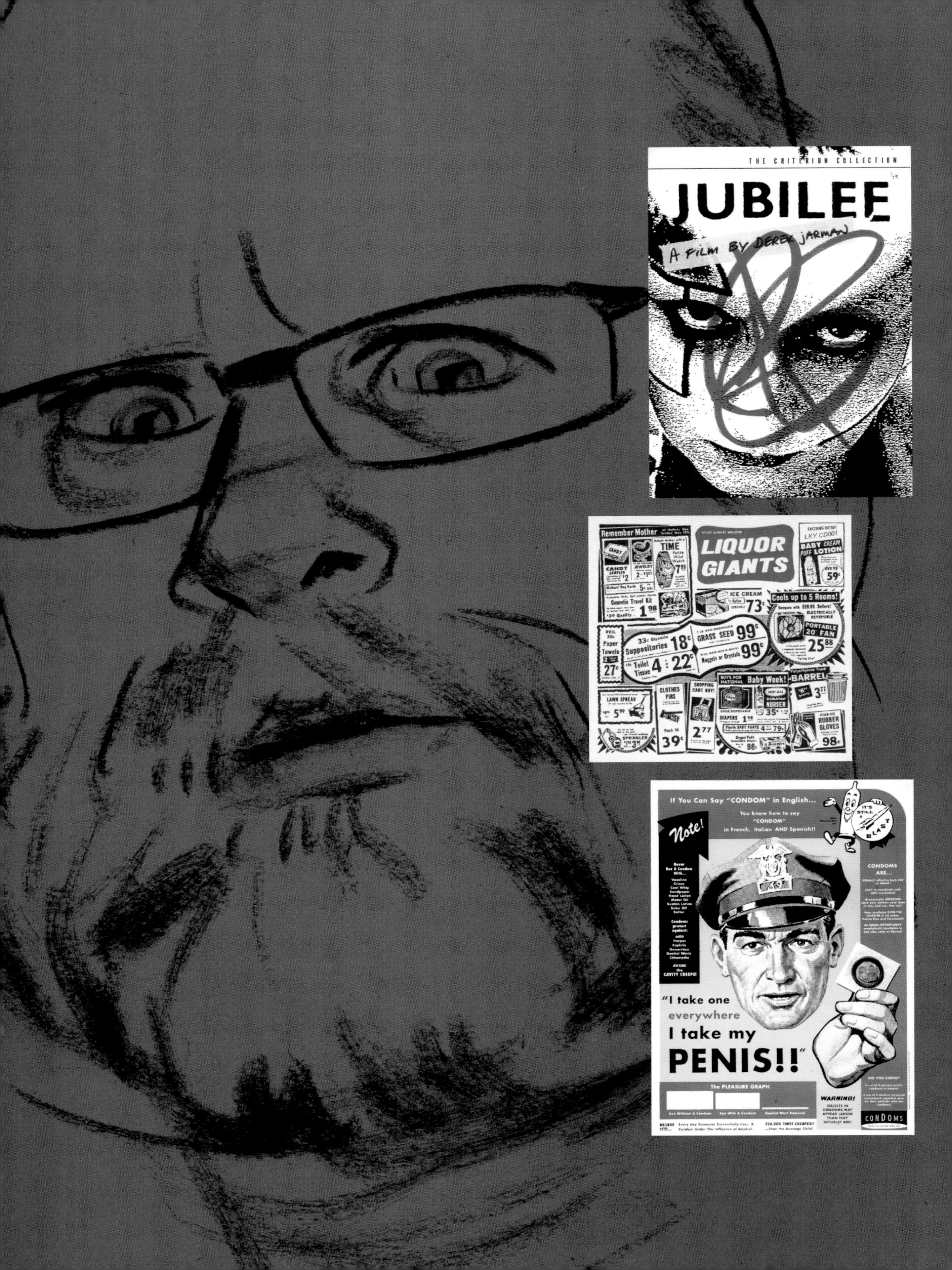
THE CRITERION COLLECTION
JUBILEE
A FILM BY DEREK JARMAN
Remember Mother
LIQUOR GIANTS
LKY CD001
BABY PUFF CREAM LOTION
ICE CREAM
Cools up to 5 Rooms!
Suppositories 18¢
GRASS SEED 99¢
Nuggets or Crystals 99¢
Toilet Tissue 4 22¢
PORTABLE 20 FAN 25.88
Baby Week!
BARREL
RUBBER GLOVES 98¢
If You Can Say "CONDOM" in English...
You know how to say "CONDOM" in French, Italian AND Spanish!!
Note!
IT'S STILL A BLAST
CONDOMS ARE...
"I take one everywhere I take my PENIS!!"
The PLEASURE GRAPH
WARNING!
DID YOU KNOW?
CONDOMS

TDC 57 JUDGE

ART CHANTRY

Raised in Tacoma, Washington, Art Chantry worked in Seattle for nearly thirty years. During that time he managed to produce a body of work that, however unorthodox, still rivals some of the best graphic design in the world. He has won hundreds of design and advertising awards, including a bronze lion at Cannes, and was named the Poster Laureate of the Colorado International Invitational Poster Exposition. His work has been collected and exhibited by some of the most prestigious museums and galleries in the world, including the Louvre, the Smithsonian, the Library of Congress, and the Rock and Roll Hall of Fame. In 1993 the Seattle Art Museum honored him with a one-man retrospective of his work and in the summer of 2003 PS1, in association with the Museum of Modern Art, did the same. His work has been published in hundreds of books and magazines, and in 2001 Chronicle Books published the monograph of his work, *Some People Can't Surf*, written by Julie Lasky. There Is Even A Book About Chantry's Work Published In China And Written Entirely In Chinese ... Though Nobody Knows What It Really Says. During his time working in Seattle, Art somehow managed to carve out a style that took hold of the popular underground music scene in the early 1990s. Dubbed "grunge" by culture mavens, it was a look developed at an alternative newsweekly named *The Rocket*, where Art began as art director in 1984 and with which he continued to be involved off and on for over ten years. During that time, the magazine became the hub on the wheel of Seattle's music and culture scene. Soon his ideas extended beyond *The Rocket* to the fledgling record label Sub Pop. His ideas found further nuance in his work for the garage rock record label Estrus Records, where his style found a perfect home. Through his work with the staff of *The Rocket* and the classes he taught at the School of Visual Concepts, Art influenced an entire generation of young graphic designers in the northwest, and eventually across the United States. He has lectured extensively and traveled to present his work all over the world. He has contributed writings to a number of books about graphic design, and his own book, *Instant Litter: Concert Posters from Seattle Punk Culture*, is considered a classic in its field. To this day, his hard-edged scrappy look can be seen everywhere from punk rock record covers to corporate annual reports.

ART CHANTRY'S SELECTION

This is one of the strangest items I've ever seen entered into a typography design competition/exhibition. Fully six out of the seven judges working on this survey actually voted to put this thing in the show. *But there's no type in it!*

It's a beautiful little book with a blue cover. The title of the book has a blank space for you to fill in (you must title it). The only typography inside the entire book is some standard text in small print on the copyright page. That's it. Instead, every page has a grid in light non-photo blue lines. Every few pages the grid changes to another pattern. This goes on for a hundred or more pages. What is going on here?

The way we understood it is that this is a book about the hidden structure of typography. The blue lines are collected from available empty notebook pages from all over the world—fully 47 different ruling styles, from traditional grade-school line spacing to music staves to mathematical grid styles. These represent the underpinning structure of all writing and typography, a structure too often ignored today by fashionable high-flying digital designers (who can do literally anything—and constantly do).

This little book is a comfortable reminder of the bedrock rules underlying all typography. It's waiting for you to add the text along the guidelines required. It's essentially a typographic "Book of Rules." (Duh!)

DESIGNER'S STATEMENT

We have been collecting notebooks and writing blocks from different countries for years, and each culture has developed its own ruling system. From this collection, we have created a notebook with 47 different rulings, from the trusted DIN format to that used for mathematical notation to traditional Chinese writing blocks.

As a collection, the ruled paper is no longer seen as a blank page to be filled. Instead the diverse rulings inspire a different way of thinking, writing, and ideating.

The rulings can be used as a matrix for taking notes, sorting information, or sketching ideas, allowing for a spontaneous visual journey through different cultures.

JUDGE'S CHOICE Book

DESIGN Till Beckmann, Jenny Hasselbach, and Franziska Morlok, *Berlin* DESIGN OFFICE Rimini Berlin CLIENT Revolver Publishing
PRINCIPAL TYPE FF Schulbuch Nord DIMENSIONS 5.1 × 6.7 in. (13 × 17 cm)

TDC 57 JUDGE

AREM DUPLESSIS

Arem is currently the Design Director of *The New York Times Magazine* Division. He has held positions at *Spin*, *GQ*, and *Blaze* magazines. His work has been recognized by the Society of Publication Designers, Communication Arts Magazine, the Type Directors Club, the AIGA, and the ADC, where *The New York Times Magazine* was awarded the 2010 Design Team of the Year Gold Cube.

Arem is an Instructor at the School of Visual Arts and teaches a yearly Masters Design Workshop in Copenhagen. He has lectured in New York, Washington, D.C., and Louisville, Kentucky.

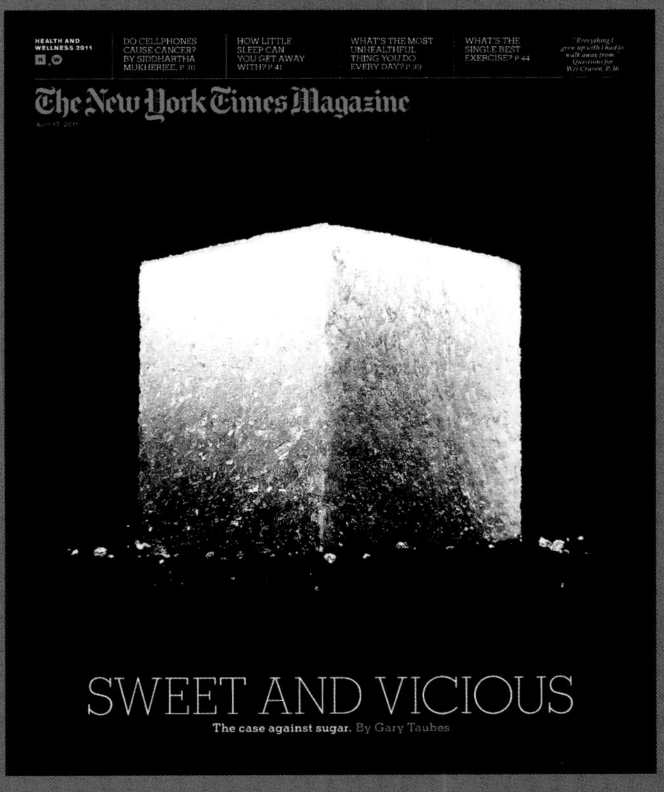

AREM DUPLESSIS'S SELECTION

verything the Ace Hotel does is spot on. The crowd, the music, the restaurant, the vibe . . . the list goes on and on.

I guess I'm a sucker for obsession. The time and focus it must have taken to execute this project floors me. The average artist would have quit after maybe twenty-seven drawings, but ninety-nine of them? All done by hand with black paint! The drawings themselves are simple interpretations, yet the scale of the work makes everything seem so detailed and right. This project excites me; maybe it's because we live in such a new digital world. It makes me happy to know that a designer made a conscious decision to go at it by hand, one stroke at a time, armed with nothing but a few black paint markers and a tenacious appetite for perfection.

DESIGNER'S STATEMENT

he Ace Hotel opened its doors in New York City last year. With locations already in Seattle, Portland, and Palm Springs, Ace is known for its hipster and motorcycle chic aesthetic. The lobby buzzes with lots of people, furniture, music, laptops, and espressos. Their café, Stumptown, has gained lots of praise, along with their British gastropub, the Breslin—which is run by the owners of the Spotted Pig in the West Village. Oh, and Q-Tip spins every Friday night. Not bad, right?

While brainstorming in the weeks before, it was important to ask some larger questions before I started my sketch: What's its relevancy? What's its importance? Can it become engaging or participatory? Having an idea for a mural that's both relative to the space it exists in and reflective of the culture around it is not an easy task to accomplish. However, I felt it was something I had to account for.

With those questions in mind, I hand-drew 99 picture frames to create a dense wall of "discovery" about NYC that could be passed to the common tourist staying in the room. Each frame contains a different fact / love / tidbit / thing of interest / shout-out to a place I dig in the city. At roughly 120 square feet, the art was drawn imprecisely to capture the spontaneity and grit of the city. I used paint markers and opaque black paint to help this technique excel. Consequently, it became a labor of love, an act of obsessiveness that was pleasantly grueling.

JUDGE'S CHOICE Signage

DESIGN Timothy Goodman, *San Francisco* LETTERING Timothy Goodman ILLUSTRATION Timothy Goodman PHOTOGRAPHY Mark Dye CLIENT Ace Hotel
PRINCIPAL TYPE handlettering with paint markers and Sharpie DIMENSIONS 120 sq. ft (11.2 sq. m)

5 x
BERLIN
CYAN
ANSCHLAEGE
ATAK
ANGELA
LORENZ
FONS
HICKMANN
M23

TDC 57 JUDGE

FONS HICKMANN

Fons Hickmann is a graphic designer, photographer, and professor living and working in Berlin. The studio »Fons Hickmann m23«, which he co-founded in 2001, is among today's most awarded design studios.

The studio varies a lot in size and scope; working with seven designers at the moment—sometimes there are four, sometimes there are fourteen—the staff comes from Austria, Germany, and Italy. The work focuses on the design of complex communication systems, and the output of the studio includes corporate designs, books, posters, magazines, and digital projects. While being conceptual and analytical, the work never fails to surprise with subtle or distinctive humor.

Practically all of the works by Fons Hickmann have been awarded with prizes of international repute; he has taught at several universities, has given lectures and held workshops around the world, is a professor at the Berlin University of the Arts, and is a member of ADC, TDC New York, and Alliance Graphique Internationale. His latest publications are *Fons Hickmann—Touch Me There* and *Beyond Graphic Design*.

FONS HICKMANN'S SELECTION

ave you heard the story of the animal experiment in which they tested whether sharks could differentiate colors, and if so, what their favorite was? First, the scientists laid out colored baits. The sharks immediately ate everything and did not care if the food was green, blue, or red. Then the sharks were given a choice: two identical baits, but in different colors. One shark examined the first, then the second bleeding delicacy. Both were equally appetizing, but he had to choose one. Then something strange happened: the shark swam away. Hungry. Apparently, the choice had completely overwhelmed him. But why didn't he just eat both?

I admit that for my Judge's Choice I could not decide, and in the end picked three works. This fantastic poster triptych from Japan is even more stunning when you see the original, foil-stamped and printed in special glowing inks. Then later in the book, the amazing typographic gloves, which would be a very good present for my daughter. And the book *Post Porn Politics*, for my girlfriend perhaps . . .

DESIGNER'S STATEMENT

his work was created for Hot Stamp Processing Company (Bihaku Wabanabe Company) to promote their new foil processing technology. It is designed to raise awareness of Fluorescent Foil and experiment with new ways of using an old method. The work familiarizes the public with those new methods, and increases the value of the two-dimensional media. Fluorescent Foil has its own unique characteristics. It expresses depth and lends itself to modeling.

DESIGN Ren Takaya, *Tokyo* **ART DIRECTION** Ren Takaya **DESIGN STUDIO** AD&D **CLIENT** Bihaku Watanabe Company and Tsujikawa Co., Ltd.
PRINCIPAL TYPE Helvetica Neue Light **DIMENSIONS** 20.3 × 28.7 in. (51.5 × 72.8 cm)

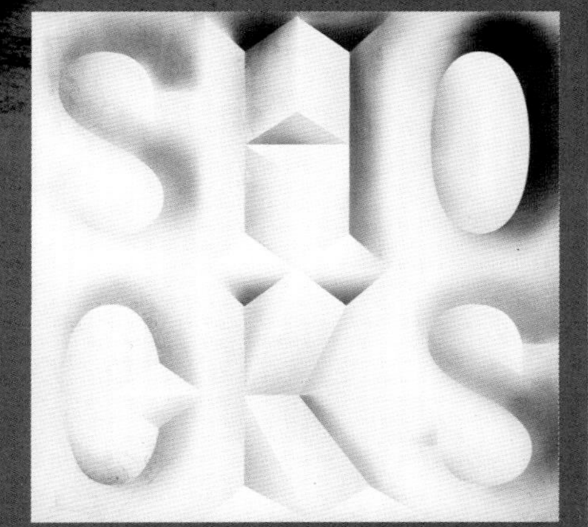

TDC 57 JUDGE

MARIO HUGO

Mario Hugo is a New York–based artist and designer. Though he spends an inordinate amount of time in front of his computer, he still feels most honest with a pencil and two or more sheets of paper. In addition to working independently, Mario is a founding partner and the creative director of Hugo & Marie, a boutique agency specializing in artist management.

MARIO HUGO'S SELECTION

adly, it's increasingly rare for us to really pick up a book and study a carefully crafted cover. Designers aside, we'd rather pinch, zoom, and get to the point. There is, however, no denying the power of a beautiful object and *The German Genius* is a monumentally intimidating tome with an absolutely intimate, ceremonial jacket.

The immaculately set black letter typography is a spiraling introduction into the enigmatic and mysterious German psyche. In fact, traversing the cover's drama doesn't even offer the promise of a title or author, and we're instead led through key themes of Germans, Nazis, Freud, and the United States in quick, curious succession.

A disjointed black and red propaganda draws us into a series of conflicting quotes, at once cocky and confessional, but each quote blends into the next to suggest a universal presence of German thinking. Maybe, maybe not—but it's a cover one might feel intimately attached to; it's the cover of a book you pick up, love, and form a bond with.

To put it simply, the jacket is beautiful and mysterious, and the object itself is a quintessential reminder of the rift between the immediacy of digital books and the intimacy of physical ones (and that each has its place).

DESIGNER'S STATEMENT

eter Watson's *The German Genius* is a survey of German thinkers and thought spanning 250 years. Confronted with a long and abstract subtitle—and a manuscript that was nearly a thousand pages long—I was worried that, despite its engaging content, the book might scare off readers.

My solution was to design for the entire "object," not just the front cover. Keeping the uncommon heft of the book in mind, I moved all of the information that was supposed to be on the cover (title, subtitle, author) onto the sizable spine. I then selected quotes about Germans and Germany from within the manuscript and created a kind of typographic "face" for the front cover. My goal/hope was to spark curiosity in the viewer, while also reflecting the dizzying volume and variety of German thought contained within. The final jacket is two flat colors, printed on an uncoated paper stock.

I am greatly indebted to Archie Ferguson, the art director at Harper, for helping to champion this unorthodox design—and of course to the author, editor, and publisher, for approving it!

The Germans dive deeper–
The planet is in flames . . . Only from the Germans can come the world-historical
The Nazis are un-German.
Our intellectual skyline has been altered by German thinkers
Freud is better
German suffering and Jewish
The U.S.
THE
GENIUS

EUROPE'S
THIRD
RENAISSANCE,
THE SECOND
SCIENTIFIC
REVOLUTION,
AND THE
TWENTIETH
CENTURY

●

PETER WATSON

JUDGE'S CHOICE Book Jacket

DESIGN Christopher Sergio, *New York* **DESIGN OFFICE** Christopher Sergio Design **PUBLISHER** HarperCollins Publishers
PRINCIPAL TYPE Fette deutsche Schrift and Knockout **DIMENSIONS** 6.25 × 9.25 in. (15.9 × 23.5 cm)

Jason Kernevich is a founding partner of the design and illustration studio The Heads of State. Since 2002, he has been creating posters, books, illustrations, and identities for the likes of *The New York Times*, *Wired*, Penguin, Vintage, Starbucks, Ogilvy and Mather, BBDO, the School of Visual Arts, and the New York Public Library, as well as music groups like R.E.M., Wilco, and The National. He has won awards from Communication Arts, *Print* magazine, *American Illustration*, and the Society of Illustrators. He studied at Tyler School of Art, where he currently teaches design and illustration. Born and raised in Pennsylvania's coal country, he has lived and worked in Brooklyn, Rome, Los Angeles, and Philadelphia, where he roots for his beloved Phillies.

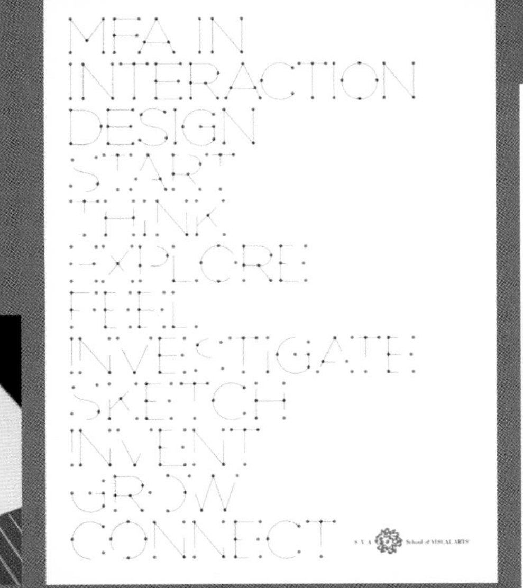

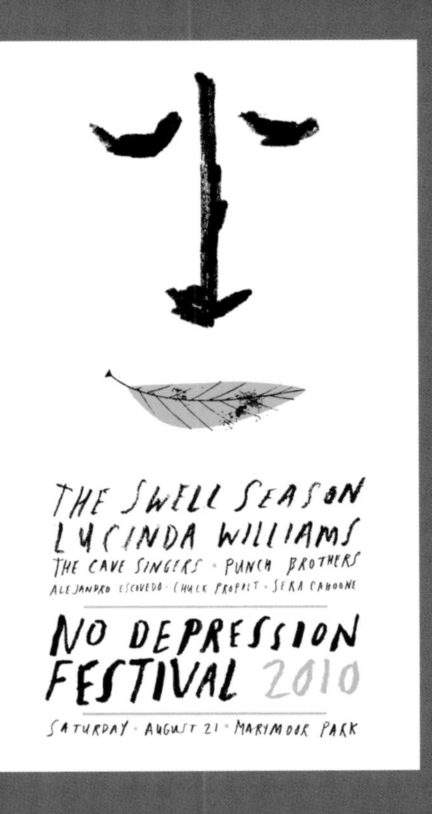

JASON KERNEVICH'S SELECTION

First and foremost I was drawn to this label design for its quality as an image. It stands out from what we've all come to expect from even well-designed wine labels simply by being a charming and abstract graphic. But it's also a bit devious. Spend a little time with it, and thin rules and slight angles reveal letterforms. By the time you make out the words—about half the time it normally takes to decipher the make and model of anything good, red, and French—you're hooked. Turn the bottle over and you're told the story of Tilly Devine, the infamous madam, bootlegger, jailbird, and wino from Down Under whose name has become Aussie slang for wine. You can almost hear her cackling as you read.

DESIGNER'S STATEMENT

When Antipodean Vintners produced a super premium McLaren Vale Shiraz, they named it Tilly Devine after the notorious Sydney madam and bootlegger of the 1920s. So successful was Tilly's bootlegging operation that her name was adopted as rhyming slang for wine. In her heyday, Tilly Devine could be found either behind prison bars or in cocktail bars. We chose this idea to drive the packaging solution. The label features what at first look appear to be prison bars. Closer inspection reveals the words Tilly Devine appearing behind the bars. To continue the theme, the label copy is written in Australian rhyming slang.

JUDGE'S CHOICE Packaging *39*

DESIGN Kellie Campbell-Illingworth, *Adelaide, Australia* CREATIVE DIRECTION Matthew Remphrey LETTERING Kellie Campbell-Illingworth
DESIGN OFFICE Parallax Design CLIENT Antipodean Vintners PRINCIPAL TYPE Akzidenz-Grotesk, Newzald, and handlettering DIMENSIONS 7.7 × 6.7 in. (19.5 × 17 cm)

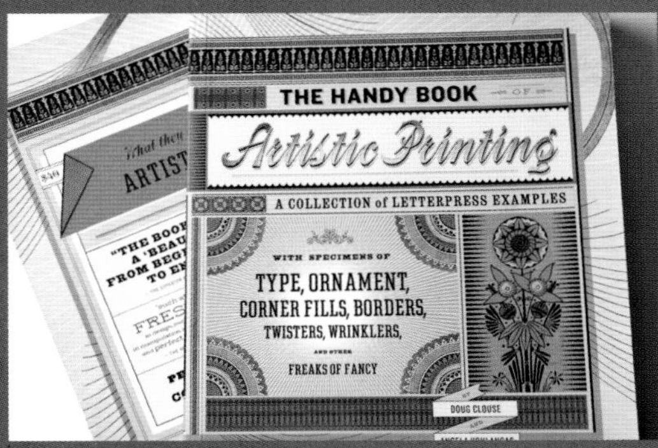

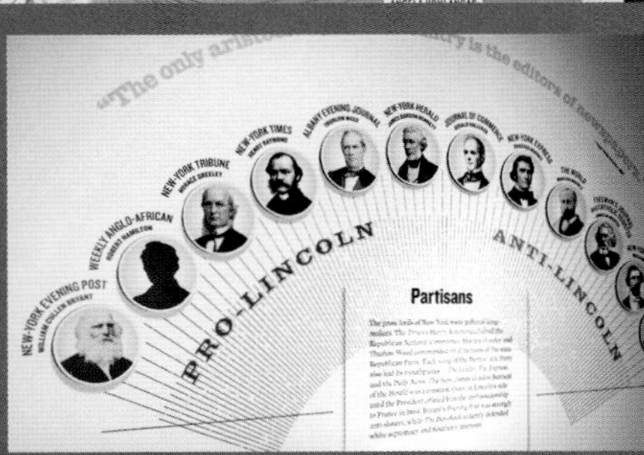

ANGELA VOULANGAS

Angela Voulangas is a graphic designer and writer based in Brooklyn, New York. She has worked with art galleries, publishers, and such cultural institutions as the New-York Historical Society, the Lower East Side Tenement Museum, and the New York Transit Museum, creating everything from banners to books, invitations to exhibitions. Her work has been recognized by the AIGA in the 50 books/50 covers and Communication Graphics shows as well as by the American Association of Museums.

The Handy Book of Artistic Printing, a study of nineteenth-century artistic letterpress design (co-written and designed by Angela with Doug Clouse), was published by Princeton Architectural Press in 2010. *The Handy Book* received a publication award from the Victorian Society in America and has been honored by the Type Directors Club. Angela and Doug also created and printed a line of letterpress cards using nineteenth-century ornament under the brand typeHigh.

Angela maintains an online miscellany of visual bric-a-brac, worthy erudition, and probably justly forgotten obscurities. She is a native New Yorker.

ANGELA VOULANGAS'S SELECTION

t was funny that we were judging the best typography of 2011 and several of us were ogling this series of letterpress business cards that looked like they were designed on a typewriter or a Commodore 64 computer. In a competition where entries often outdo one another in production values, concept, and complexity, it was refreshing to see some loose, low-tech humor.

Whimsy, nicely executed.

DESIGNER'S STATEMENT

n an industry full of uptight designers, one of the most effective ways to set yourself apart is to not take yourself too seriously. Most people think they're "delightful" and "surprising"—only letterpress could make ASCII spam look classy—which makes it memorable and gets people chatting. And really, isn't that the whole point of having a business card to begin with? I haven't gotten any new unicorn grooming business from them, but designers seem to like them.

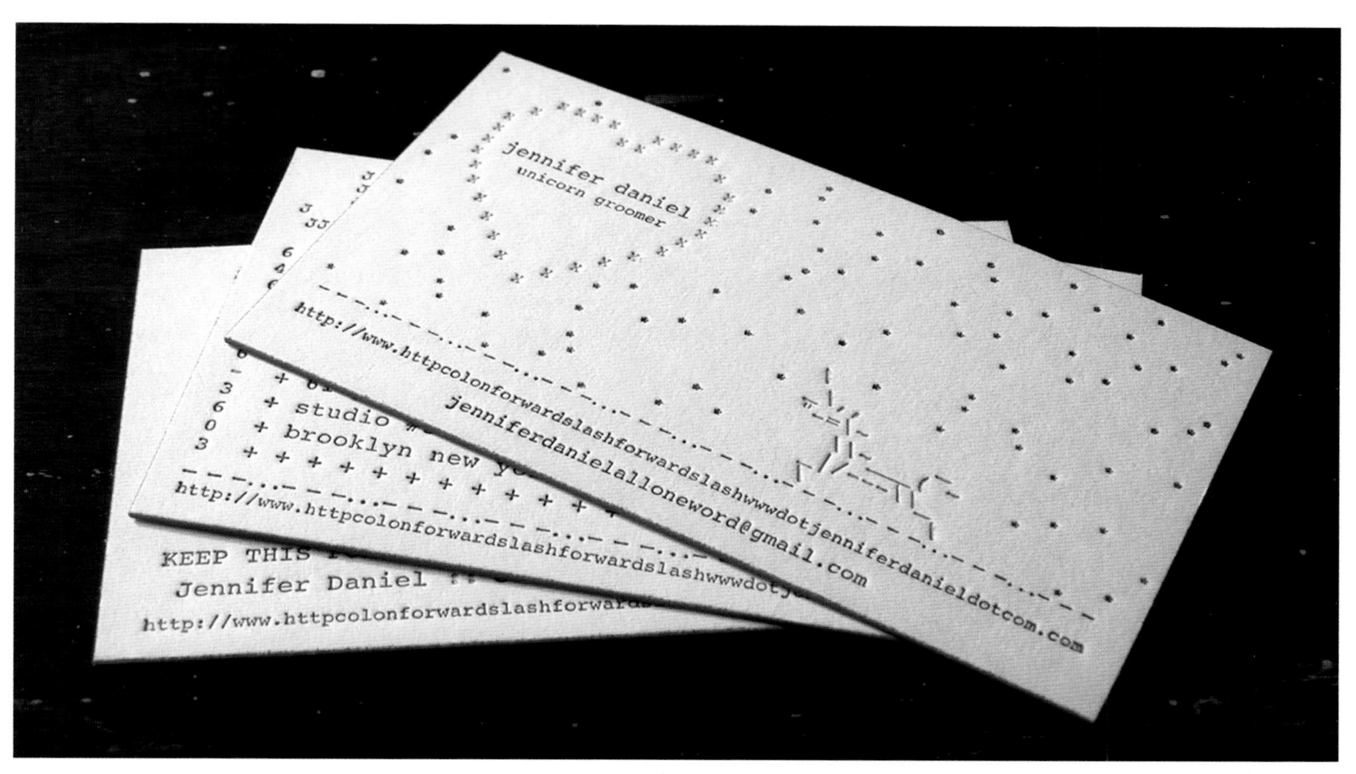

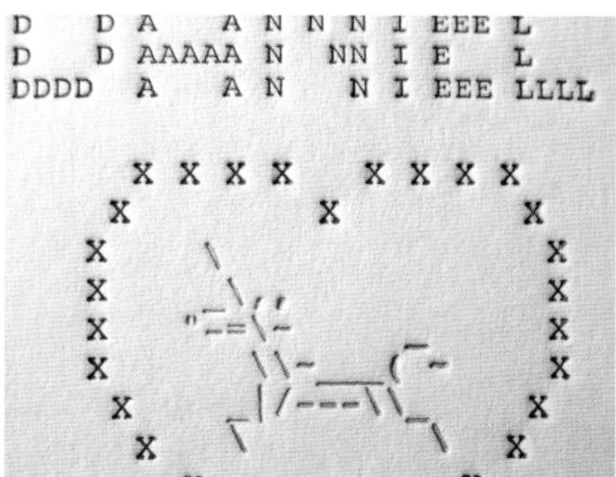

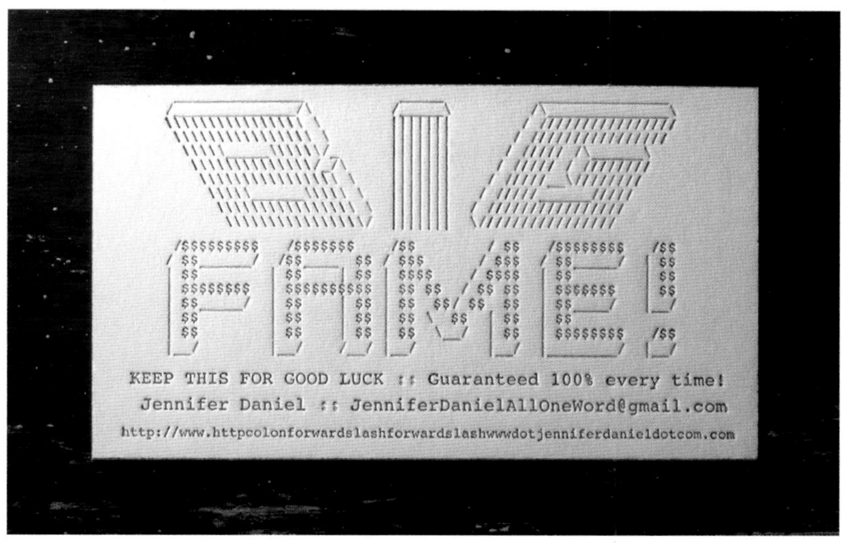

JUDGE'S CHOICE Self-Promotion

DESIGN Jennifer Daniel, *Brooklyn, New York* PRINCIPAL TYPE Courier
DIMENSIONS 3.5 × 2 in. (8.9 × 5.1 cm)

TDC 57 JUDGE

BRUCE WILLEN

Bruce Willen is co-founder of Post Typography, a multi-disciplinary studio specializing in graphic design, conceptual typography, illustration, and custom lettering, with additional forays into art, apparel, music, curatorial work, design theory, and vandalism. Post Typography's work has received numerous fancy design awards and has been featured in such books as Ellen Lupton's *Graphic Design: The New Basics*, Phaidon's *Area 2*, and Taschen's *Contemporary Graphic Design*, as well as a monograph of the studio's work by European publisher Pyramyd Éditions. Willen and Post Typography co-founder Nolen Strals are authors of *Lettering & Type*, a book on lettering and typeface design, which was published by Princeton Architectural Press in 2009. Post Typography have appeared in multiple design and art exhibitions, and their posters are collected by high-school punk rockers and prominent designers (whom they consider equally important). Willen and Strals teach classes in Experimental Lettering and Typography at the Maryland Institute College of Art, and have lectured at the Cooper Union, Minneapolis College of Art and Design, and Harvard University among others.

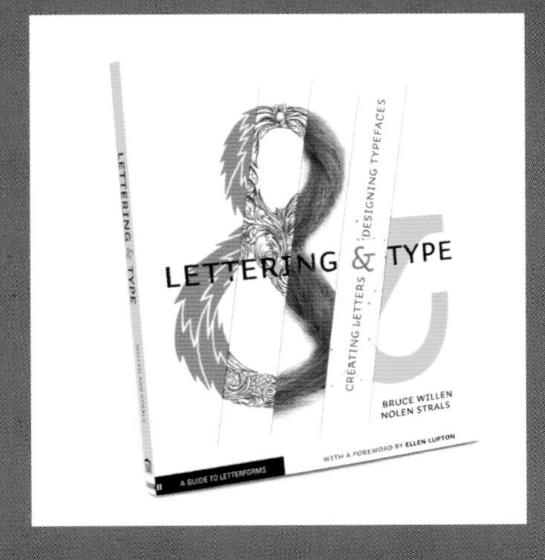

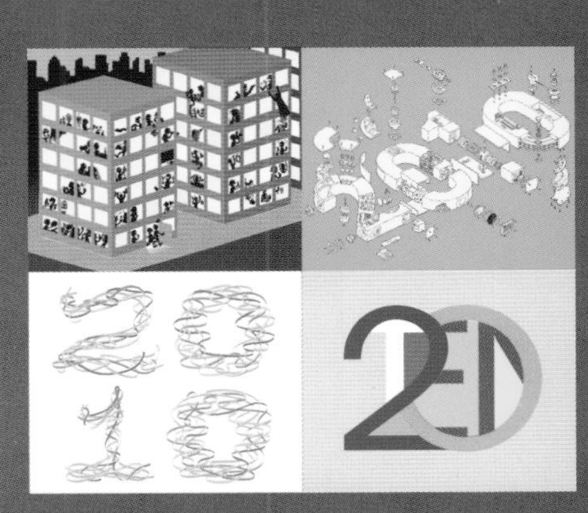

BRUCE WILLEN'S SELECTION

I almost overlooked this piece at first; it was a quiet moment between some of the bold and confrontational typography of other posters in the competition. But Justus Oehler's design with its camouflaged lettering snuck up on me and burrowed its message into my brain.

The poster hits the trifecta for being subtle, smart, and visually striking, all while employing inventive lettering. It's a perfect example of text and image joining forces to deliver a larger narrative. With minimalist elegance, the lettering conveys both the suggestion of violent, seismic upheaval and the massive interruption of the life of an entire country. The poster's concept and execution are great, and the disrupted handwriting vividly references the physical output of a seismograph machine. The designer was wise to keep the overall design spare and minimal, allowing the lettering-cum-illustration to speak for itself and give the viewer enough room to take in and digest the poster's concept.

Oehler's Haiti poster stood out to me, not just for its simplicity, but also for its thoughtful marriage of text and with concept. While many other pieces in the competition showcased stylish typography or used lettering to tell a more complex story, few managed to do both as well as Oehler did in this poster. We will definitely be making it an example for our students next semester.

DESIGNER'S STATEMENT

This poster for "The Haiti Poster Project" is part of a goodwill benefit campaign for Haiti after its devastating earthquake. The poster motif created by Justus Oehler is based on the impressive visualization of unexpected brutal earth tremors. Just like Haiti was suddenly and surprisingly shaken and destroyed by the earthquake, the word "Haiti" in the poster is suddenly subject to strong jolting and vibrations; handwritten with a fountain pen, it shows strong seismographic deflections in the middle. Oehler: "I wanted the design to be as merciless and naturally forceful as earthquakes are. I had to try several times . . . my fountain pen just about survived it.

Haiti
HELP REBUILD HAITI!
POSTER DESIGNED BY JUSTUS OEHLER FOR
THE HAITI POSTER PROJECT

JUDGE'S CHOICE Poster

DESIGN Justus Oehler, *Berlin* LETTERING Justus Oehler DESIGN OFFICE Pentagram Design Berlin CLIENT The Haiti Poster Project
PRINCIPAL TYPE handlettering DIMENSIONS 17.7 × 23.6 in. (45 × 60 cm)

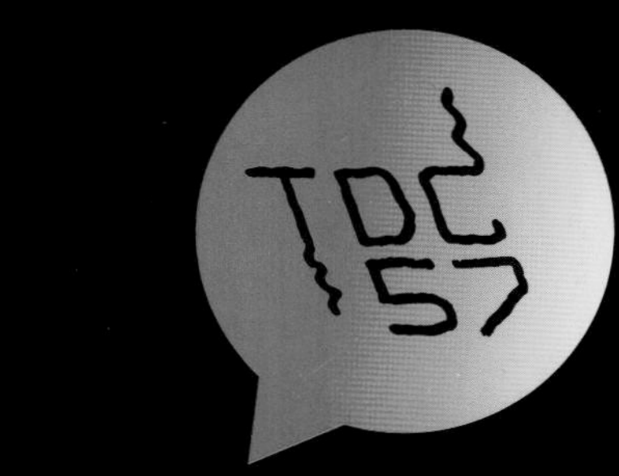

WINNING ENTRIES

DESIGN Catherine Casalino, *New York* CREATIVE DIRECTION Anne Twomey PHOTOGRAPHY Ryann Cooley DESIGN OFFICE Catherine Casalino Design PUBLISHER Grand Central Publishing PRINCIPAL TYPE Briem Mono and custom metal letters DIMENSIONS 6 × 9 in. (15.2 × 22.9 cm)

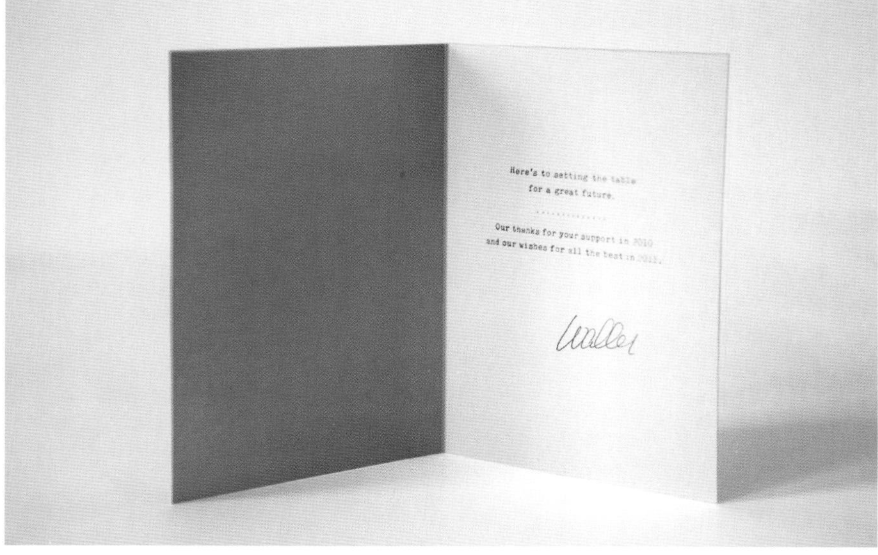

 Greeting Card

DESIGN Katy Fischer, Eric Thoelke, *St. Louis, Missouri* COPYWRITER Geoff Story STUDIO TOKY Branding + Design
CLIENT St. Louis Public Library Foundation PRINCIPAL TYPE typewriter DIMENSIONS 4.5 × 6.25 in. (11.4 × 15.9 cm)

WE BELIEVE IN POSSIBLE
INSPIRED TO DO GOOD THINGS
WOULD LIKE YOUR HELP

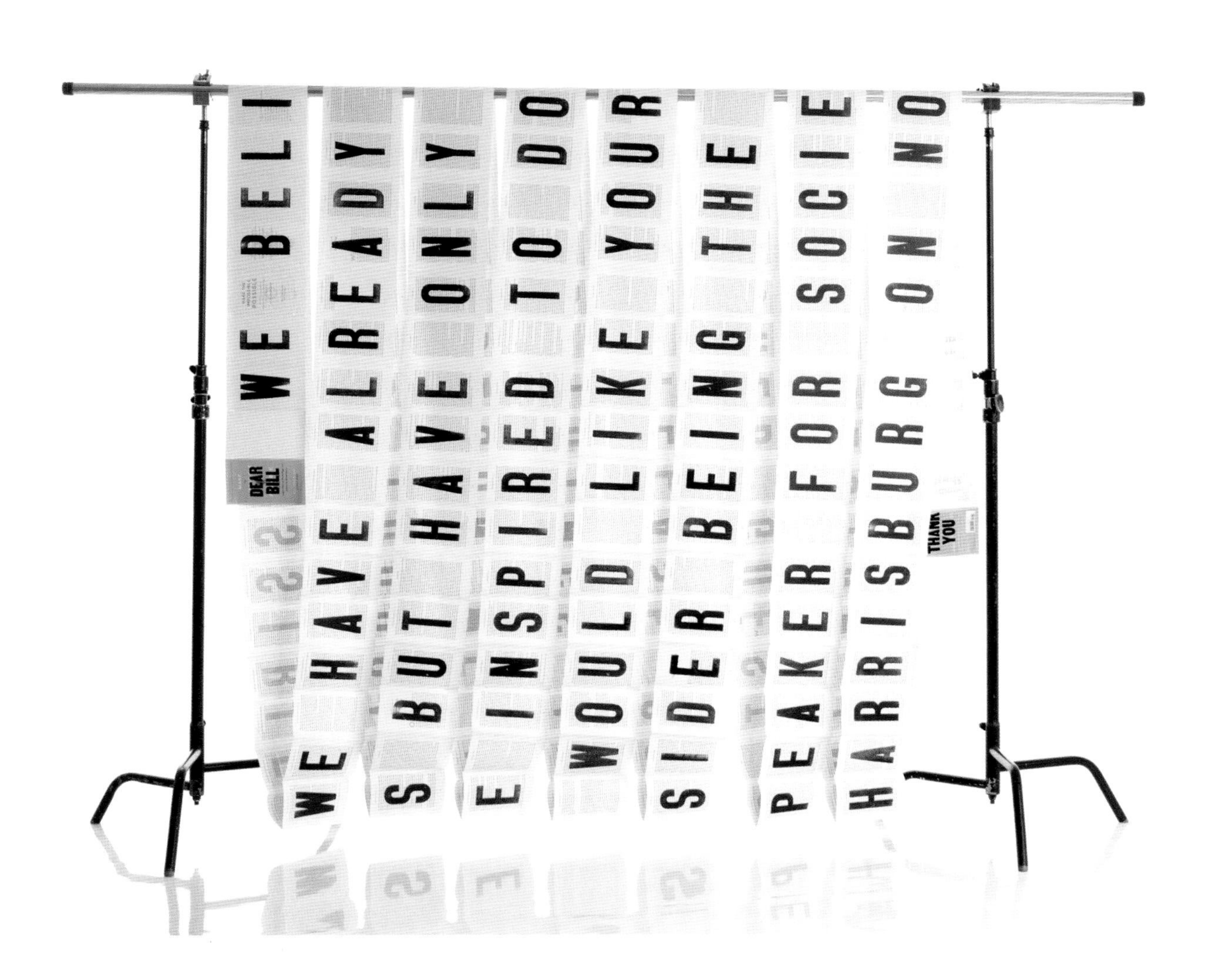

DESIGN Craig Welsh, *Lancaster, Pennsylvania* STUDIO Go Welsh CLIENT Society of Design PRINCIPAL TYPE Gothic wood type
DIMENSIONS Closed: 5 × 8 in. (12.7 × 20.3 cm), Opened: 100 × 8 in. (254 × 20.3 cm)

 Business Card

DESIGN Oliver Munday, *New York* CLIENT Robson Desouza
PRINCIPAL TYPE Univers DIMENSIONS 3.5 × 2 in. (8.9 × 5.1 cm)

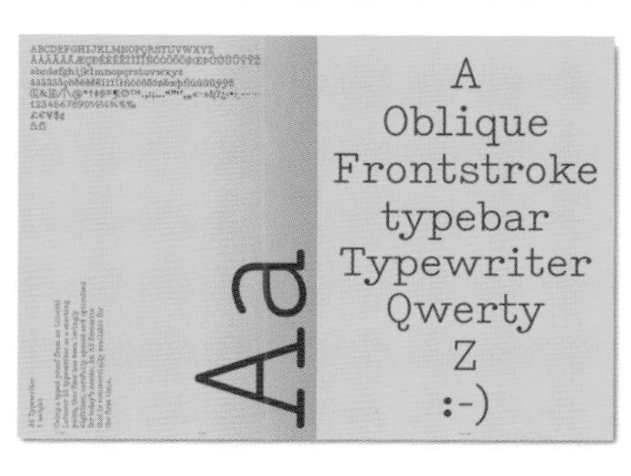

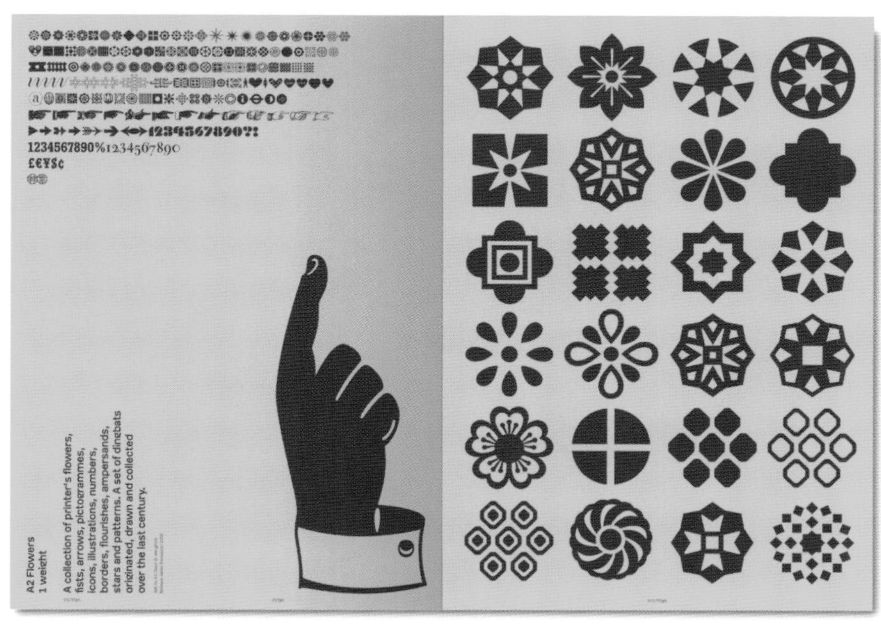

DESIGN Henrik Kubel and Scott Williams, *London* DESIGN OFFICE A2/SW/HK CLIENT A2-TYPE
PRINCIPAL TYPE various DIMENSIONS 5.9 × 8.3 in. (15 × 21 cm)

 Book Jacket

DESIGN Melissa Chang, *New York* ART DIRECTION Hana Nakamura CREATIVE DIRECTION Matteo Bologna LETTERING Melissa Chang DESIGN OFFICE Mucca Design
CLIENT Rizzoli PRINCIPAL TYPE handlettering DIMENSIONS 8.75 × 5.5 in. (22.2 × 14 cm)

DESIGN Demetri Martin, *New York* ART DIRECTION Elizabeth Connor CREATIVE DIRECTION Anne Twomey PUBLISHER Grand Central Publishing
PRINCIPAL TYPE Electra and handlettering DIMENSIONS 5.75 × 8.5 in. (14.6 × 21.6 cm)

 Book Jacket

DESIGN Gregg Kulick, *New York* ILLUSTRATION Gregg Kulick PUBLISHER Penguin Group (USA)
PRINCIPAL TYPE Gotham Rounded and hand drawn found types DIMENSIONS 6.1 × 9.25 in. (15.6 × 23.5 cm)

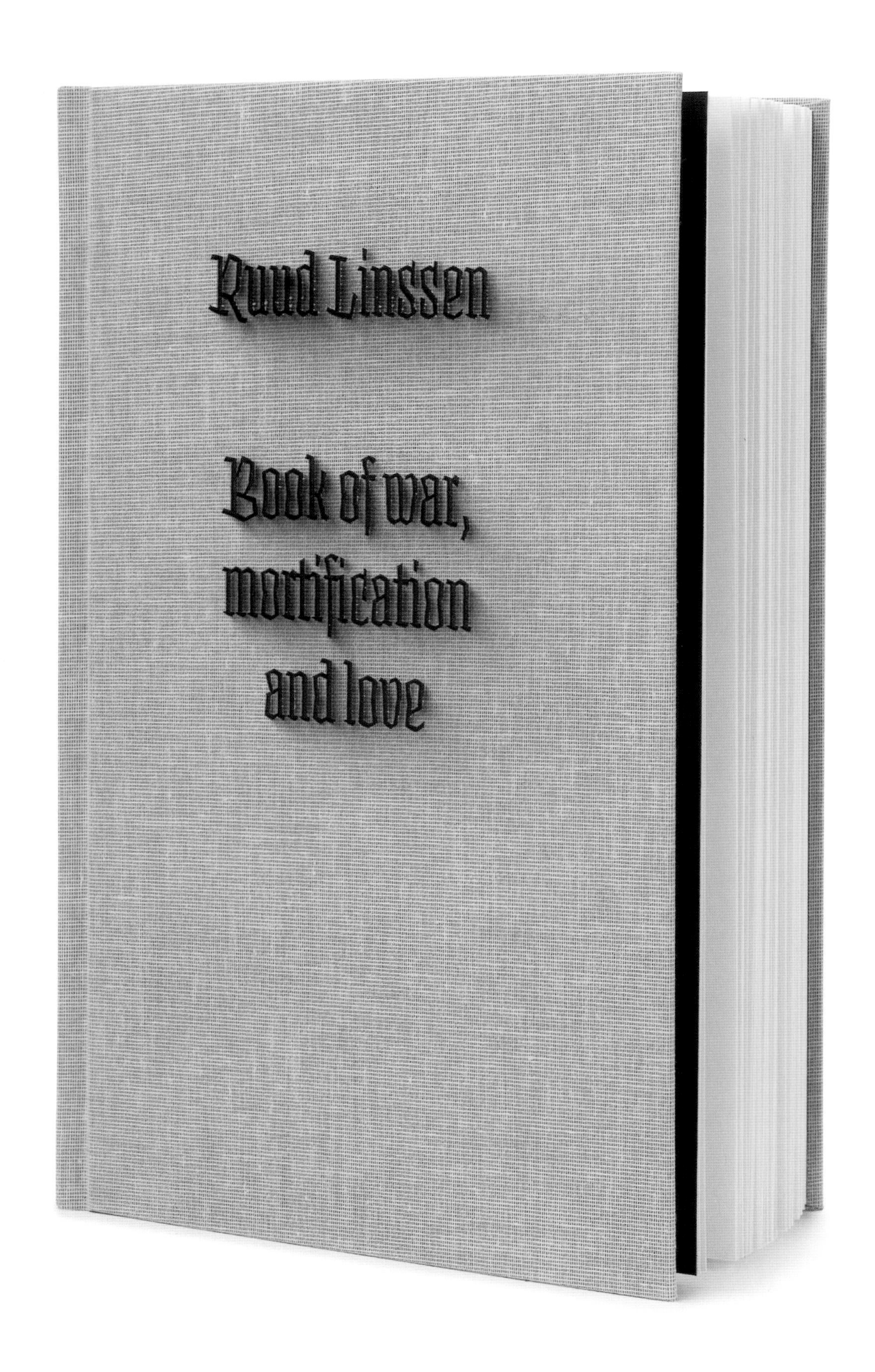

Book *57*

DESIGN Underware, *The Hague, Netherlands*
PRINCIPAL TYPE Fakir DIMENSIONS 5.3 × 8.3 in. (13.5 × 21.1 cm)

ART DIRECTION Reginald Wagner, *Hamburg* CREATIVE DIRECTION Katrin Oeding PHOTOGRAPHY Ulrike Kirmse and Guido Stanke ILLUSTRATION Sarah Gossner COPYWRITERS Till Grabsch and Delia D. Marti AGENCY Kolle Rebbe/KOREFE CLIENT Borkebjs.com PRINCIPAL TYPE Borkebjs DIMENSIONS 4.8 × 5.9 in. (12.2 × 15 cm)

ESTABLISHED 2010 · NEW YORK CITY

WALL & WATER

LUNCH

MANHATTAN *is a* NARROW ISLAND *off the coast of* NEW JERSEY *devoted to the* PURSUIT OF LUNCH.
– RAYMOND SOKOLOV –

2 COURSES } $35 + TAX
INCLUDES coffee or tea

3 COURSES } $44 + TAX
INCLUDES coffee or tea

APPETIZERS

'S & SALADS

'D PUMPKIN SOUP
'ram, carrots, goat cheese
–8–

' MUSHROOMS
s, arugula, *roasted* garlic,
ne, hazelnuts

/FRISÉE SALAD
g, anchovies,
'k olives

CHARCUTERIE & CHEESES

homemade chutney *of the day*
pickled seasonal vegetables
grilled farm bread

OLD CHATHAM black sheep camembert 12
BERKSHIRE unpasteurized jersey blue 11
HAWTHORNE VALLEY raw milk organic cheddar 11
salted, cured HUDSON VALLEY duck salami 12
housemade foie gras terrine 17
smoked pork lo...

STARTERS

SEARED SCALLOPS
slow-cooked peppers, mussels, parsley,
roasted garlic, lemon preserves
–17–

SALT CURED PACIFIC SALMON
dill, grapefruit, chili, black olives
–13–

SMOKED VENISON
broccoli, apple slaw, must...

DESIGN Christy Thrasher, *Santa Monica, California* CREATIVE DIRECTION Robert Louey and Regina Rubino
VICE PRESIDENT FOOD & BEVERAGE INTERNATIONAL OPERATIONS Achim Lenders, *Chicago* VICE PRESIDENT CULINARY OPERATIONS Susan Terry, *Chicago*
GENERAL MANAGER Toni Hinterstoisser, *New York* DESIGN OFFICES Regina Rubino/IMAGE: Global Vision LLC and Robert Louey Design/Pagenova
CLIENTS Andaz Wall Street, *New York*, and Grand Hyatt New York PRINCIPAL TYPE ATChevalier Regular (modified) and Engravers MT Regular DIMENSIONS various

Deklaration für einen Kurswechsel in der Meinungslandschaft

| Dek 21

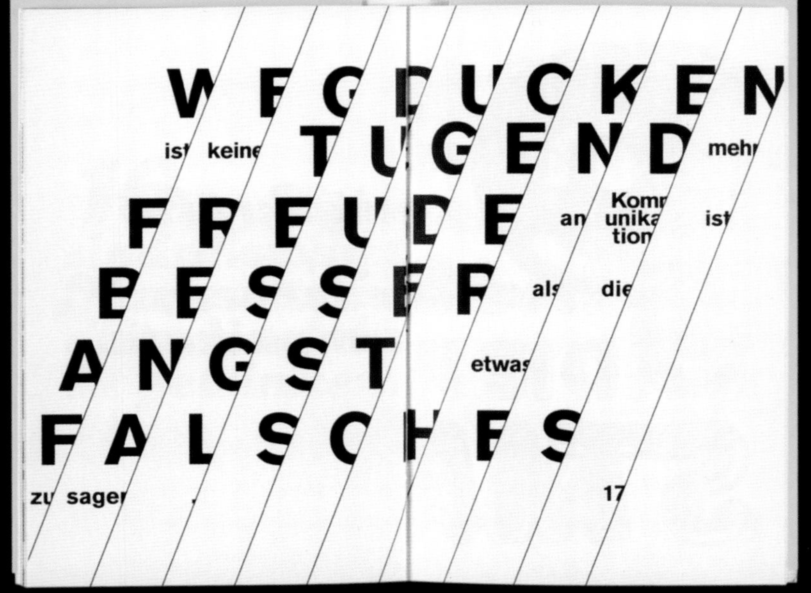

60 Brochure

DESIGN Tobias Heidmeier, *Hamburg* CREATIVE DIRECTION Jan Kruse AGENCY Ligalux GmbH CLIENT fischerAppelt, relations GmbH
PRINCIPAL TYPE Various DIMENSIONS 3.8 × 5.8 in. (9.6 × 14.8 cm)

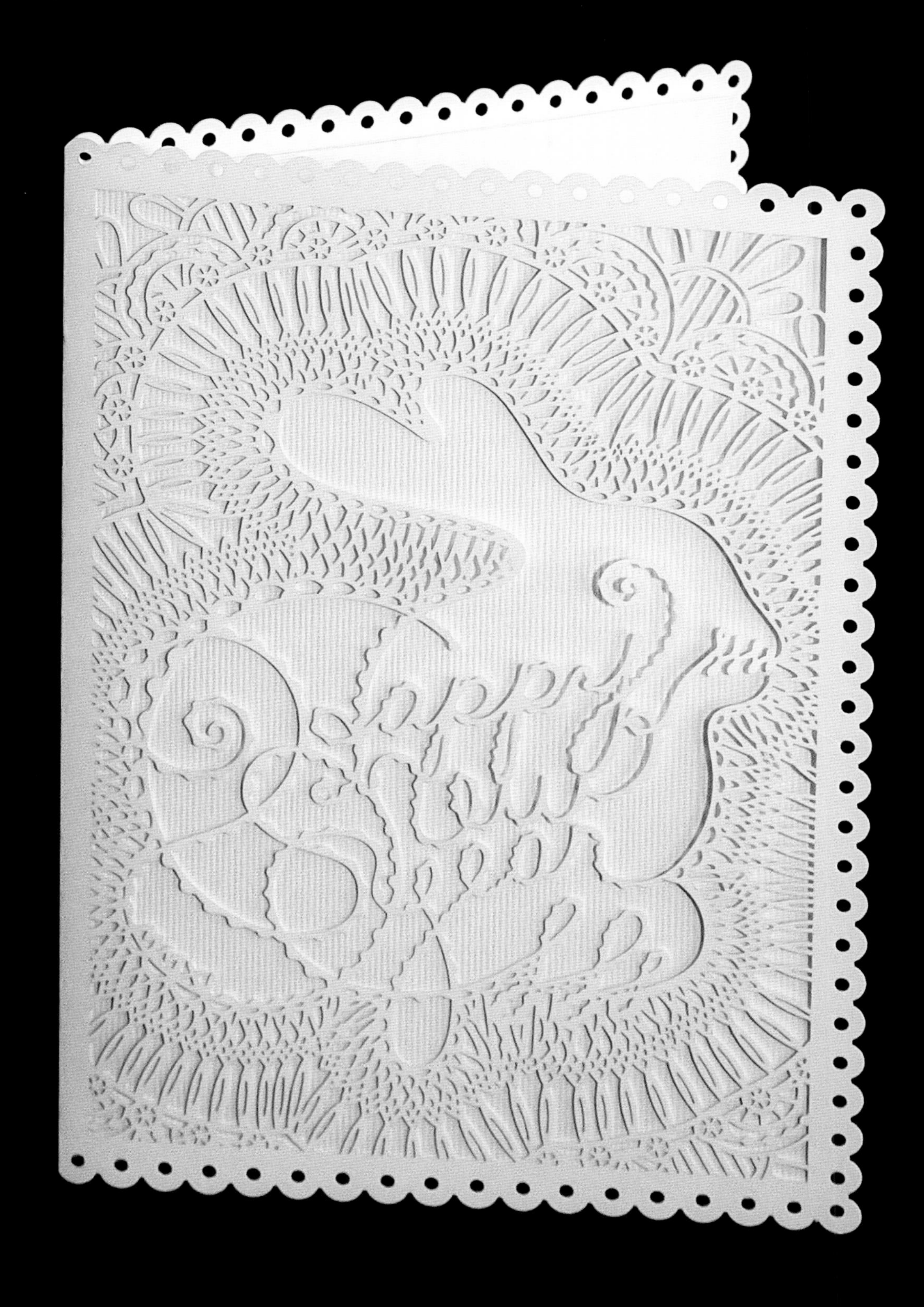

Greeting Card *61*

DESIGN Masayo Anton-Ozawa, *New York* LETTERING Masayo Anton-Ozawa PHOTOGRAPHY Theresa Stebe, *Deer Park, New York*
PRINCIPAL TYPE handlettering DIMENSIONS 5 × 7 in. (12.7 × 17.8 cm)

DESIGN Christy Thrasher, *Santa Monica, California* CREATIVE DIRECTION Robert Louey and Regina Rubino VICE PRESIDENT & MANAGING DIRECTOR Matt Adams, *New York* VICE PRESIDENT CULINARY OPERATIONS Susan Terry, Chicago DESIGN OFFICES Regina Rubino/IMAGE: Global Vision LLC and Robert Louey Design/Pagenova CLIENT Grand Hyatt New York PRINCIPAL TYPE various DIMENSIONS various

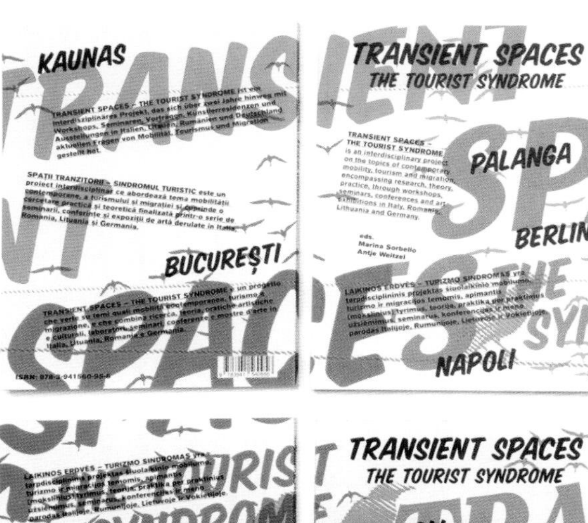

INTERNATIONAL COMMUTERS, SEASONAL WORKERS, "SUITCASE MIGRANTS", TOURISTS, FOREIGN RESIDENTS, AND OTHERS

and internal borders of the EU necessitate longer or shorter periods of immobilizations (deportation camps, waiting for the opportunity to cross borders etc.): yet they also create a space for informal kinds of mobility (transnational migrant networks, immigrant smuggling organizations etc.), which are stimulated not least by the economic demand for "cheap" labor.

In this combination of limiting and loosening the circulation of non-EU residents, mobility is revealed in a particularly evident way as a double effect of *projection* (geographical and social mobility of individuals as economic resource) and *reaction* (geographical and social mobility of individuals as a threat to national hegemony and the privileged ways of life of EU residents).[6] The emblem of the x-rayed suitcase and the EURES dance diagram of mobility visualize this logic of projection and reaction in a quite vivid way. Both images seek to symbolize mobility, yet they become – no matter how unintentionally – icons of an *interplay* between mobilization and control.

THE "NEW MOBILITIES"

One reason for the difficulties caused by the theme of mobility lies in the fact that the descriptions and definitions of mobility always also possess a normative core. Mobility *should* exist, not only because mobility is tied to the fundamental value of freedom, but because mobility is deemed useful and profitable. Interest-driven concepts envision mobility as a resource of economic productivity, as a key factor of a radical reordering of economic-political and social relations – according to neoliberal economics. The paradigm of mobility is constantly *programmatically turned*, i.e., declared a requirement in times of globalization that "is demanded of all organizations as a structural feature and expected of more and more individuals as a personal feature".[7]

In the field of tension between the "pressure to be mobile" and "the readiness to be mobile", a "mobility culture" emerges, in which differentiated flexibility becomes part of the requirement profile. The change between circulation and migration, the transitions between *transfer* (temporary or permanent movement at one place) and *transport* (routine flexibility that does not interrupt everyday life) bring experiences and values with them, the sum of which can be called "mobility".[7] Society – often grasped more statically than dynamically – can no longer be adequately understood without acknowledging the geographic, regional, professional, and social mobility of its members. Instead of "mobility" in the singular, talk is increasingly of (new) "mobilities". This pluralization of mobility can be put down to, amongst others, the replacement of a Fordist concept of mobility that was based on routine and being bound to one place, by a post-Fordist destabilization of space-time relations. In the wake of the intensified dynamism of globalization after 1989, the "new mobilities" articulate themselves in "new types of migrations": international commuters, seasonal workers, "suitcase migrants", tourists, foreign residents, and others traveling to and fro engender a unique typology of traversing space and time inside and outside the EU's borders that is in turn oriented toward different border functions and regimes: arriving, departing, entering, and leaving, tourist stays, second place of residence, remigration, vague, nomadic vagabonding.[8]

The multiple mobilities restructuring economic and social life in the form of a network are grasped as productive forces that are to be unleashed, on the one hand, yet observed, registered, and theorized, on the other. The sociologist John Urry sharpens the debate by contending that, under the impression of new mobilities, the social as society is being replaced by the social as mobility. He claims that the global movements of individuals, companies, and goods creates a space beyond society and institutions.[9] Urry repeatedly stresses that

WHAT DOES MOBILITY MEAN?

90

the transformation of the social to mobility is not a linear, uniform process of liquefaction. The dialectics of mobility and immobility does remain – along with the social and economic inequalities caused by different accesses to the technologies and infrastructures of mobility.

Yet the analysis of the "new mobilities paradigm", which is currently expanding to become an interdisciplinary research field of its own,[10] is not free of mobility euphoria. At times, current mobility research is reminiscent of postmodern thinkers such as Paul Virilio, Michel de Certeau, Gilles Deleuze/Félix Guattari, James Clifford, or Iain Chambers, who envisioned "a wonderful new mobile world of nomads and travelers".[11] Michael Hardt and Antonio Negri, the authors of *Empire*, also position themselves in this tradition of a subversive twist given to the epos of mobility. They write that in the global empire a resistive, tactically operating, "transversal mobility" engenders "new, nomadic desires", which the state and society have a hard time disciplining.[12] The biopolitics of mobility, of which there are signs in this vision of a transversal mobility, potentially works toward a "mechanism that can coordinate politically the new dynamics of the global domain of capital and the subjective dimension of the actors".[13] Of course, in this call for coordination, Hardt and Negri reveal a socio-technical moment which one must also presume behind the restructuring of social sciences necessitated by mobility. The new, allegedly deterritorializing mobility is thus *reterritorialized* – in sociological typologies and philosophical-political projects. And it is exploited where state institutions produce and control mobility. For, government mobility policies no longer consist merely in restrictive and immobilizing measures, they instead adapt to the general developments and processes of mobility from case to case. The "strategic application of immobility to specific cases" is thus "coupled with the production of (certain kinds of) mobility" that promise dynamizing and deregulating effects.[14]

In a symptomatic co-production between the different collective and individual actors of mobility who observe and learn from each other, an informal and irregular sphere emerges, a specific mobility culture. This sphere gives rise to peculiar architectures and infrastructures in and through which mobility is embodied and performed. These spaces of mobility should not be mistaken for the virtual landscapes of a techno-imaginary in which individuals float in a bodiless fashion; the materiality of these spaces and the individuals and groups populating and traversing them is unquestionable. Equally, one must not criminalize, precarize, marginalize, or simply write off the informal spaces and the subjects circulating in them. What is instead at issue here is to examine how the geography and practices of mobility change in view of population-political and border-police regulations; how, in the informal sphere, a "political economy of migration" arises, increasingly supplementing the older subjectivization patterns as labor migrants with the subject position of the entrepreneur[15]; and how totally new dance steps are rehearsed in this space, which one cannot get hold of using the old graphics.

ARRIVING, DEPARTING, ENTERING, AND LEAVING, TOURIST STAYS, SECOND PLACE OF RESIDENCE, REMIGRATION, VAGUE, NOMADIC VAGABONDING

MOBILITY IS "FROZEN MOVEMENT"

So what is the special feature of what today can be called mobility? First, it may have become clear that it is not only about flexibility as in the prevailing demands for "professional mobility", but also not exclusively about movement in the sense of shifting from one place to another, be it in daily transport or long-term transfer. While individuals do change their location by moving from one point to another, they simultaneously remain at that other place where their movement began. This quite evidently applies to tourists. But it is also true of immigrants who, in a number of respects, maintain

TOM HOLERT / MARK TERKESSIDIS

91

DESIGN Sascha Thoma, Ben Wittner, and Bjoern Wolf, *Berlin* STUDIO Eps51 graphic design studio CLIENT uqbar, *Berlin* PRINCIPAL TYPE Akzidenz-Grotesk, House Slant, Rosewood, and Soda Script DIMENSIONS Books: 7.9 × 10.2 in. (20 × 26 cm) Posters: 33.1 × 23.4 in. (84.1 × 59.4 cm)

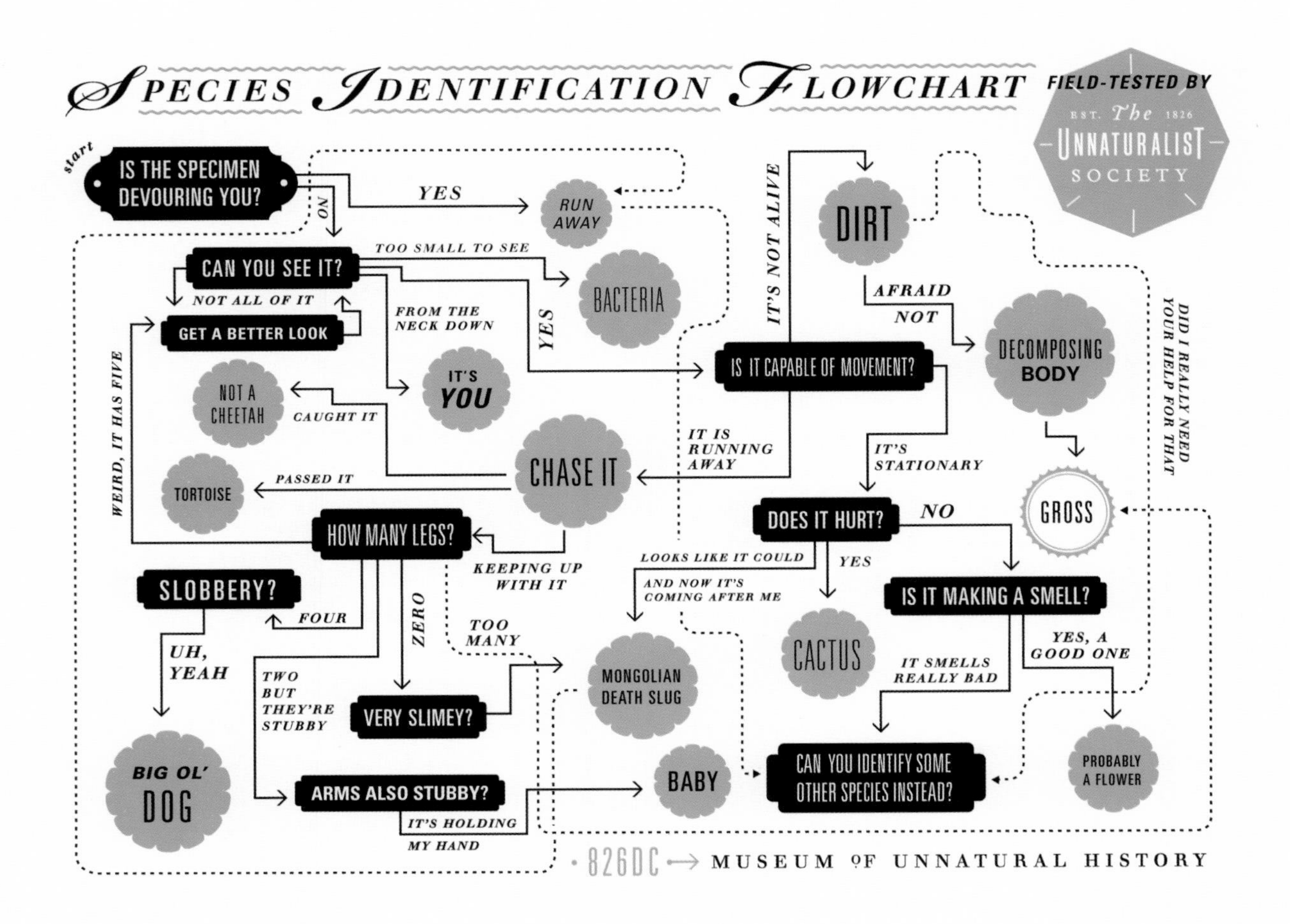

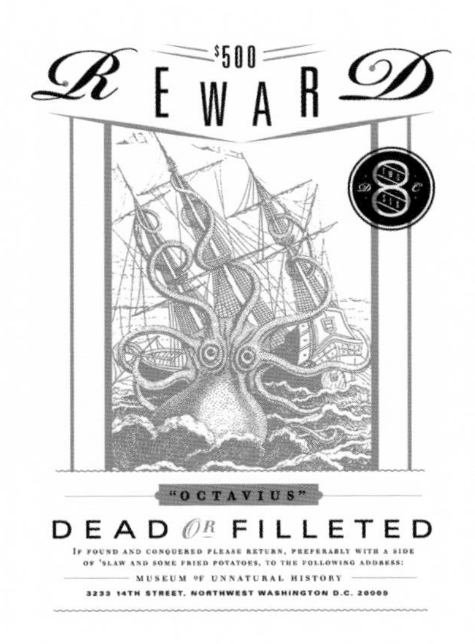

DESIGN Oliver Munday, *New York* CLIENT 826DC PRINCIPAL TYPE Bickham Script, Univers, and Walbaum
DIMENSIONS 18 × 24 in. (45.7 × 61 cm)

ONE ATL
ANTIC C
HARDON
NAY SAN
TA BARB
ARA COU
NTY
20 09

ONE ATL
ANTIC C
ABERNET
SAUVIGN
ON NAPA
VALLEY
20 08

DESIGN Christine Celic Strohl, *New York* ART DIRECTION Christine Celic Strohl CREATIVE DIRECTION Matteo Bologna DESIGN OFFICE Mucca Design CLIENT Icon Group
PRINCIPAL TYPE One Atlantic Book, One Atlantic Text Light, One Atlantic Text Light Italic DIMENSIONS 2 × 4 in. (5.1 × 10.2 cm)

DESIGN Eduardo del Fraile Carbajo and Andrés Guerrero, *Murcia, Spain* STUDIO Eduardo del Fraile CLIENT Soso Salt PRINCIPAL TYPE Helvetica Bold
DIMENSIONS 4.9 × 3.5 in. (12.5 × 9 cm)

dtv C.H.Beck

FRIEDRICH NIETZSCHE

ALSO SPRACH ZARA-THUS-TRA

MAN MUSS NOCH CHAOS IN SICH HABEN,
UM EINEN TANZENDEN STERN GEBÄREN ZU KÖNNEN.

PLATON

VON DER UNSTERBLICHKEIT DER SEELE
WENN DIE SEELE UNSTERBLICH IST, SO BEDARF SIE SORGSAMER PFLEGE.

dtv C.H.Beck

Arthur Schopenhauer

Willig tun was man kann und
willig leiden was man muß.

dtv C.H.Beck

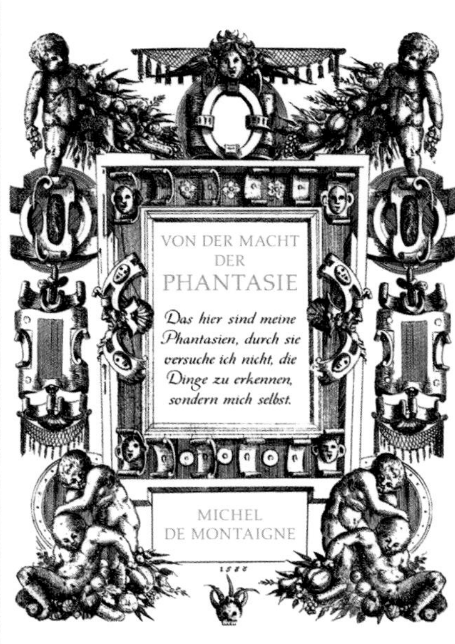

dtv C.H.Beck

Lew Tolstoi

Herr und Knecht

Was man in einer Stunde
versäumt hat, bringt man in
einem Jahr nicht wieder ein.

DESIGN Michaela Kneissl and Christian Otto, *Munich* DESIGN OFFICE Geviert CLIENT C.H.Beck oHG dtv PRINCIPAL TYPE various
DIMENSIONS 4.3 × 7.1 in. (11 × 18 cm)

DESIGN Masumi Briozzo and Angus Hyland, *London* DESIGN OFFICE Pentagram Design London CLIENT Barbican Art Gallery
PRINCIPAL TYPE Archer, Bickham Script Pro, Caslon Pro, and Lettres ombrées ornées DIMENSIONS 7.1 × 9.1 in. (18 × 23 cm)

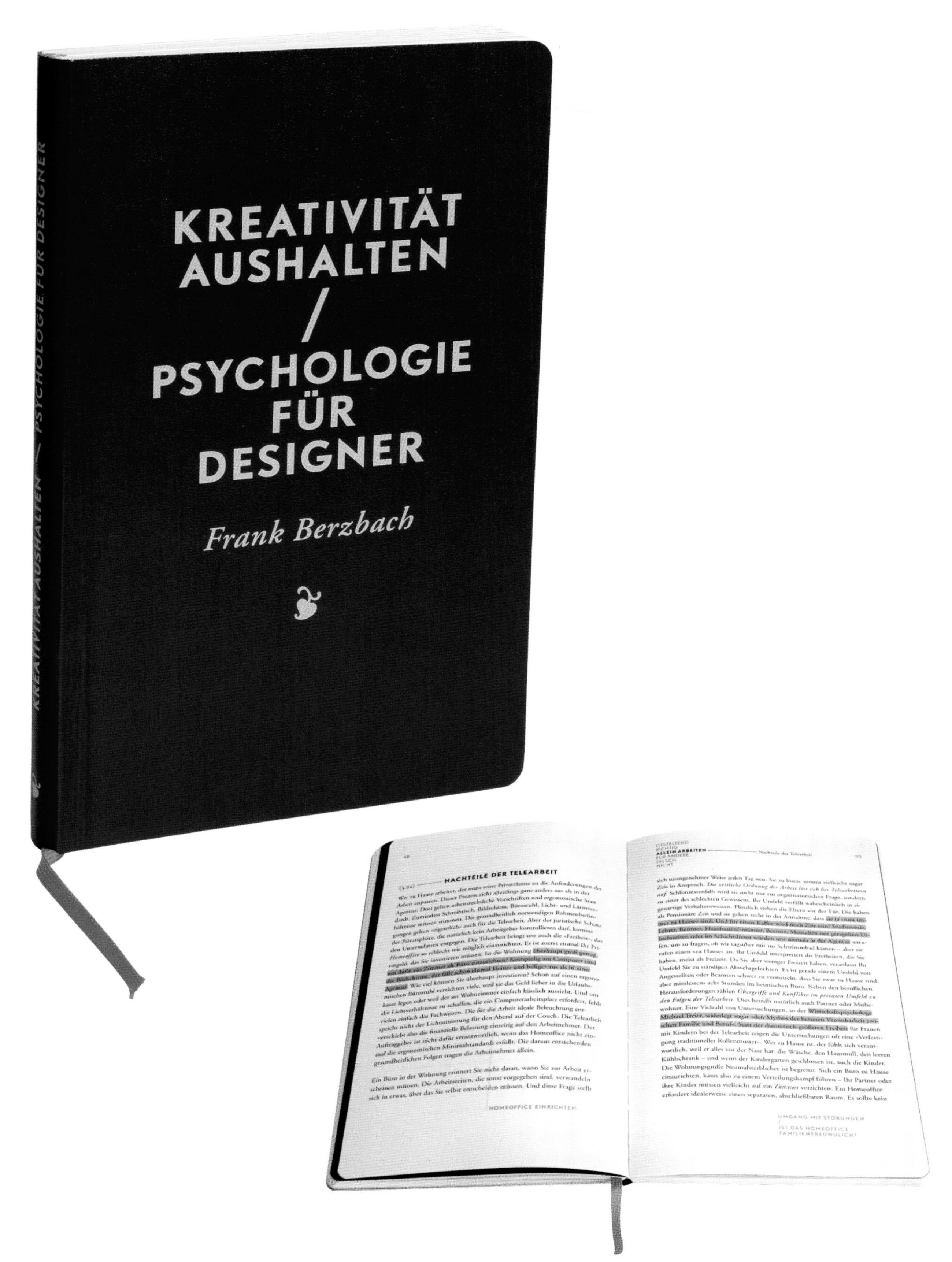

DESIGN Katrin Schacke, *Offenbach, Germany* **AUTHOR** Dr. Frank Berzbach, *Bonn, Germany* **MARKETING** Karin Schmidt-Friderichs, *Mainz, Germany*
PRINTER Universitaetsdruckerei H. Schmidt, *Mainz* **PUBLISHER** Verlag Hermann Schmidt, *Mainz* **PRINCIPAL TYPE** Adobe Garamond and DTL Nobel T
DIMENSIONS 5.3 × 8.2 in. (13.5 × 21 cm)

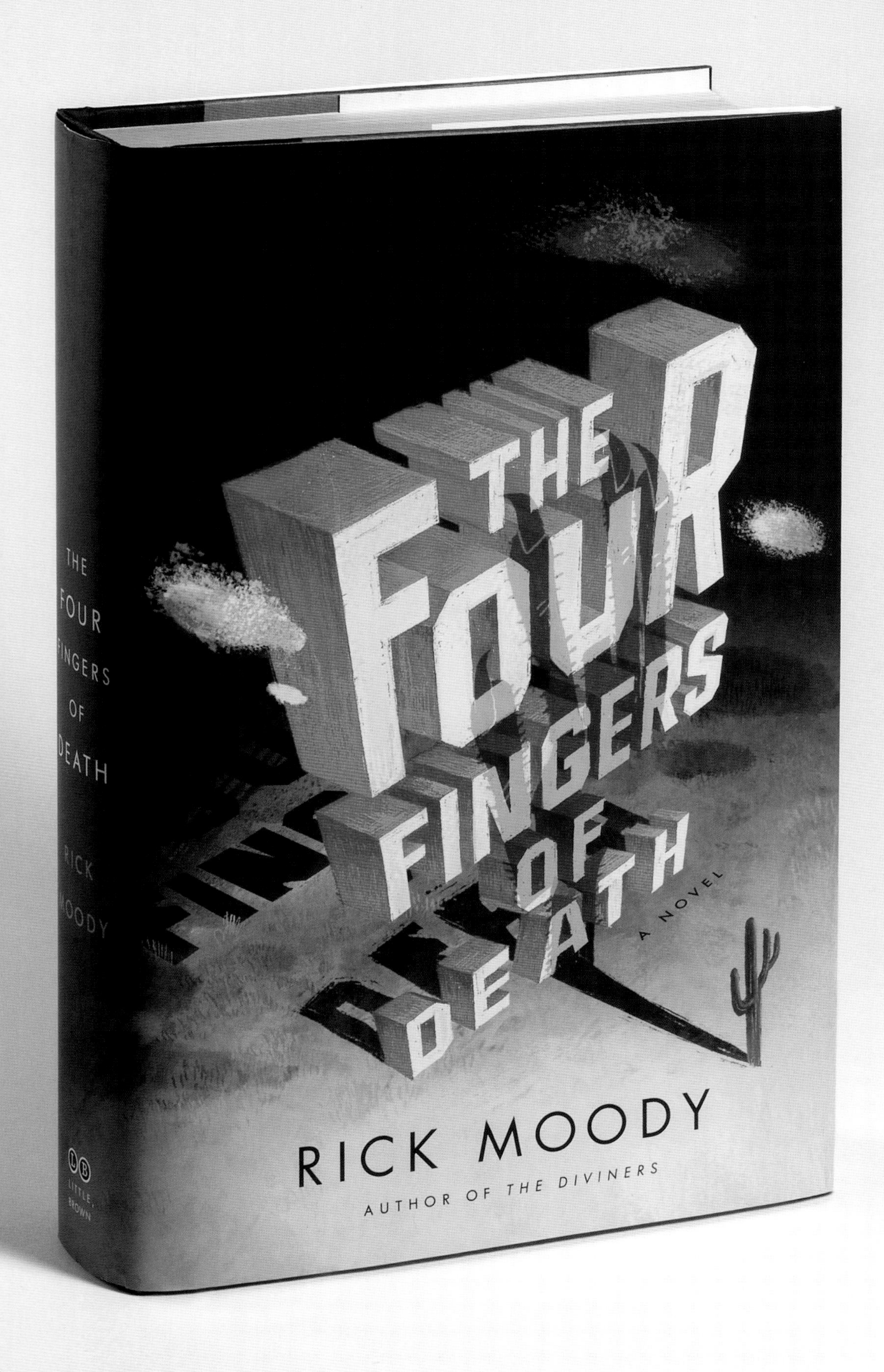

70 Book Jacket

DESIGN Keith Hayes, *New York* LETTERING Keith Hayes and Ronald Kurniawan ART DIRECTION Keith Hayes CREATIVE DIRECTION Mario J. Pulice ILLUSTRATION Ronald Kurniawan PUBLISHER Hachette Book Group / Little, Brown and Company PRINCIPAL TYPE Futura Book and handlettering DIMENSIONS 6.1 × 9.5 in. (15.6 × 24.1 cm)

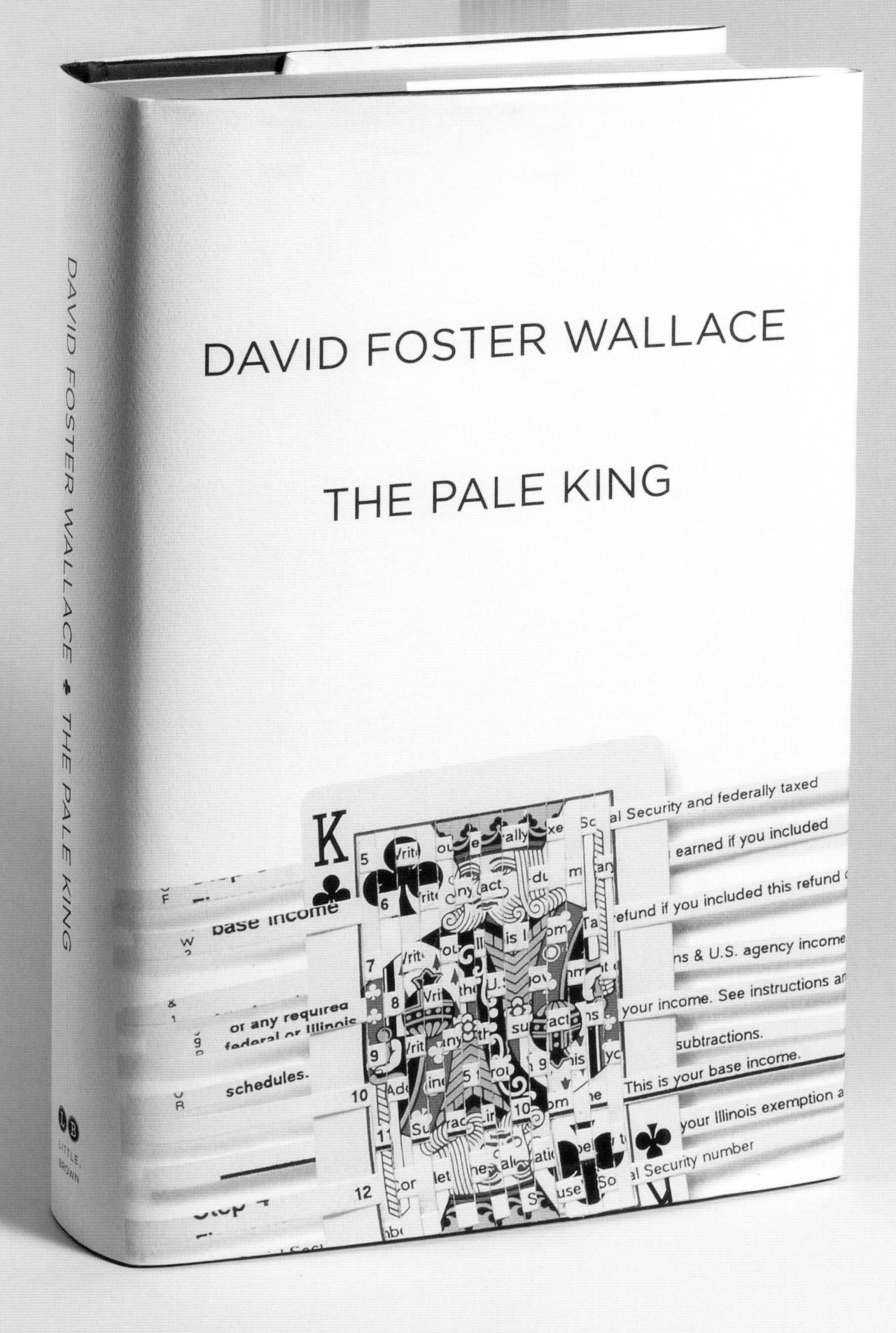

Book Jacket

DESIGN Mario J. Pulice, *New York* CREATIVE DIRECTION Mario J. Pulice ARTWORK Karen Green PUBLISHER Hachette Book Group / Little, Brown and Company
PRINCIPAL TYPE Gotham Book DIMENSIONS 6.1 × 9.5 in. (15.6 × 24.1 cm)

 Brochure

CREATIVE DIRECTION Karlheinz Müller and Paul Wagner, *Munich* TRANSLATOR Ross M. Benjamin, *New York* AGENCY Freie Radikale Werbung
CLIENT Heidelberger Druckmaschinen AG PRINCIPAL TYPE United Stencil DIMENSIONS 7.9 × 7.9 in. (20 × 20 cm)

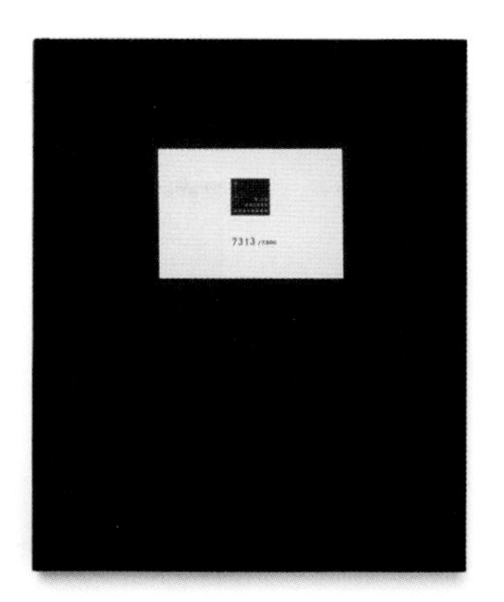

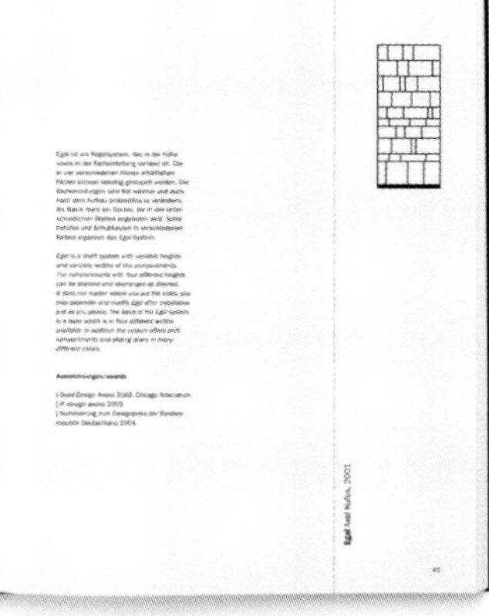

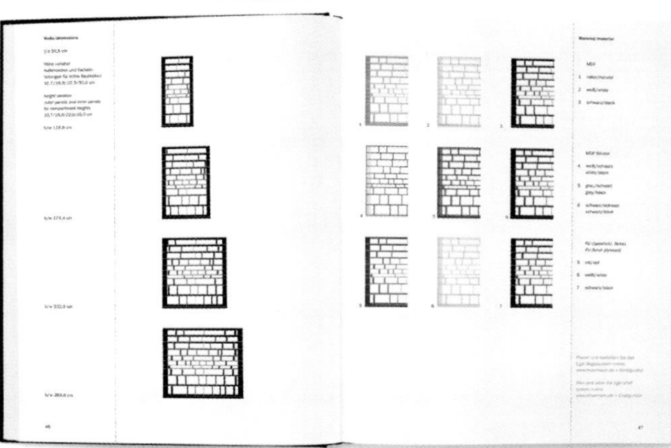

DESIGN Olaf Jäger and Regina Jäger, *Überlingen, Germany* AGENCY Jäger & Jäger CLIENT Nils Holger Moormann GmbH PRINCIPAL TYPE ITC Franklin Gothic
DIMENSIONS 8.9 x 11.2 in. (22.5 x 28.5 cm)

 Book Jacket

DESIGN Charlotte Strick, *New York* PUBLISHER Farrar, Straus and Giroux PRINCIPAL TYPE Pelso
DIMENSIONS 6.1 × 9.2 in. (15.6 × 23.3 cm)

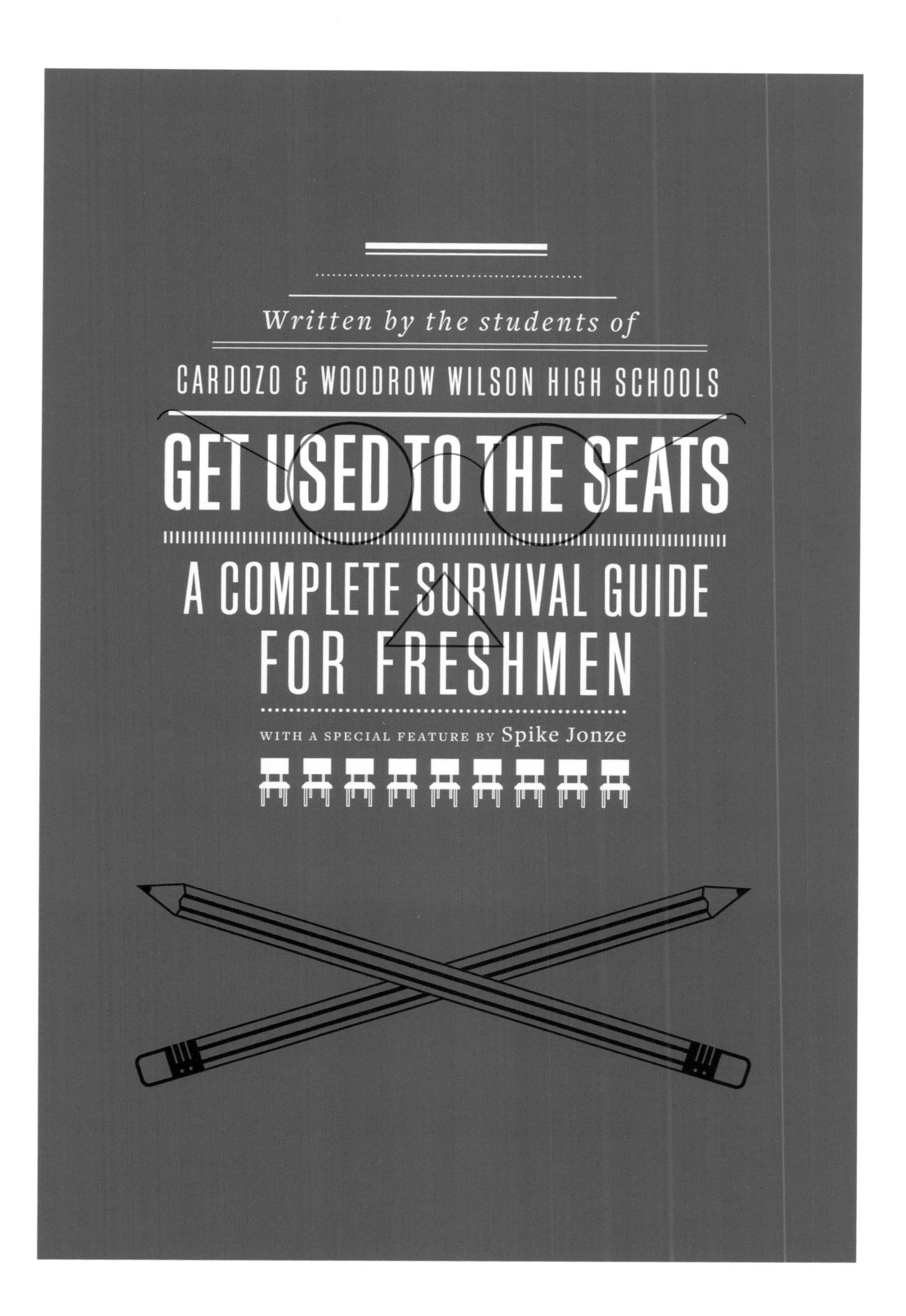

DESIGN Oliver Munday, *New York* **CLIENT** 826DC **PRINCIPAL TYPE** Block Gothic, and Freight Micro
DIMENSIONS 6 × 9 in. (15.2 × 22.9 cm)

 Catalog

DESIGN Bondé Prang, *Philadelphia* **ART DIRECTION** Andy Cruz, *Wilmington, Delaware* **PHOTOGRAPHY** Carlos Alejandro
PHOTOGRAPHY STUDIOS Carlos Alejandro Photography and The Herman Miller Archive **TEXT SHOWINGS** Erik van Blokland and Ben Kiel, *The Hague, Netherlands*, and *Yorklyn, Delaware* **DESIGN OFFICE** House Industries, *Yorklyn, Delaware*, and The Eames Office, *Santa Monica, California*
PRINCIPAL TYPE Eames Century Modern and Eames Exhibits **DIMENSIONS** 4.5 × 8.25 in. (11.4 × 21 cm)

DESIGN Clea Forkert, *Toronto* CREATIVE DIRECTION Claire Dawson and Fidel Peña DESIGN OFFICE Underline Studio
CLIENT The Robert McLaughlin Gallery, McMaster Museum of Art PRINCIPAL TYPE Helvetica Neue, Hoefler Text, and Hoefler Titling
DIMENSIONS Flat 39.2 × 10 in. (99.45 × 25.4 cm), Folded 7.5 × 10 in. (19.1 × 25.4 cm)

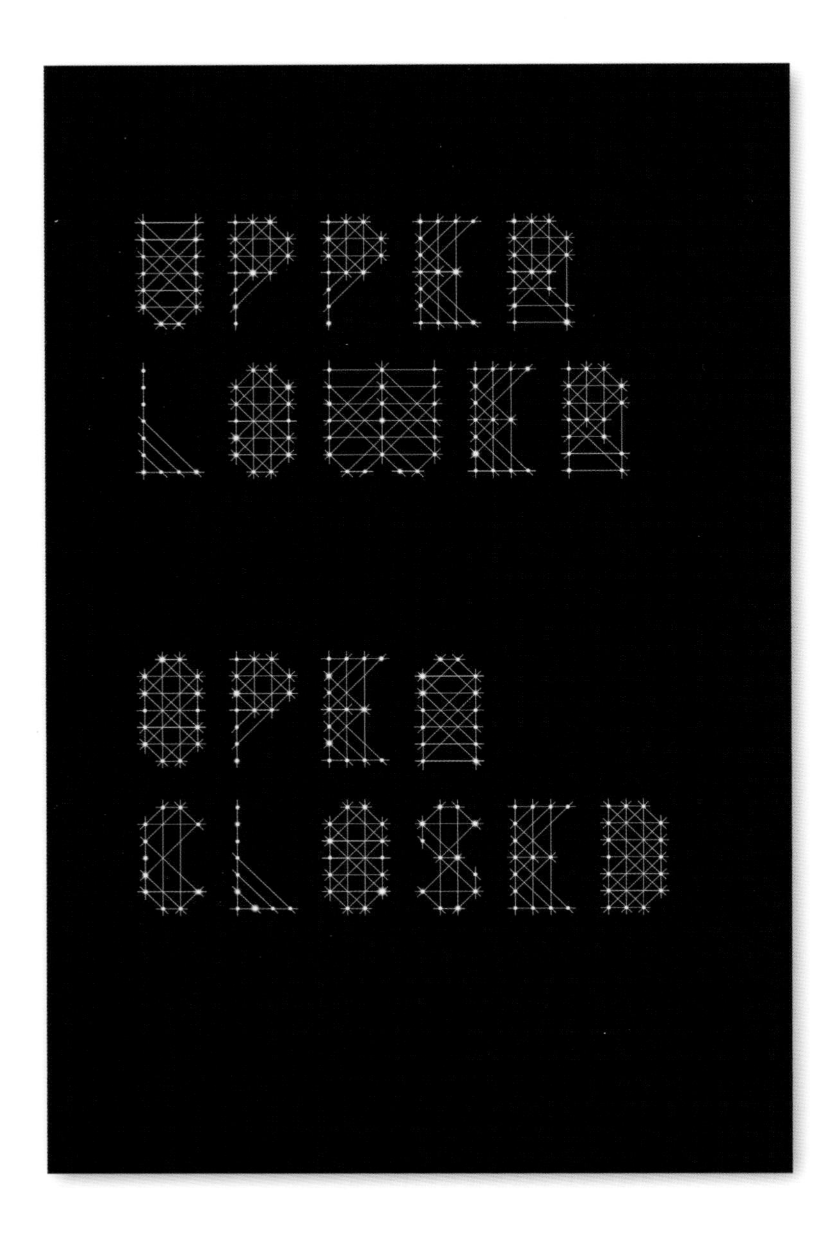

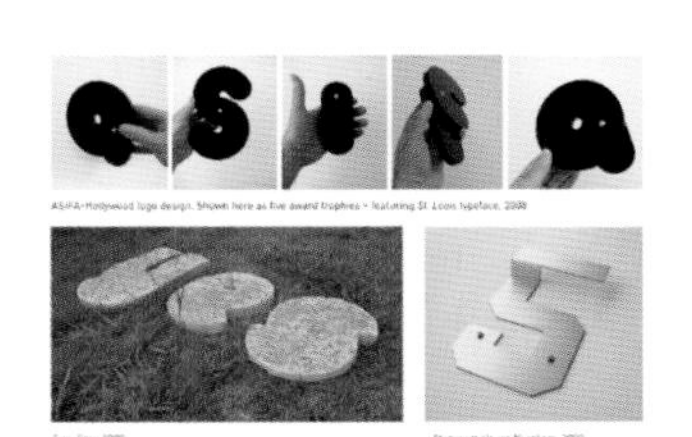

I always think of type or lettering as two-dimensional, flat, on a piece of paper ... Oh yes, it might have a drop shadow to give the illusion of a bit of a lift off the page, but that's about it ... until I see what Andrew Byrom does with letter forms.

Ed Fella, Graphic Designer/Artist/Educator (Los Angeles)

Other cultures adopted – and adapted – the Sumerian system and the alphabet we know today slowly began to take shape. Later, the Romans standardized the design with a system for carving letters onto their architecture. These developments were again brought about by practical and physical needs. Here the constraints of a reed scraping clay are replaced by those of a chisel chipping away at stone.

In traditional, printed typography the effect of three-dimensions has been with us since the mid 1800s, by which time the Industrial Revolution had fine-tuned the printing press for mass production and its effect had spread throughout the globe – spawning new fields in affordable literature, newspaper production, and advertising. Before this period typefaces were beautifully proportioned and designed for optimum legibility on page-after-page of text. Printed advertisements

16

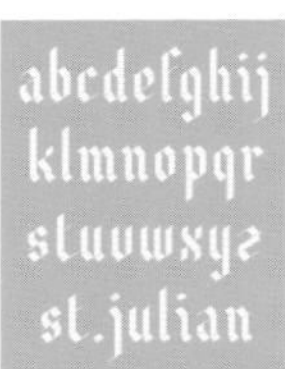

now needed new and more engaging typefaces that would draw attention to themselves and scream short, sharp messages: *Look at me! I'm new! I'm improved! I'm on sale! I'm beautiful! Buy me!*

Vincent Figgins was one of several type founders who reacted to this need for dramatic new letterforms. He designed many groundbreaking styles of lettering including *In Shade*, the first drop-shadow; *Pearl Outline*, the first outlined specimen, and in 1832 he coined the term, 'san serif'. Although the majority of this work was largely restricted to what today we might describe as 'display' faces, designers like Figgins and his contemporaries – Robert Thorne, William Caslon IV, and William Thorowgood – can be seen as the first experimental typographers. Their contribution to typography was immense. They were the first to design self-conscious typefaces: letterforms that drew attention not just to the message they carried, but to their own design.

The new technologies and visual trends of the 1950s, 60s, and 70s saw a wave of type designs that took inspiration from three-dimensional forms: examples include Roger Excoffon's *Calypso* (1958), which would later become a Letraset favorite, and Milton Glaser's *Baby Curls* (1975).

17

DESIGN Andrew Byrom, *Long Beach, California* WRITERS Andrew Byrom and Renée Cossutta
CLIENTS La Sierra University and The University of Massachusetts Lowell PRINCIPAL TYPE various DIMENSIONS 5.5 × 8.5 in. (14 × 21.6 cm)

DESIGN Tom Ising, *Munich* AGENCY Herburg Weiland Design Agency CLIENT Martin Wöhrl
PRINCIPAL TYPE Helvetica DIMENSIONS 7.1 × 9.1 in. (18 × 23 cm)

DESIGN Mette Hornung Rankin, *Portland, Oregon* **LETTERING** Mette Hornung Rankin **DESIGN OFFICE** Bureau of Betterment
PRINCIPAL TYPE handlettering **DIMENSIONS** 17.25 × 23 in. (43.8 × 58.4 cm)

DESIGN Richard The, *New York* **ART DIRECTION** Stefan Sagmeister **STUDIO** Sagmeister Inc.
PRINCIPAL TYPE custom

DESIGN Yoichi Kondo, Minato-ku, *Japan* AGENCY ENJIN Inc. CLIENT LOTTE Co., LTD. PRINCIPAL TYPE custom
DIMENSIONS 3 × 0.8 in. (7.5 × 2 cm)

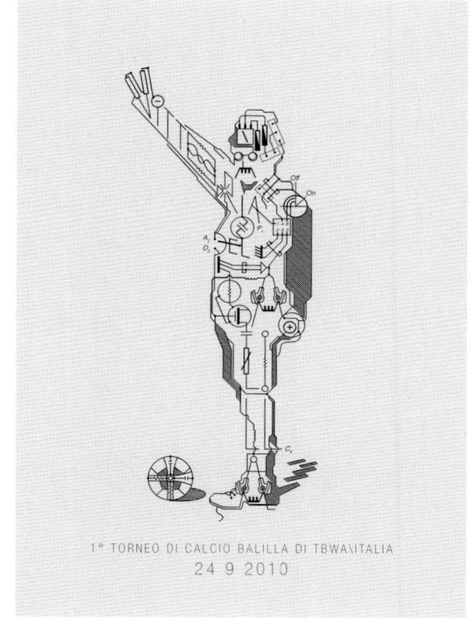

1° TORNEO DI CALCIO BALILLA DI TBWA\ITALIA
24 9 2010

DESIGN Mattia Montanari, *Milan* **ART DIRECTION** Mattia Montanari **CREATIVE DIRECTION** Francesco Guerrera and Nicola Lampugnani **AGENCY** TBWA\ITALIA SPA
CLIENT FirstFloorUnder.com **PRINCIPAL TYPE** Oblio **DIMENSIONS** 27.6 x 39.4 in. (70 x 100 cm)

RENOIR
The Late Years
A new exhibit explores why art aficionados lost their taste for Renoir—and why they should reconsider.
BY SARA ROMANO
"Girl in Red Ruff" (1896)
24 FRANCE • WINTER 2009-10

84 Magazine Spread

DESIGN Todd Albertson, *Washington, D.C.* **STUDIO** Todd Albertson Design **CLIENT** *France Magazine* **PRINCIPAL TYPE** custom
DIMENSIONS 9 × 10.9 in. (22.9 × 27.7 cm)

SAILOR
←
Jean Paul Gaultier has an abiding passion for sailor stripes. Here he poses in the hallway of the ELLE Décoration apartment at Paris's Cité de l'Architecture, which he recently swathed in the iconic blue-and-white fabric.
THIS YEAR'S HOT TREND WAS LAUNCHED IN EUROPE—150 YEARS AGO.
BY SARA ROMANO
FRANCE • SUMMER 2010 33

DESIGN Todd Albertson, *Washington, D.C.* STUDIO Todd Albertson Design CLIENT *France Magazine* PRINCIPAL TYPE custom
DIMENSIONS 9 × 10.9 in. (22.9 × 27.7 cm)

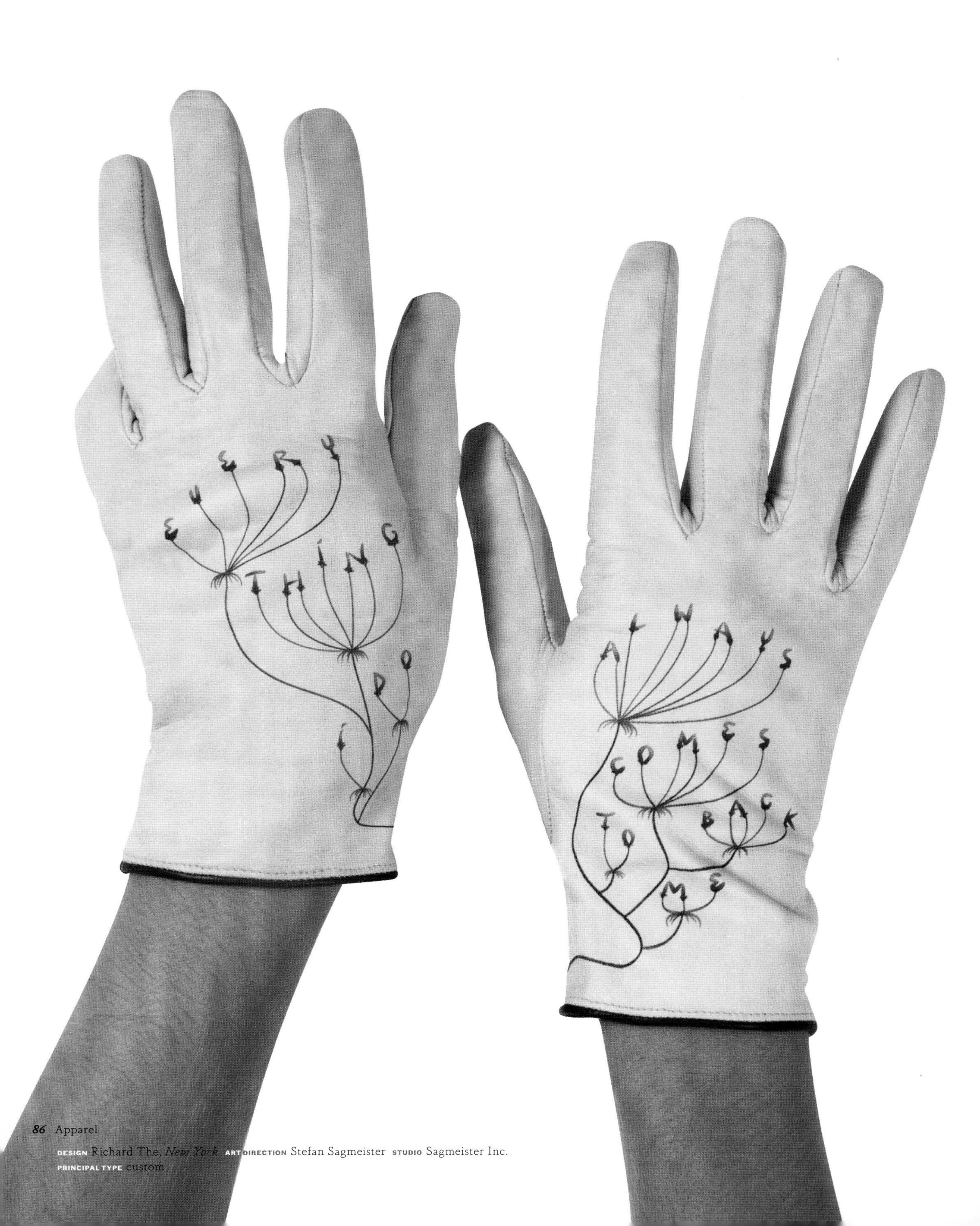

DESIGN Richard The, *New York* **ART DIRECTION** Stefan Sagmeister **STUDIO** Sagmeister Inc.
PRINCIPAL TYPE custom

DESIGN Kathryn Bernadette Fabrizio, *Philadelphia* IN-HOUSE DEPARTMENT Anthropologie PRINCIPAL TYPE Helvetica Neue
DIMENSIONS 3 × 2 in. (7.5 × 5 cm)

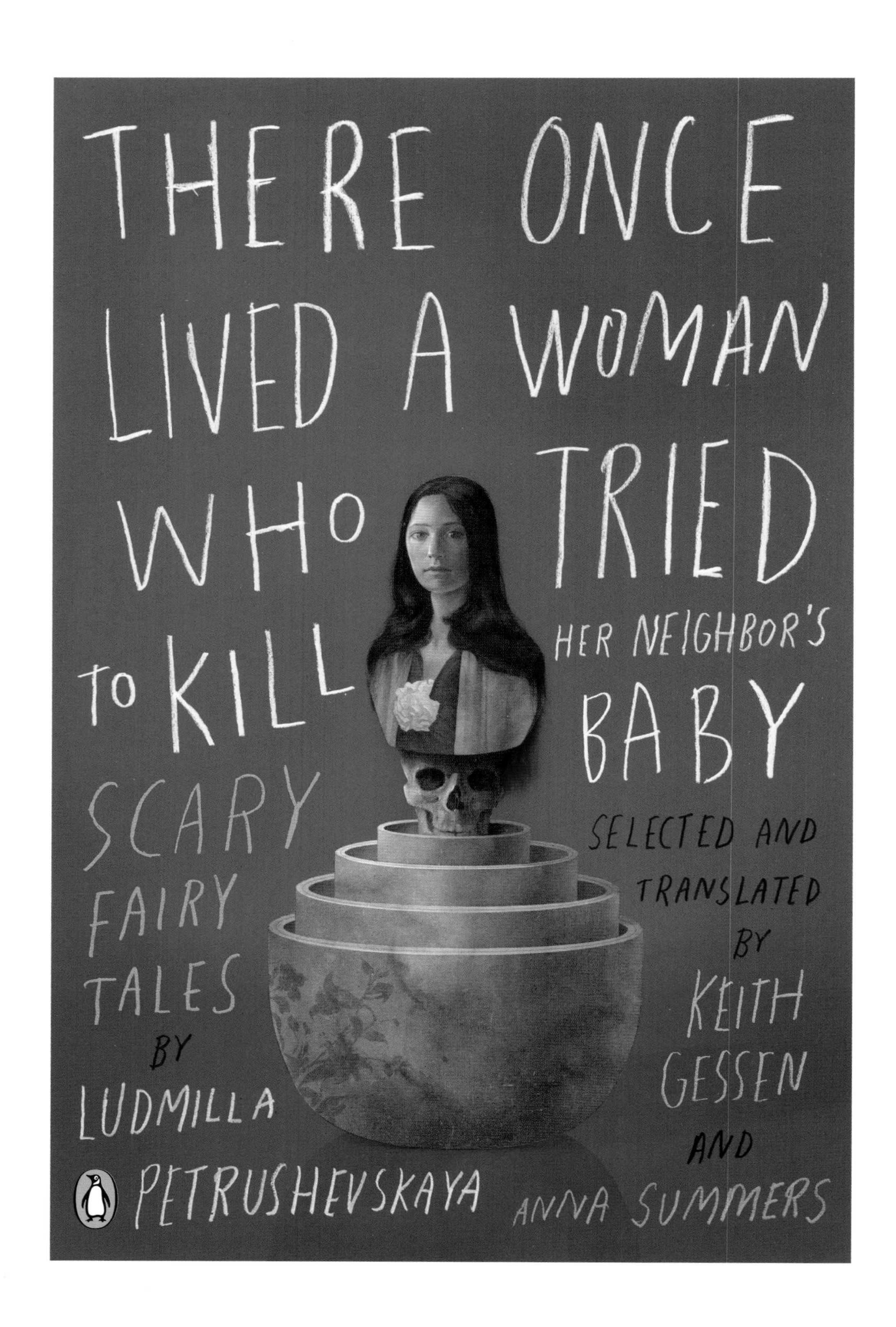

 Book Jacket

DESIGN Christopher Brand, *New York* ART DIRECTION Roseanne Serra CREATIVE DIRECTION Paul Buckley LETTERING Christopher Brand ILLUSTRATION Sam Weber PUBLISHER Penguin Books PRINCIPAL TYPE handlettering DIMENSIONS 5.1 in × 7.75 in. (13 × 19.7 cm)

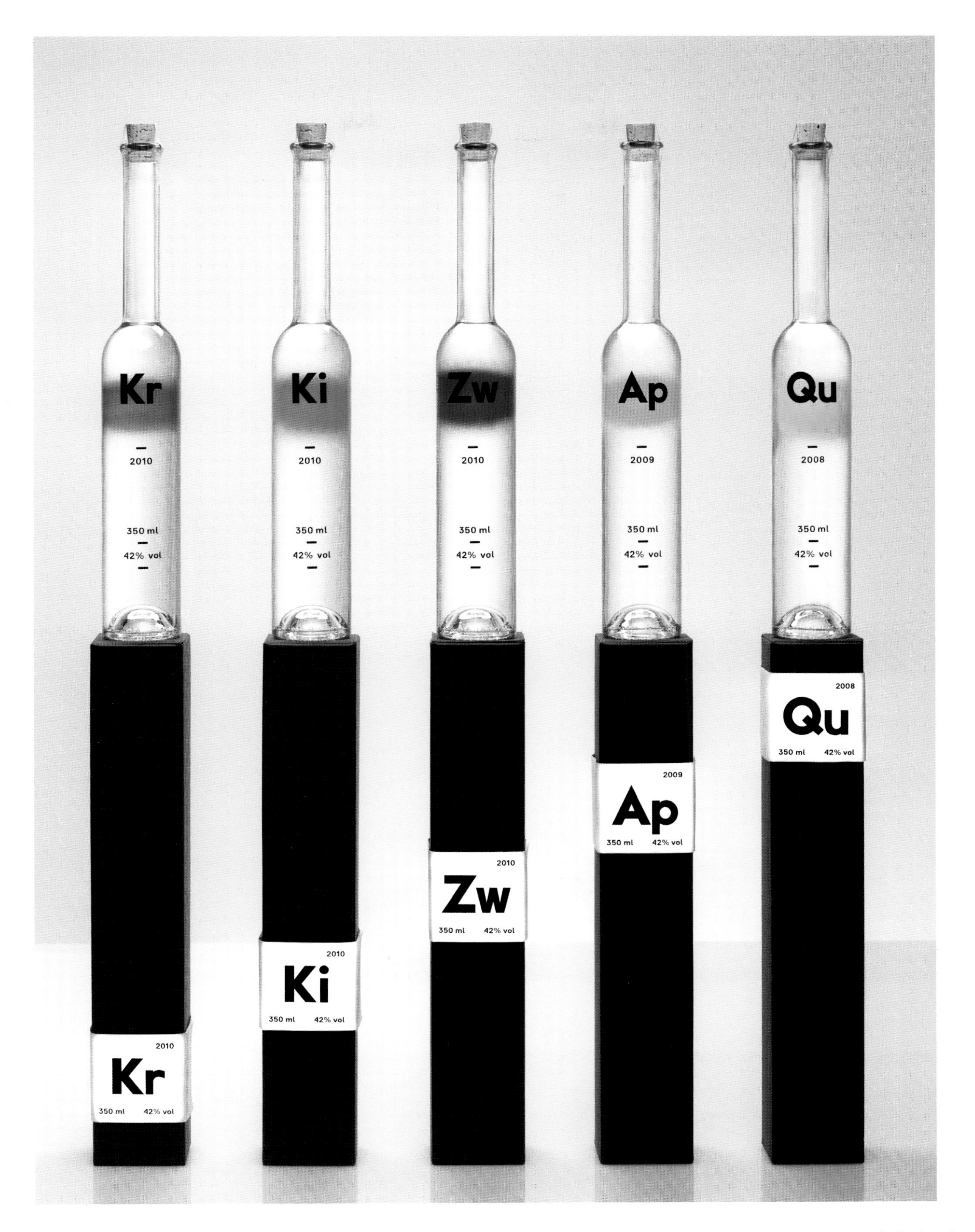

DESIGN Thomas Lehner, *Berlin* FINE ARTS Christine Gertsch, *Zürich* PHOTOGRAPHY Michael Koritschan, Studio Koritschan COPYWRITER Julius Weiss
DESIGN OFFICE Thomas Lehner, Visual Communications CLIENT Rezept-Destillate, Wettingen, *Switzerland*
PRINCIPAL TYPE Apotheke and Replica DIMENSIONS 2.4 x 14.8 x 2.4 in. (6 x 37.5 x 6 cm)

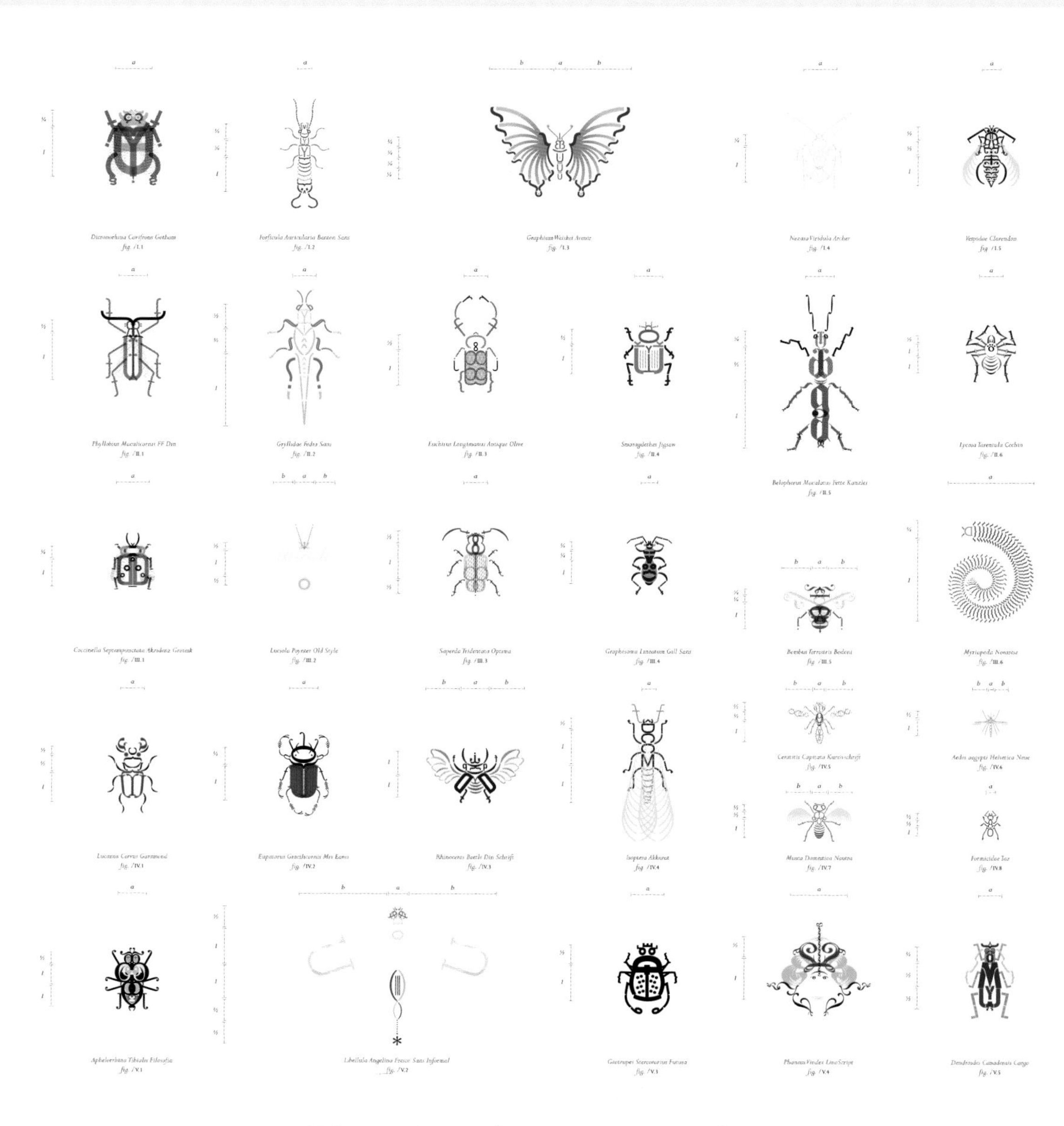

Typographic Entomology

DESIGN Valentina Ascione, Cristiano Bottino, Serena Brovelli, Libero Corti, Luigi Farrauto, Barbara Forni, Sergio Menichelli, and Paolo Tesei, *Milan*
PRINTER CTS Grafica **STUDIO** studio FM milano **PRINCIPAL TYPE** Insects **DIMENSIONS** 18.9 × 26.5 in. (47.9 × 67.3 cm)

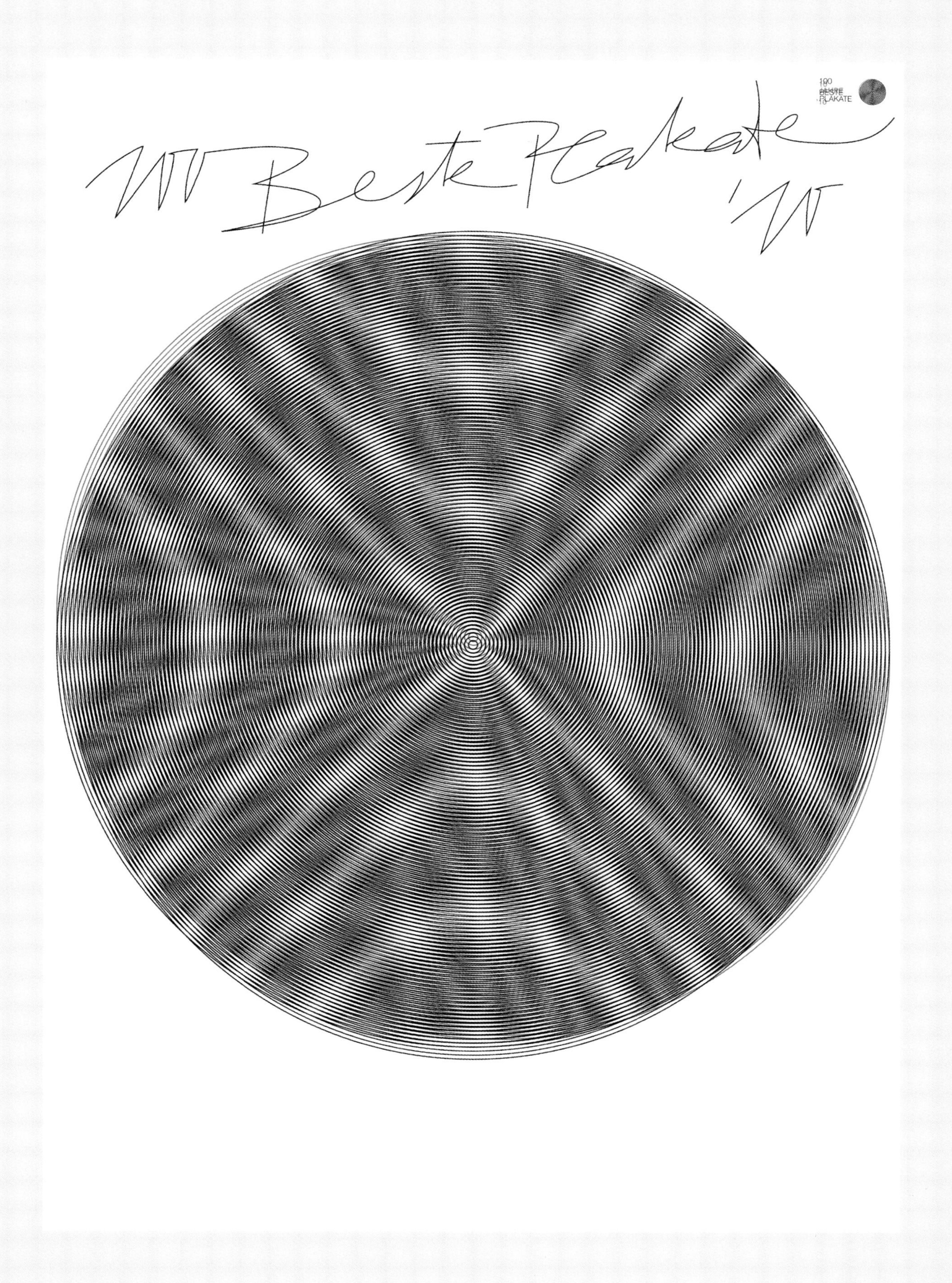

DESIGN Sascha Lobe and Dirk Wachowiak, *Stuttgart* ART DIRECTION Simon Brenner CREATIVE DIRECTION Sascha Lobe LETTERING Sascha Lobe and Simon Brenner STUDIO L2M3 Kommunikationsdesign GmbH CLIENT 100 Beste Plakate e. V. PRINCIPAL TYPE handlettering DIMENSIONS 16.5 × 23.4 in. (42 × 59.4 cm)

DESIGN Joshua C. Chen, Debbie Ladas, and Max Spector, *San Francisco* **CREATIVE DIRECTION** Joshua C. Chen **DESIGN OFFICE** Chen Design Associates
CLIENT Tell Tale Preserve Company **PRINCIPAL TYPE** Bickham Script, Craw Modern, Joanna, and Knockout **DIMENSIONS** various

CREATIVE DIRECTION Kirsten Dietz, *Stuttgart* DESIGN OFFICE Strichpunkt Design CLIENT Taschen PRINCIPAL TYPE Adobe Garamond Pro, FF Scala Sans, and Vineta
DIMENSIONS 6.9 × 8.6 in. (17.5 × 21.8 cm)

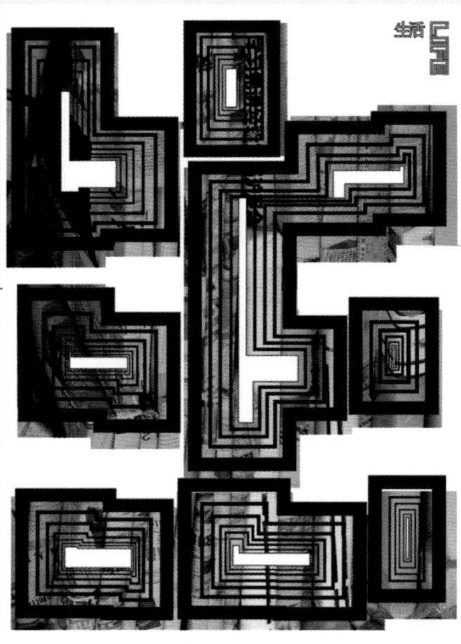

DESIGN Chen Pingbo, *Shenzhen, China* AGENCY Chen Pingbo Graphic Design CLIENT Shenzhen Graphic Design Association (SGDA)
PRINCIPAL TYPE Blackbold DIMENSIONS 27.6 × 39.4 in. (70 × 100 cm)

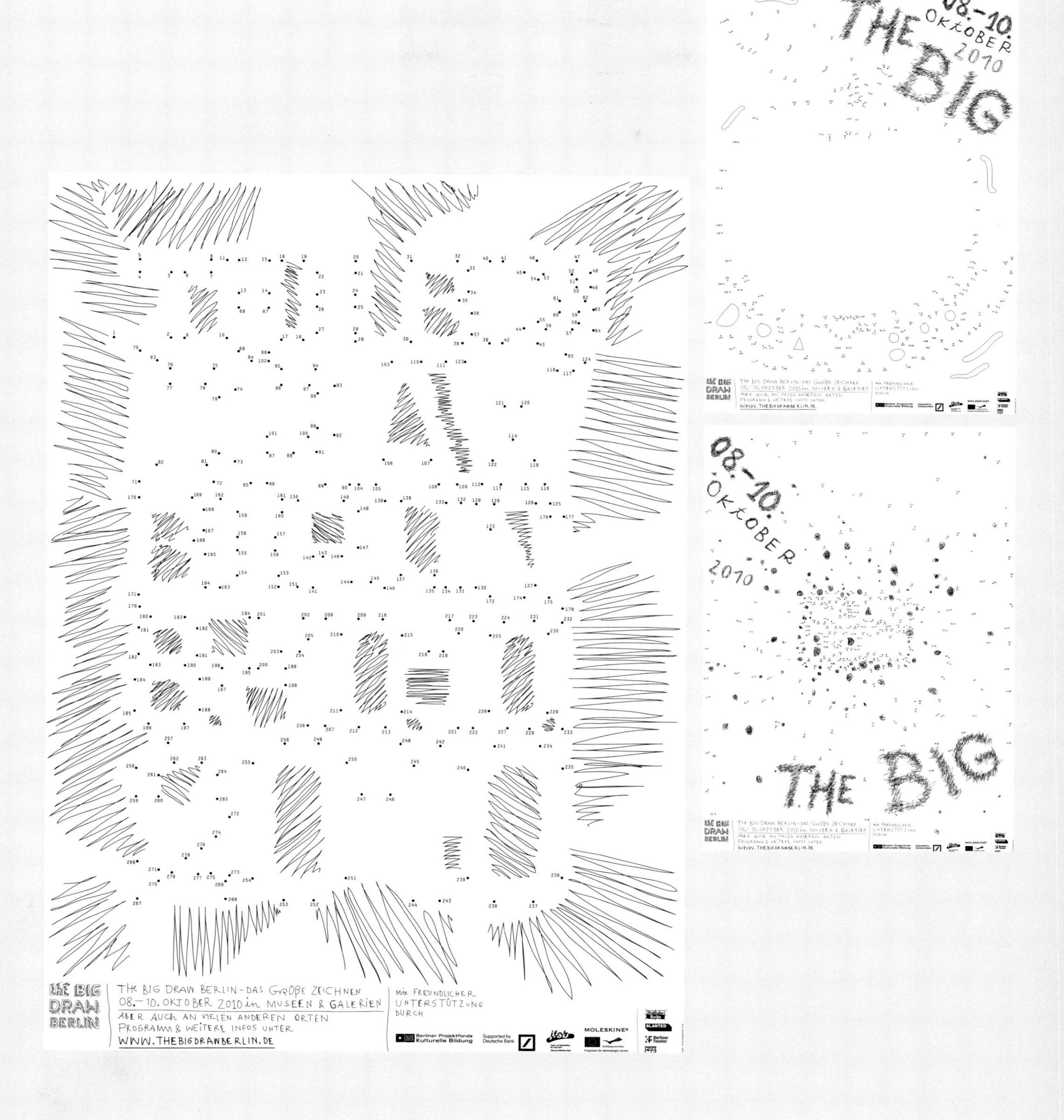

DESIGN Ariane Spanier, *Berlin* **LETTERING** Ariane Spanier **DESIGN OFFICE** Ariane Spanier Design **CLIENT** Kulturlabor e.V. **PRINCIPAL TYPE** handlettering
DIMENSIONS 23.4 × 33.1 in. (59.4 × 84 cm)

DESIGN Harry Pearce, *London* PHOTOGRAPHY Richard Foster DESIGN OFFICE Pentagram Design London CLIENT Haiti Poster Project
PRINCIPAL TYPE Courier and handdrawn DIMENSIONS 27.3 × 39.1 in. (69.4 × 99.4 cm)

ART DIRECTION Flo Gaertner and Patrick Hubbuch, *Karlsruhe and Ubstadt-Weiher, Germany* **DESIGN OFFICE** MAGMA Brand Design GmbH & Co. KG
CLIENT b_books, Tim Stüttgen (editor) **PRINCIPAL TYPE** Monotype Grotesque and Times New Roman **DIMENSIONS** 6.3 × 9.1 in. (16 × 23 cm)

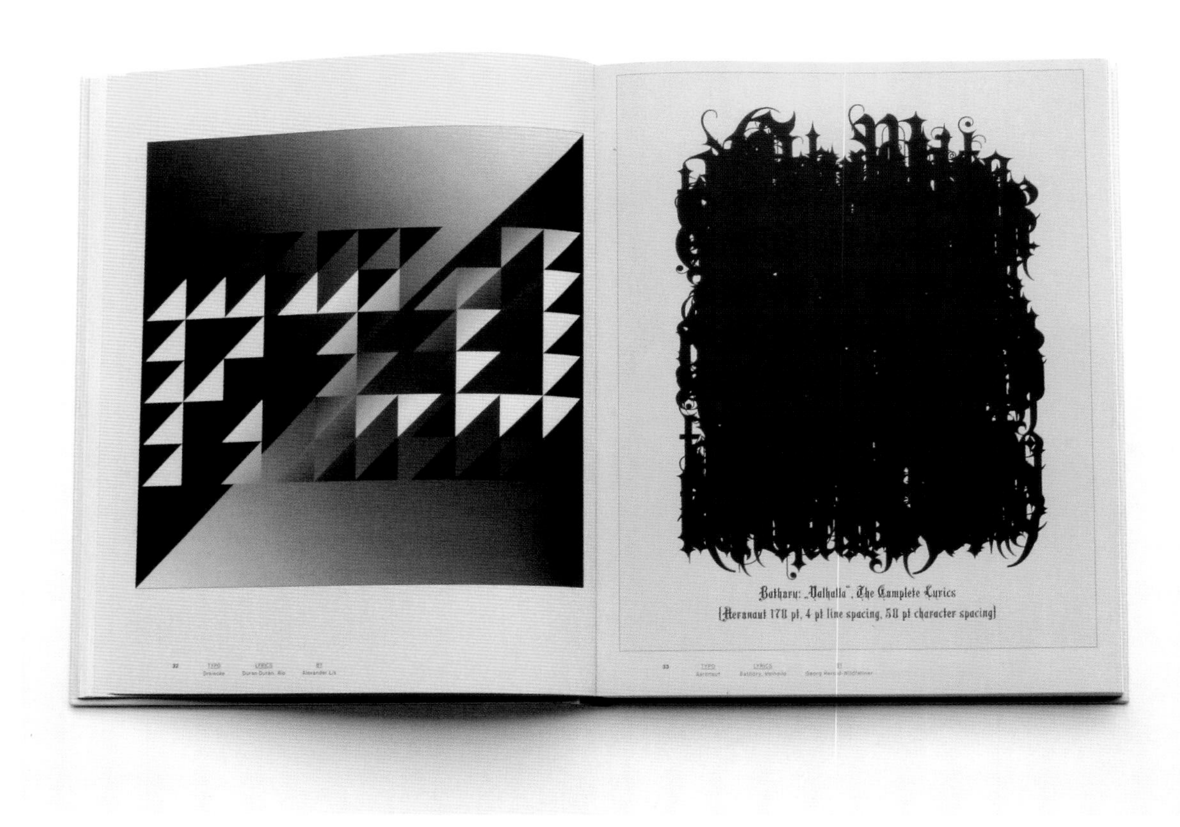

98 Book

DESIGN Jan Kiesswetter, Karlsruhe, *Germany* **ART DIRECTION** Lars Harmsen and Flo Gaertner **ASSISTANT EDITOR** Julia Kahl
DESIGN OFFICES MAGMA Brand Design GmbH & Co. KG **CLIENT** Birkhäuser Verlag **PRINCIPAL TYPE** Executive **DIMENSIONS** 8.9 × 11.2 in. (22.5 × 28.5 cm)

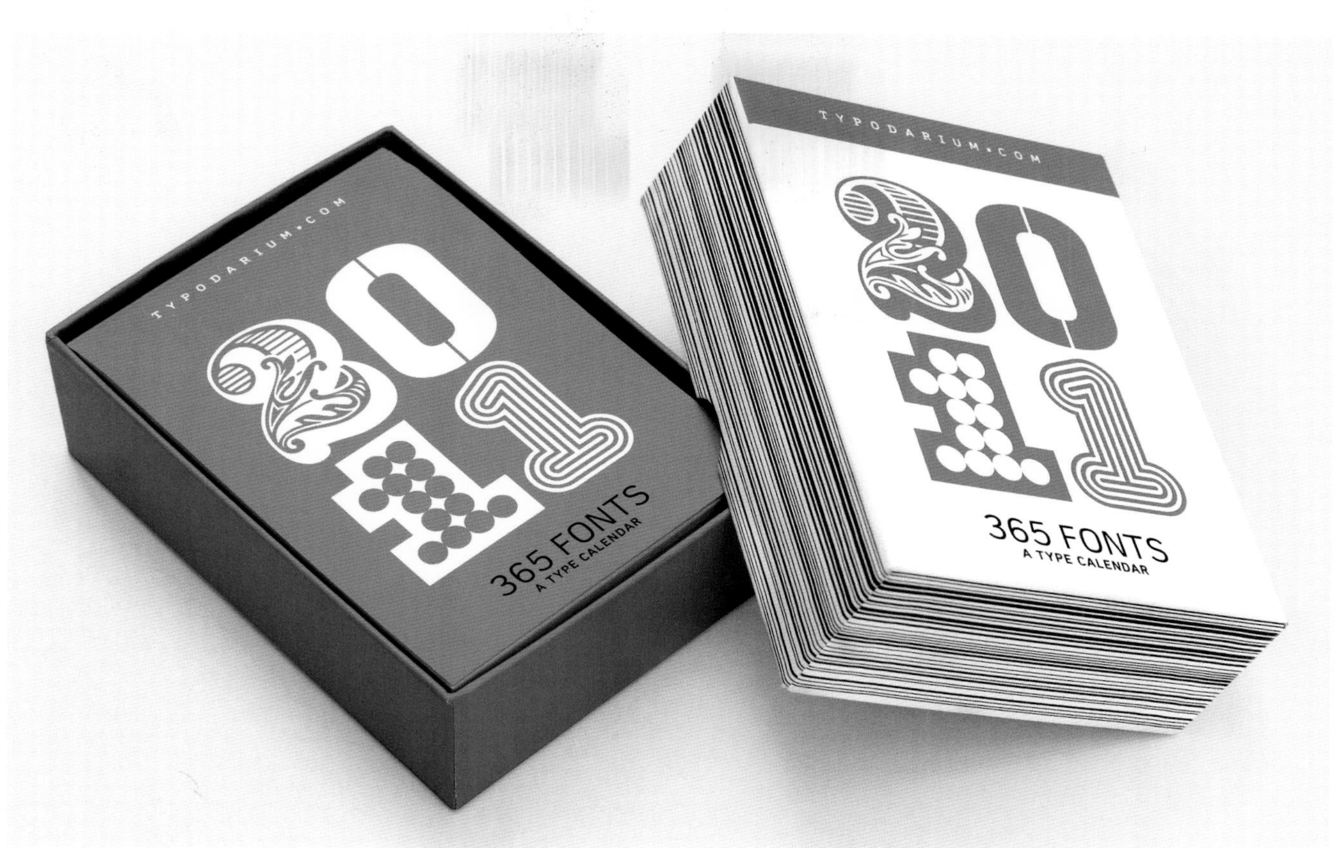

ART DIRECTION Boris Kahl, *Karlsruhe, Germany* **CREATIVE DIRECTION** Lars Harmsen and Raban Ruddigkeit, *Karlsruhe and Berlin, Germany*
PROJECT MANAGER Marina Friedrich **DESIGN OFFICES** MAGMA Brand Design GmbH & Co. KG, and ruddigkeit corporate ideas
CLIENT Verlag Hermann Schmidt, Mainz **PRINCIPAL TYPE** Copy **DIMENSIONS** 3.7 × 5.1 × 1.6 in. (9.5 × 13 × 4 cm)

CCA CALIFORNIA COLLEGE OF THE ARTS

extended education - winter/spring 2010

Courses take place on CCA's San Francisco and Oakland campuses.
Register early to ensure your place in class.
Gift certificates are available. They make great holiday gifts!

- architecture
- ceramics
- computer courses
- drawing
- graphic design
- illustration
- interior design
- jewelry / metal arts
- painting
- photography
- sculpture
- textiles
- writing
- courses for high school students

Offerings range from one-session workshops to more comprehensive courses.
For course listings and registration info, visit **www.cca.edu/extended** or call **510.594.3710.**

Registration for summer 2010 youth programs begins soon: **www.cca.edu/summer**

NONPROFIT ORGANIZATION
US POSTAGE
PAID
SAN FRANCISCO, CA
PERMIT NO. 271

DESIGN: CCA SPUTNIK / JAMES PROVENZA

 Student Project

DESIGN James Provenza, *San Francisco* **SCHOOL** California College of the Arts **INSTRUCTOR** Bob Aufuldish
PRINCIPAL TYPE FF Meta and FF Meta Serif **DIMENSIONS** 4 × 9 in. (10.2 × 22.9 cm)

DESIGN Stefan Sagmeister, *New York* PHOTOGRAPHY Karim Charlebois-Zariffa TEXT Stefan Sagmeister MANUFACTURER Bali Rattan, *Bali, Indonesia*
PRINCIPAL TYPE custom DIMENSIONS 47.2 × 31.1 in. (120 × 79 cm)

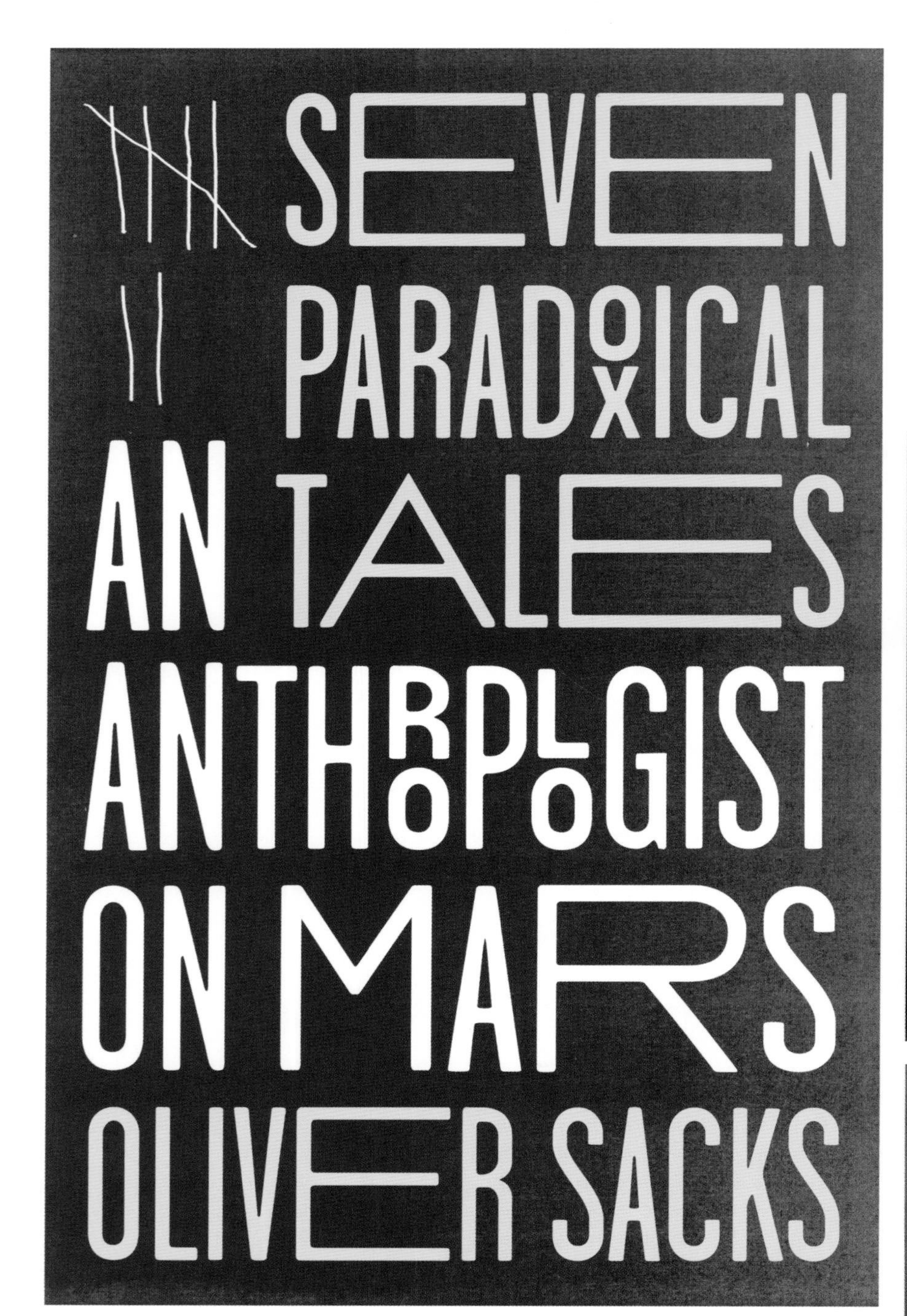

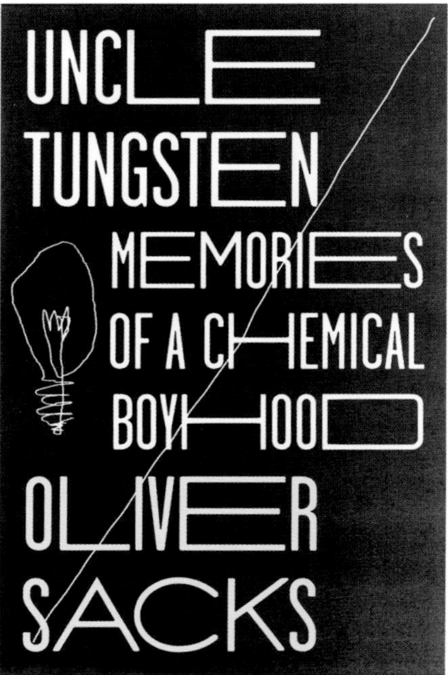

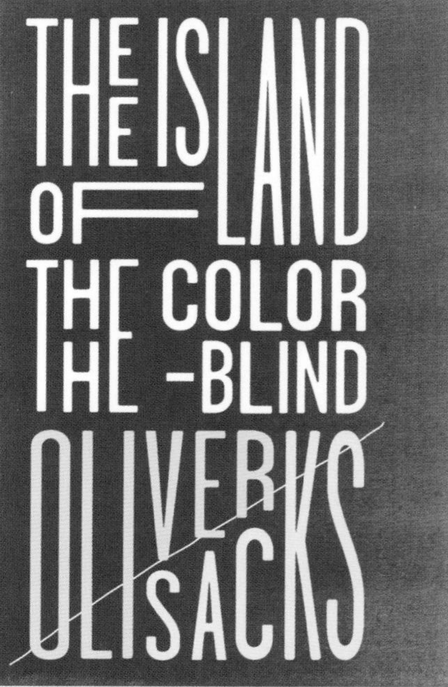

DESIGN Cardon Webb, *East Elmhurst, New York* CLIENT Vintage/Anchor Books PRINCIPAL TYPE Garage Gothic Regular
DIMENSIONS 5.2 × 8 in. (13.2 × 20.3 cm)

DESIGN Patricia Kim, Gina Maniscalco, Maayan Pearl, and Lee Wilson, *New York* DESIGN DIRECTION Cynthia Hoffman DESIGN MANAGER Emily Anton ART DIRECTION Robert Vargas CREATIVE DIRECTION Richard Turley ILLUSTRATION Nick White PUBLICATION *Bloomberg Businessweek* PRINCIPAL TYPE Neue Haas Grotesque DIMENSIONS 10.5 × 7.9 in. (26.7 × 20.1 cm)

DESIGN Elina Asanti, *New York* ART DIRECTION Jacob Wildschiødtz STUDIO NR2154 CLIENT *S Magazine*
PRINCIPAL TYPE Akkurat, Austin, and Austin–S Display DIMENSIONS 9.1 × 11.8 in. (23 × 30 cm)

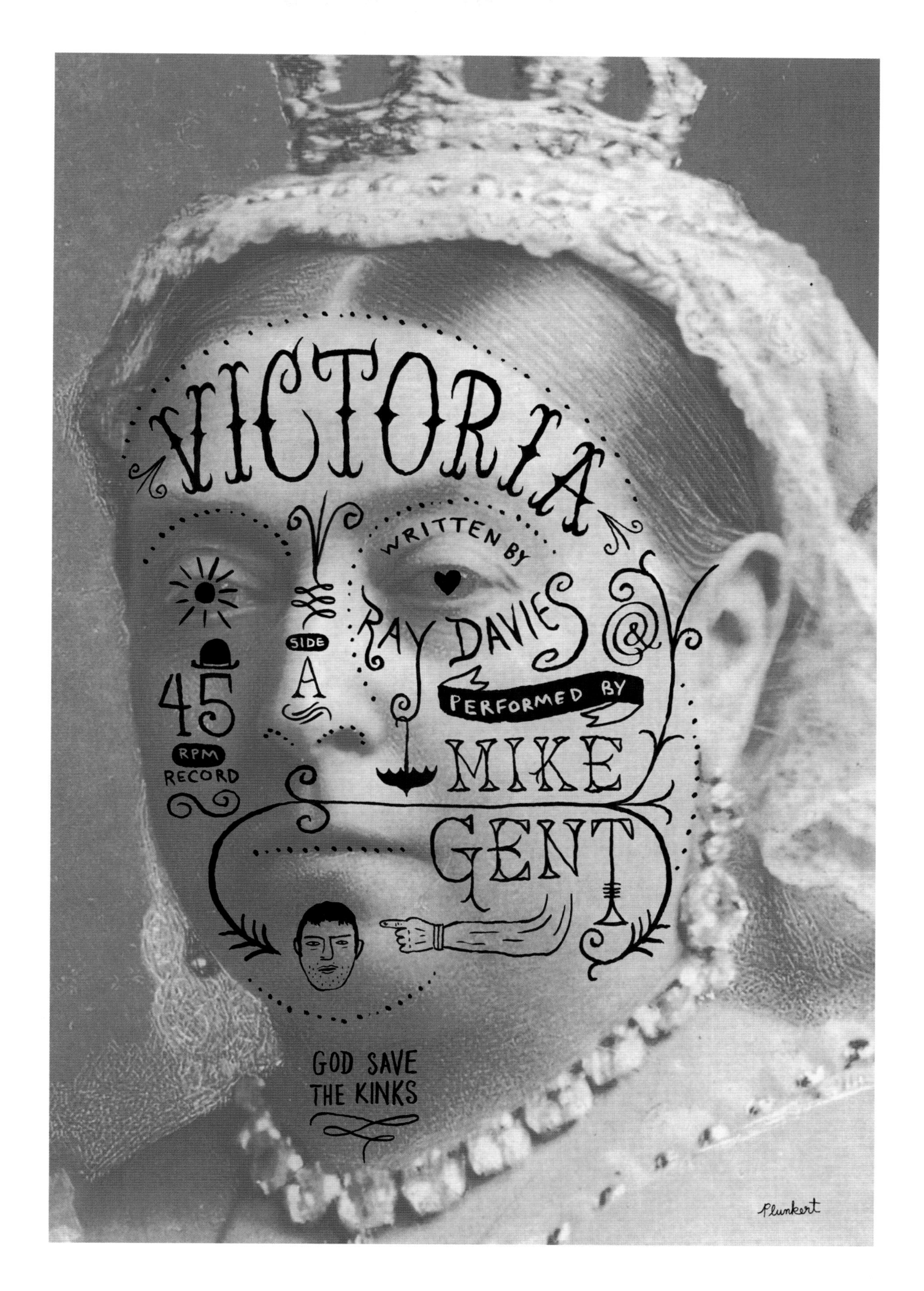

DESIGN David Plunkert, *Baltimore* ART DIRECTION David Plunkert LETTERING David Plunkert PHOTOGRAPHY Alexander Bassano, owned by Library of Congress
ILLUSTRATION David Plunkert based on Thomas Gainsborough STUDIO Spur Design CLIENT Film Shack PRINCIPAL TYPE handlettering DIMENSIONS 14.75 × 22 in. (37.5 × 55.9 cm)

DESIGN Michael Croxton, *Brooklyn, New York* SCHOOL School of Visual Arts, *New York* INSTRUCTOR Milton Glaser
PRINCIPAL TYPE Odeon Condensed DIMENSIONS 18 × 24 in. (45.7 × 61 cm)

DESIGN Christopher Silas Neal, *Brooklyn, New York* **LETTERING** Christopher Silas Neal **CLIENT** Shout Out Louds **PRINCIPAL TYPE** handlettering
DIMENSIONS 19 × 25 in. (48.3 × 63.5 cm)

DESIGN Kei Takimoto, *Tokyo* ART DIRECTION Kei Takimoto CREATIVE DIRECTION Kei Takimoto LETTERING Kei Takimoto PRINCIPAL TYPE handlettering
DIMENSIONS 23.4 × 33.1 in. (59.4 × 84.1 cm)

"DUALPHABET" Capital letter × Small letter_Experimental work POSTER 2010. Copyright © 2010 Kei Takimoto All Rights Reserved.

DESIGN Kei Takimoto, *Tokyo* **ART DIRECTION** Kei Takimoto **CREATIVE DIRECTION** Kei Takimoto **LETTERING** Kei Takimoto **PRINCIPAL TYPE** handlettering
DIMENSIONS 23.4 × 33.1 in. (59.4 × 84.1 cm)

DESIGN Djoko Hartioko, Jordan Marzuki, and Ignatius Hermawan Tanzil, *Jakarta, Indonesia* ART DIRECTION Ignatius Hermawan Tanzil CREATIVE DIRECTION Ignatius Hermawan Tanzil ILLUSTRATION Djoko Hartioko, Radhinal Indra, and Jordan Marzuki DESIGN OFFICE LeBoYe CLIENT dialogue PRINCIPAL TYPE Triumph Tippa DIMENSIONS various

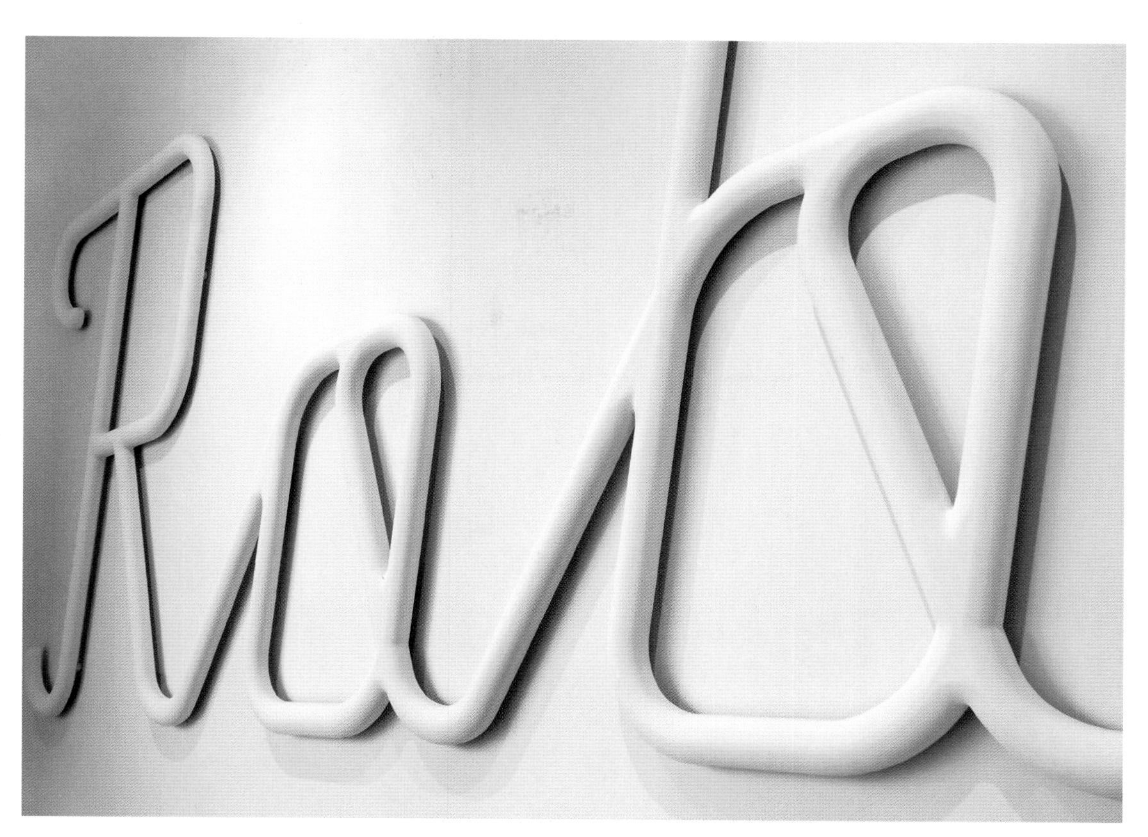

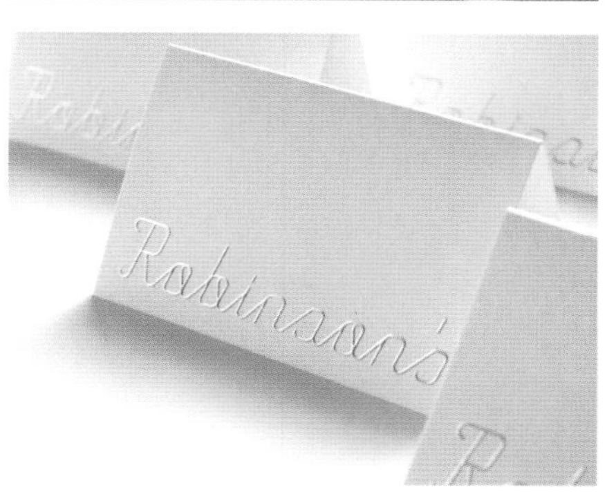

DESIGN Kellie Campbell-Illingworth, *Adelaide, Australia* CREATIVE DIRECTION Matthew Remphrey LETTERING Kellie Campbell-Illingworth DESIGN OFFICE Parallax Design CLIENT Robinson's Accident Repair Centre PRINCIPAL TYPE Akkurat Mono and handlettering DIMENSIONS various

 Poster

DESIGN Underware, *The Hague, Netherlands* PRINCIPAL TYPE Liza
DIMENSIONS 32 × 46 in. (81.3 × 116.8 cm)

DESIGN René Clément, *Montréal* CREATIVE DIRECTION Louis Gagnon LETTERING Sériepop AGENCY Paprika CLIENT Galerie Anatome
PRINCIPAL TYPE Helvetica and handlettering DIMENSIONS 24 × 34 in. (61 × 86.4 cm)

AN
OBJECT
OF
BEAUTY

a novel

STEVE
MARTIN

CREATIVE DIRECTION Anne Twomey, *New York* LETTERING Darren Booth, *St. Catharines, Canada* PUBLISHER Grand Central Publishing
PRINCIPAL TYPE Neutraface and handlettering DIMENSIONS 6 × 9 in. (15.2 × 22.9 cm)

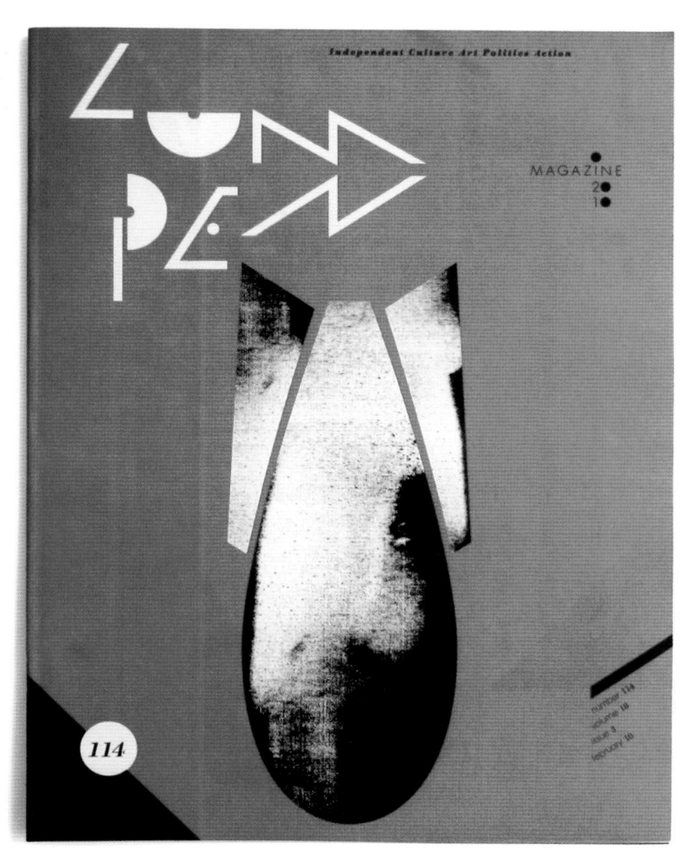

ART DIRECTION Jeremiah Chiu and Renata Graw, *Chicago* EDITOR/PUBLISHER Ed Marszewski STUDIO Plural Design CLIENT Lumpen
PRINCIPAL TYPE Berthold Bodoni Antiqua BE, ITC Golden Type, Univers, and custom DIMENSIONS 10 × 13 in. (25.4 × 33 cm)

The Magazine of
Architecture and Design
TWO SCHOOLS That Give Us Hope
METROPOLIS
WE WILL GROW FOOD IN AND ON OUR BUILDINGS.
WE WILL PROTECT OUR COASTLINES WITH FLEXIBLE DEFENSES.
WE WILL REDESIGN THE ENERGY GRID.
WE WILL CREATE BUILDINGS THAT MAKE ENERGY INSTEAD OF BURNING IT.
WE WILL CUSTOMIZE OUR HOTEL ROOMS.
WE WILL URBANIZE THE SUBURBS.
WE WILL DESIGN SLOW ROADS.
WE WILL REIMAGINE THE SCENT OF HOSPITALS.
WE WILL REENERGIZE DEAD URBAN SPACES.
THE 1•5•10 ISSUE
What we must do immediately and in the near and long term to preserve our future
USA $5.95 | CANADA $5.95
January 2010 METROPOLIS
THE MAGAZINE OF ARCHITECTURE AND DESIGN

DESIGN Post Typography, *Baltimore* ART DIRECTION Dungjai Pungauthaikan, *New York* CREATIVE DIRECTION Criswell Lappin PUBLICATION *Metropolis*
PRINCIPAL TYPE Scout DIMENSIONS 9 × 10.75 in. (22.9 × 27.3 cm)

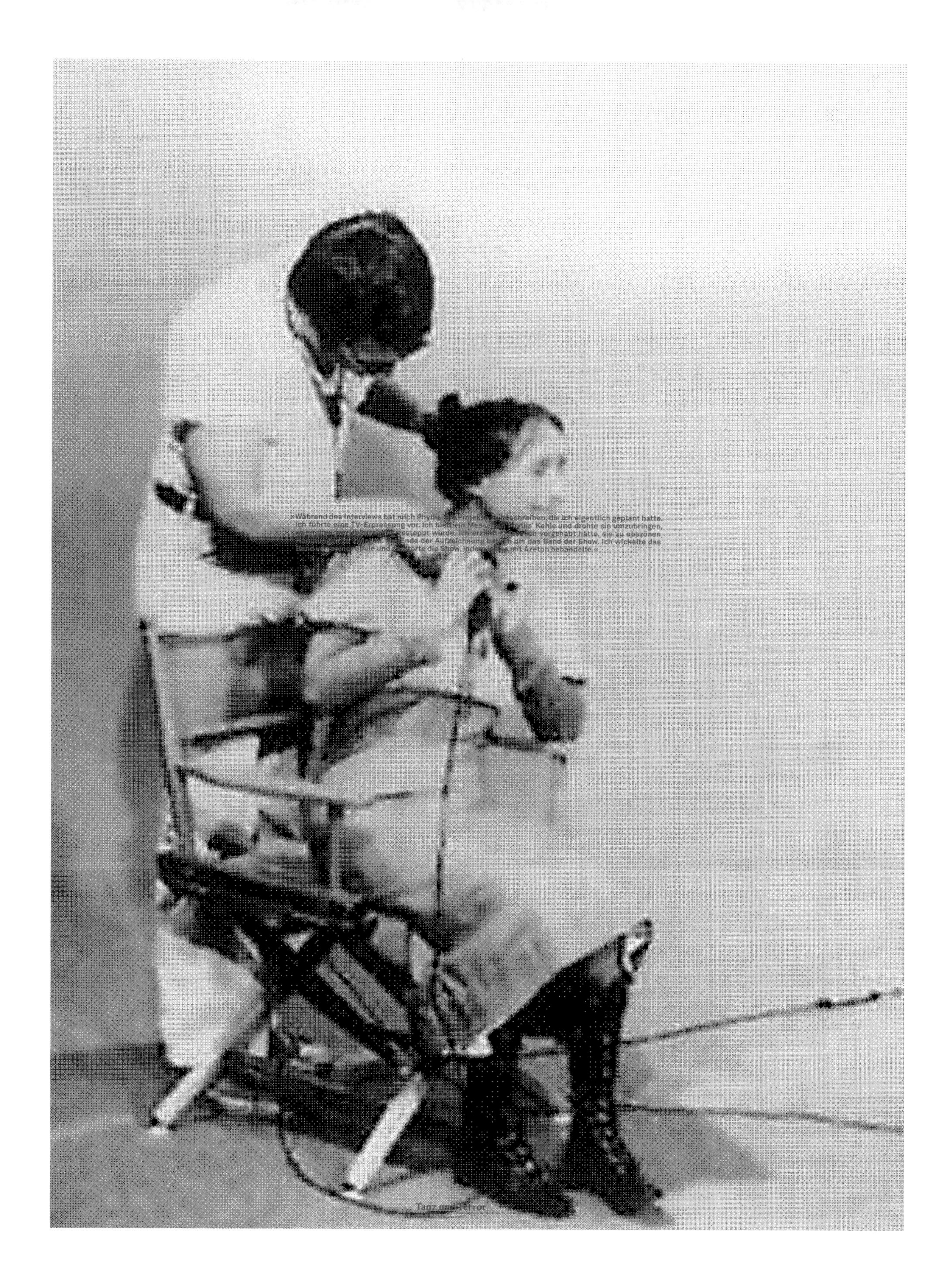

DESIGN Sven Quadflieg, *Neuss, Germany* SCHOOL Folkwang Universität der Künste PROFESSORS Thomas Rempen and Peter Wippermann
PRINCIPAL TYPE Akkurat Bold and DTL Albertina Bold DIMENSIONS 23.4 × 33.1 in. (59.4 × 84.1 cm)

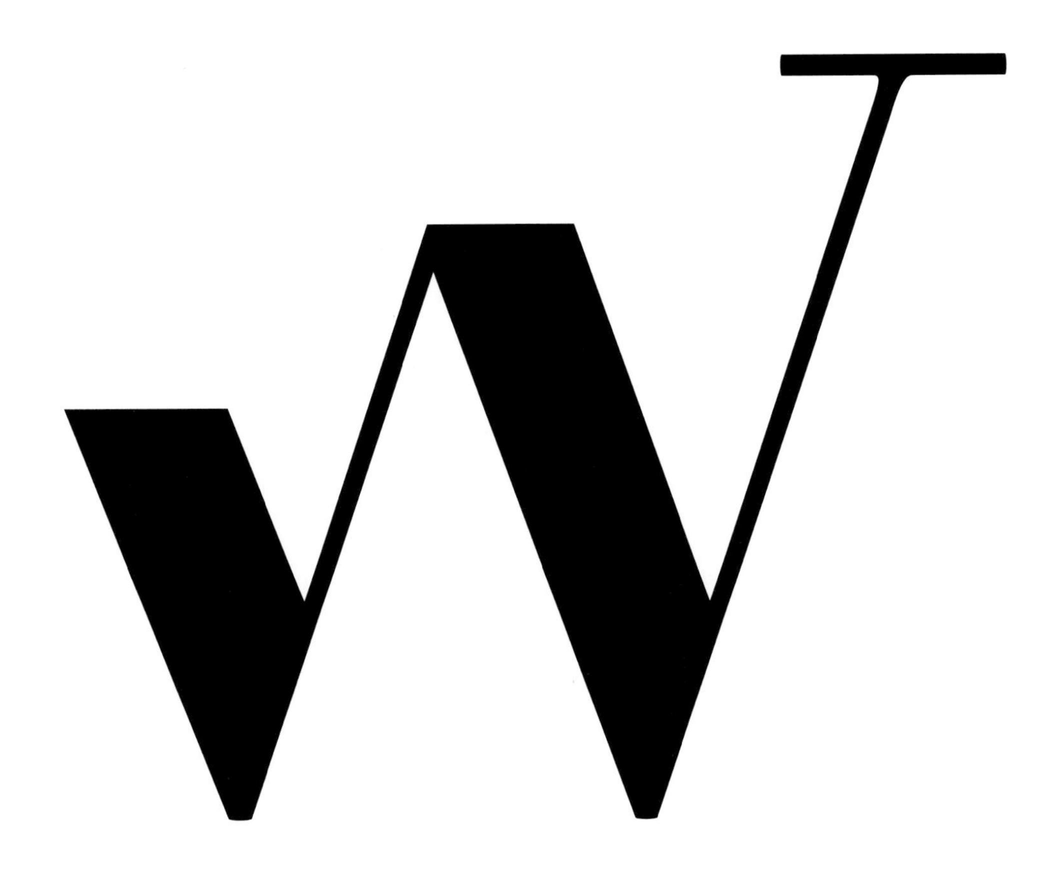

DESIGN Elizabeth diGiacomantonio and Joseph Traylor, *Brooklyn, New York* ART DIRECTION Joseph Traylor STUDIO Ville
CLIENT Walk Up Press PRINCIPAL TYPE custom

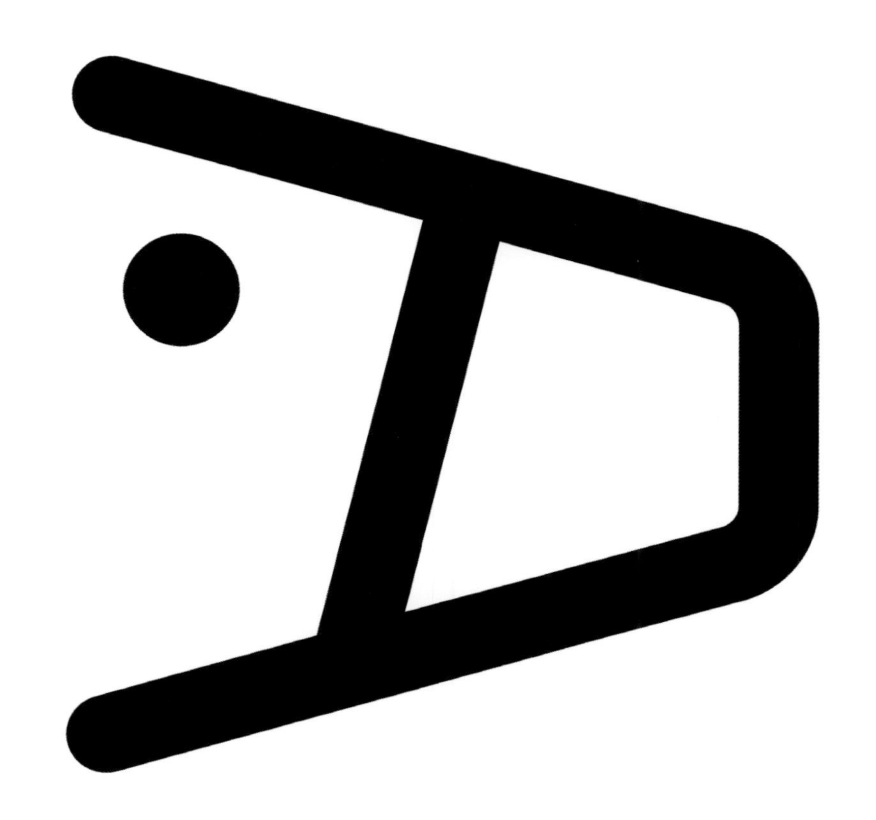

DESIGN Ken DeLago **CLIENT** Archer Stables
PRINCIPAL TYPE handlettering

Tri-Shop-Saar
Weinbergweg 11 /// D-66119 Saarbrücken
Telefon: +49 (0)681 | 68 74 698 /// Telefax: +49 (0)681 | 68 74 698
www.trishopsaar.de /// info@trishopsaar.de

III

TRI-
SHOP-
SAAR

3.86
180
42.195
km

Geschäftsinhaber: MARTIN MALCHAREK
Sparkasse Saarbrücken /// BLZ 590 501 01 /// KTO 74 333 626
IBAN DE71590501010074333626 /// BIC SAKSDE55
St.-Nr. 040/247/30722 /// USt.-ID.-Nr. DE267825959

TRIATHLON
only

DESIGN Patrick Bittner, *Saarbrücken, Germany* **CLIENT** Martin Malcharek, Tri-Shop-Saar
PRINCIPAL TYPE Romain BP **DIMENSIONS** various

Europäischer Tag der jüdischen Kultur
5. September 2010, 11–18 Uhr
Journée européenne de la culture juive
5 septembre 2010, 11h–18h
Foto-Ausstellung von André Mailänder
Exposition photo par André Mailänder
Kennenlernen – Verstehen: eine erste fotografische Spurensuche in der ehemaligen Synagoge von Fénétrange
Découvrir et comprendre: une première lecture photographique de l'ancienne synagogue de Fénétrange
Tage der offenen Tür:
Journées portes ouvertes:
Tag des offenen Denkmals
12. September 2010, 10–18 Uhr
Journée du monument historique
12 septembre 2010, 10h–18h
Europäische Tage des Kulturguts
18.–19. September 2010, 10–18 Uhr
Journées européennes du patrimoine
18–19 septembre 2010, 10h–18h
INITIATIVE
SYNAGOGUE
FÉNÉTRANGE
DIE SYNAGOGE
www.synagogue-fenetrange.org
Herzlichen Dank an unsere Partner für ihr Engagement Nous remercions nos partenaires de leur précieux soutien
Ville de Fénétrange, Jüdisches Museum Berlin, Consulat Général de France à Sarrebruck
Saarländische Galerie Berlin – Europäisches Kunstforum e.V., Union Stiftung, repa druck, Hahnemühle FineArt

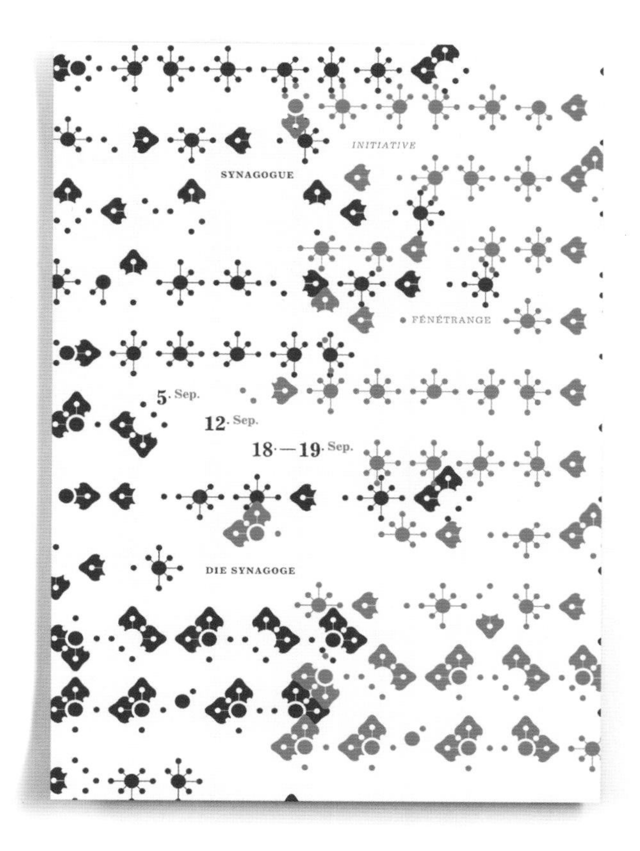

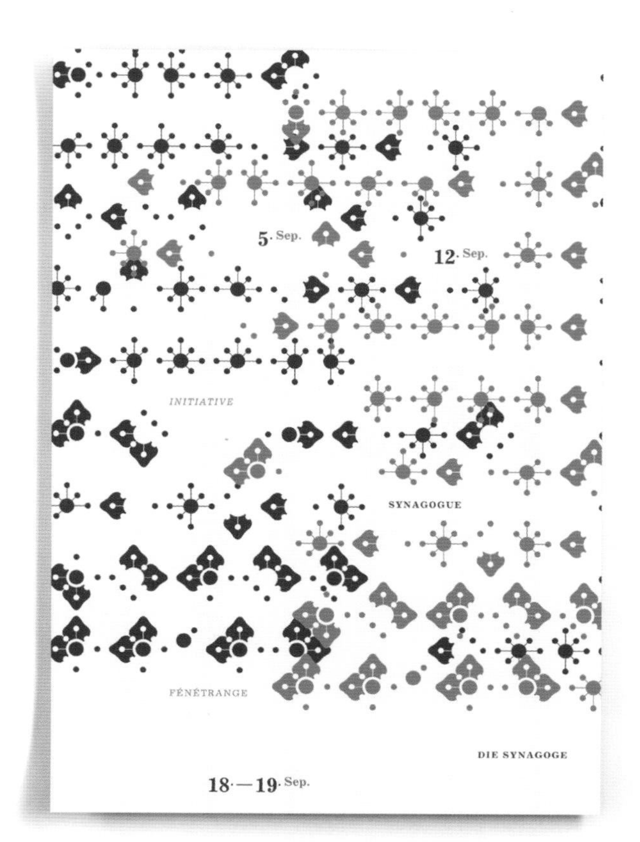

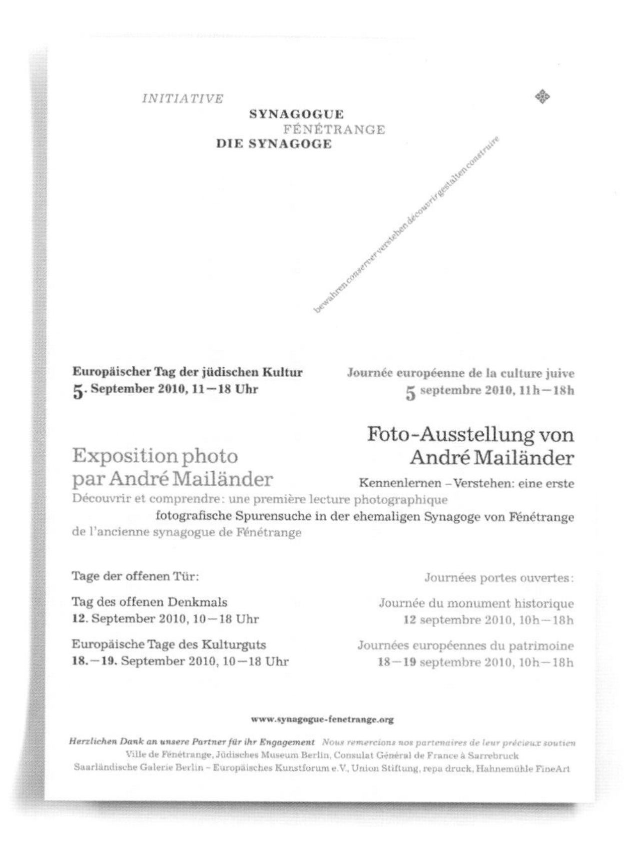

INITIATIVE
SYNAGOGUE
FÉNÉTRANGE
DIE SYNAGOGE
Europäischer Tag der jüdischen Kultur
5. September 2010, 11–18 Uhr
Journée européenne de la culture juive
5 septembre 2010, 11h–18h
Foto-Ausstellung von André Mailänder
Exposition photo par André Mailänder
Kennenlernen – Verstehen: eine erste fotografische Spurensuche in der ehemaligen Synagoge von Fénétrange
Découvrir et comprendre: une première lecture photographique de l'ancienne synagogue de Fénétrange
Tage der offenen Tür:
Journées portes ouvertes:
Tag des offenen Denkmals
12. September 2010, 10–18 Uhr
Journée du monument historique
12 septembre 2010, 10h–18h
Europäische Tage des Kulturguts
18.–19. September 2010, 10–18 Uhr
Journées européennes du patrimoine
18–19 septembre 2010, 10h–18h
www.synagogue-fenetrange.org
Herzlichen Dank an unsere Partner für ihr Engagement Nous remercions nos partenaires de leur précieux soutien
Ville de Fénétrange, Jüdisches Museum Berlin, Consulat Général de France à Sarrebruck
Saarländische Galerie Berlin – Europäisches Kunstforum e.V., Union Stiftung, repa druck, Hahnemühle FineArt

DESIGN Patrick Bittner, *Saarbrücken, Germany* CLIENT Bettina Hanstein, Initiative Synagoge Fénétrange PRINCIPAL TYPE Excelsior and Synagogue-F
DIMENSIONS 5.8 × 8.3 in. (14.8 × 21 cm)

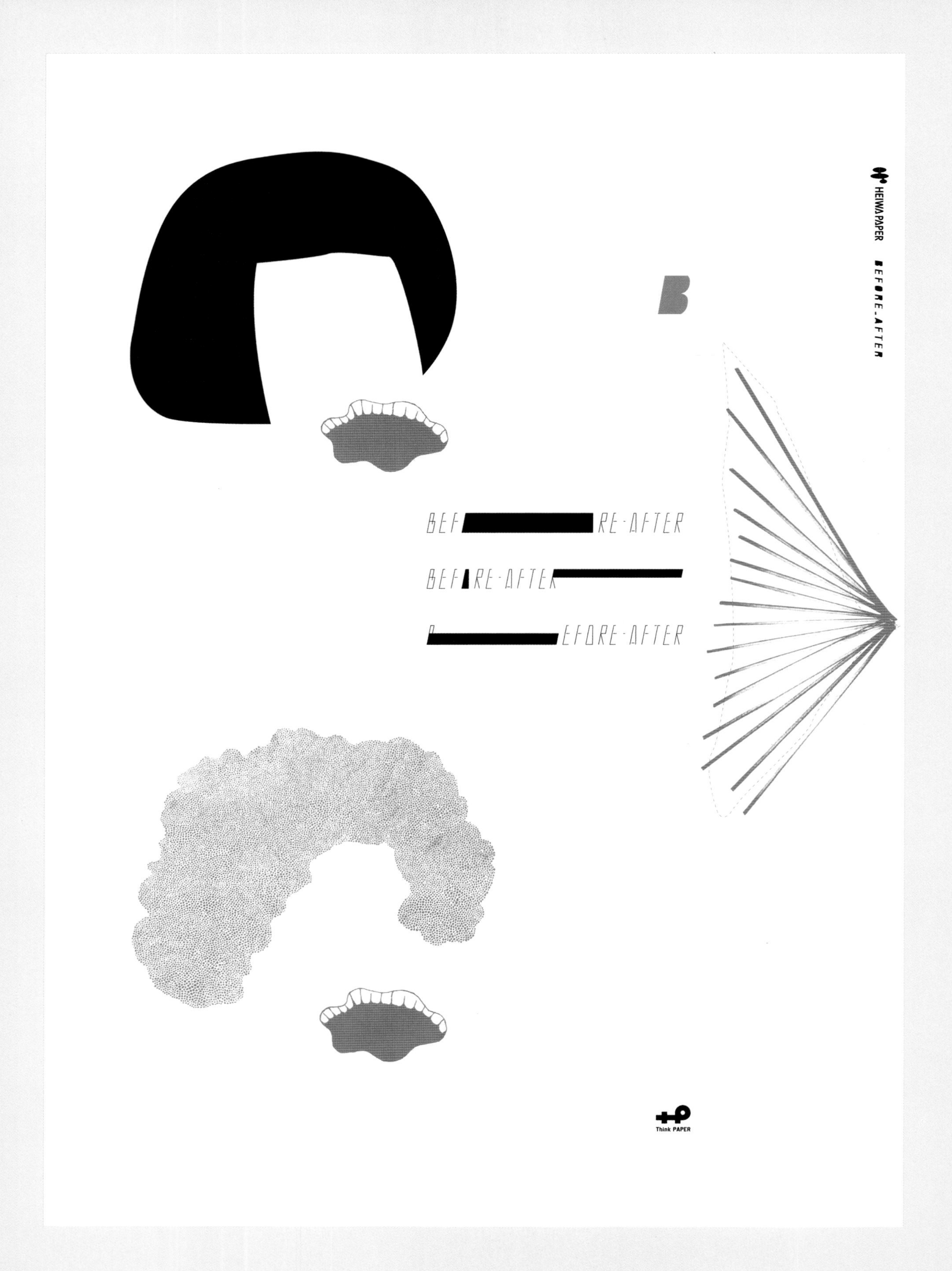

DESIGN Akiko Masunaga, *Osaka, Japan* ART DIRECTION Akiko Masunaga ILLUSTRATION Akiko Masunaga CLIENT Heiwa Paper Co., Ltd.
PRINCIPAL TYPE original DIMENSIONS 28.7 × 40.6 in. (72.8 × 103 cm)

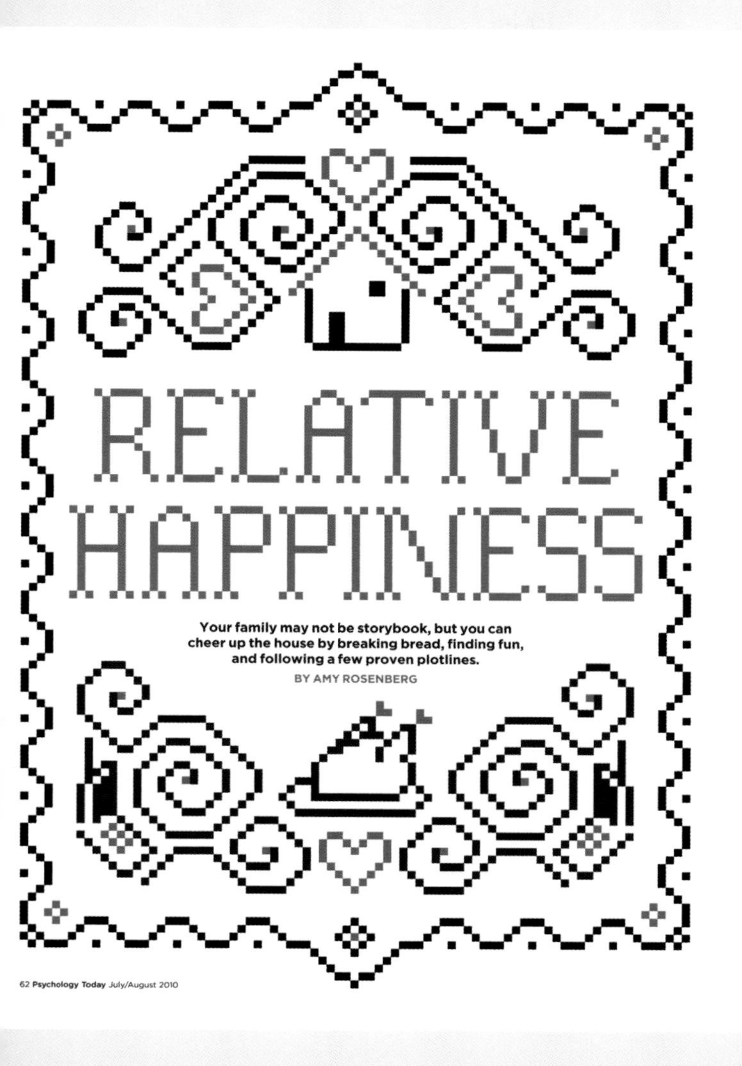

RELATIVE HAPPINESS
Your family may not be storybook, but you can cheer up the house by breaking bread, finding fun, and following a few proven plotlines.
BY AMY ROSENBERG
62 Psychology Today July/August 2010

THE LANDSGAARD FAMILY Olive Branch, Miss.: Kristen and Peter with their children, Michael, 10; Mary Claret, 8; Ann Catherine, 6; Peter, 5; Joseph, 3; and Margaret, 3.

Photograph by **BRAD JONES**

ART DIRECTION Katherine Bigelow, *New York* CREATIVE DIRECTION Edward Levine STUDIO Levine Design Inc. CLIENT *Psychology Today*
PRINCIPAL TYPE Gotham and custom DIMENSIONS 16 × 10.5 in. (40.6 × 26.7 cm)

DESIGN Andrew Freeman and Paula Scher, *New York* ART DIRECTION Paula Scher LETTERING Paula Scher DESIGN OFFICE Pentagram Design New York
CLIENT New York City Department of Cultural Affairs, New York City Department of Education, and New York City School Construction Authority
PRINCIPAL TYPE handlettering

DESIGN Andrew Freeman and Paula Scher, *New York* ART DIRECTION Paula Scher LETTERING Paula Scher DESIGN OFFICE Pentagram Design New York
CLIENT New York City Department of Cultural Affairs, New York City Department of Education, and New York City School Construction Authority
PRINCIPAL TYPE handlettering

ART DIRECTION Drue Wagner, *New York* CREATIVE DIRECTION Dirk Barnett PUBLICATION *Maxim* PRINCIPAL TYPE McKloud Black
DIMENSIONS 15.25 × 10.5 in. (38.7 × 26.7 cm)

DESIGN Jessica Walsh, *New York* ART DIRECTION Stefan Sagmeister STUDIO Sagmeister Inc. CLIENT Levi's PRINCIPAL TYPE custom
DIMENSIONS 19.5 × 44 ft. (5.9 × 13.4 m)

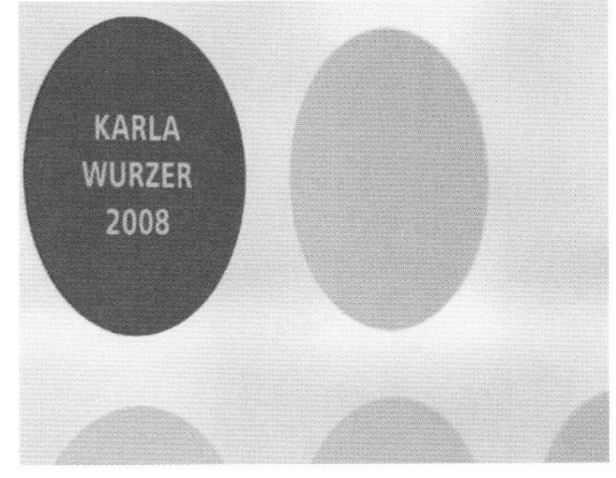

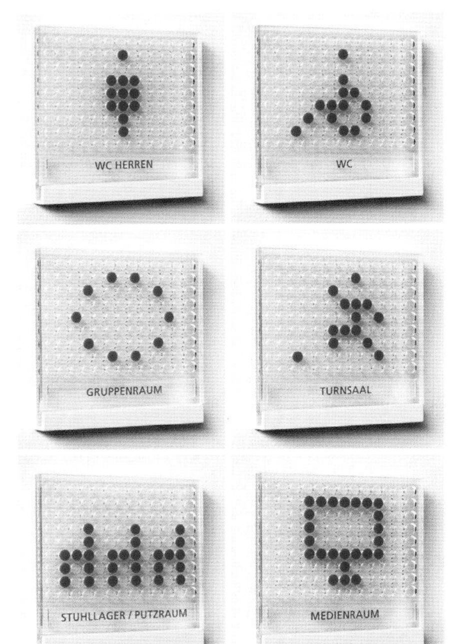

DESIGN Angelika Mathis and Verena Petrasch, *Dornbirn, Austria* ART DIRECTION Angelika Mathis and Verena Petrasch
ARCHITECTURE Arge HEIN-TROY & Thurnher ZT, *Bregenz, Austria* CLIENT Elementary School and Nursery School Satteins
PRINCIPAL TYPE Dilthey Dot (self-created dot font) and Frutiger Next LT
DIMENSIONS Glass wall: 15.5 × 78.7 × 1102.4 in. (39.4 × 200 × 2800 cm), Doorplates: 5.7 × 5.9 in. (14.5 × 15 cm)

¥€$
WE SAVE !!
HALOID
THANKS TO XEROGRAPHY...
You can save the time & the money because of xerography,
the technology which started the office copying revolution,
was born unheralded on October 22, 1938, the inspiration
of a single man working in his spare time.
10.-22.-38
ASTORIA
FUJI xerox

DESIGN Yuki Nishimura, *Osaka, Japan* DESIGN TEAM D+ DESIGN OFFICE TryKID'S, Inc. CLIENT Fuji Xerox Co., Ltd. PRINCIPAL TYPE Helvetica Neue
DIMENSIONS 28.7 × 40.6 in. (72.8 × 103 cm)

 Student Project

DESIGN Grant Gold, *New York* SCHOOL School of Visual Arts, *New York* INSTRUCTOR Olga Mezhibovskaya
PRINCIPAL TYPE handlettering DIMENSIONS 11 × 15 in. (27.9 × 38.1 cm)

COLOR OF THE
FLOWER HAS
ALREADY FADED
AWAY WHILE I
IDLE THOUGHTS
MY LIFE PASSES
VAINLY BY
AS I WATCH
THE LONG
RAINS
FALL

DESIGN Hiroko Sakai, *Tokyo* ART DIRECTION Hiroko Sakai DESIGN OFFICE coton design PRINCIPAL TYPE Utsuroi
DIMENSIONS 28.7 × 40.6 in. (72.8 × 103 cm)

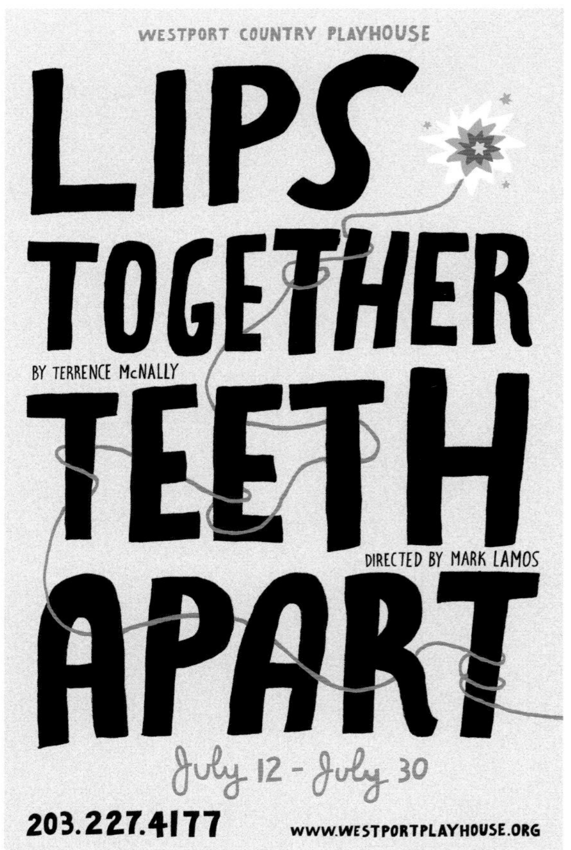

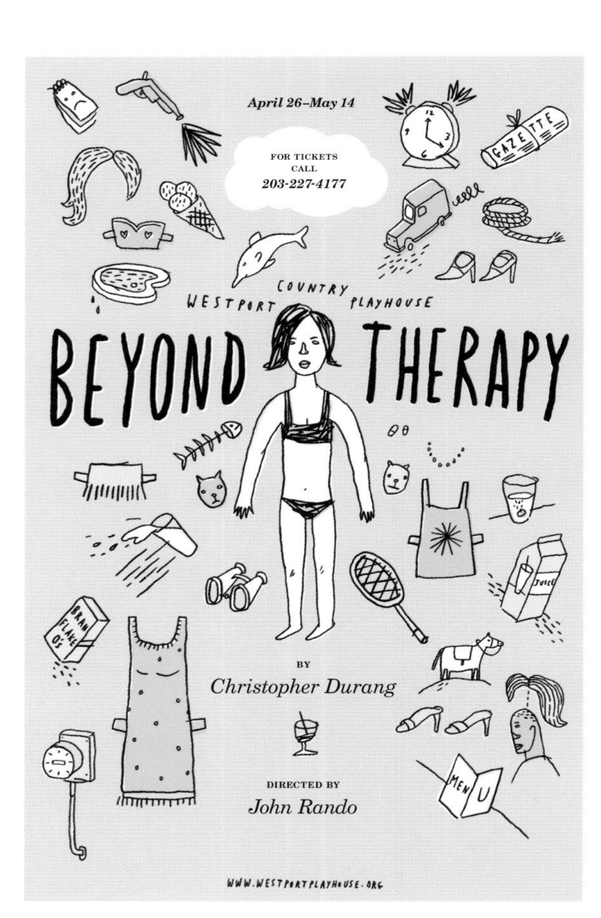

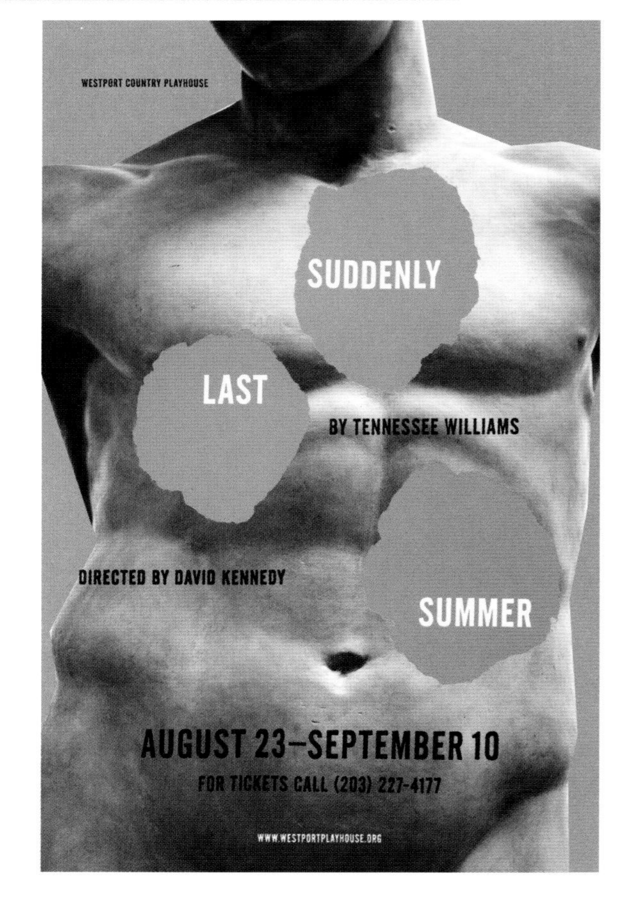

DESIGN Kevin Brainard, Christopher Brand, Darren Cox, and John Fulbrook III, *Norwalk, Connecticut*
ILLUSTRATION Brian Rea (Beyond Therapy) PHOTOGRAPHY Darren Cox STUDIO Pleasure CLIENT Westport Country Playhouse
PRINCIPAL TYPE Alternate Gothic, Century Schoolbook, and handlettering DIMENSIONS 28 × 44 in. (71.1 × 111.8 cm)

DESIGN Andrew Freeman and Paula Scher, *New York* ART DIRECTION Paula Scher DESIGN OFFICE Pentagram Design New York
CLIENTS Society of Typographic Arts and International Council of Graphic Design Associations PRINCIPAL TYPE Akkurat DIMENSIONS 24 × 36 in. (61 × 91.4 cm)

DESIGN Hiroko Sakai, *Tokyo* **ART DIRECTION** Hiroko Sakai **DESIGN OFFICE** coton design
PRINCIPAL TYPE Futura **DIMENSIONS** 28.7 × 40.6 in. (72.8 × 103 cm)

DESIGN Seung Hee Lee, *New York* SCHOOL School of Visual Arts, *New York* INSTRUCTORS Kevin Brainard and Darren Cox
PRINCIPAL TYPE handlettering DIMENSIONS 8 × 10 in. (20.3 × 25.4 cm)

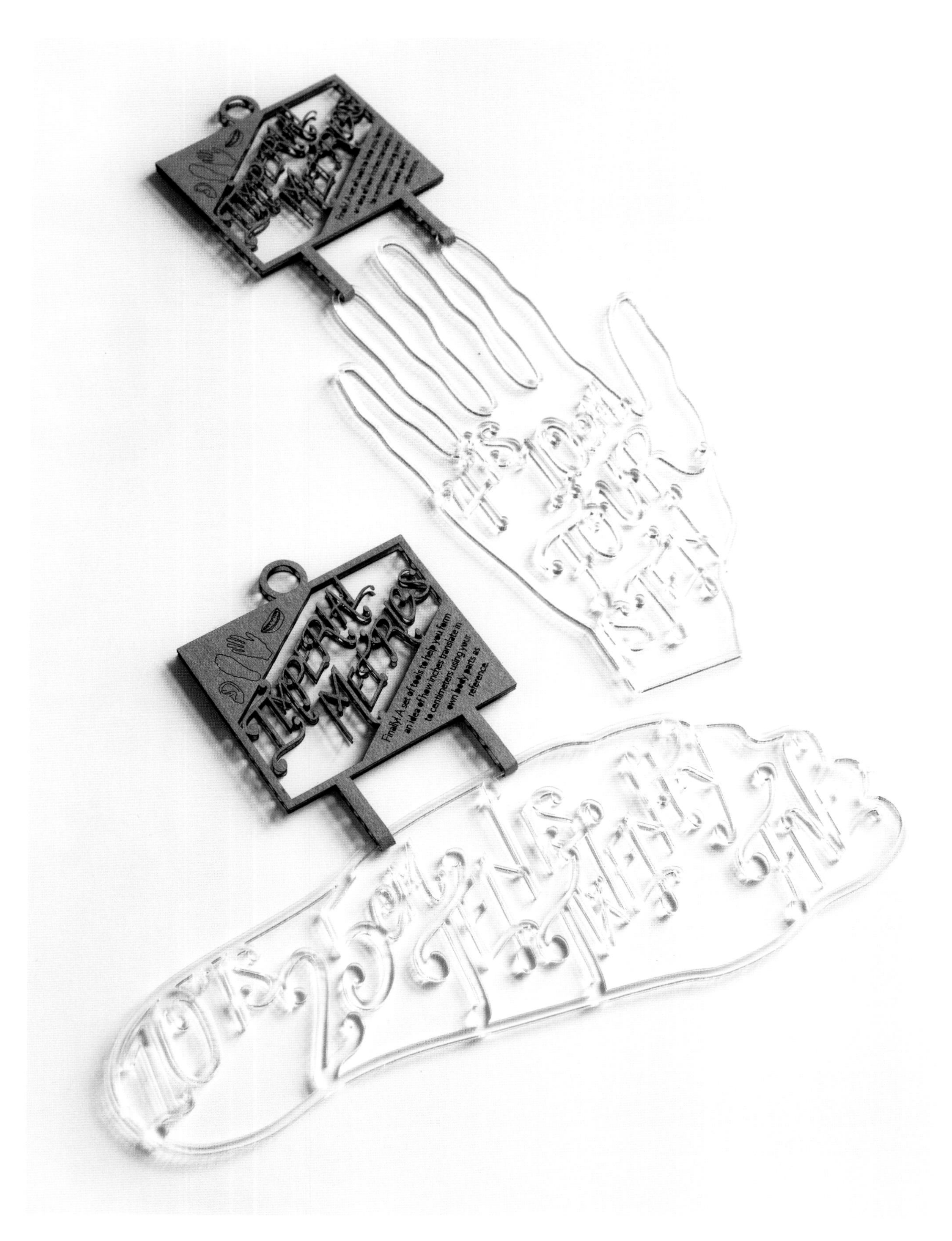

DESIGN Cristina Vasquez, *New York* **SCHOOL** School of Visual Arts, *New York* **INSTRUCTORS** Stephen Doyle and Erik Guzman
PRINCIPAL TYPE custom **DIMENSIONS** Foot: 10 × 3.5 in. (25.4 × 8.9 cm), Hand: 4 × 8 in. (10.2 × 20.3 cm)

DESIGN Anja Geier and Marta Marek, *Augsburg, Germany* ART DIRECTION Christoph Sauter and Mara Weyel CREATIVE DIRECTION Artur Gulbicki BRAND CONSULTING Tobias Sommer DESIGN OFFICE KW Neun Grafikagentur CLIENT Stadtjugendring Augsburg KdöR PRINCIPAL TYPE Sabon Next DIMENSIONS 23.4 × 33.1 in. (59.4 × 84.1 cm)

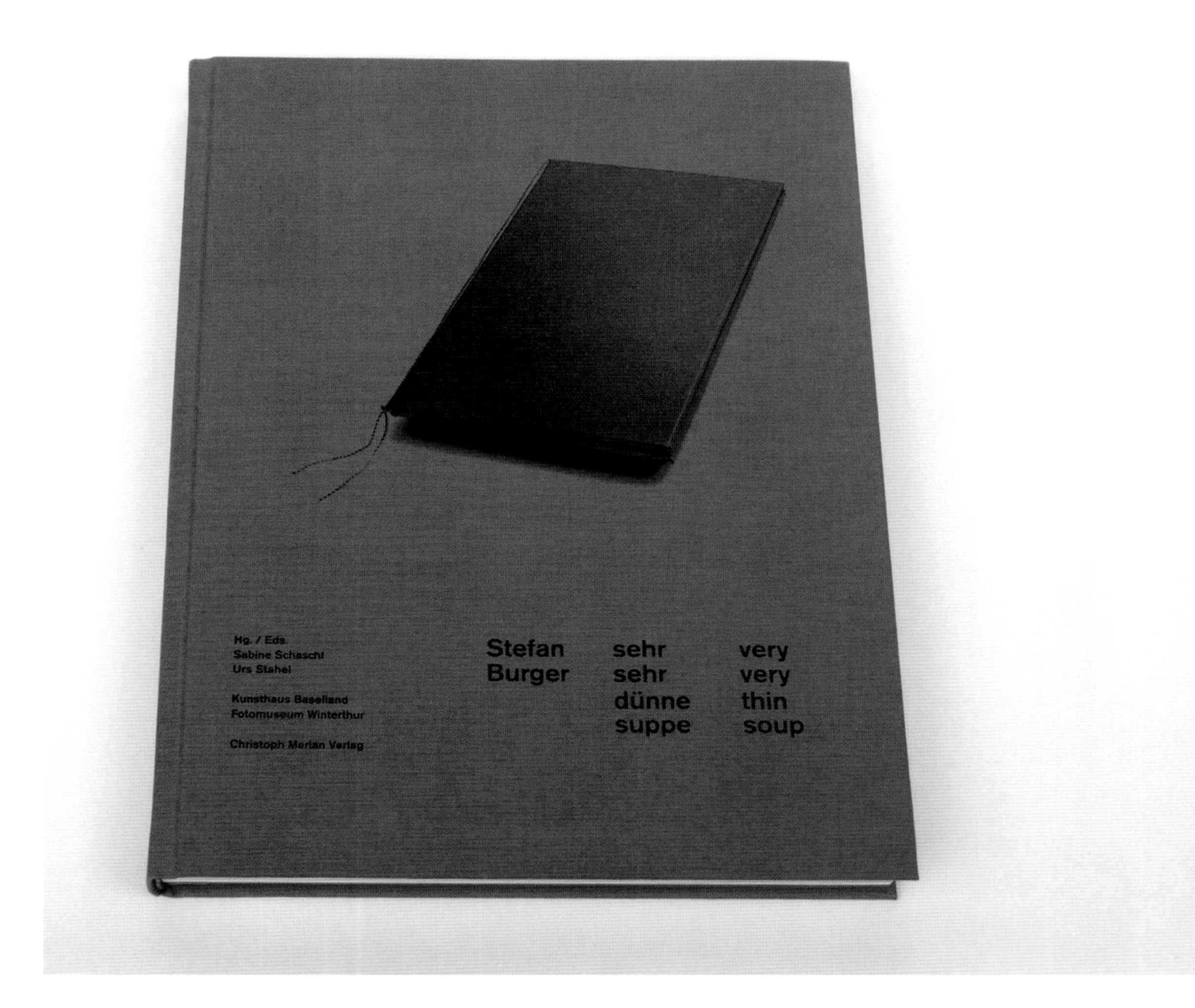

138 Book

DESIGN Friedrich-Wilhelm Graf and Alina Günter, *Zürich* **PHOTOGRAPHY** Stefan Burger **PRINTING AND BINDING** DZA, Druckerei zu Alternburg **LITHOGRAPHY** Daniele Kaehr **EDITORS** Urs Stahel, Fotomuseum, and Sabine Schaschl, *Kunsthaus* **PUBLISHER** Christoph Merian Verlag, *Basel, Switzerland* **DESIGN OFFICE** unfolded **CLIENTS** Fotomuseum Winterthur and Kunsthaus Baselland **PRINCIPAL TYPE** Akzidenz Grotesk **DIMENSIONS** 8.3 × 10.6 in. (21 × 27 cm)

DESIGN Erica Heitman-Ford, *New York* ART DIRECTION Erica Heitman-Ford CREATIVE DIRECTION Matteo Bologna
LETTERING Erica Heitman-Ford DESIGN OFFICE Mucca Design CLIENT Rizzoli USA PRINCIPAL TYPE handlettering
DIMENSIONS *La Cuisine*: 10.25 × 7.25 in. (26 × 18.4 cm), *La Cucina*: 10.25 × 7.25 in. (26 × 18.4 cm)

 Book Jacket

DESIGN Christopher Silas Neal, *Brooklyn, New York* LETTERING Christopher Silas Neal CLIENT Vintage Books
PRINCIPAL TYPE handlettering DIMENSIONS 5 × 8 in. (12.7 × 20.3 cm)

DESIGN Christopher Silas Neal, *Brooklyn, New York* **LETTERING** Christopher Silas Neal **CLIENT** Vintage Books **PRINCIPAL TYPE** handlettering
DIMENSIONS 5 × 8 in. (12.7 × 20.3 cm)

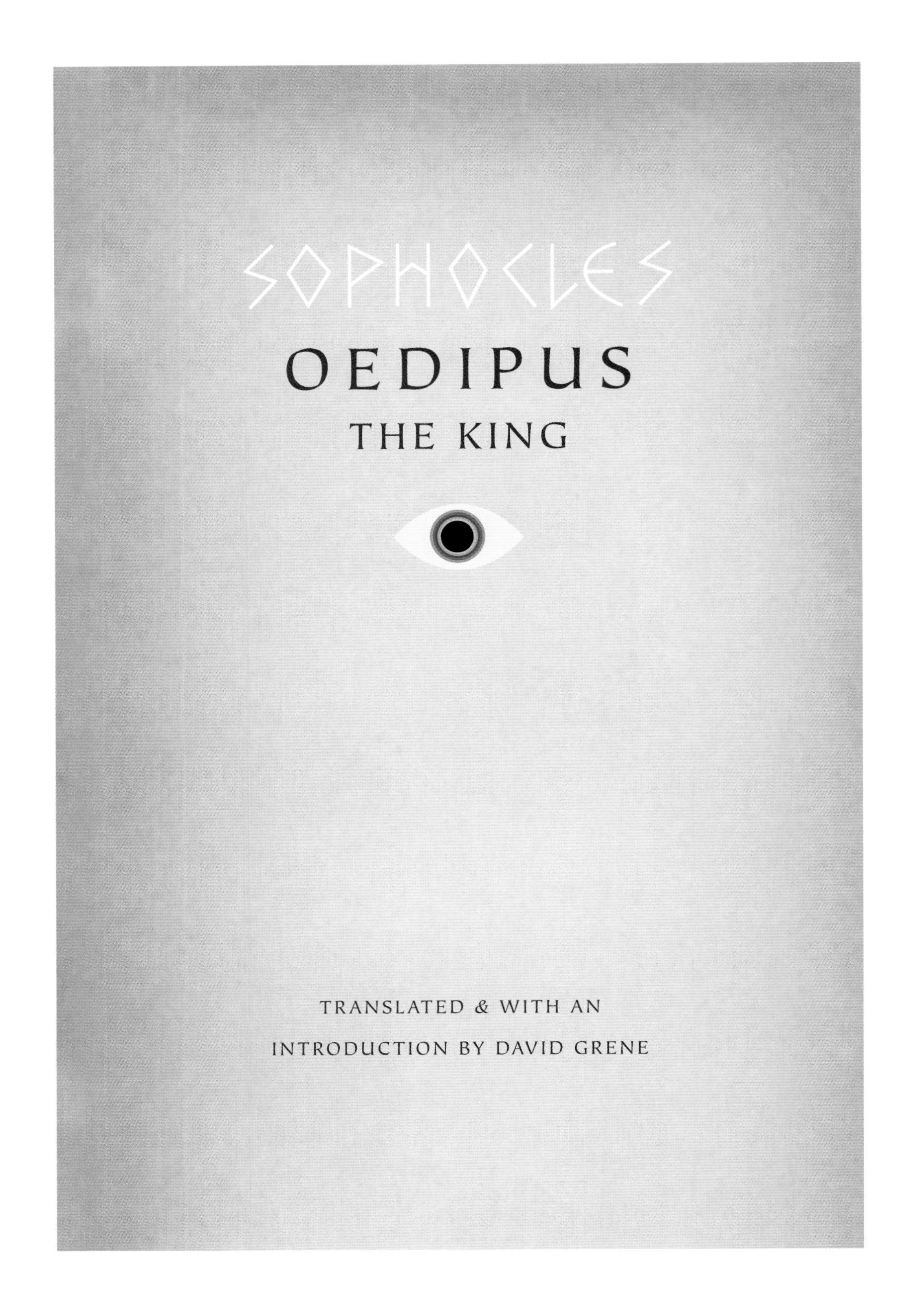

 Book Jacket

DESIGN Dustin Kilgore, *Chicago* ART DIRECTION Jill Shimabukuro LETTERING Dustin Kilgore PUBLISHER The University of Chicago Press
PRINCIPAL TYPE ITC Tiepolo and handlettering DIMENSIONS 5.25 × 8 in. (13.3 × 20.3 cm)

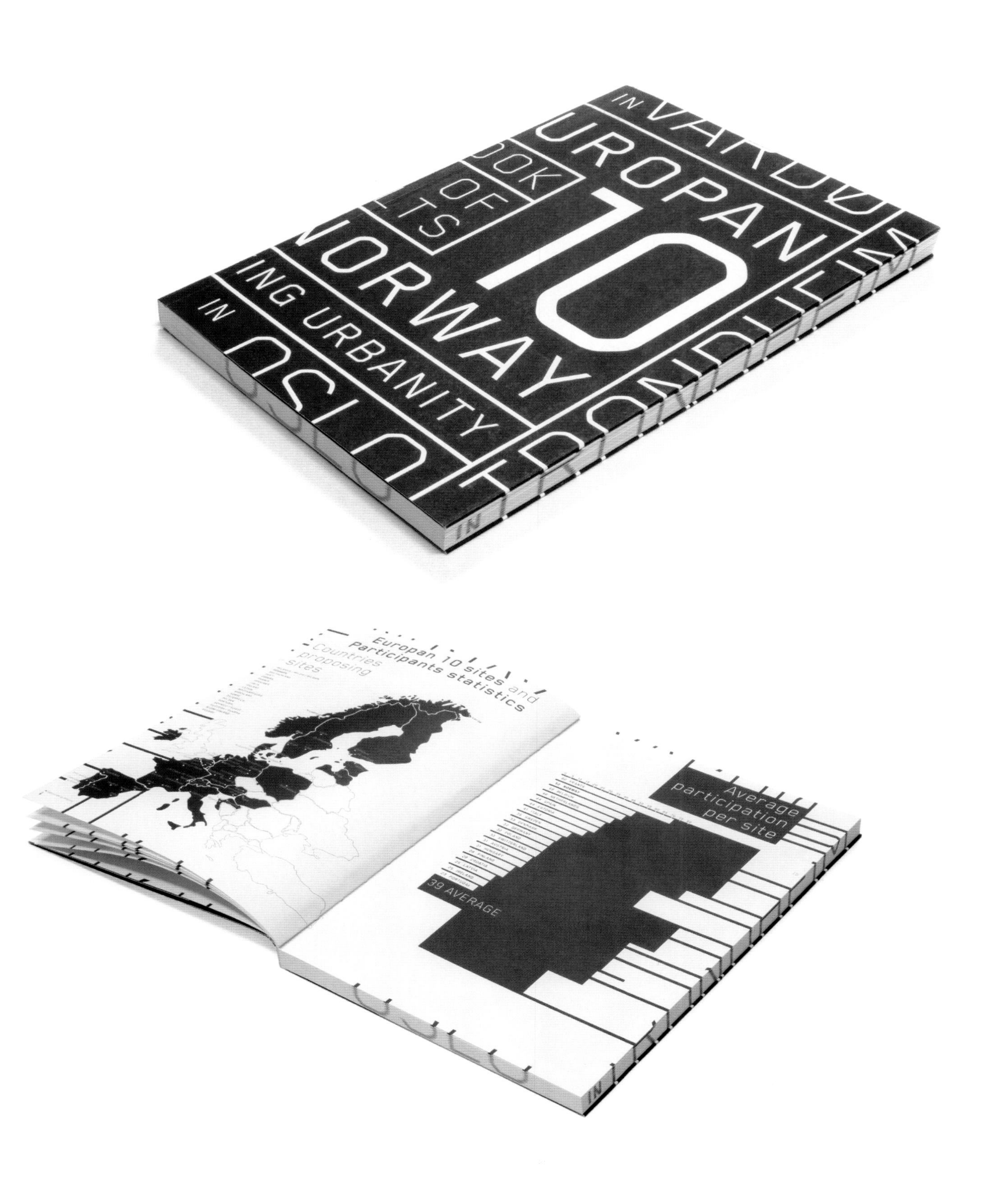

DESIGN Ariane Spanier **DESIGN OFFICE** Ariane Spanier Design **CLIENT** Europan Norway **PRINCIPAL TYPE** Blender Pro
DIMENSIONS 7.1 x 10.2 in. (18 x 26 cm)

144 Book

DESIGN Jiri Adamik-Novak, *Stockholm, Sweden* **ART DIRECTION** Jiri Adamik-Novak **CLIENT** Konstfack University Press
PRINCIPAL TYPE Lexicon **DIMENSIONS** 5.4 × 9 in. (13.8 × 22.8 cm)

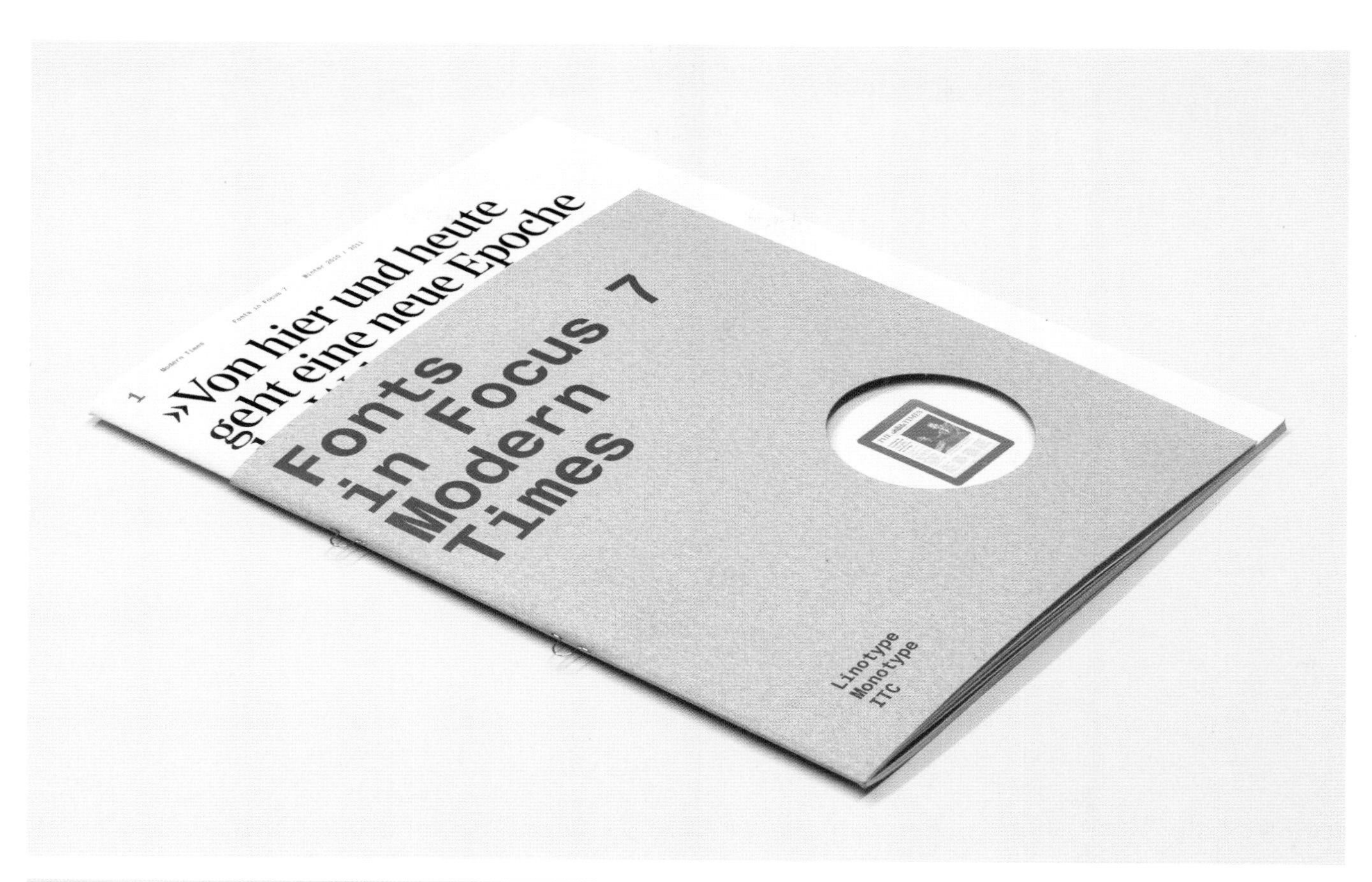

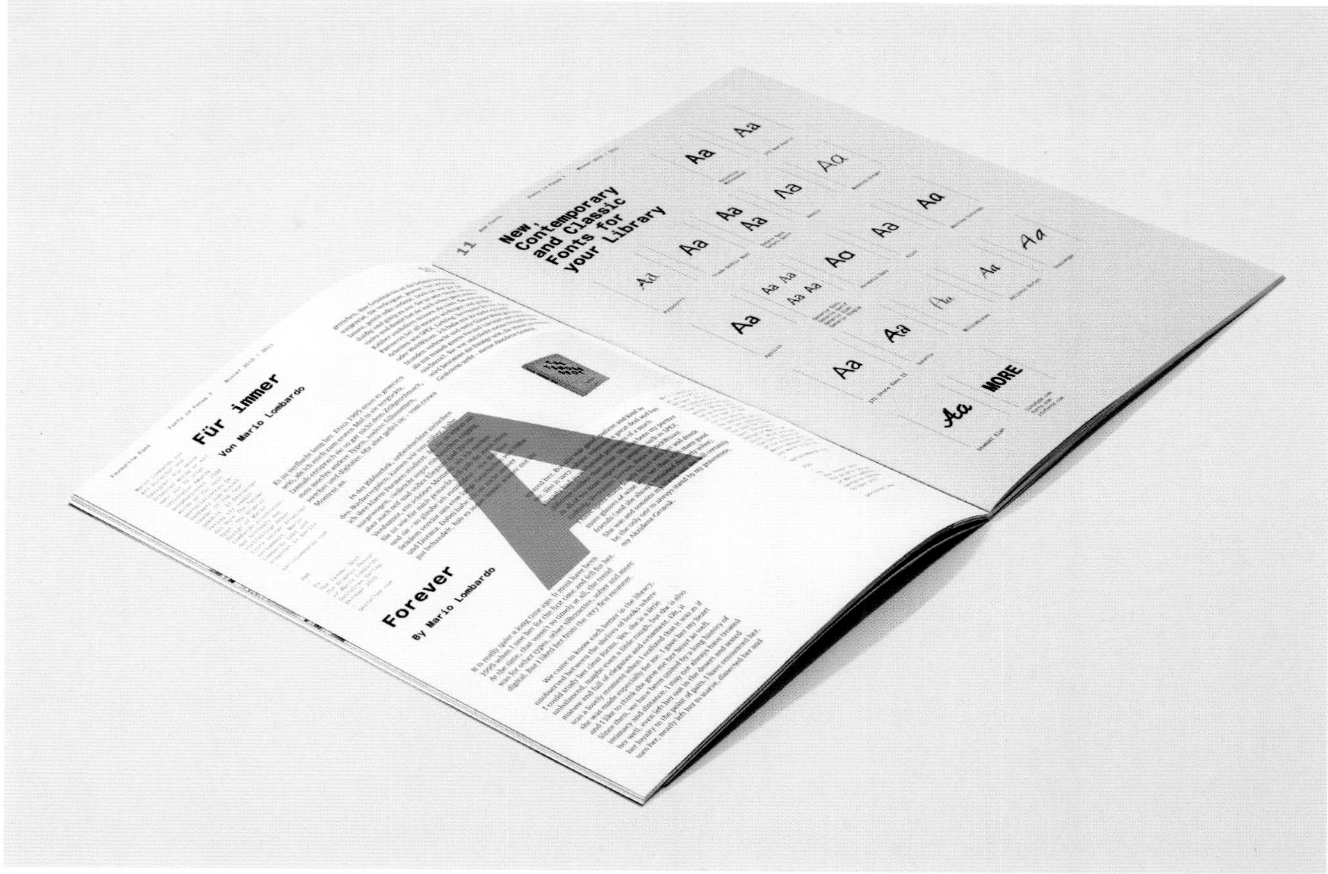

ART DIRECTION Flo Gaertner, *Karlsruhe, Germany* **SECOND ART DIRECTION** Matthias Kantereit **DESIGN OFFICE** MAGMA Brand Design GmbH & Co. KG
CLIENT Linotype GmbH **PRINCIPAL TYPE** ITC Charter, Helvetica Monospaced, and Times Modern **DIMENSIONS** 8.1 × 11 in. (20.5 × 28 cm)

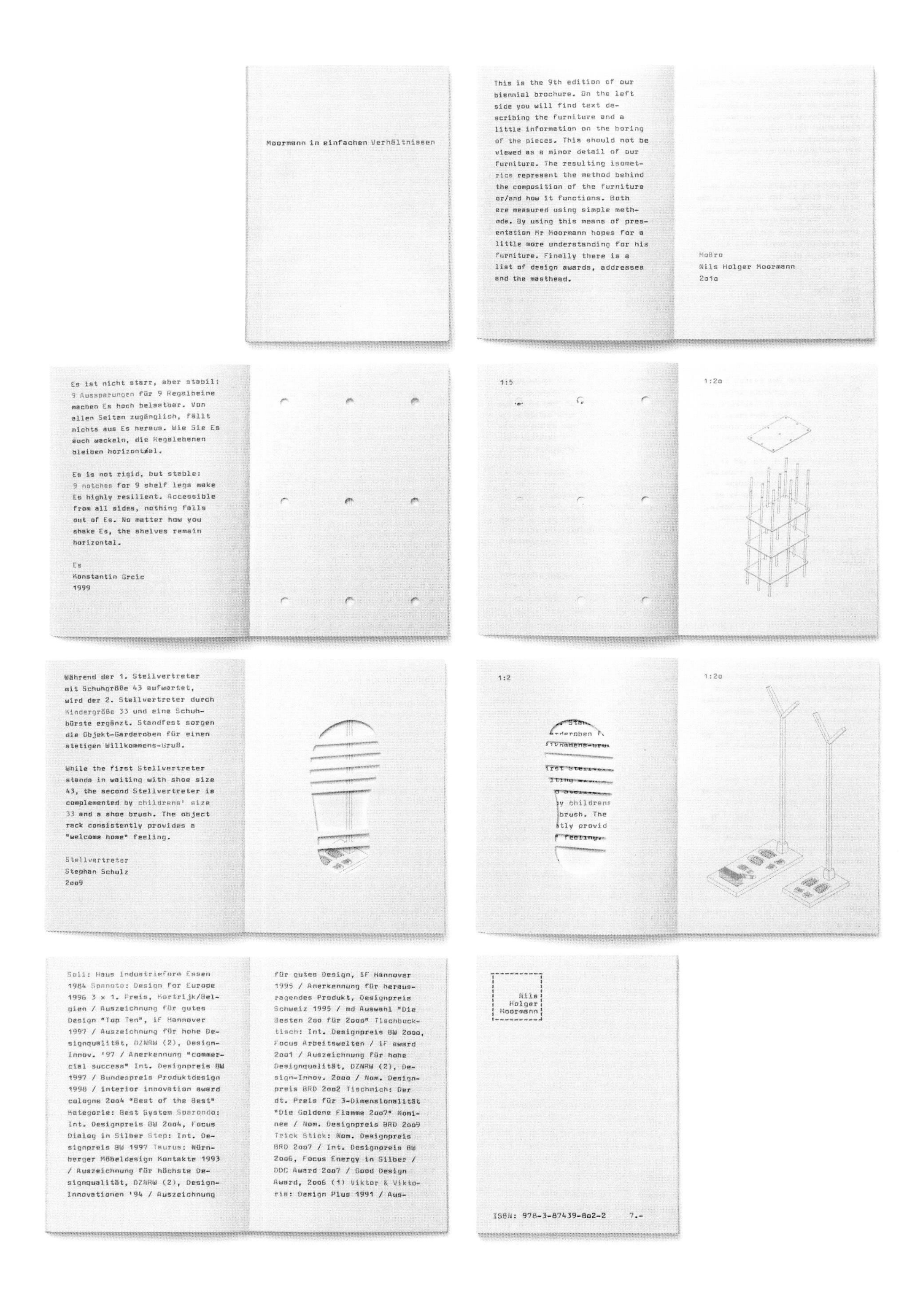

DESIGN Olaf Jäger and Regina Jäger, *Überlingen, Germany* **AGENCY** Jäger & Jäger **CLIENT** Nils Holger Moormann GmbH
PRINCIPAL TYPE Olympia Report de Luxe electric typewriter type **DIMENSIONS** 4.1 × 5.8 in. (10.5 × 14.8 cm)

Plate *147*

CREATIVE DIRECTION Christopher Simmons, *San Francisco* LETTERING Danielle Davis, *Lawton, Oklahoma* DESIGN OFFICE MINE™
PRINCIPAL TYPE handlettering DIMENSIONS 8-inch (20.3-cm) diameter

 Poster

DESIGN Niklaus Troxler, *Willisau, Switzerland* LETTERING Niklaus Troxler DESIGN OFFICE Niklaus Troxler Design CLIENT Jazz in Willisau
PRINCIPAL TYPE handlettering DIMENSIONS 35.4 × 50.4 in. (90 × 128 cm)

Mut zur Wut. Plakataktion Heidelberg 2010. Niklaus Troxler

DESIGN Niklaus Troxler, *Willisau, Switzerland* LETTERING Niklaus Troxler DESIGN OFFICE Niklaus Troxler Design
CLIENT Mut Zur Wut, Götz Gramlich, *Heidelberg, Germany* PRINCIPAL TYPE handlettering DIMENSIONS 33.1 × 46.9 in. (84 × 119 cm)

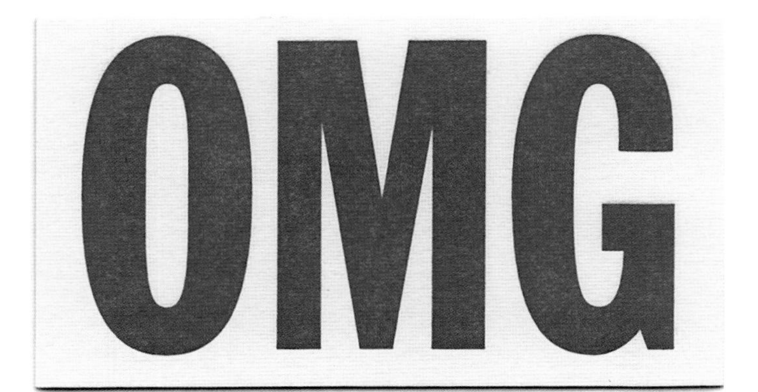

Oliver Munday (group) 147 W. 35th St Suite 202 New York NY 10018
202.294.4534 | OLIVER.MUNDAY@GMAIL.COM | OLIVERMUNDAY.COM

 Business Card

DESIGN Oliver Munday, *New York* PRINCIPAL TYPE Franklin Gothic
DIMENSIONS 2 × 3.5 in. (5.1 × 8.9 cm)

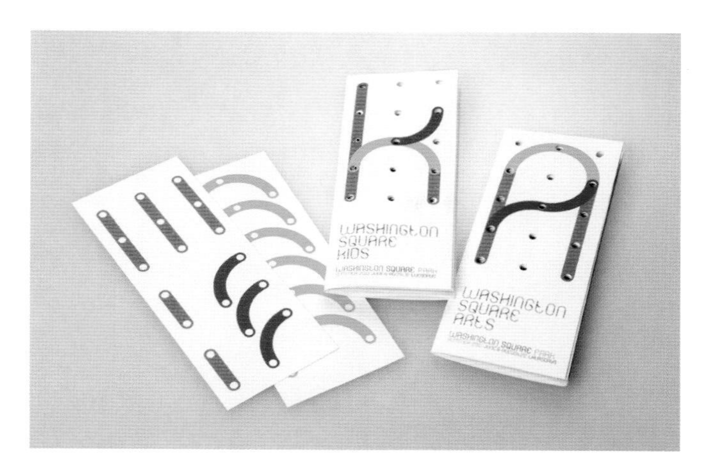

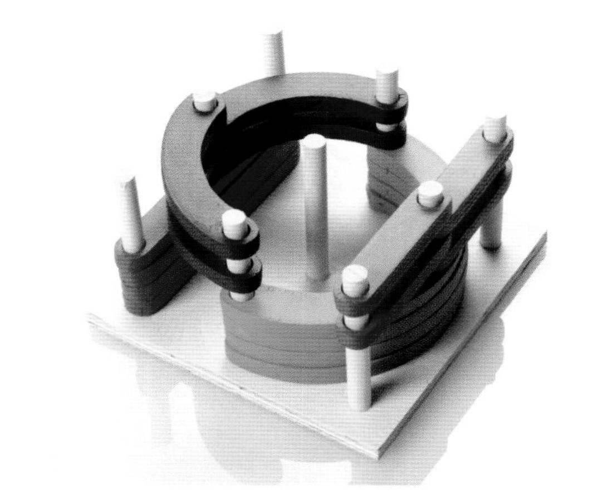

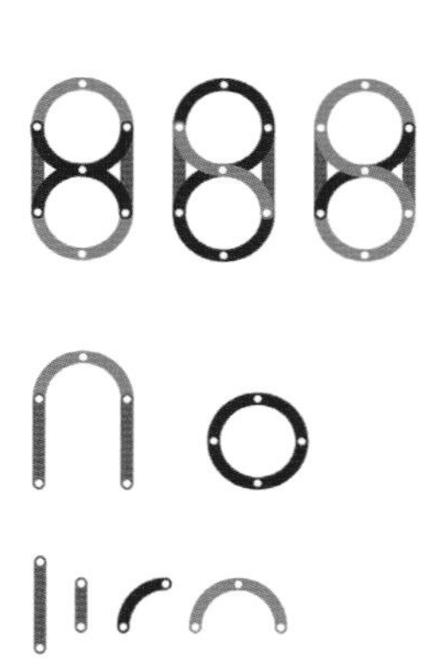

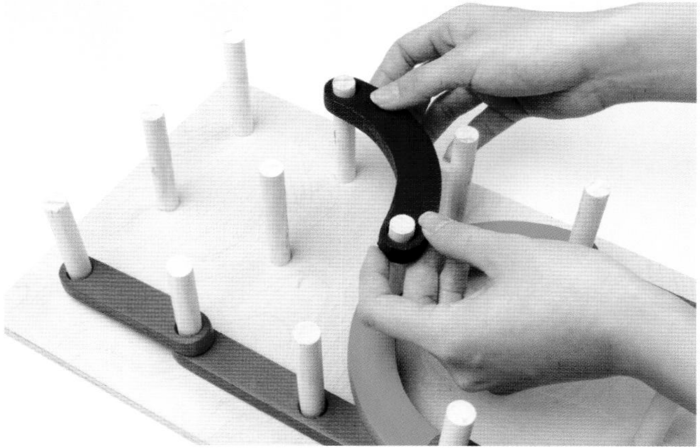

DESIGN Jiwon Kim, *New York* SCHOOL School of Visual Arts, *New York* INSTRUCTOR Paula Scher
PRINCIPAL TYPE custom DIMENSIONS various

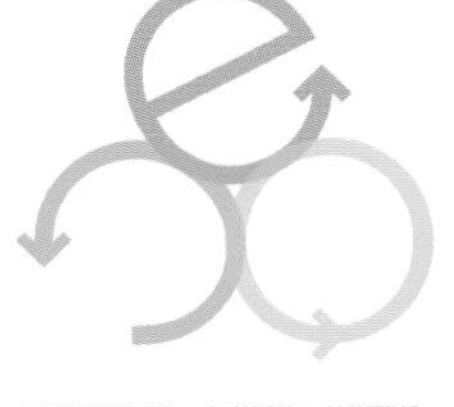

CONTENTS >>
> INTRODUCTION
> PAPER IN ARCHITECTURE
> PAPER IN FASHION
PAPER DRESS

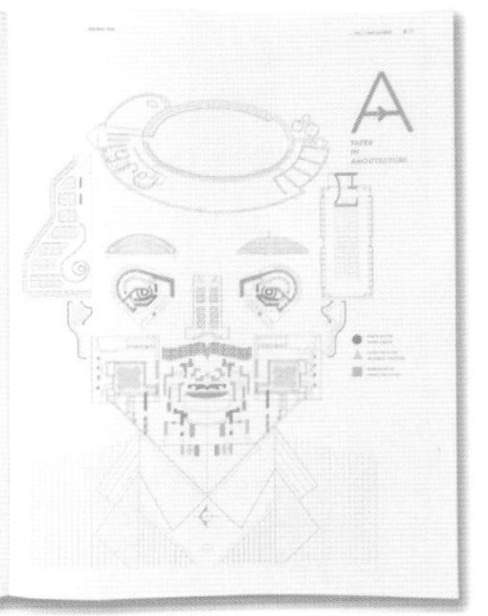

"Paper
is made
out of trees,"
Shigeru Ban says.
"Humans create
architecture
out of trees, so it must
be possible to create
architecture
out of paper."

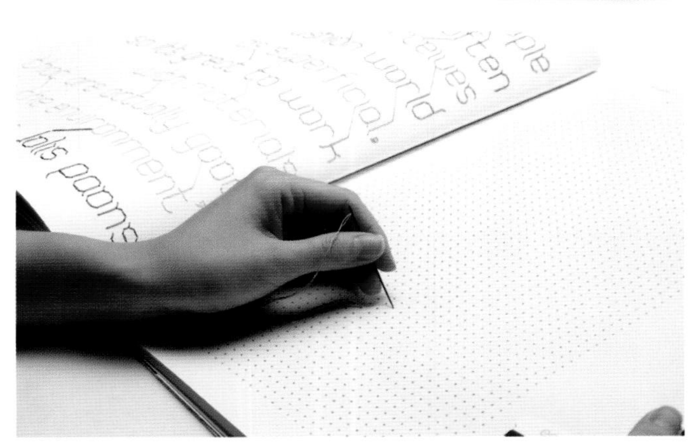

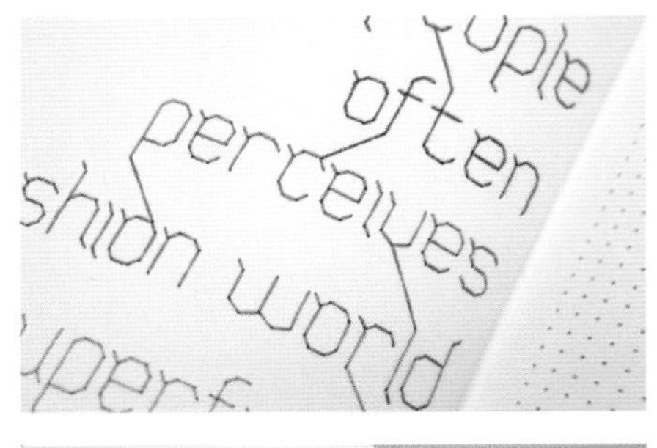

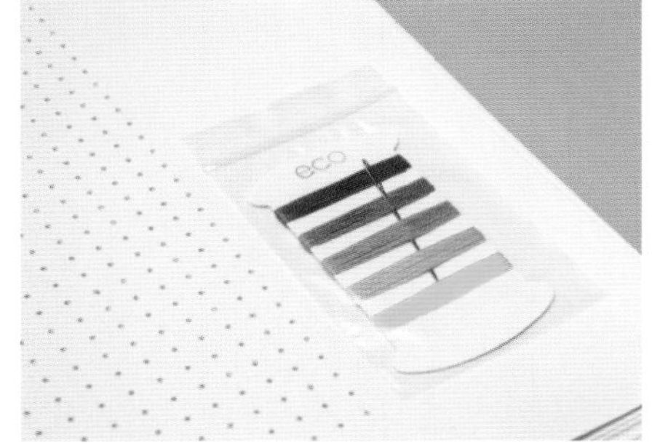

 Student Project

DESIGN Jiwon Kim, *New York* **SCHOOL** School of Visual Arts, *New York* **INSTRUCTOR** Julia Hoffmann **PRINCIPAL TYPE** custom
DIMENSIONS 12 × 15 in. (30.5 × 38.1 cm)

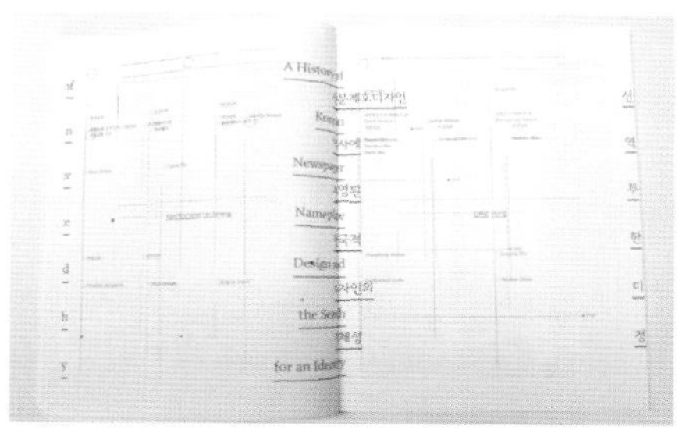

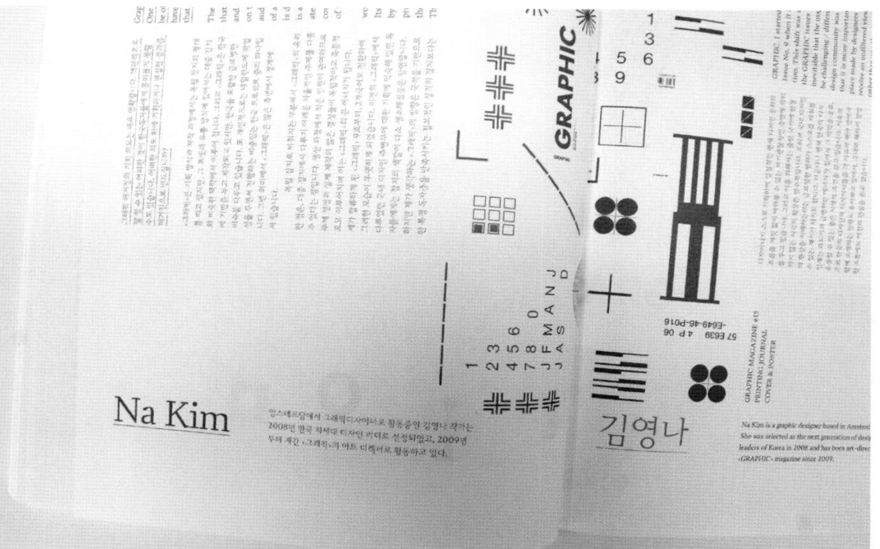

DESIGN Sangwon Bae, Geehyun Joo, Dajeong Kim, and Sukju Lee, *Seoul* **ART DIRECTION** Jiwon Huh, Hyesoo Kim, Joonki Min, and Jisung Park **CREATIVE DIRECTION** Deborah Kim, Yujin Kim, and Jiyoung Lee **LETTERING** Hyeran Choi, Suyeon Kim, Ryunghwa Rhee, and Chris Ro **TYPOGRAPHERS** Haewon Ahn, Jihae Kim, Eunjung Lee, and Songeun Lee **EDITORS** Jin Yeol Jung and Yunim Kim **SCHOOL** Better Days Institute **INSTRUCTORS** Chris Ro and Jae Hyouk Sung **PRINCIPAL TYPE** handlettering **DIMENSIONS** 7.5 × 10 in. (19 × 25.5 cm)

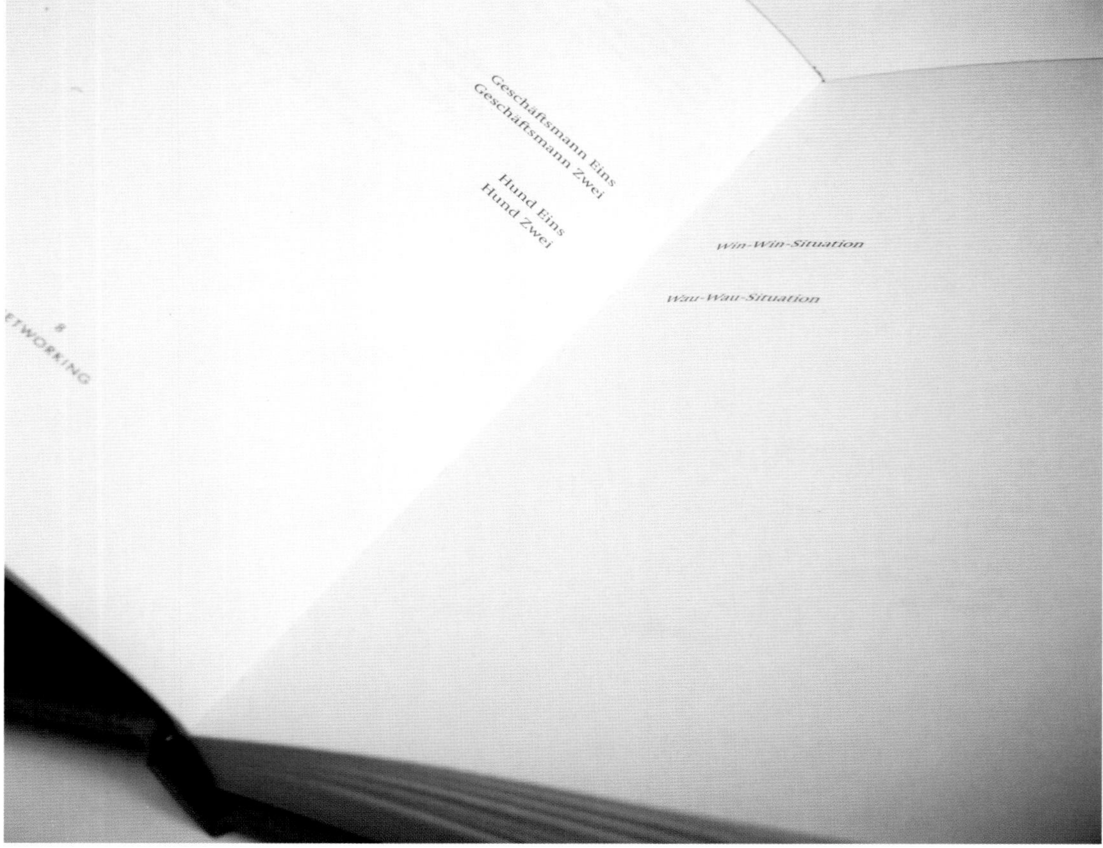

DESIGN Jenna Gesse, *Bielefeld, Germany* SCHOOL Fachhochschule Bielefeld/Fachbereich Gestaltung PROFESSOR Dirk Fütterer
PRINCIPAL TYPE Futura and Swift DIMENSIONS 4.3 × 7.1 in. (11 × 18 cm)

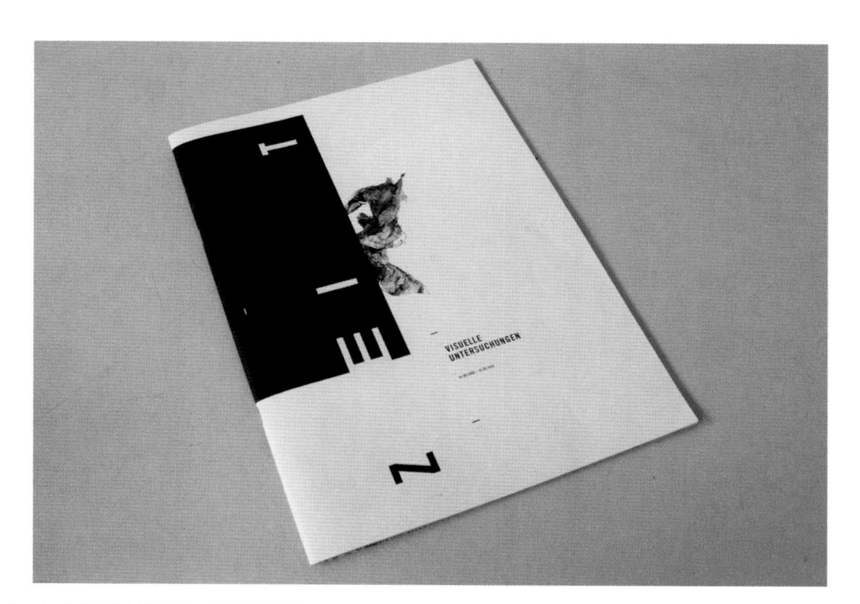

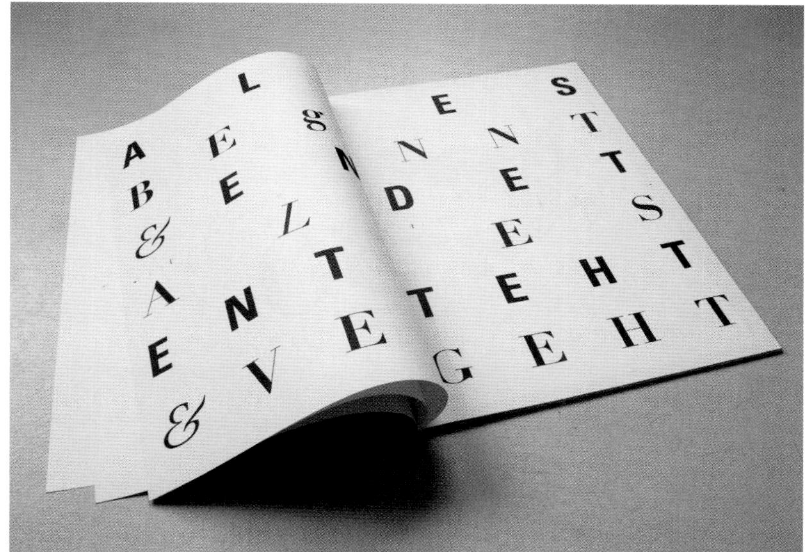

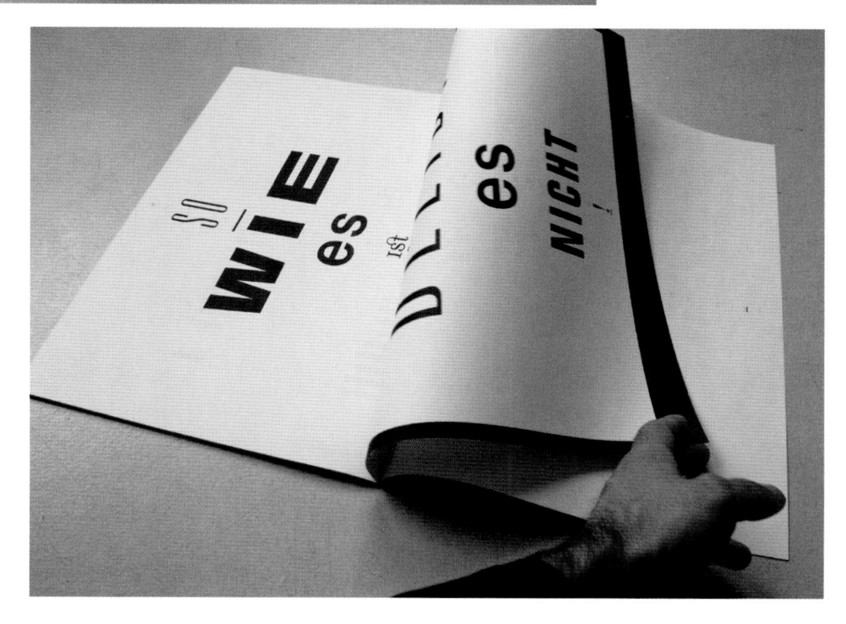

DESIGN Stefan Kaetz, *Hamburg* SCHOOL University of Applied Sciences, *Hamburg* PROFESSOR Heike Grebin PRINCIPAL TYPE Trade Gothic
DIMENSIONS 10.4 × 14.8 in. (26.5 × 37.5 cm)

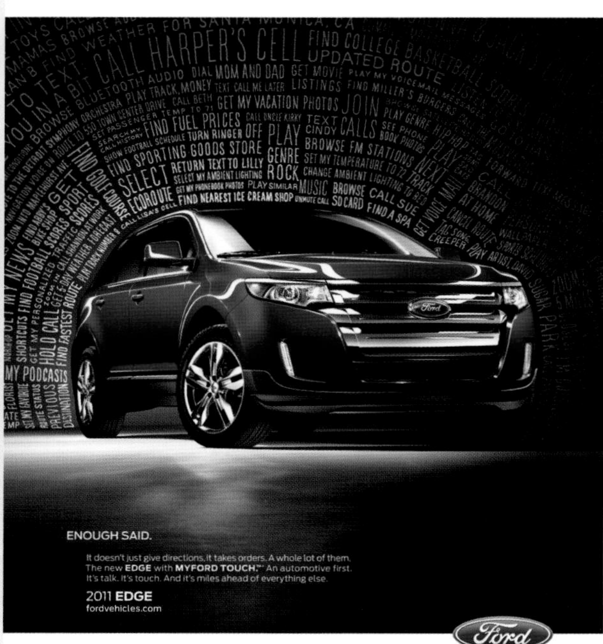

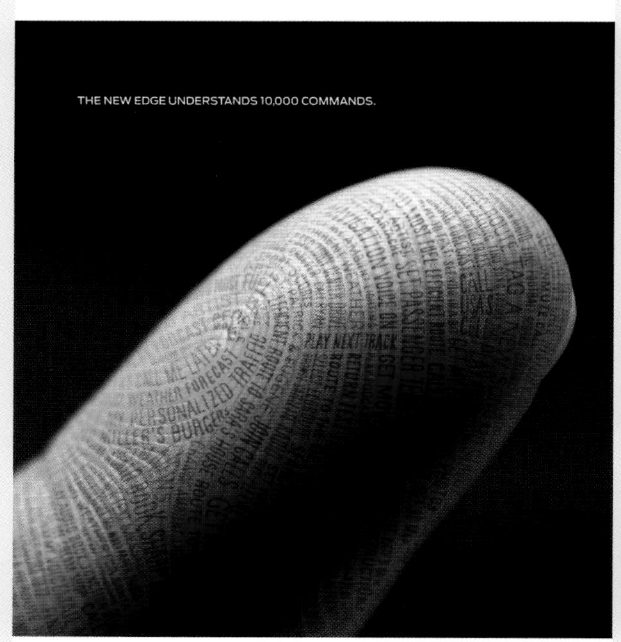

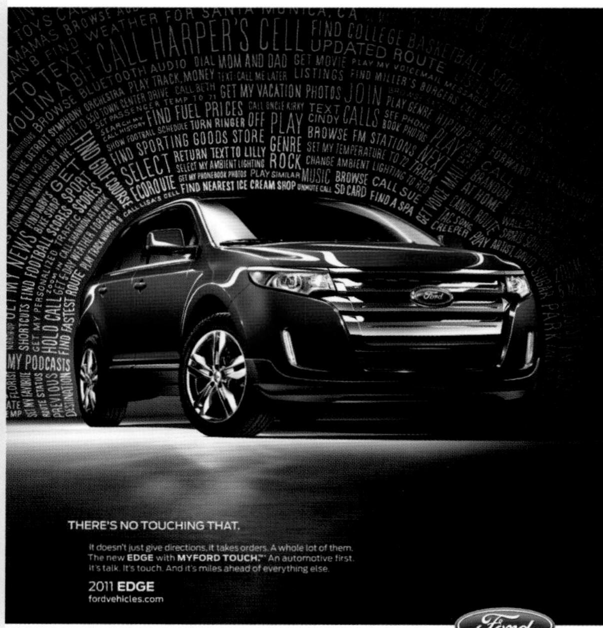

LETTERING Graham Clifford DESIGN Christine Jones and Tim McCaffrey, *Dearborn, Michigan* DESIGN DIRECTION Michele Silvestri ART DIRECTION Beth Hambly CHIEF CREATIVE OFFICER Toby Barlow CREATIVE DIRECTION Eric McClellan PHOTOGRAPHY John Roe, Farmington Hills, Michigan COPYWRITER Susan Mersch RETOUCHER Armstrong-White STRATEGY Emilie Hamer DESIGN OFFICE Graham Clifford Design, *New York* AGENCY Team Detroit CLIENT Ford Motor Company PRINCIPAL TYPE Ford Antenna and handlettering DIMENSIONS 8.5 × 11 in. (21.6 × 27.9 cm)

Roger Dutilleul's passion for collecting art was evident the moment one entered his apartment on Paris's rue Monceau.

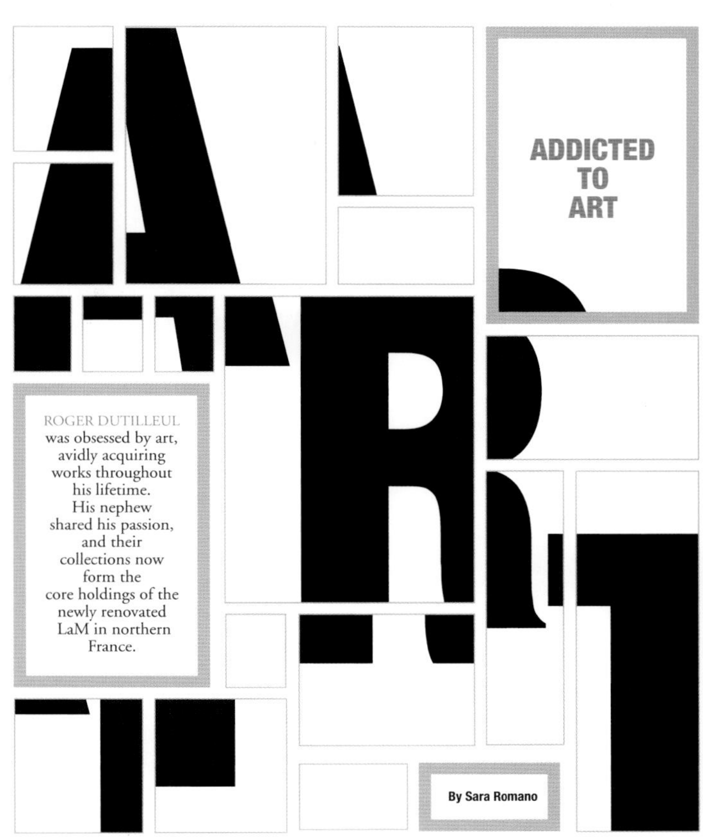

ADDICTED TO ART
ROGER DUTILLEUL was obsessed by art, avidly acquiring works throughout his lifetime. His nephew shared his passion, and their collections now form the core holdings of the newly renovated LaM in northern France.
By Sara Romano
FRANCE • FALL 2010 49

DESIGN Todd Albertson, *Washington, D.C.* **STUDIO** Todd Albertson Design **CLIENT** *France Magazine* **PRINCIPAL TYPE** Helvetica Neue
DIMENSIONS 9 × 10.9 in. (22.9 × 27.7 cm)

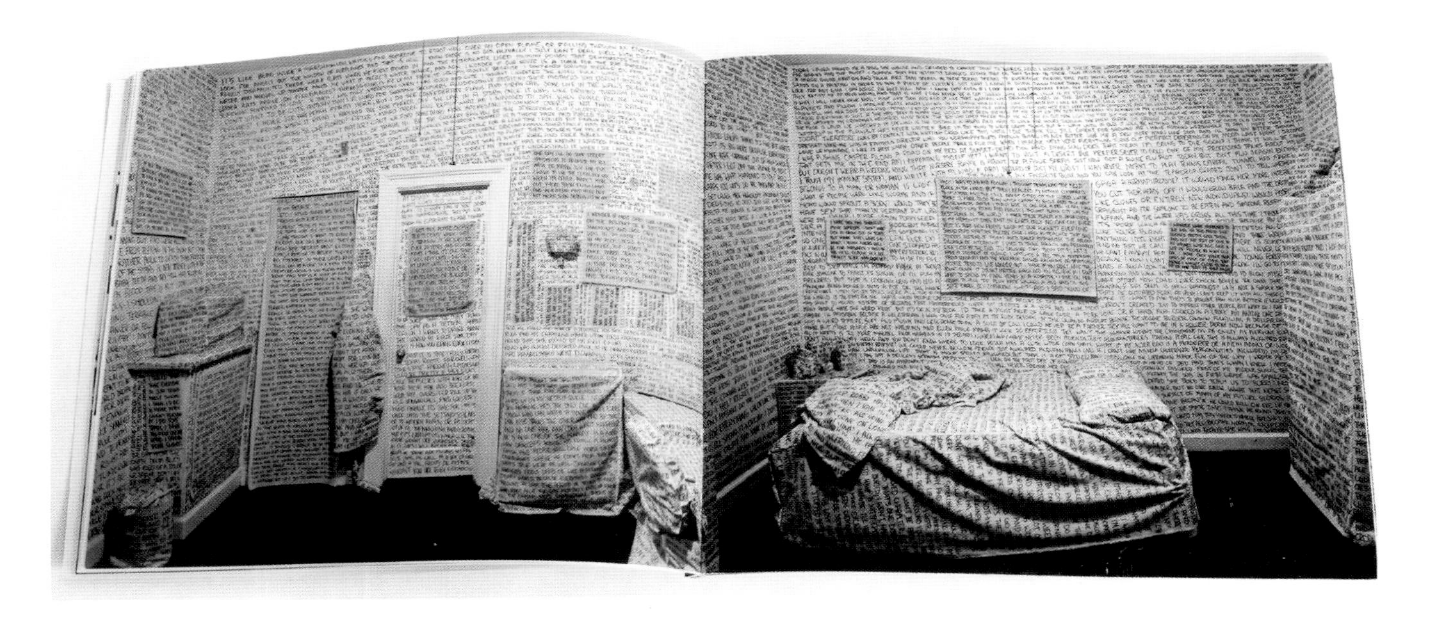

DESIGN Tara Odorizzi SCHOOL Savannah College of Art and Design INSTRUCTOR Rhonda Arntsen PRINCIPAL TYPE handlettering
DIMENSIONS 10 × 24 in. (25.4 × 61 cm)

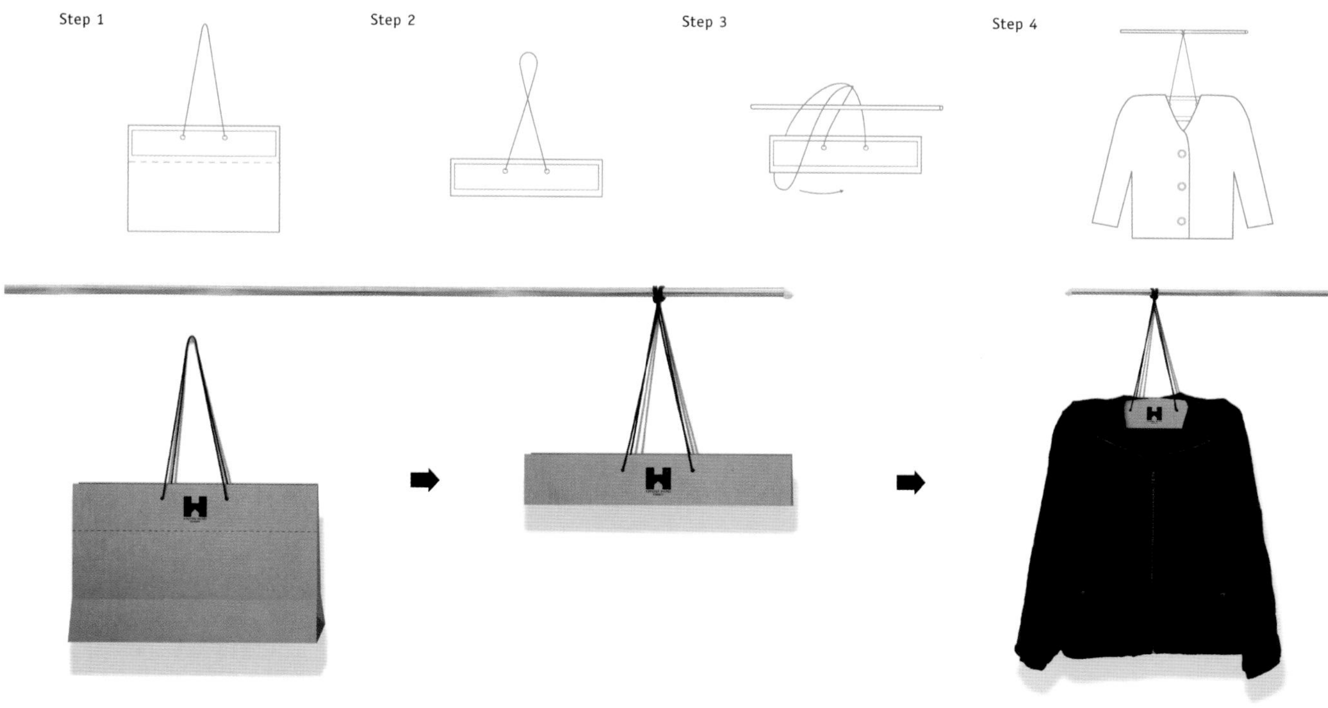

DESIGN Hiu Chui, *Weehawken, New Jersey* SCHOOL School of Visual Arts, *New York* INSTRUCTORS Kristina DiMatteo and Carin Goldberg
PRINCIPAL TYPE ITC Officina Sans DIMENSIONS various

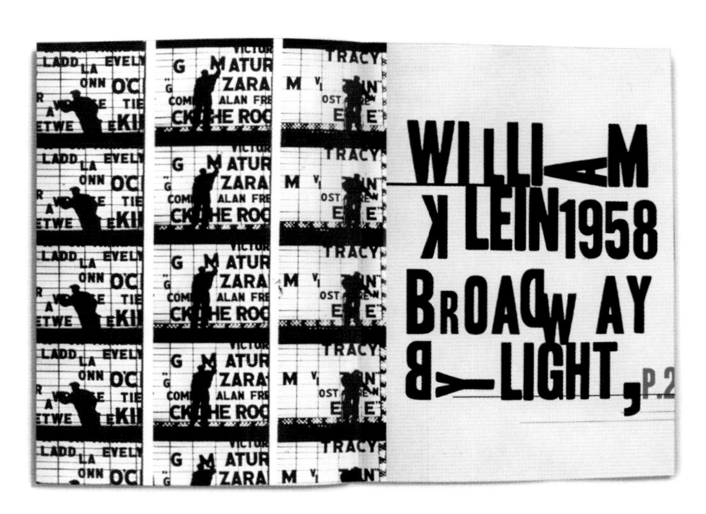

THE KINETIC QUALI TY OF NEW Y
RK,THE K IDS,DIR T, M DN E SS-
I DIDN'T SE E CLEAN TE CHNIQU
BEING RIGHT FOR NEW YORK. I TR
ED TO FIN D A PHOTOGRA HI
STYLE THAT WOULD COME CLOS
TO IT." WILLIAM KLEI N

160 Student Project

DESIGN Yoonbin Lee, *New York* SCHOOL School of Visual Arts, *New York* INSTRUCTOR Carin Goldberg PRINCIPAL TYPE woodtype
DIMENSIONS 20 × 25 in. (50.8 × 63.5 cm)

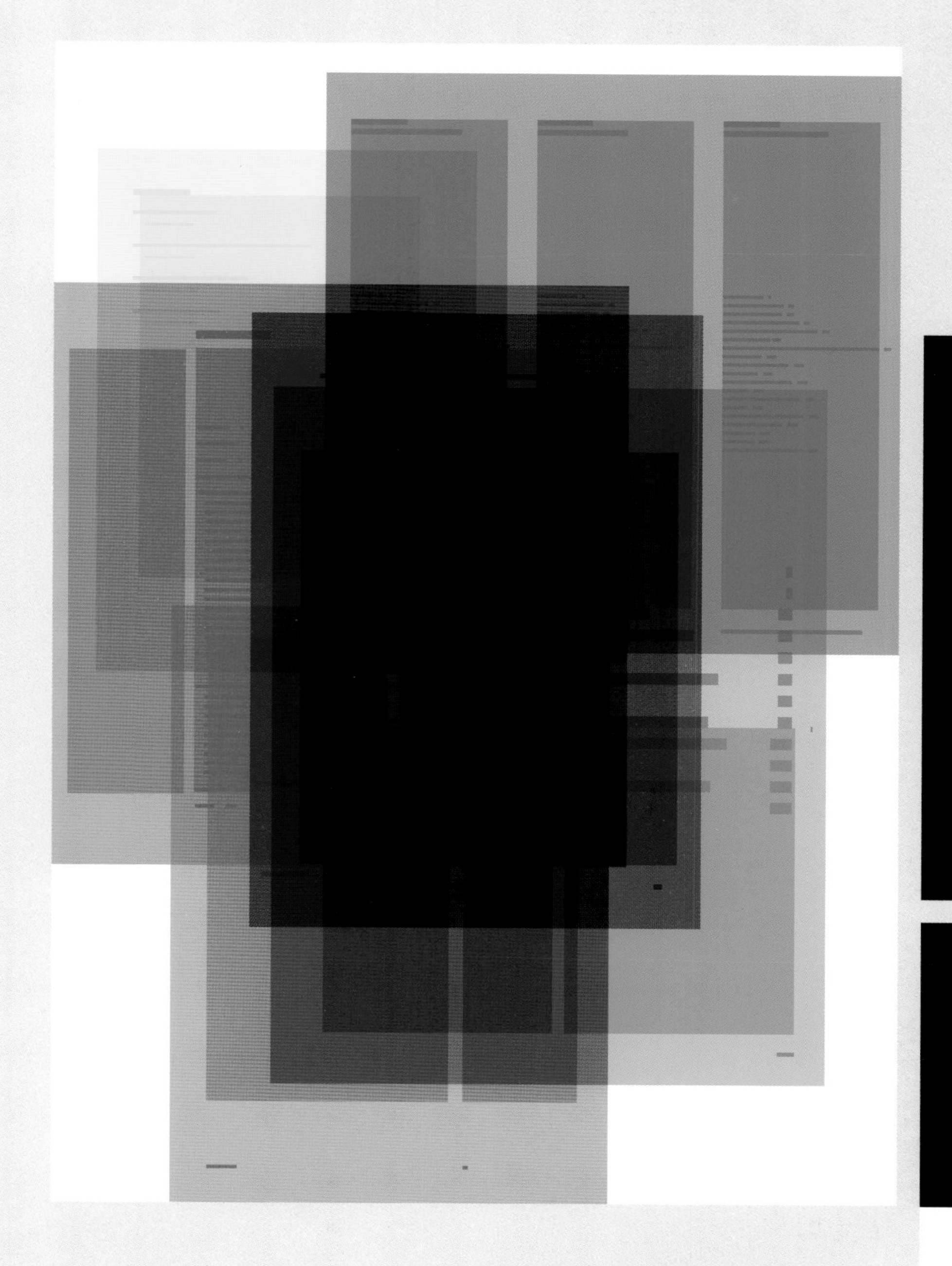

DESIGN Yujin Kim, *Seoul* SCHOOL Kookmin University Graduate School INSTRUCTOR Chris Ro PRINCIPAL TYPE various
DIMENSIONS 23.4 × 33.1 in. (59.4 × 84.1 cm)

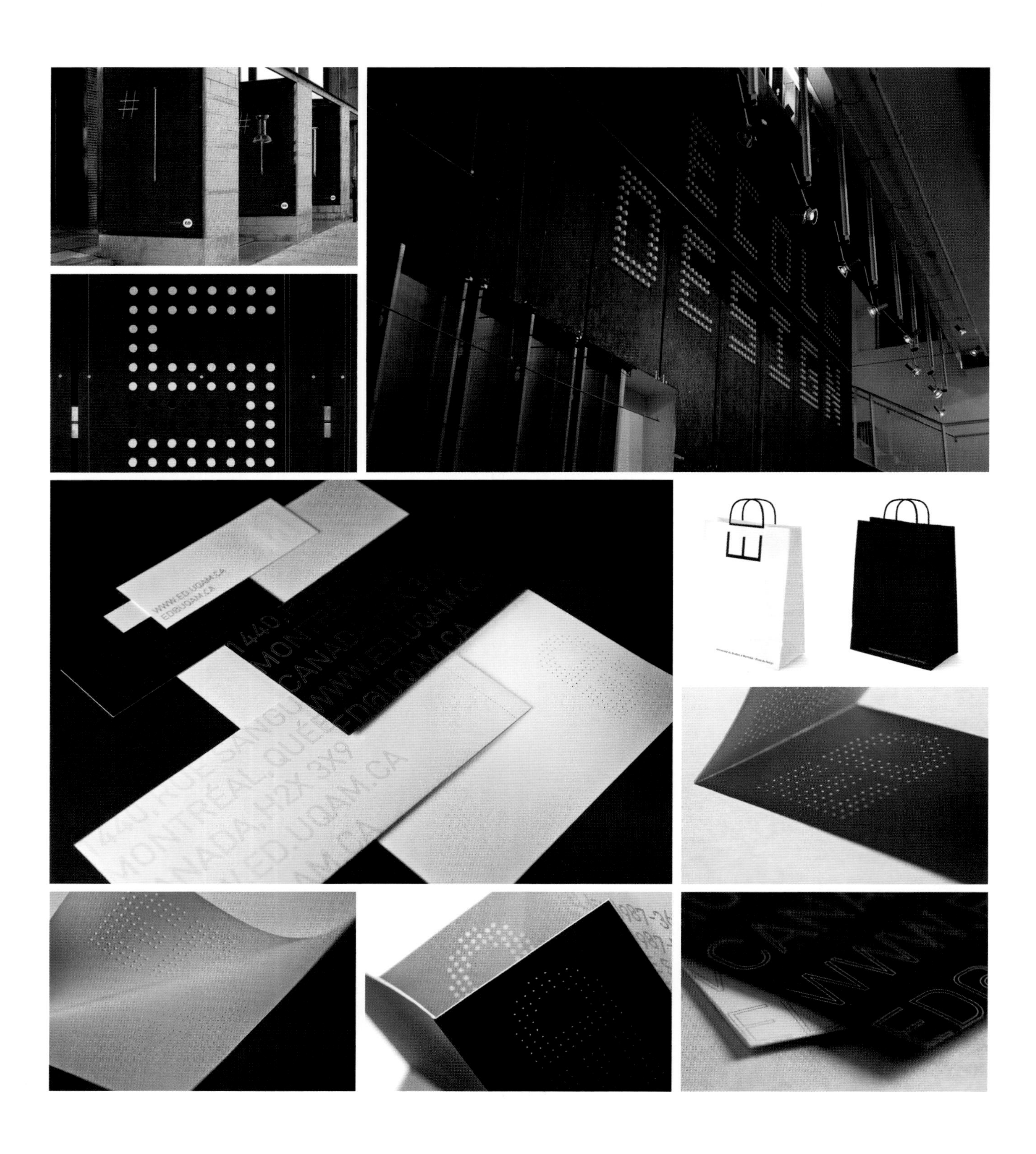

DESIGN Jean Tran, *Montréal* SCHOOL Université du Québec à Montréal (UQÀM) INSTRUCTOR Louis Gagnon
PRINCIPAL TYPE DIN (modified), Helvetica Neue (modified), and custom DIMENSIONS various

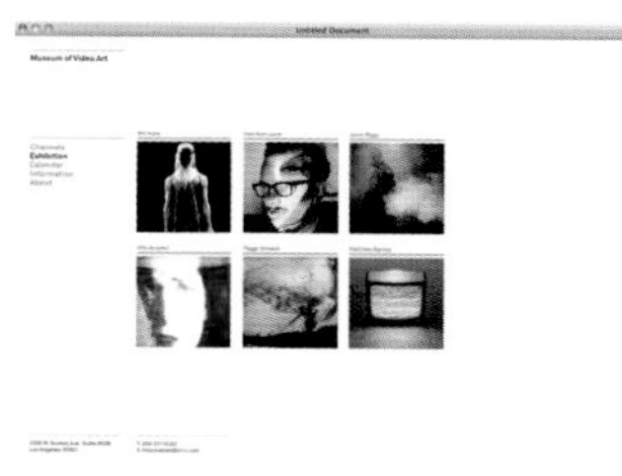

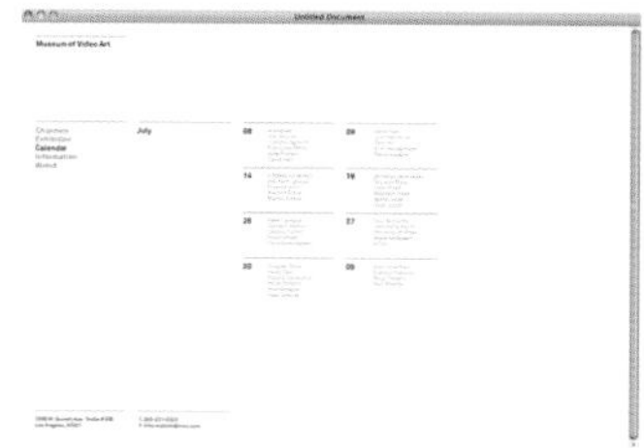

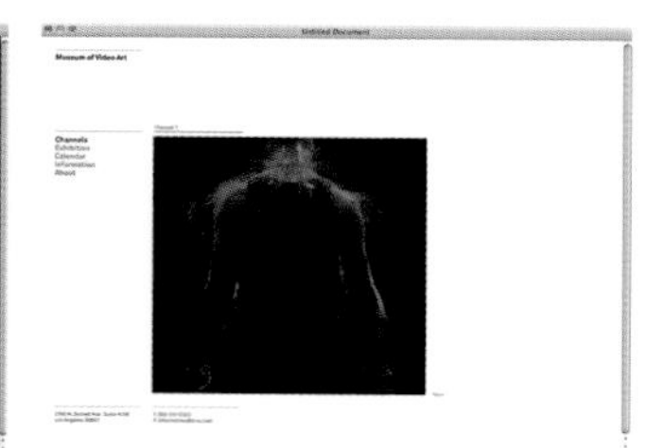

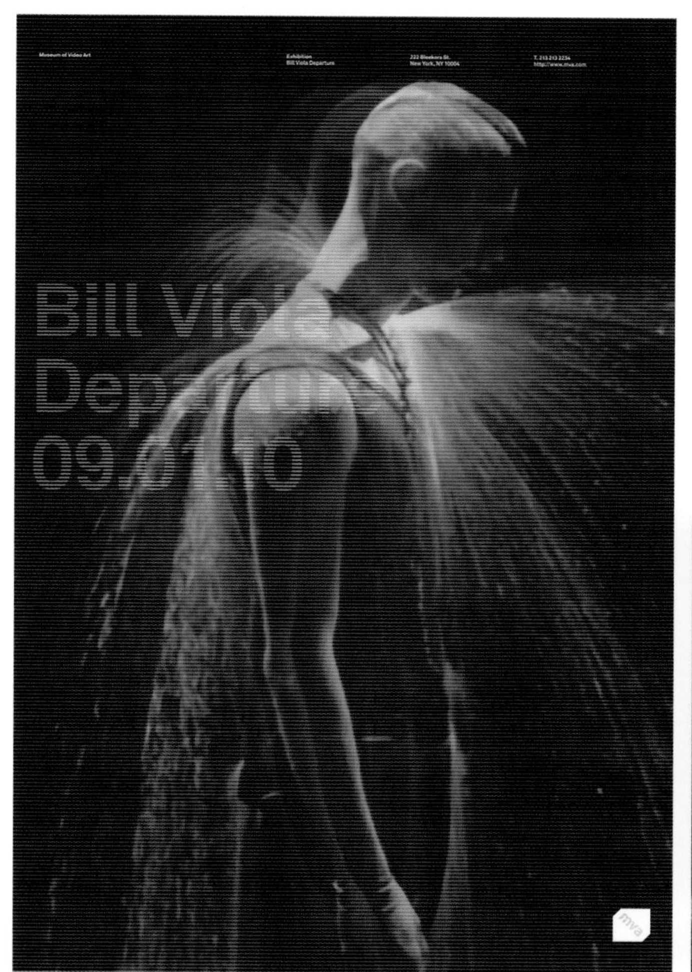

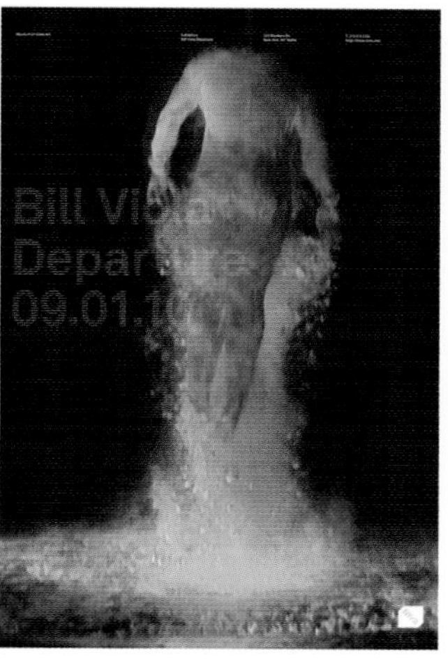

DESIGN Jee Won Kim, *Pasadena, California* SCHOOL Art Center College of Design INSTRUCTOR Brad Bartlett
PRINCIPAL TYPE Akkurat DIMENSIONS 24 × 36 in. (61 × 91.4 cm)

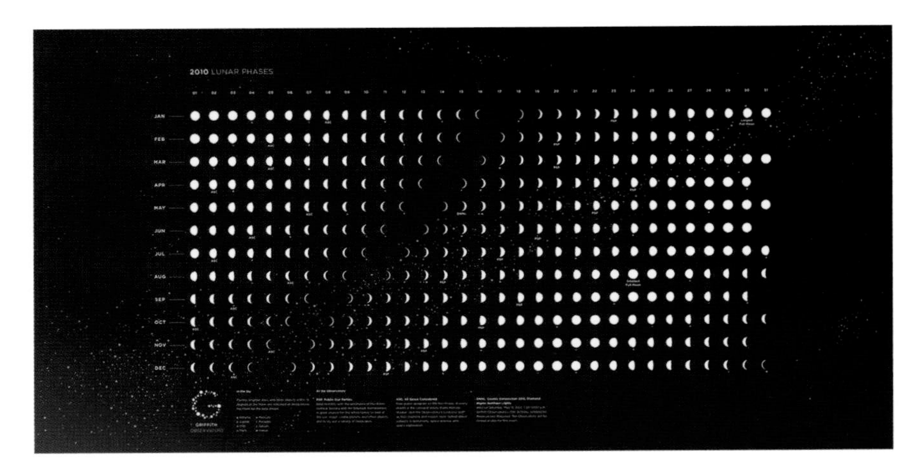

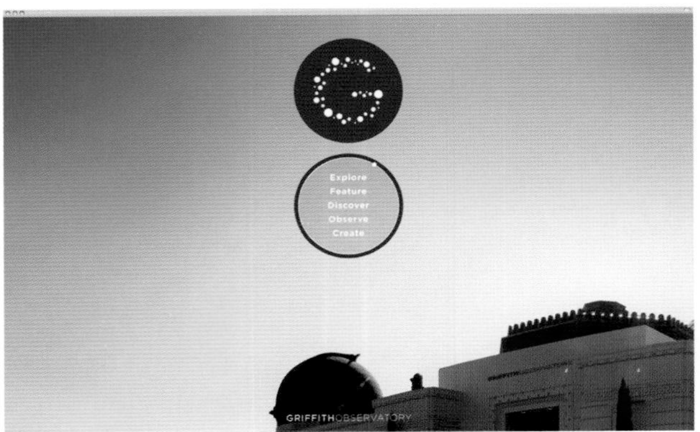

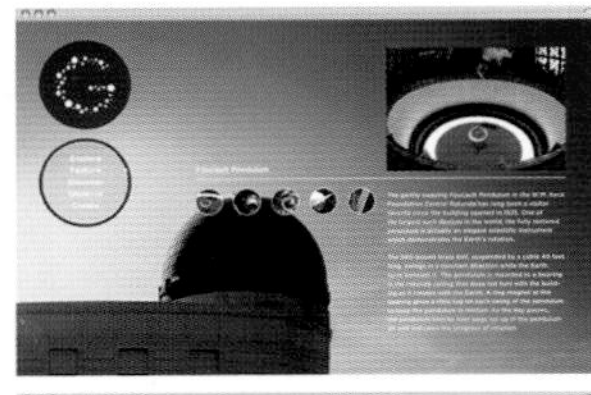

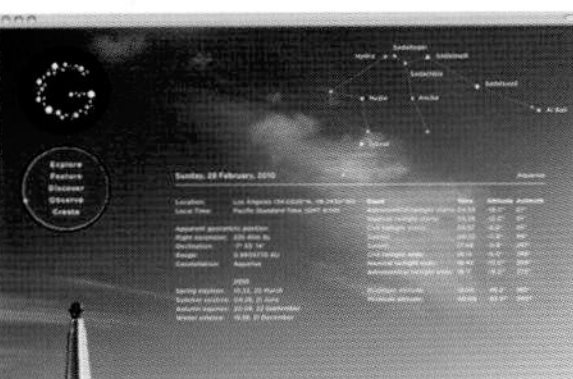

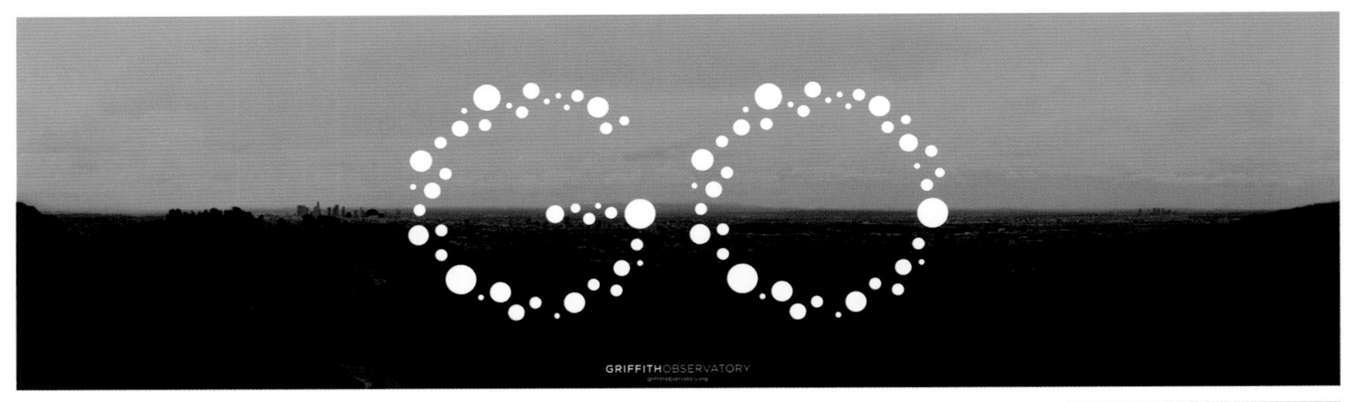

DESIGN Tomoko Ogino, *Pasadena, California* PHOTOGRAPHY Kai Iwamoto SCHOOL Art Center College of Design INSTRUCTOR Brad Bartlett
PRINCIPAL TYPE Gotham DIMENSIONS Posters: 40 × 11.8 in. (101.6 × 30 cm), Calendar: 40 × 20.5 in. (101.6 × 52.1 cm)

DESIGN Rocco Cambareri, *New York* SCHOOL School of Visual Arts, *New York* INSTRUCTOR Andrew Castrucci PRINCIPAL TYPE Distorted type
DIMENSIONS 24 × 30 in. (61 × 76.2 cm)

WA
FABRIC
COLLEC-
TION
2011
WA INTERNATIONAL FABRIC COLLECTION 2011
有限会社 わ／〒107-0062 東京都港区南青山3-15-17 Wa.Ltd.／3-15-17 Minami Aoyama Minato-ku, Tokyo Japan 107-0062 TEL.03-6912-0440 FAX.03-3746-4151 URL.www.wallart.co.jp

166 Poster

DESIGN Gaku Ohsugi and Michi Takahashi, *Tokyo* ART DIRECTION Gaku Ohsugi CREATIVE DIRECTION Fumiko Shirahama
DESIGN OFFICE 702 Design Works CLIENT Wa ltd. PRINCIPAL TYPE custom DIMENSIONS 28.7 × 40.6 in. (72.8 × 103 cm)

DESIGN Henrik Kubel, *London* LETTERING Henrik Kubel DESIGN OFFICE A2/SW/HK CLIENT Royal College of Art
PRINCIPAL TYPE Fern Italic, Fern Regular, and handlettering DIMENSIONS 27.6 × 39.4 in. (70 × 100 cm)

 Poster

DESIGN Rocco Piscatello, *New York* DESIGN OFFICE Piscatello Design Centre CLIENT Fashion Institute of Technology
PRINCIPAL TYPE Akzidenz Grotesk DIMENSIONS 23.4 × 33.1 in. (59.4 × 84.1 cm)

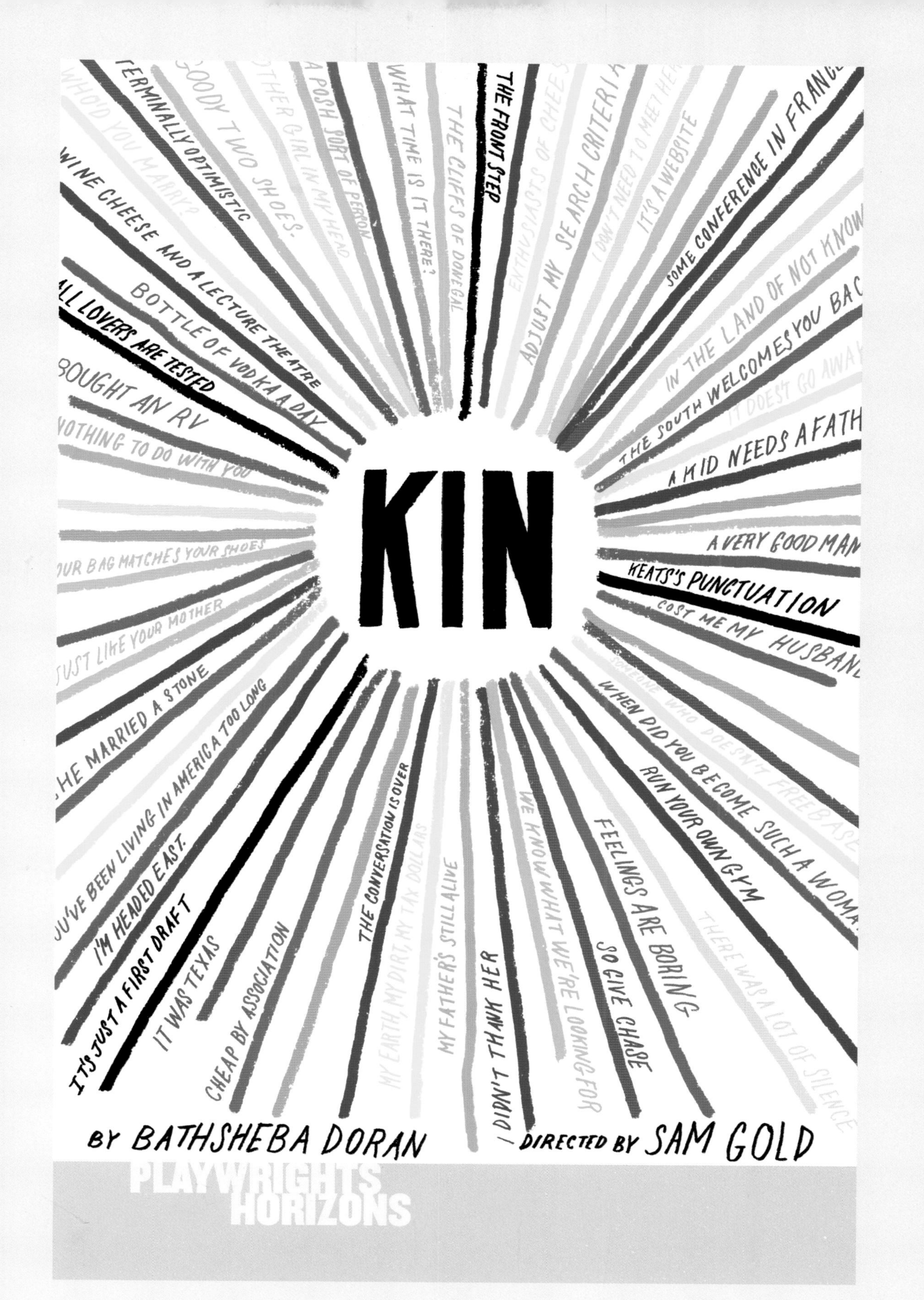

DESIGN Jamus Marquette, *New York* ART DIRECTION Sam Eckersley CREATIVE DIRECTION Stuart Rogers DESIGN OFFICE Rogers Eckersley Design
CLIENT Playwrights Horizons PRINCIPAL TYPE Knockout No. 70 Full Welterweight DIMENSIONS 22 × 36 in. (55.9 × 91.4 cm)

DESIGN Alice Genaud, Jean-Paul Lehfeld, Jason Little, and Brad Stevens, *Paris* DESIGN DIRECTION Brad Stevens CREATIVE DIRECTION Jason Little
AGENCY Landor Associates CLIENT Iggesund PRINCIPAL TYPE Arete Mono DIMENSIONS 23.4 × 33.1 in. (59.4 × 84 cm)

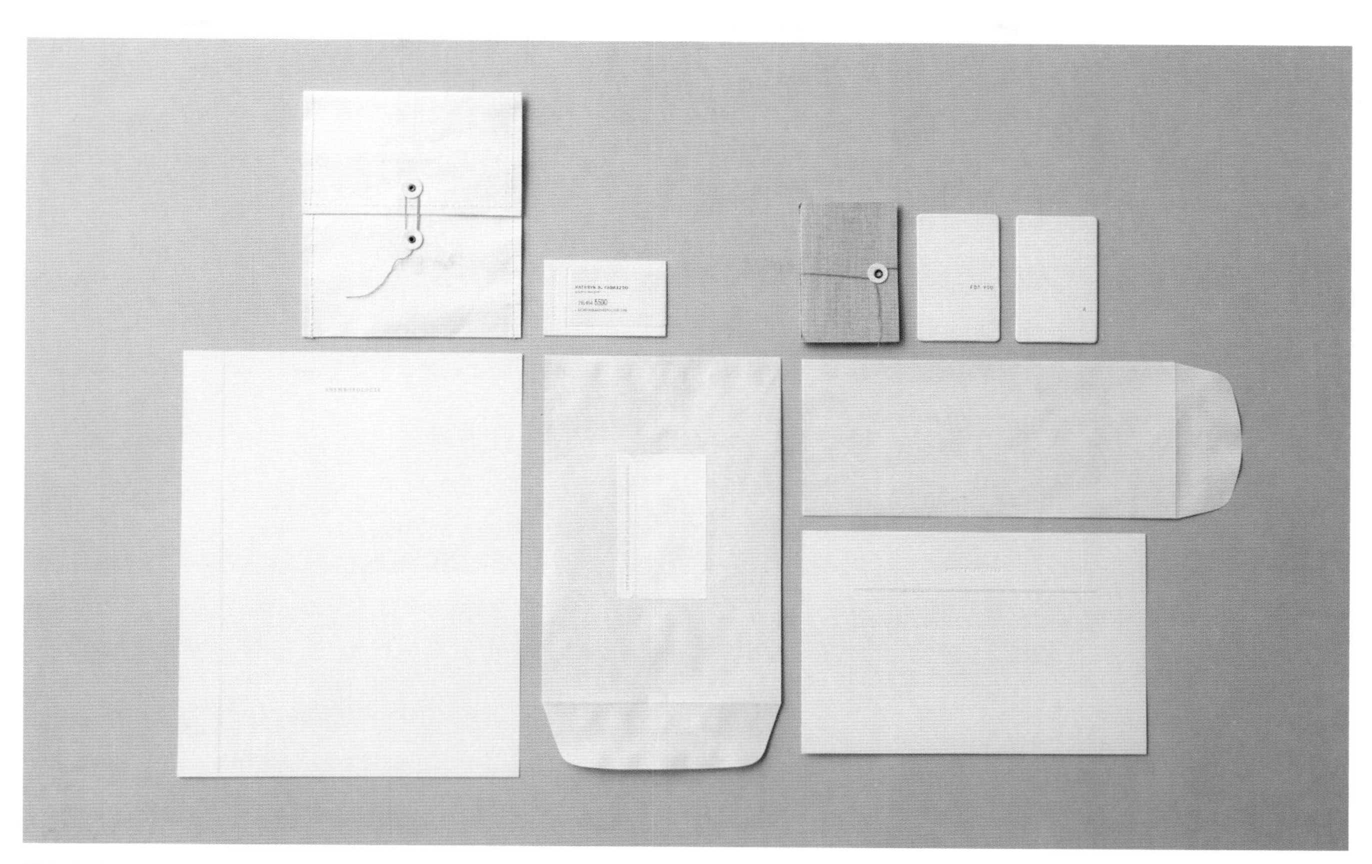

DESIGN Becky Berkheimer and Kathryn Bernadette Fabrizio, *Philadelphia* **SENIOR DESIGN DIRECTION** Alana McCann **ART DIRECTION** Carolyn Keer
IN-HOUSE STUDIO Anthropologie **PRINCIPAL TYPE** Akzidenz Grotesk **DIMENSIONS** various

DESIGN Edmond Ng, *Toronto* CREATIVE DIRECTION Diti Katona and John Pylypczak STUDIO Concrete Design Communications CLIENT Fabbrica
PRINCIPAL TYPE ITC American Typewriter, Blender Pro, and custom DIMENSIONS various

NEW YORK

SPECIAL DOUBLE ISSUE

DECEMBER 20–27, 2010

REASONS TO LOVE NEW YORK RIGHT NOW

6th Edition

New York

REASONS TO LOVE NEW YORK

DECEMBER 20–27, 2010

$4.99 USA/CANADA

NYMAG.COM

0 74808 01912 0 01

DESIGN John Gall, *New York* DESIGN DIRECTION Chris Dixon EDITOR-IN-CHIEF Adam Moss PUBLICATION *New York* PRINCIPAL TYPE HTF Didot Light
DIMENSIONS 7.6 × 10.5 in. (19.3 × 26.7 cm)

THE
AMERICAN
B A K
HEIST
IT'S A WEEKLY OCCURRENCE THESE DAYS: THE KOOKY BANK ROBBERY AS SEEN ON THE LOCAL NEWS.
GQ
194
BUT EVERY SO OFTEN ALONG COMES A SCHEME OF SUCH INGENUITY, SUCH PRECISION, THAT YOU CAN'T HELP BUT STOP AND APPRECIATE THE CRAFTSMANSHIP. DAVID KUSHNER TELLS THE TALE OF THE FALLEN FOOTBALL HERO WHO CAME UP WITH THE (ALMOST) PERFECT CAPER
ILLUSTRATION BY JOHN RITTER

174 Magazine Spread

DESIGN Anton Ioukhnovets, *New York* DESIGN DIRECTION Fred Woodward PUBLICATION *GQ* PRINCIPAL TYPE handlettering
DIMENSIONS 16 × 10.75 in. (40.6 × 27.3 cm)

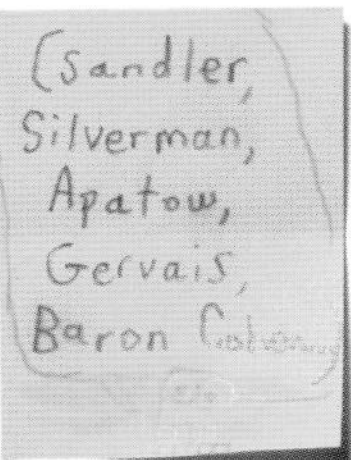

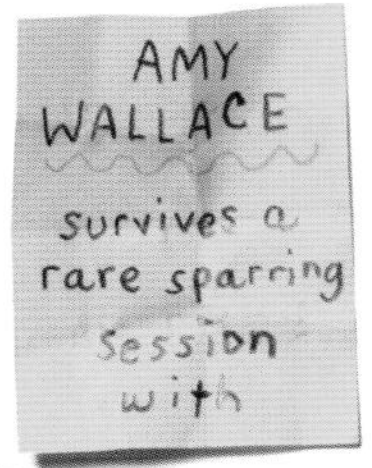

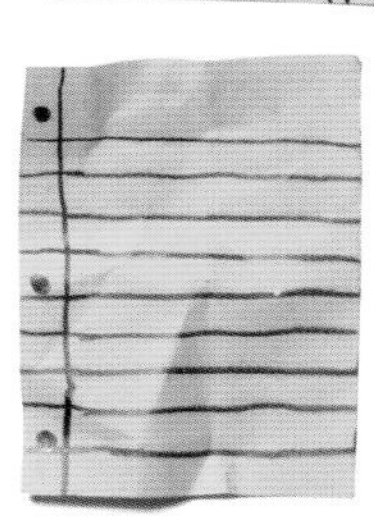

DESIGN Delgis Canahuate, *New York* DESIGN DIRECTION Fred Woodward ILLUSTRATION Mark Todd PUBLICATION *GQ*
PRINCIPAL TYPE handlettering DIMENSIONS 16 × 10.75 in. (40.6 × 27.3 cm)

176 Student Project

DESIGN Rukiye Sahin, *New York* SCHOOL School of Visual Arts, *New York* INSTRUCTOR Paul Sahre PRINCIPAL TYPE unknown
DIMENSIONS 11 × 15 in. (27.9 × 38.1 cm)

RAISING NEW YORK'S CHOLESTEROL SINCE **1929**

FREE DELIVERY!
We Accept all major credit cards. Corporate Account Welcome. Catering Available

174 FIFTH AVENUE Between 22nd & 23rd Street New York, NY 10010 TEL: 212-675-5096 FAX: 212-675-0276

EISENBERG'S SANDWICH SHOP

SOUPS

Chicken Noodle......3.50
Split Pea......3.50
Tomato......3.50
Matzo Ball......4.00
Borscht......4.00
Manhattan Clam Chowder (Fridays only)......4.00
Vegetarian Vegetable......3.50 (Tuesdays, Thursdays, Fridays)

SANDWICHES

2 Eggs......4.00
2 Eggs with Cheese......4.50
2 Eggs with Bacon, Sausage Or Ham......5.00
2 Eggs with Cheese And Bacon, Sausage Or Ham......5.50
Sliced Hard Boiled Egg......3.50
Lettuce & Tomato......3.00
Bacon, Lettuce & Tomato......6.00
Peanut Butter & Jelly......3.50
Peanut Butter & Bacon......4.50
Cream Cheese......2.50
Cream Cheese & Chopped Olives......3.50
Lox & Cream Cheese......7.50
Cheese Sandwich......4.25
Ham......6.00
Ham & Cheese......6.50
Bologna......6.00
Salami......6.00
Liverwurst......6.00
Sliced Turkey......7.50
Sliced White Meat Chicken......7.50
Roast Beef......7.50
Egg Salad......6.50
Tuna Salad......7.25
Chicken Salad......7.25
Can Tuna Or Sardines......7.25
Chopped Liver from Bubbe Eisenberg's Original Recipe......8.00
Single Frank (Mondays & Wednesdays)......5.00
Meatloaf (Tuesday's & Thursdays)......7.50
Shrimp Salad (Fridays only)......7.50

GRILLED SANDWICHES

Grilled Cheese......5.00
Grilled Cheese with Tomato......5.25
Grilled Cheese with Bacon Or Ham......7.00
Grilled Cheese with Turkey......7.25
Tuna Melt......7.50
Open Face Tuna Melt......9.00
Reuben......9.00
Turkey Reuben......9.00
Corned Beef/Pastrami Combo Reuben......9.75
Philly Cheese Steak......8.50
Cuban Sandwich......8.50
Chicken Cutlet......7.50
Grilled Chicken......8.50
Fried Filet Of Fish......7.00
Fried Salami Or Bologna......7.00

CLASSICS

Hot Pastrami......8.50
Hot Corned Beef......8.50
Hot Brisket......8.50
Hot Tongue......9.00
The Pick Two Combo pastrami, corned beef or brisket......9.50
Pastrami, Corned Beef, Swiss & Slaw......10.00

CLASSIC COMBOS

Tuna & Egg Salad Combo......8.00
Bacon & Egg Salad......7.25
Bacon & Chicken Salad......7.75
Chopped Liver & Turkey......9.00
Chopped Liver & Pastrami......9.75
Turkey Club......8.50
Roast Beef, Turkey, Swiss & Slaw......9.00
Turkey, Swiss & Slaw......8.00

The Eisen BURGERS

A Full Half Pound Of Ground Sirloin Grilled To Perfection Over An Open Flame. Served With Lettuce & Tomato

Plain Burger......6.50
Deluxe With French Fries......8.00
Cheese Burger......7.00
Deluxe With French Fries......8.50
Veggie or Turkey Burger......7.50
Deluxe With French Fries......9.50

Choose Your Cheese: American, Cheddar, Swiss, Muenster Or Provolone. Substitute Onion Rings For Fries $1. Add Bacon $1.50

Eggs & Omelets

Served With French Fries Or Lettuce & Tomato
(Egg Whites Only Add $0.50)

2 Eggs Any Style......5.00
With Ham, Bacon or Sausage......6.75
Cheese Omelet......6.50
With Ham, Bacon Or Sausage......8.00
Western Omelet......7.50
Mushroom Omelet......7.00
Veggie Omelet......7.50
Salami & Eggs......8.00
Pastrami Or Corned Beef & Eggs......9.00
Lox, Onions, And Eggs......9.50
Eisenberg's Special Omelet 3 egg whites, mushrooms, muenster cheese, tomato and onion......9.50
Matzo Brei......7.0

COLD PLATTERS

Tuna Plate served with egg salad or cottage cheese......8.50
Chicken Salad Plate served with egg salad or cottage chees......8.50
Chopped Liver Plate served with egg salad or cottage cheese......9.50
Shrimp Salad (Fridays only)......9.00
House Salad......5.00
Chopped Vegetables with cottage cheese or sour cream......6.50
Scoop Of Tuna Or Chicken Salad Over Lettuce And Tomato......7.50
Scoop Of Egg Salad Over Lettuce And Tomato......6.75
Cottage Cheese & Fruit Salad......7.50
Chef's Salad roast beef, turkey, ham, swiss cheese, and hard boiled egg......9.50
Triple Treat tuna, chicken & egg salad over lettuce and tomato......10.50
Sliced Grilled Or Poached Chicken over house salad......9.25
With Crispy Bacon......10.00

Hot Platters

Meat Loaf with gravy, mashed potatoes and vegetables (Tuesday and Thursdays only)......8.50
Hebrew National Kosher Knockwurst & Beans (Mondays and Fridays only)......8.50
Fried Fish Filet with mac & cheese (Fridays only)......8.50
Hot Turkey Platter with gravy, mashed potatoes & vegetables......9.25
Hot Brisket Platter with gravy, mashed potatoes & vegetables......9.25
Fried Fish Filet with fries, lettuce, And Tomato......8.50
Fried Clams with fries, slaw and tartar sauce......9.25

SIDES & SWEETS

Potato Salad......2.00
Cole Slaw......2.00
Cottage Cheese......2.50
Rice Pudding......2.50
Pie Or Cake......3.50
Babka......4.50
French Fries......3.00
Onion Rings......3.50
Fries & Rings......4.00
Knish......2.50
Stuffed Derma......5.75
Fruit Salad......4.50

RISE & SHINE
Served 'Til 11 AM

STARTERS & SIDES

Coffee/Decaf/Tea......1.00/1.50
Herbal Tea......1.25/1.75
Juice......1.50/2.25
Hot Chocolate......1.75
Milk......1.50
Chocolate Milk......2.00
Iced Tea/Coffee......2.00
Egg Cream......2.00
Muffins, Danish, Donut......1.25
Oatmeal......2.50/3.00
Cold Cereal......2.50
Side Order Bacon, Sausage Or Ham......3.00
Side Order Grits......2.50/3.00
Side Order Home Fries......3.00
Side Order Corned Beef Hash......3.00
Banana......50
Fresh Fruit Salad......4.50
Bagel/Bialy......1.50

BREAKFAST SANDWICHES

Bagel, Bialy or English Muffin Add $0.50. Two Eggs or Egg Whites Only Add $0.50

Egg Sandwich......2.00
Egg & Cheese......2.50
Egg & bacon, sausage or ham......3.00
Egg & Cheese with bacon, sausage Or ham......3.50
Turkey & Egg......6.00
Turkey, Egg & Cheese......6.50
Salami & Egg......5.50
Lox & Egg Sandwich......6.75

DAILY SPECIALS

Monday & Wednesday

Hebrew National Jumbo Frank & Beans......8.50
Single Frank & Beans......7.50
Single Frank Sandwich......5.00

Tuesday & Thursday

Meatloaf Platter......8.50
Served with Mashed, Gravy & Vegetables
Meatloaf Sandwich......7.50

Friday

Fried Fish Filet......8.50
Served with Mac & Cheese
Shrimp Salad Platter......9.00
Served with Egg Salad or Cottage Cheese
Shrimp Salad Sandwich......7.50

BEVERAGES

Coffee/Decaf/Tea......1.00/1.50
Herbal Tea......1.25/1.75
Soda......1.25
Fountain Coke, Diet Coke......1.25
Iced Tea/Coffee......2.00
Arnold Palmer......2.00
Lime Rickey......2.00
Lemonade......2.00
Egg Cream......2.00
Milk Shake......4.00
Ice Cream Soda......4.00
Hot Chocolate......1.75
Milk......1.50
Juice......1.50/2.25
Chocolate Milk......2.00
Bottled Water......1.50
Outgoing Platters Add $.25

Pastrami & Egg......6.25
Bacon, Lettuce & Tomato......5.50
Breakfast B.L.T bacon, lettuce, and tomato with a fried egg......6.00
Cream Cheese On A Bagel......2.50
Lox & Cream Cheese On A Bagel......6.75

BREAKFAST PLATTERS

Served With Toast & Homefries Or Grits. Bagel, Bialy Or English Muffin Add $0.50

Two Eggs Any Style......3.50
with Bacon, Sausage or Ham......4.50
with Corned Beef Hash......5.00
Cheese Omelet......5.00
with Bacon, Sausage or Ham......6.25
Mushroom Omelet......6.50
Western Omelet......6.50
Veggie Omelet......7.00
Lox & Eggs......8.50
Eisenberg's Special Omelet 3 egg whites, mushrooms, muenster cheese, tomato and onion......8.50
I Want It All: 3 eggs, bacon, sausage & a short stack......10.75
Matzo Brei......6.50
Pastrami & Eggs......7.50
Turkey & Eggs......6.50
Salami & Eggs......6.50
French Toast Or Pancakes......4.00
with Bacon, Sausage or Ham......5.50
with Sliced Banana......4.50
with Home Fries......4.75

DESIGN Elizabeth Chan, *New York* SCHOOL School of Visual Arts, *New York* INSTRUCTOR Genevieve Williams PRINCIPAL TYPE Trade Gothic
DIMENSIONS 11 × 15 in. (27.9 × 38.1 cm)

DESIGN Jennifer Kinon and Bobby C. Martin Jr., *New York* CREATIVE DIRECTION Jennifer Kinon and Bobby C. Martin Jr. ILLUSTRATION Joe Finocchiaro and Jasper Goodall, *Brighton, UK* AGENCY OCD | The Original Champions of Design CLIENT Girl Scouts of the USA PRINCIPAL TYPE Avenir (modified) and Omnes

DESIGN Vanessa Eckstein and Patricia Kleeberg, *Toronto* **CREATIVE DIRECTION** Vanessa Eckstein **DESIGN OFFICE** Blok Design **CLIENT** Oveja Negra Lowe **PRINCIPAL TYPE** Blender Bold, Helvetica, Helvetica Bold, and Univers Light Ultra Condensed **DIMENSIONS** various

B

ORN

CROSS

-EYED!

WITH HIS

SKEWED VIEW OF

THE WORLD, DAVID

CROSS HAS BEEN CRACKING

UP FANS—AND FELLOW COMEDIANS—FOR

TWO DECADES. IS HE READY FOR HIS CLOSEUP?

BY JOSH EELLS PHOTOGRAPHS BY CHRIS BUCK

 Magazine Spread

ART DIRECTION Drue Wagner, *New York* CREATIVE DIRECTION Dirk Barnett PUBLICATION *Maxim* PRINCIPAL TYPE Granat
DIMENSIONS 15.25 × 10.5 in. (38.7 × 26.7 cm)

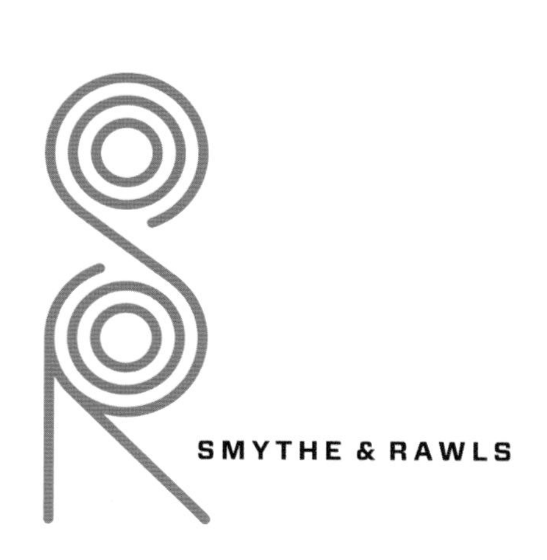

DESIGN Craig Bailey, *New York* ART DIRECTION Craig Bailey CREATIVE DIRECTION David Schimmel PHOTOGRAPHY Kristy Leibowitz STUDIO And Partners CLIENT Smythe & Rawls PRINCIPAL TYPE Forza and PNM Caecilia DIMENSIONS various

DESIGN Koshi Ogawa, *Tokyo* CLIENT The Society of Publishing Arts PRINCIPAL TYPE custom
DIMENSIONS 10.2 × 8.5 in. (25.8 × 21.6 cm)

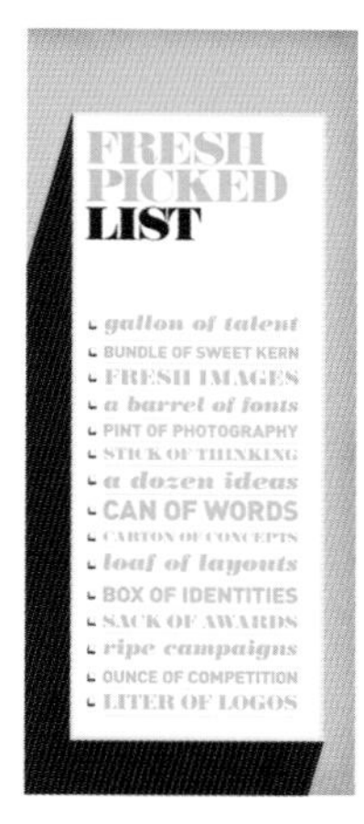

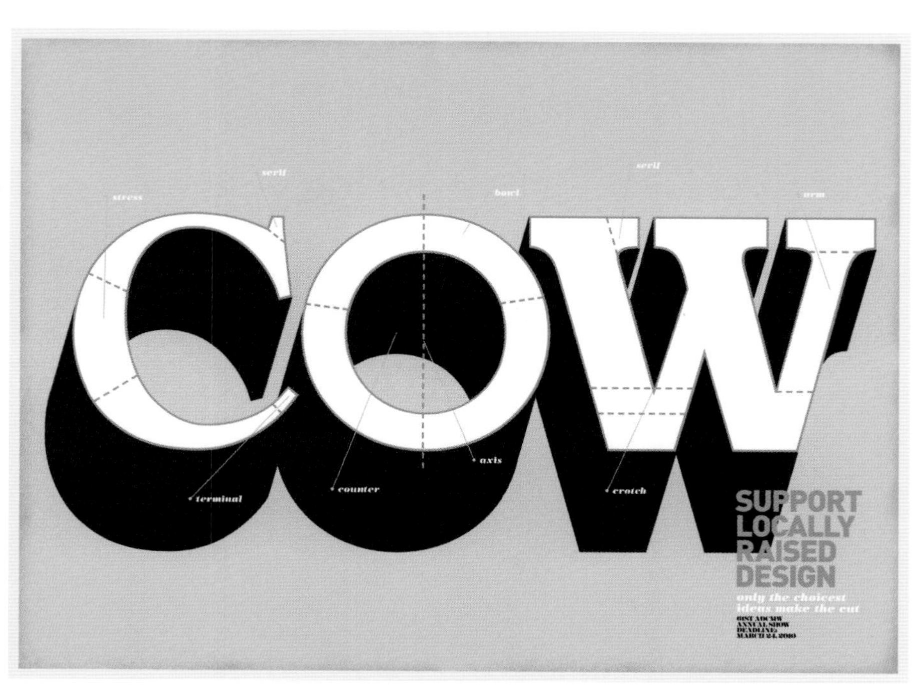

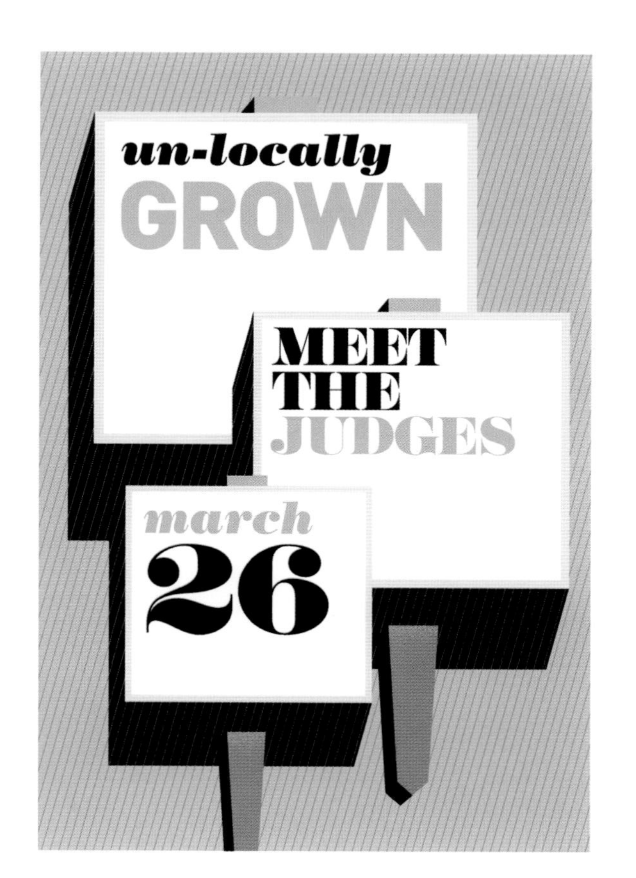

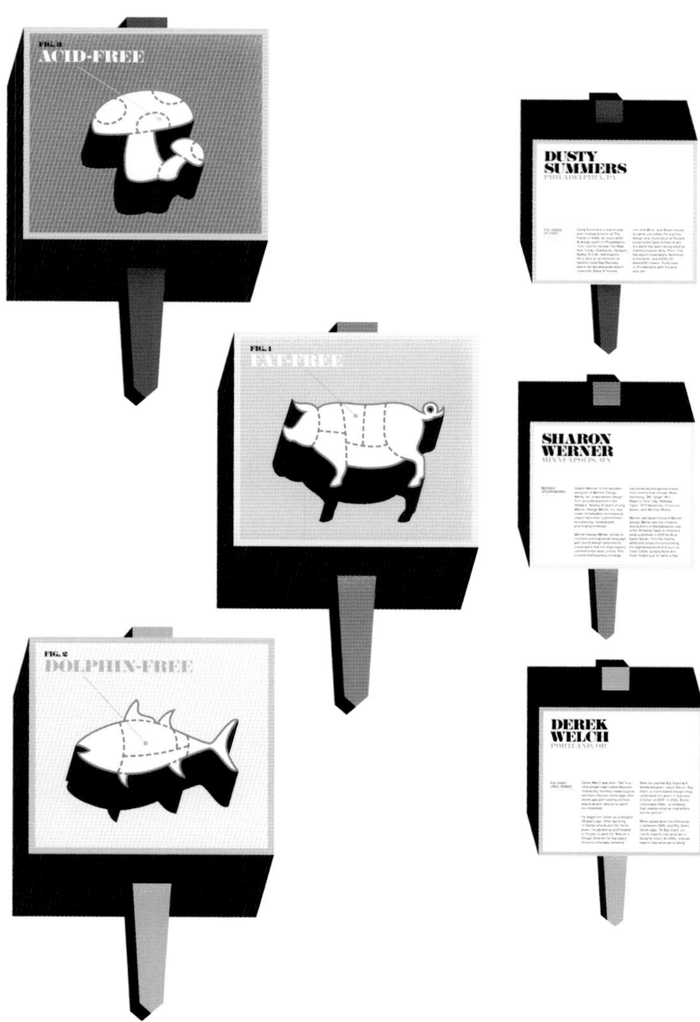

DESIGN Taylor Buckholz, *Washington, D.C.* ART DIRECTION Pum Lefebure CREATIVE DIRECTION Jake Lefebure and Pum Lefebure WRITER Wayne Geyer
PRINTER Westland Enterprises AGENCY Design Army CLIENT Art Directors Club of Metropolitan Washington (ADCMW) Annual Show 61
PRINCIPAL TYPE Bodoni Poster, DIN, and Sahara Bodoni DIMENSIONS various

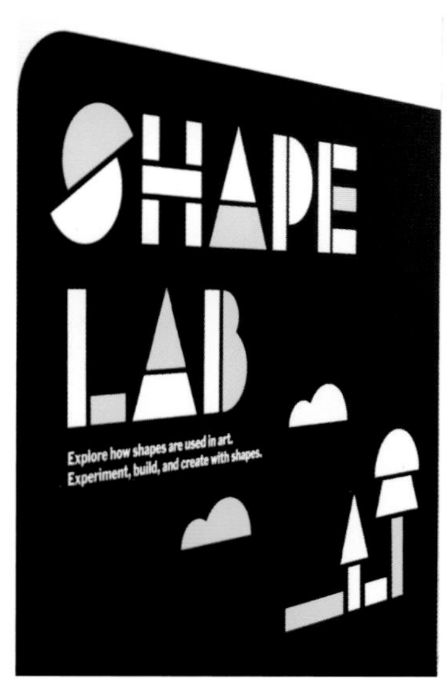

DESIGN Natalie Herrera, *New York* ART DIRECTION Ingrid Chou CREATIVE DIRECTION Julia Hoffmann PHOTOGRAPHY Michael Nagle
MUSEUM The Museum of Modern Art (MoMA), Department of Advertising and Graphic Design CLIENT Department of Education, The Museum of Modern Art (MoMA) PRINCIPAL TYPE MoMA Gothic Display and custom DIMENSIONS 354 x 87 ft. (107.9 x 26.5 m)

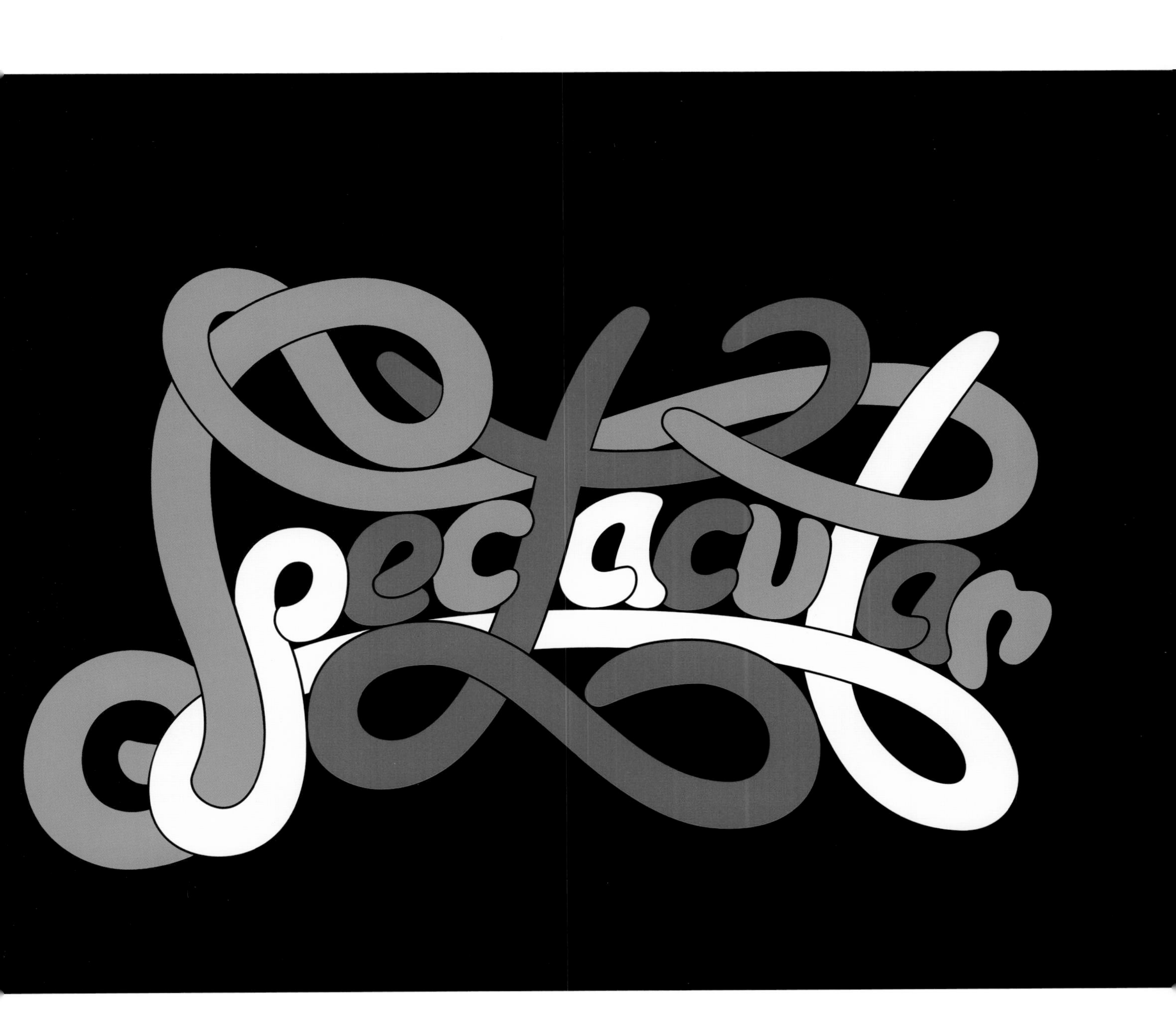

LETTERING Erik Marinovich, *San Francisco* STUDIO Friends of Type CLIENT Graniph
PRINCIPAL TYPE handlettering

ABCDEFG
HIJKLMN
OPQRSTU
VWXYZ

Salutations
Type experiment exploring social interaction
and communication through common gestures.

DESIGN Kevin Chan, *Alhambra, California* STUDIO Sublurban PRINCIPAL TYPE Akzidenz Grotesk and Gill Sans
DIMENSIONS 18 × 24 in. (45.7 × 61 cm)

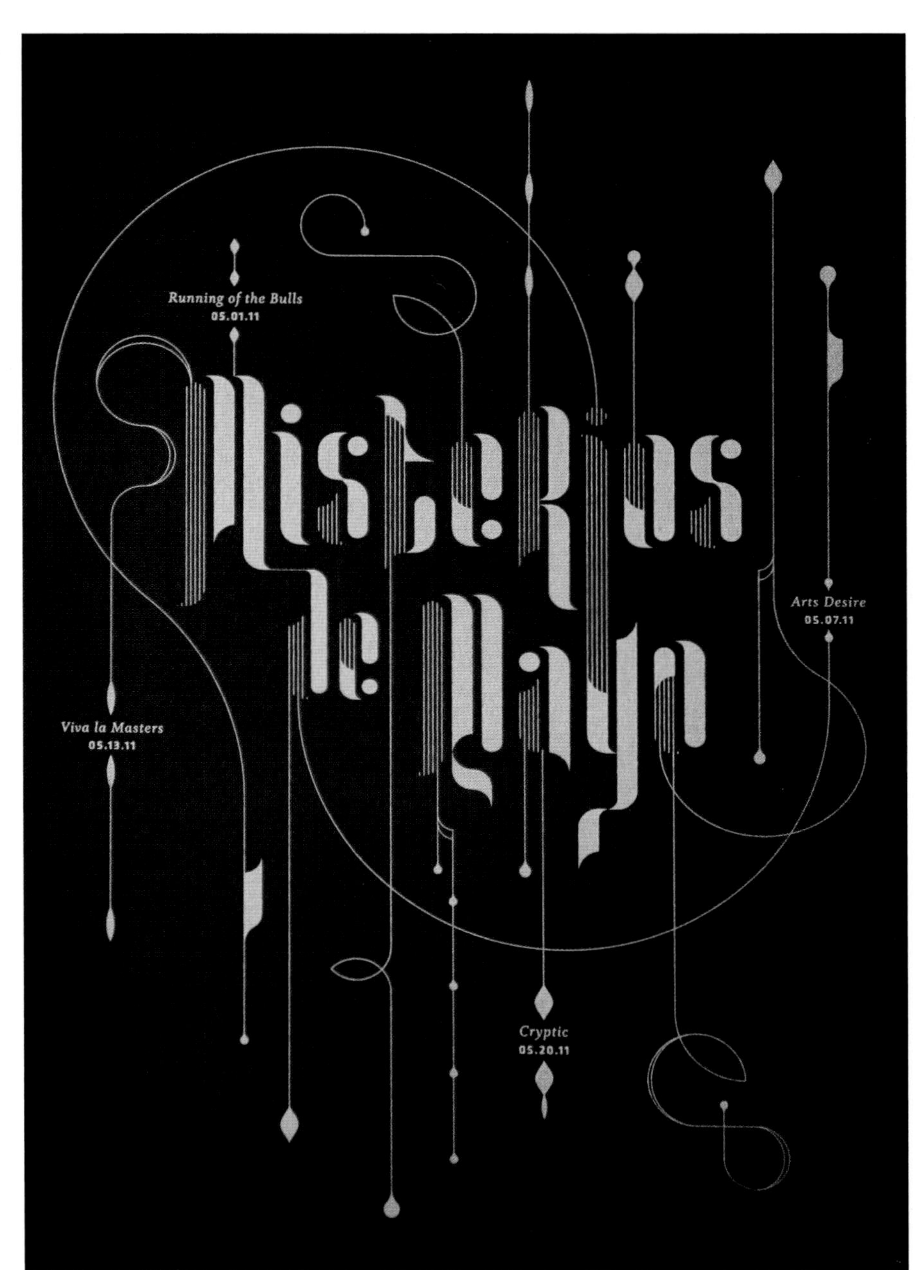

DESIGN Bruce Burton and Katy Fischer, *St. Louis, Missouri* CREATIVE DIRECTION Eric Thoelke STUDIO TOKY Branding + Design
CLIENT Contemporary Art Museum St. Louis PRINCIPAL TYPE handlettering

DESIGN Klaus Hesse, *Düsseldorf* DESIGN OFFICE Hesse Design GmbH CLIENT Hochschule für Gestaltung Offenbach
PRINCIPAL TYPE GE Arista and Replica Pro Bold DIMENSIONS 27.6 × 39.4 in. (70 × 100 cm)

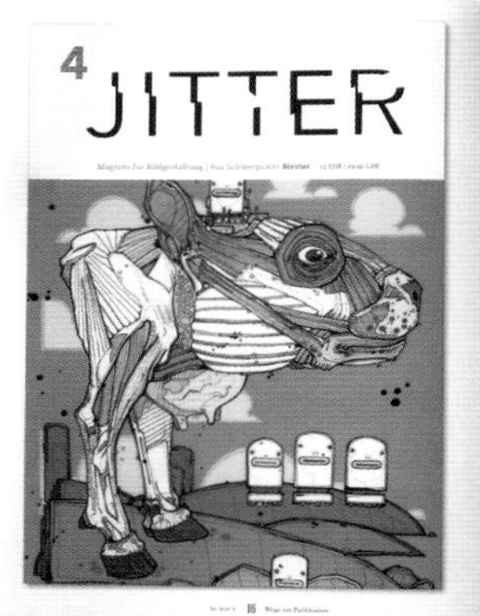

Magazine **189**

STUDIO leomaria grafikdesign **CLIENT** Alliance of German Designers (AGD) **PRINCIPAL TYPE** Helvetica Extra Compressed, Neoprint M319, and Sabon **DIMENSIONS** 9.2 × 11.8 in. (23.4 × 30 cm)

 Poster

DESIGN Akihiko Tsukamoto, *Tokyo* ART DIRECTION Akihiko Tsukamoto LETTERING Akihiko Tsukamoto ILLUSTRATION Harumi Kimura DESIGN OFFICE Zuan Club CLIENT Hatter TORAYA PRINCIPAL TYPE handlettering DIMENSIONS 28.7 × 40.6 in. (72.8 × 103 cm)

DESIGN Henning Kreitel and Daniel Strohhäcker, *Stuttgart* SCHOOL Staatliche Akademie der Bildenden Künste Stuttgart
PROFESSOR Hans-Georg Pospischi PRINCIPAL TYPE handlettering DIMENSIONS 23.4 × 33.1 in. (59.4 × 84.1 cm)

 Poster

DESIGN Michael Bierut and Yve Ludwig, *New York* ART DIRECTION Michael Bierut DESIGN OFFICE Pentagram Design New York
CLIENT Yale School of Architecture PRINCIPAL TYPE News Gothic (BT) and Titling Gothic Compressed DIMENSIONS 22 × 34 in. (55.9 × 86.4 cm)

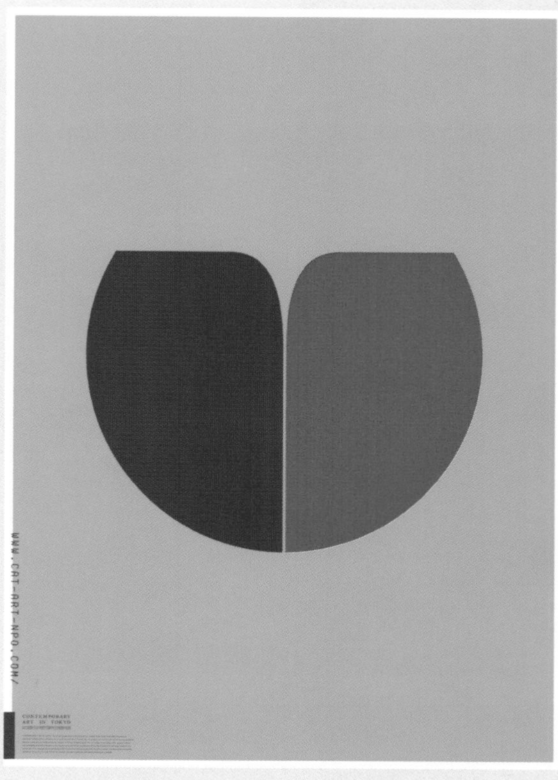

DESIGN Tomoya Kaishi, *Tokyo* **ART DIRECTION** Tomoya Kaishi **STUDIO** room-composite **CLIENT** Contemporary Art in Tokyo
PRINCIPAL TYPE Fake Receipt Regular and custom **DIMENSIONS** 28.7 × 40.6 in. (72.8 × 103 cm)

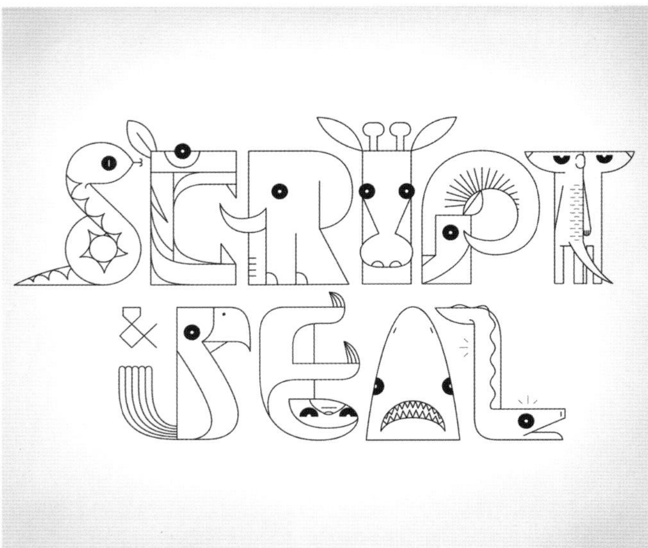

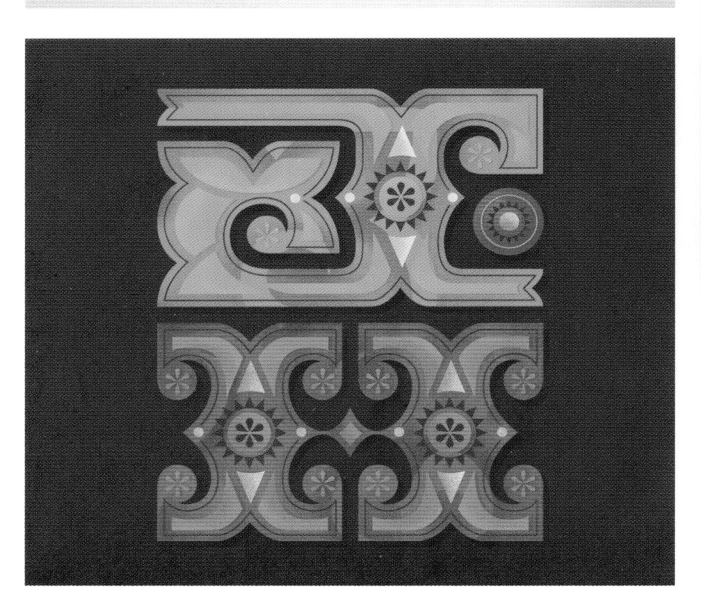

LETTERING Erik Marinovich, *San Francisco* STUDIO Friends of Type PRINCIPAL TYPE handlettering
DIMENSIONS various

LETTERING Erik Marinovich, *San Francisco* STUDIO Friends of Type PRINCIPAL TYPE handlettering
DIMENSIONS 27 × 30 in. (68.6 × 76.2 cm)

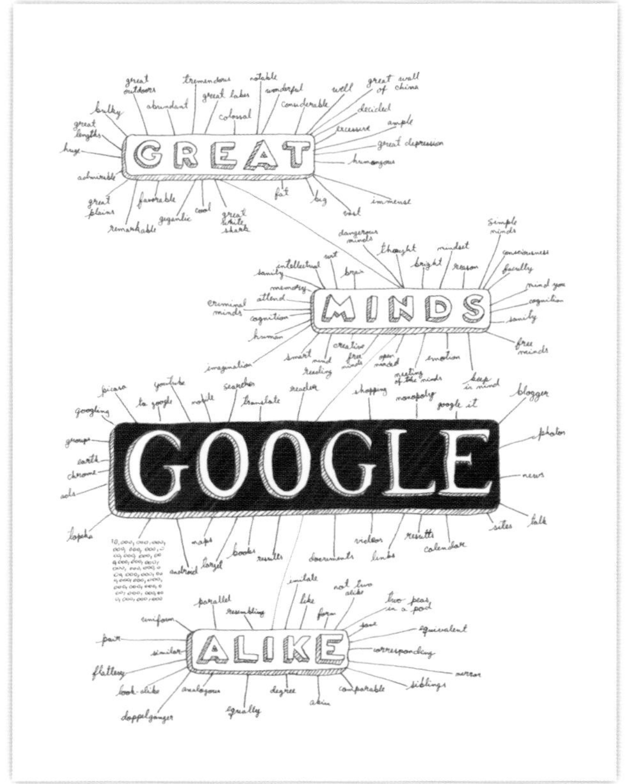

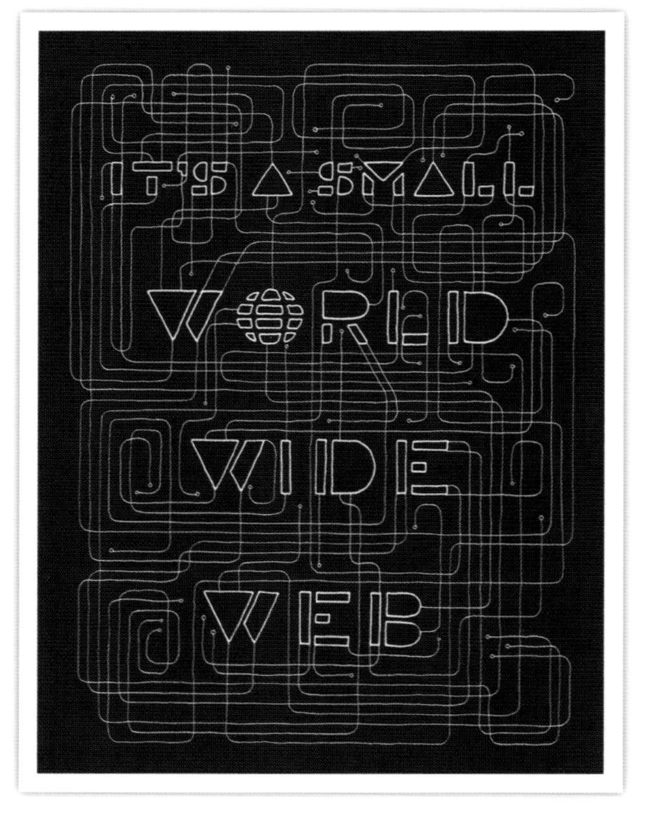

DESIGN Bernardo Margulis, *Philadelphia* ART DIRECTION Kelly Holohan LETTERING Bernardo Margulis COPYWRITER Bernardo Margulis
PRINCIPAL TYPE handlettering DIMENSIONS 12 × 16 in. (30.5 × 40.6 cm)

DESIGN Anja Geier, Nelli Gulbicki, Markus Hasel, and Daniel Schäfer, *Augsburg, Germany* ART DIRECTION Christoph Sauter and Mara Weyel CREATIVE DIRECTION Artur Gulbicki BRAND CONSULTING Tobias Sommer DESIGN OFFICE KW Neun Grafikagentur CLIENT Kulturamt der Stadt PRINCIPAL TYPE Generika Mono DIMENSIONS 33.1 × 46.8 in. (84.1 cm × 118.9 cm)

TOPHER
IN
FALVEY HALL
April
19
th
DELANEY
THE EDGE EFFECT
AT
6:30 PM
MONDAY
SEAM STUDIO | TDELANEY.COM
MICA

 Poster

DESIGN Oliver Munday, *New York* CLIENT Maryland Institute College of Art (MICA) PRINCIPAL TYPE Century Schoolbook and custom
DIMENSIONS 12 × 19 in. (30.5 × 48.3 cm)

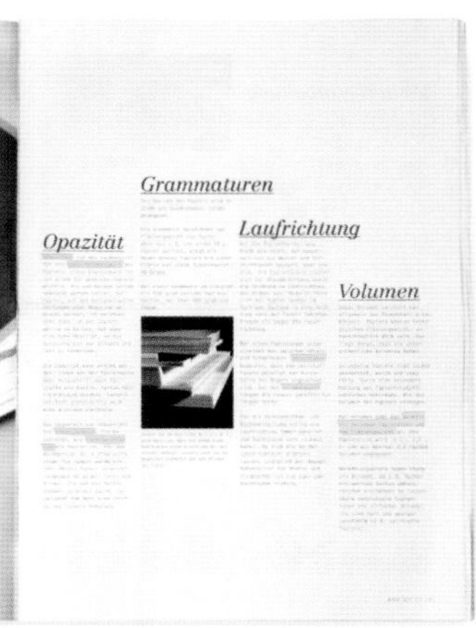

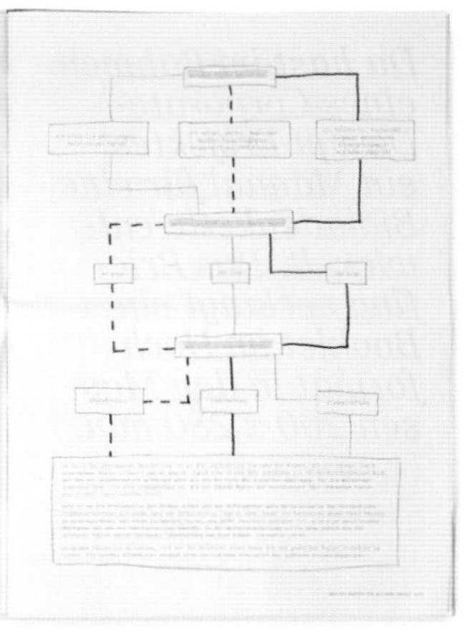

Du warst mit deinem Fotokurs auf Exkursion in Holland. Ihr habt viele Aufnahmen von bunten Tulpenfeldern gemacht. Zur Ausstellung soll ein Katalog mit etwa 150 Seiten im Format DIN A4 erscheinen.

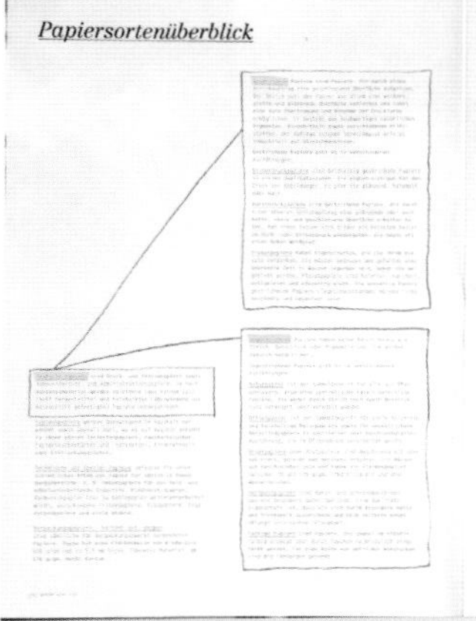

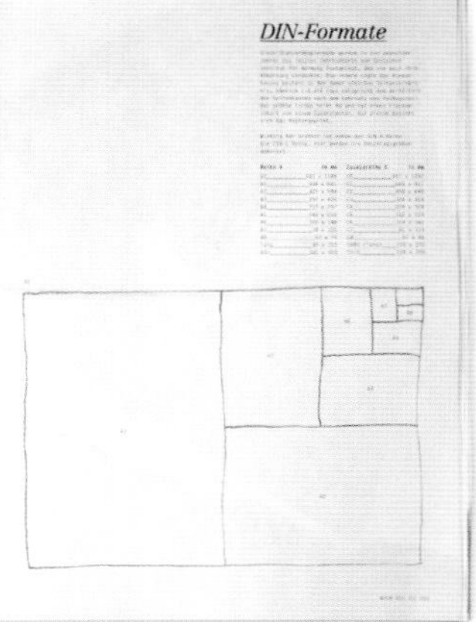

DESIGN Sonja Fritsch and Stephan Günther, *Mainz, Germany* **SCHOOL** Fachhochschule Mainz **PROFESSOR** Ulysses Voelker
PRINCIPAL TYPE Linotype Centennial and Letter Gothic LT **DIMENSIONS** 10.6 × 15 in. (27 × 38 cm)

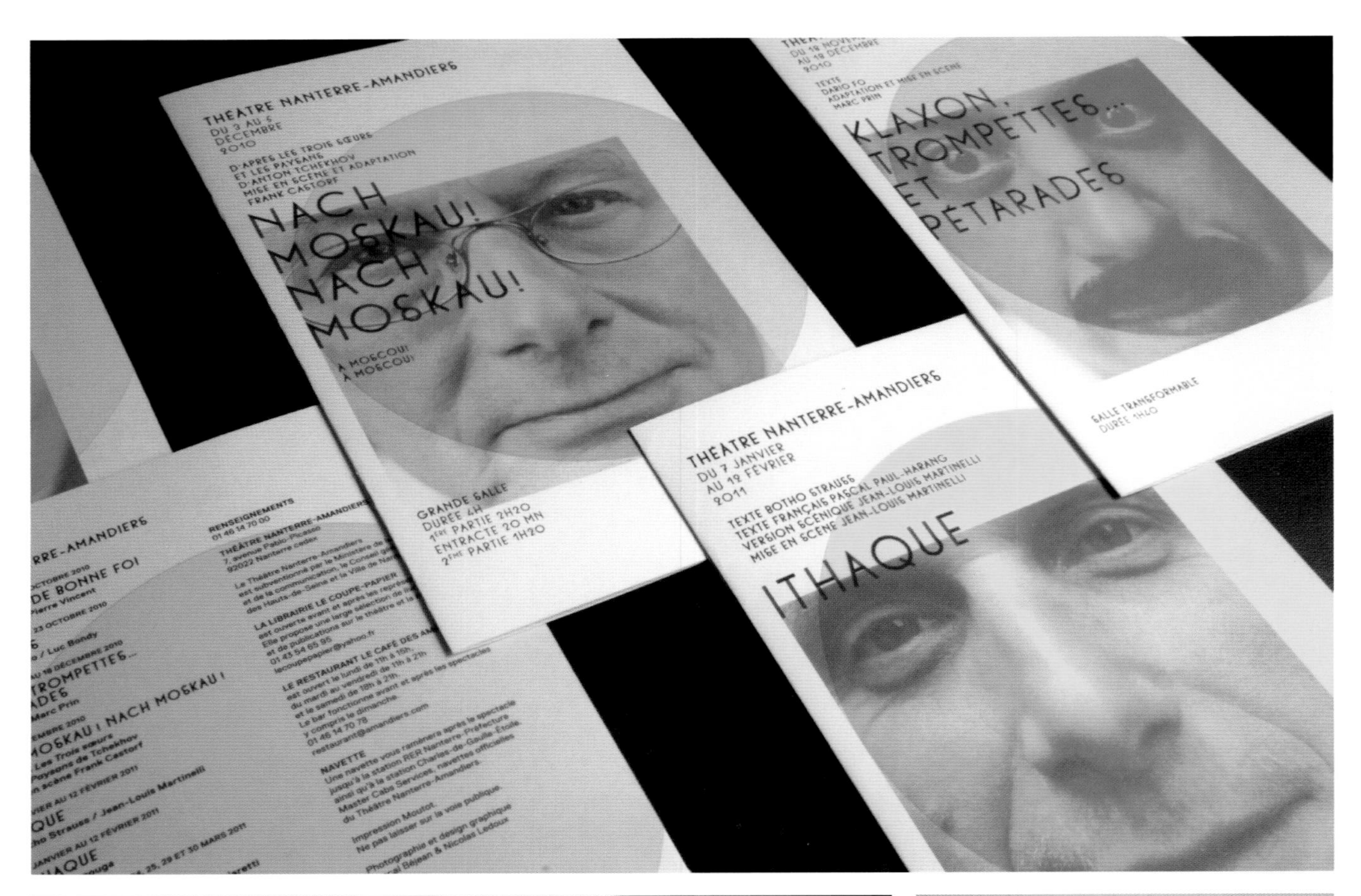

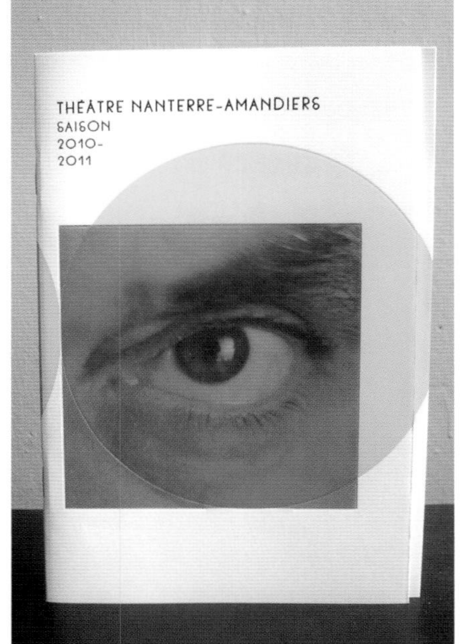

DESIGN Pascal Béjean, Olivier Körner, and Nicolas Ledoux, *Paris* CREATIVE DIRECTION Pascal Béjean, Olivier Körner, and Nicolas Ledoux
STUDIO Pascal Béjean, Olivier Körner & Nicolas Ledoux CLIENT Théâtre Nanterre-Amandiers PRINCIPAL TYPE Marcelle and Replica Norm DIMENSIONS various

DESIGN Rob Alexander, Will Ecke, and Jason Schulte, *Boston and San Francisco* EXECUTIVE CREATIVE DIRECTOR Tom Godici and Greg Ketchum, *New York* WORLDWIDE EXECUTIVE CREATIVE DIRECTOR Susan Westre ART DIRECTION Tom Godici, Jason Schulte, and Lew Willig CREATIVE DIRECTION Michael Paterson VICE CHAIRMAN OF CREATIVE Chris Wall WRITERS Rob Jamieson, Greg Ketchum, and Mike Wing AGENCY Ogilvy & Mather, *New York* STUDIO Office: Jason Schulte Design CLIENT Ogilvy & Mather and IBM PRINCIPAL TYPE ITC Lubalin Graph DIMENSIONS various

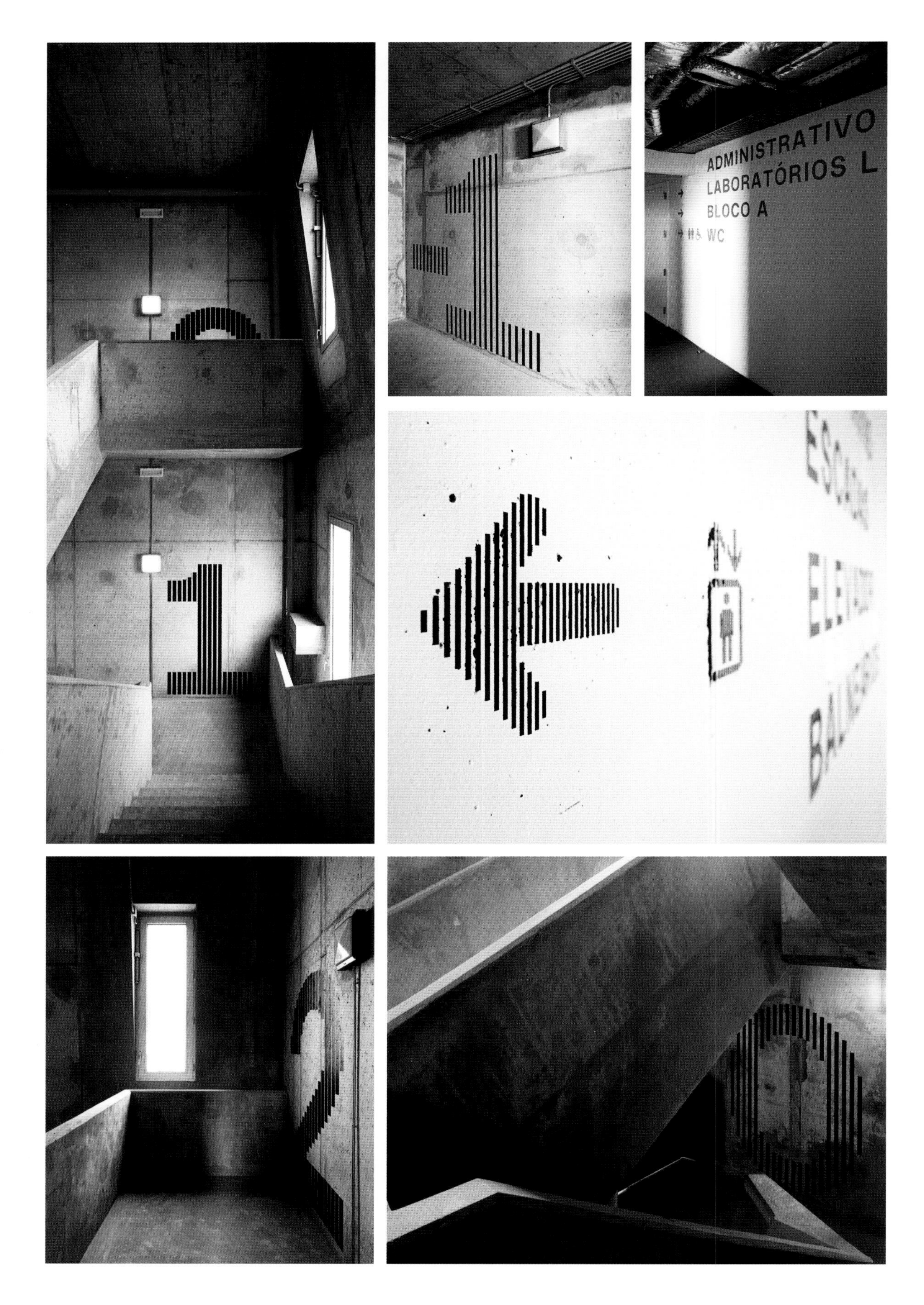

DESIGN Sebastian Fischer, Lizá Defossez Ramalho, and Artur Rebelo, *Stuttgart, Germany, and Porto, Portugal* ART DIRECTION Lizá Defossez Ramalho and Artur Rebelo CREATIVE DIRECTION Lizá Defossez Ramalho and Artur Rebelo CLIENT Parque Escolar PRINCIPAL TYPE Stripe DIMENSIONS various

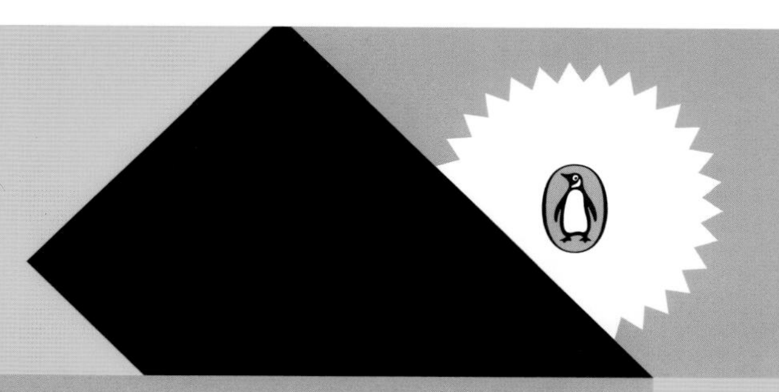

PENGUIN 75

Designers | Authors | Commentary

(the good, the bad . . .)

Edited with an Introduction by PAUL BUCKLEY

Foreword by CHRIS WARE

DESIGN Paul Buckley, *New York* ART DIRECTION Paul Buckley PUBLISHER Penguin Group (USA) PRINCIPAL TYPE Gaq and Gotham
DIMENSIONS 7.5 × 9.1 in. (19.1 × 23.1 cm)

Walter
Cronkite
is Dead.

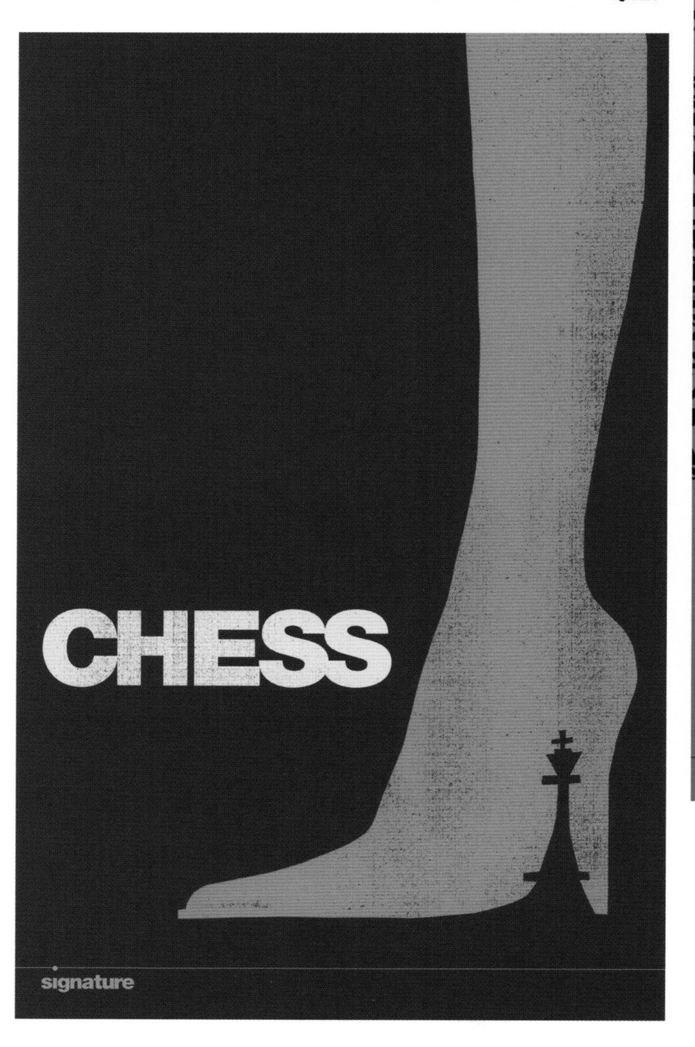

DESIGN Lucas Badger, Sucha Becky, and Eric Rother, *Washington, D.C.* ART DIRECTION Pum Lefebure CREATIVE DIRECTION Pum Lefebure and Jake Lefebure
AGENCY Design Army CLIENT Signature Theatre Season Posters PRINCIPAL TYPE Caslon Open Face and Swiss 721 DIMENSIONS 14 × 22 in. (35.6 × 55.9 cm)

WE HEAR A LOT ABOUT **BREAST CANCER**—EXCEPT WHAT IT FEELS LIKE YEARS DOWN THE ROAD, AFTER THE CRISIS HAS PASSED AND LIFE MIRACULOUSLY CONTINUES. FOUR SURVIVORS TELL HOW THEY'VE LEARNED TO DEAL WITH TENACIOUS FEAR, DANGEROUS FRIENDSHIPS AND THE SUDDEN HAPPY PROSPECT OF A RIPE OLD AGE

PHOTOGRAPHED BY ELINOR CARUCCI

NOVEMBER 2010 | *more.com* *117*

DESIGN Cláudia de Almeida, *New York* CREATIVE DIRECTION Debra Bishop LETTERING Cláudia de Almeida PUBLICATION *MORE* PRINCIPAL TYPE Affair and Miller
DIMENSIONS 16.5 × 10.9 in. (41.9 × 27.7 cm)

DESIGN Michael Bierut and Jennifer Kinon, *New York* ART DIRECTION Michael Bierut DESIGN OFFICE Pentagram Design New York
CLIENT Saks Fifth Avenue, *New York* PRINCIPAL TYPE Gotham Light DIMENSIONS various

FOLDING BASICS

Scoring and folding capabilities differ by printer. Many printers maintain in-house bindery operations but, depending on the type and complexity of folds involved, may outsource folds that exceed their technical capabilities or production capacity to specialty binderies and contract out hand-folding steps to independent shops. No matter where the work is done, printers typically incorporate all bindery processes in their cost estimates, so it is rarely necessary to seek a separate bindery bid. This section focuses on issues that designers should consider during the concept development phase and as they prepare digital files for the printer.

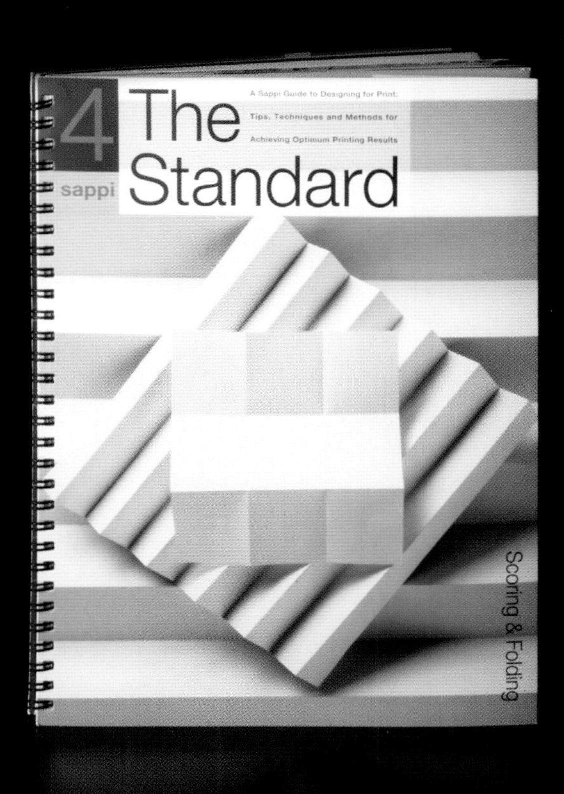

DESIGN Belle Chock and Gloria Hiek, *San Francisco* **CREATIVE DIRECTION** Kit Hinrichs **PHOTOGRAPHY** Terry Heffernan **ILLUSTRATION** Elwood Smith, *Rhinebeck, New York* **COPYWRITER** Delphine Hirasuna **DESIGN OFFICE** Studio Hinrichs **CLIENT** Sappi Fine Paper North America **PRINCIPAL TYPE** Champion Gothic, Franklin Gothic BT, Helvetica Neue, and News Gothic BT **DIMENSIONS** 7.5 × 10.4 in. (19.1 × 26.4 cm)

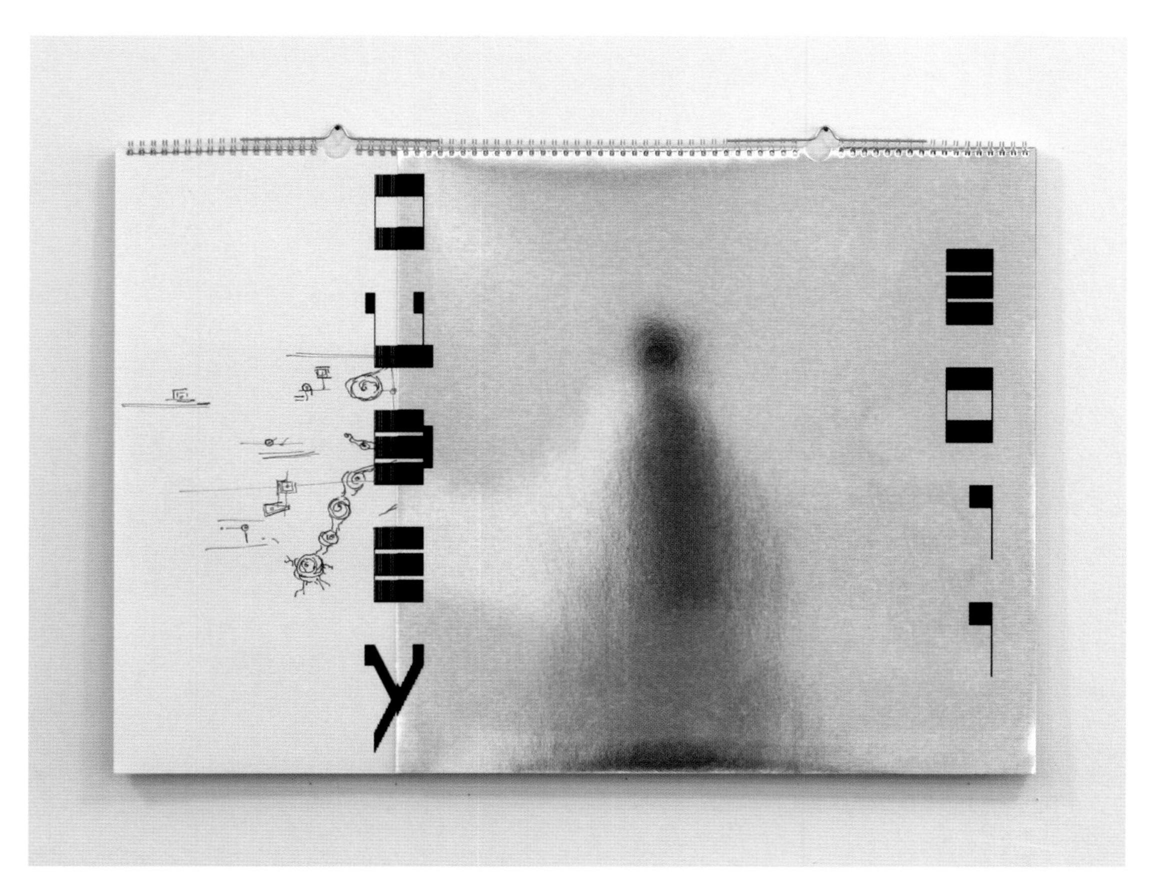

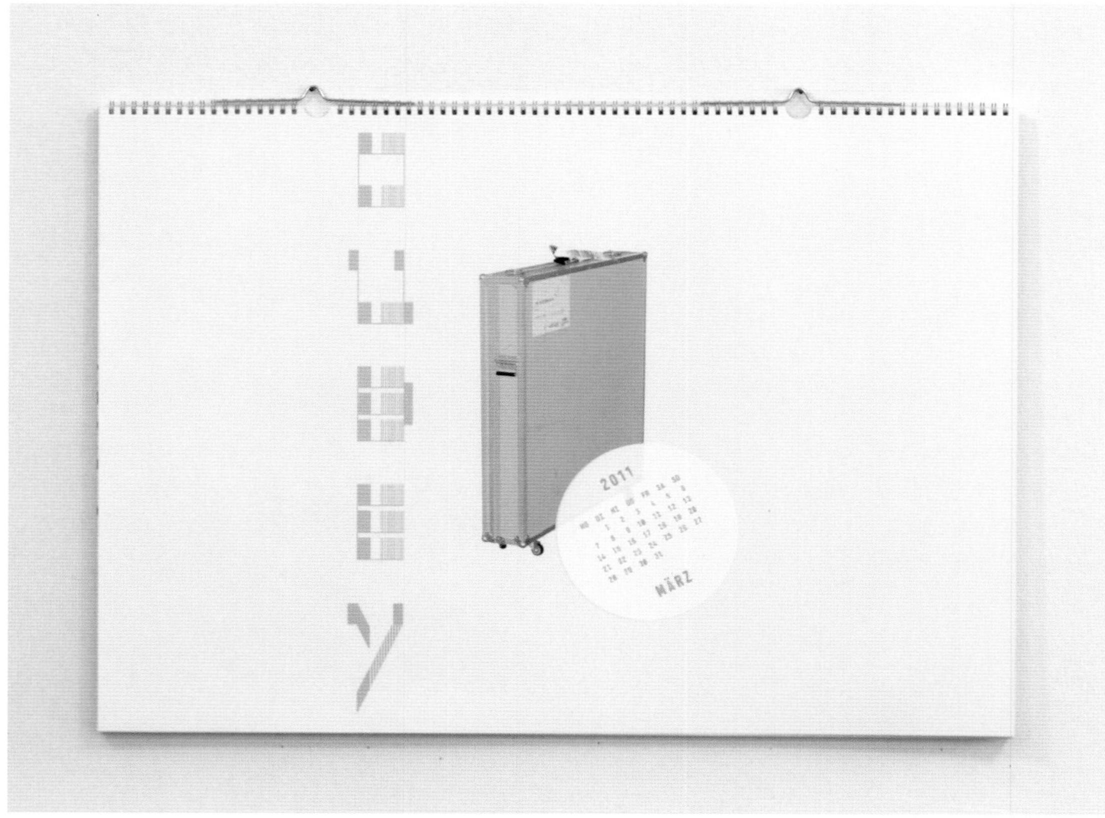

ART DIRECTION Flo Gaertner, *Karlsruhe, Germany* FINAL ART WORK Silke Hensel, Jan Kiesswetter, and Anna Straetmans DESIGN OFFICE MAGMA Brand Design GmbH & Co. KG CLIENT E&B engelhardt & bauer PRINCIPAL TYPE OUBEY Type System and Generika MG DIMENSIONS 26.8 × 18.9 in. (68 × 48 cm)

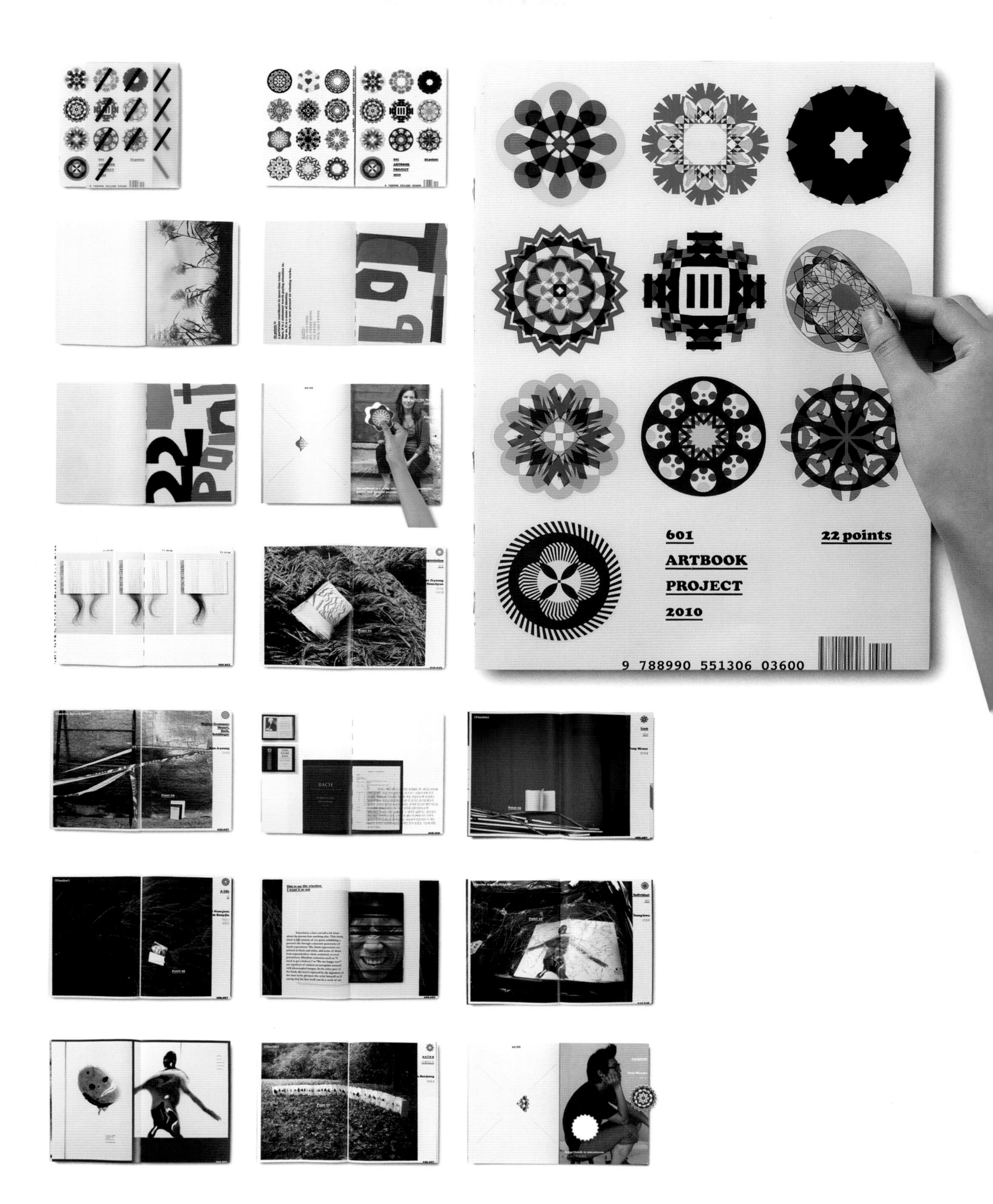

DESIGN Koo Bon-hae and Park Kum-jun, *Seoul* ART DIRECTION Park Kum-jun CREATIVE DIRECTION Park Kum-jun ILLUSTRATION Park Kum-jun and Lee Ji-hee PHOTOGRAPHY Park Kum-jun and Cho Ok-hee PHOTO REVISION Joe Sung-kwon PHOTO STUDIO Studio Dahong WRITERS Lee So-youn and Song Ji-sun PUBLISHER Jong Jong-in COORDINATORS Lee Ji-hye, Lee Jung-hye, and Nam Seung-youn DESIGN OFFICE 601bisang PRINCIPAL TYPE Cooper Black, Garamond Pro, and SM ShinShin Myung-jo DIMENSIONS 9.6 × 13.2 in (24.3 × 33.5 cm)

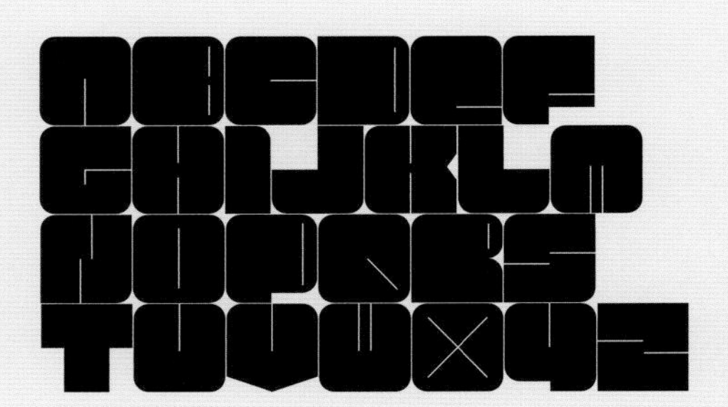

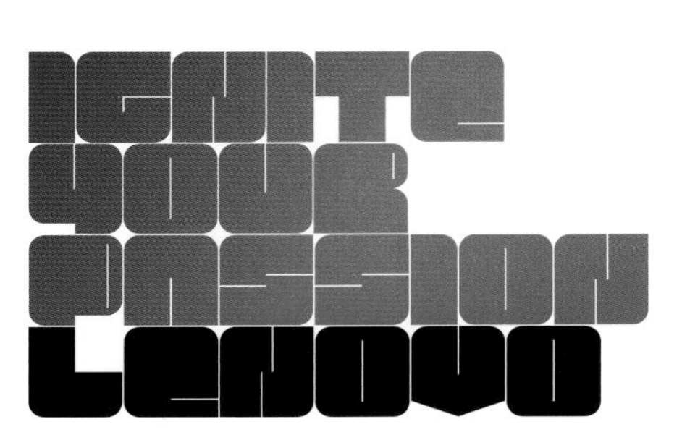

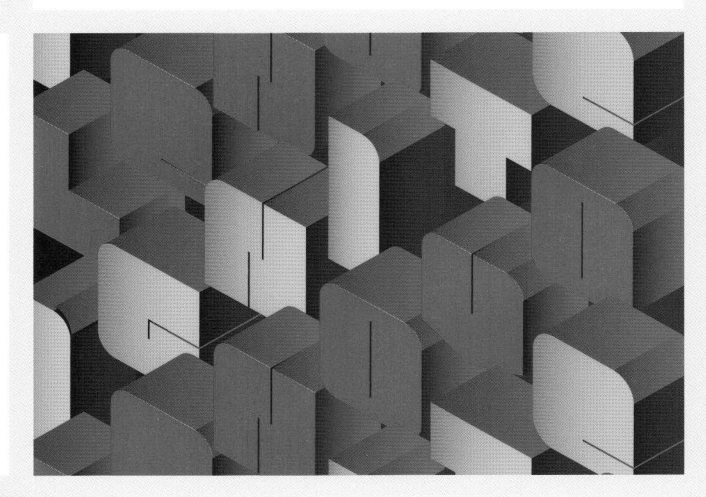

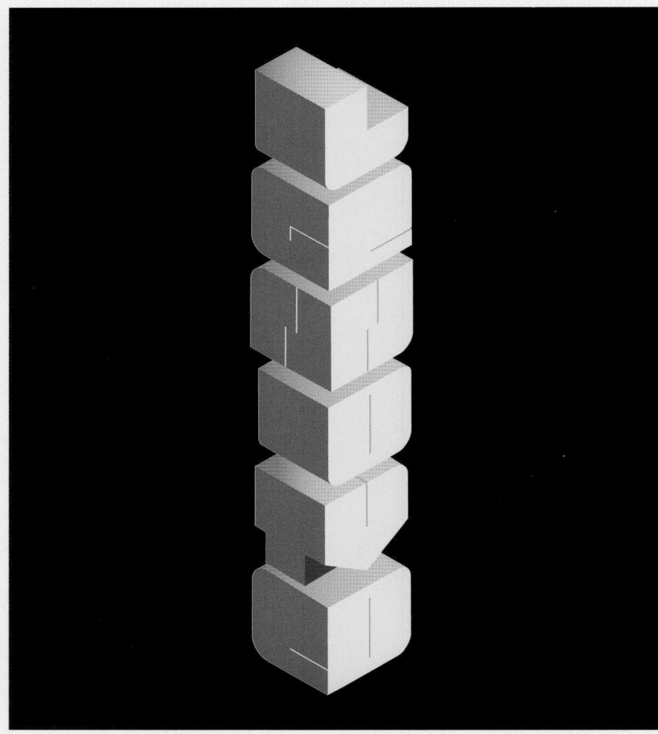

DESIGN Thomas Porostocky, *New York* CREATIVE DIRECTION Brian Collins and Leland Maschmeyer DESIGN OFFICE COLLINS: CLIENT Lenovo
PRINCIPAL TYPE Compressed Key DIMENSIONS 14 × 20 in. (35.6 × 50.8 cm)

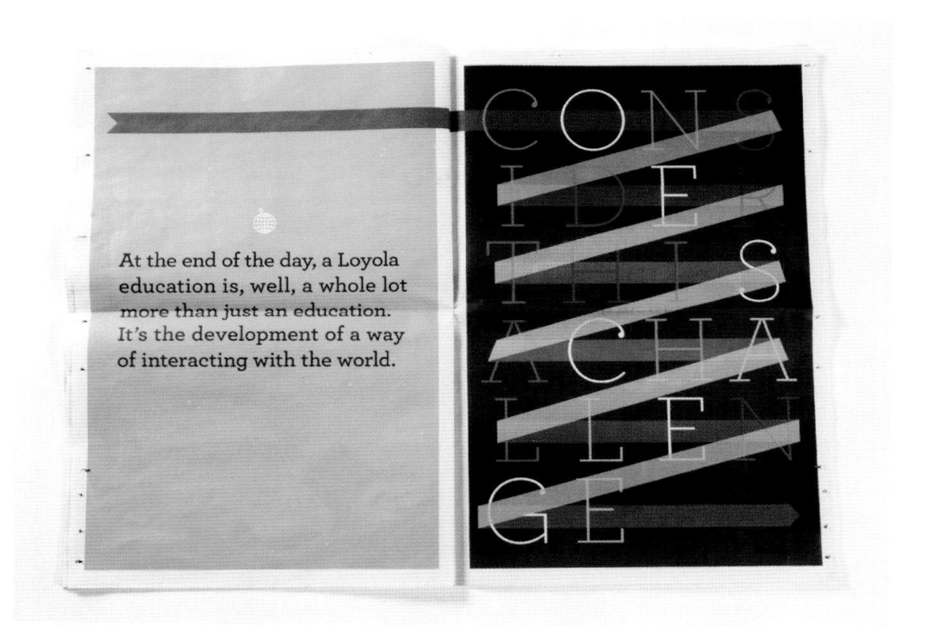

At the end of the day, a Loyola education is, well, a whole lot more than just an education. It's the development of a way of interacting with the world.
CONS
IDER
THIS
ACHA
LLEN
GE

DESIGN Kelly Dorsey, *Philadelphia* EXECUTIVE CREATIVE DIRECTION Jim Walls CHIEF CREATIVE OFFICER, PRINCIPLE Darryl Cilli CREATIVE DIRECTION Dan Shepelavy COPYWRITER Anna Hartley DIRECTOR OF PRODUCTION Rosemary Fahmie PRINTING Alcom Printing Company AGENCY 160over90 CLIENT Loyola University Maryland PRINCIPAL TYPE Archer and Gotham Narrow DIMENSIONS 17 × 11.5 in. (43.2 × 29.2 cm)

TRADICIÓN
CULTURA
ARTE
RITUAL
EMOCIÓN

TOROS SÍ

BARBARIE
MUERTE
TORTURA
CRUELDAD
MALTRATO

TOROS NO

DESIGN Ricardo Cañizares and Pepe Gimeno, *Valencia, Spain* ART DIRECTION Pepe Gimeno STUDIO Pepe Gimeno · Proyecto Gráfico
CLIENT Universitat de València PRINCIPAL TYPE Akzidenz Grotesk DIMENSIONS 19.7 × 27.6 in. (50 × 70 cm)

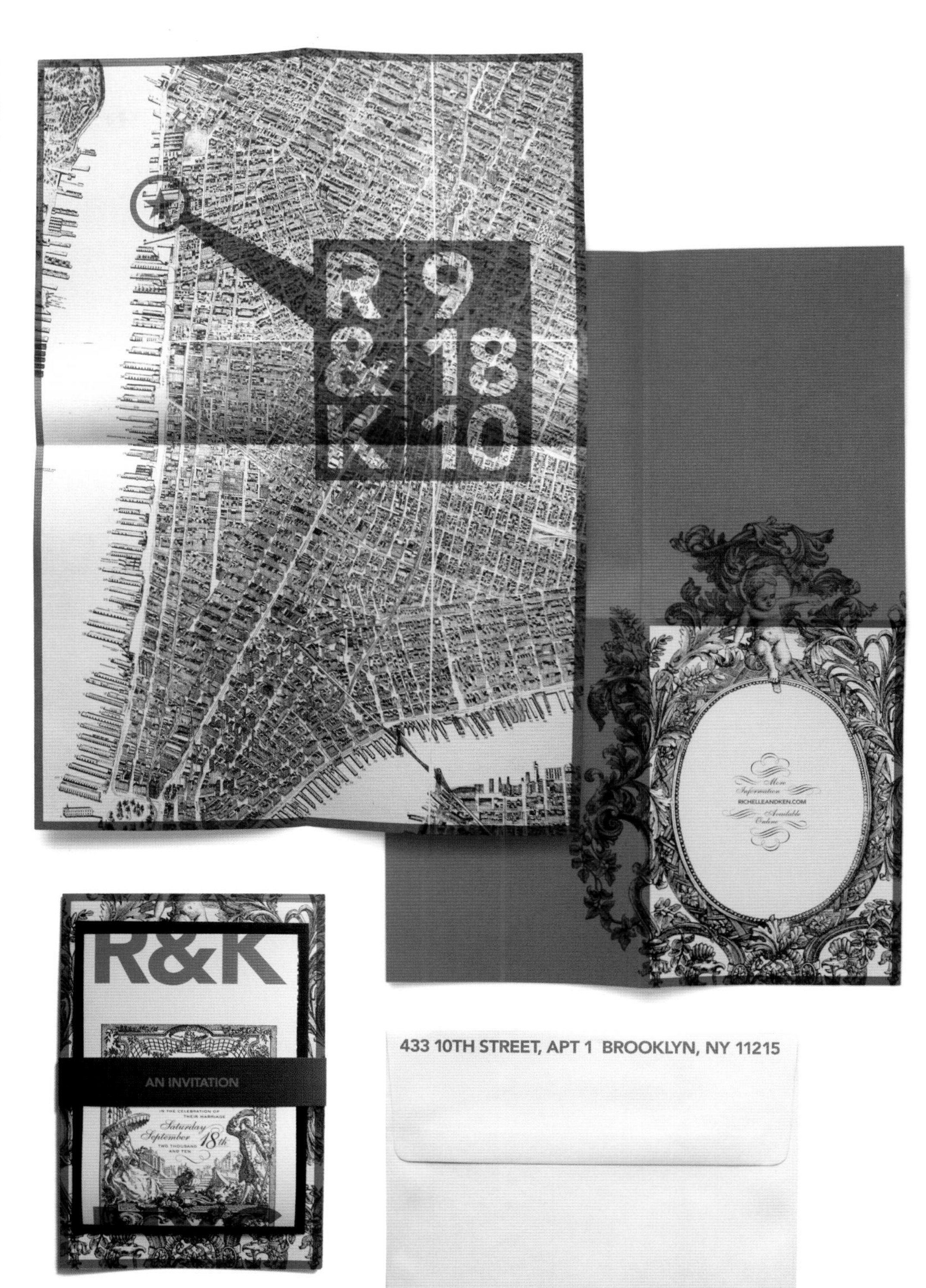

DESIGN J. Kenneth Rothermich, *Brooklyn, New York* CLIENT Richelle Singleton & Ken Rothermich PRINCIPAL TYPE Avenir, Sackers Gothic, and Shelley Script DIMENSIONS various

CREATIVE DIRECTION Konrad Angermüller, Anna Kranebitter, Jelka Kretzschmar, and Adrian Palko, *Weimar, Germany*
CLIENT HORIZONTE - Zeitschrift für Architekturdiskurs PRINCIPAL TYPE Korpus, Liberation Mono, and SangBleu BP DIMENSIONS 5.9 × 9.1 in. (15 × 23 cm)

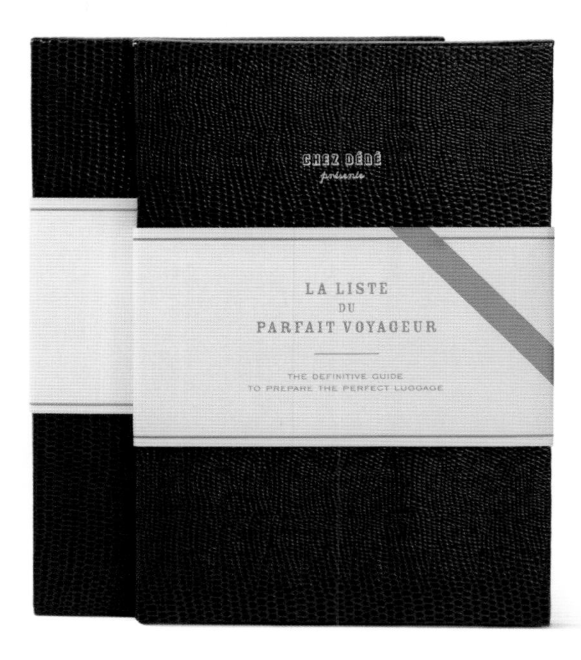

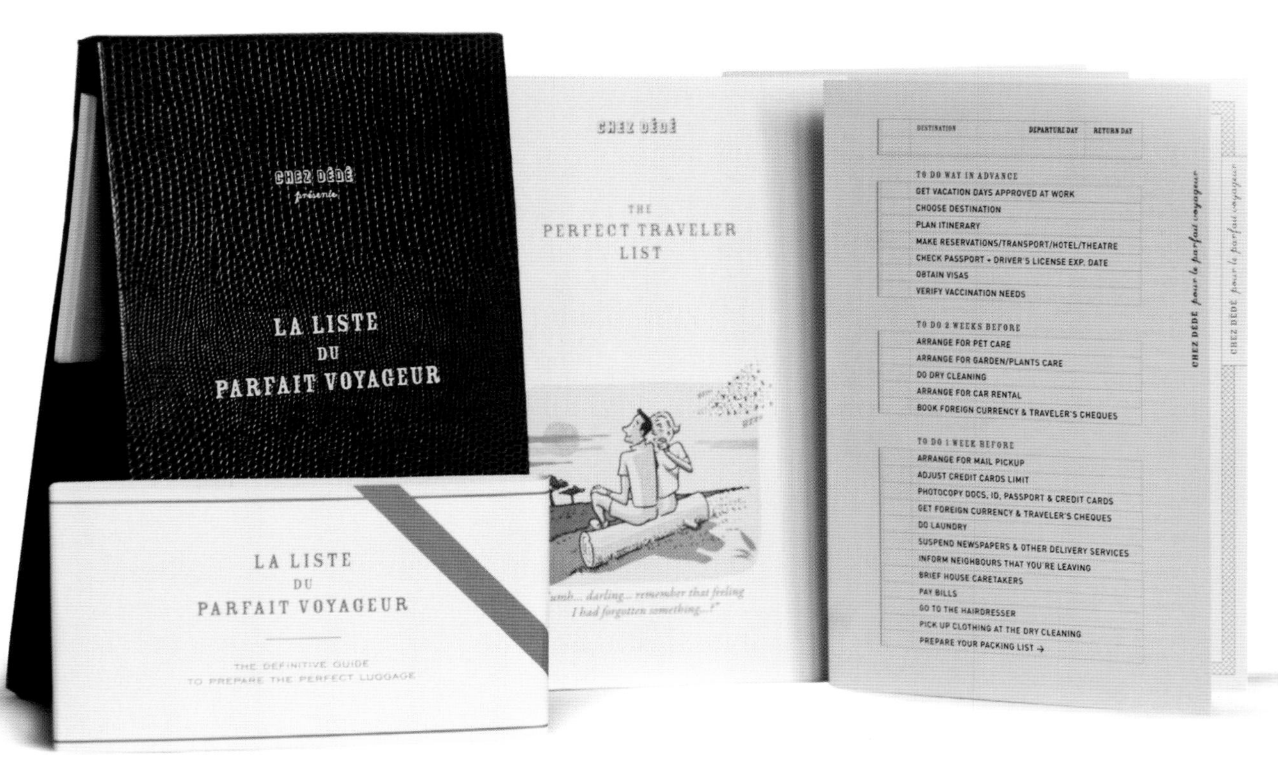

ART DIRECTION Daria Reina, *Rome, Italy* **CREATIVE DIRECTION** Andrea Ferolla and Daria Reina **ILLUSTRATION** Andrea Ferolla **DESIGN OFFICE** Ferolla Reina - Chez Dede **PRINCIPAL TYPE** Commercial Script, FF Din, Engravers Gothic, Maus, and Rosewood **DIMENSIONS** 4.3 × 6.3 in. (11 × 16 cm)

Besuch bei einer 87-jährigen Dame, die glaubt, dass ihr Nachbar sie vergasen will

FINGER
WEG VON MEINER
PARANOIA

TEXT

OLIVER GEHRS

FOTOS

BARBARA KENTNER

24

DUMMY

Hagel wohnt hier nicht mehr. Aber das ist egal, darum geht es nicht. Er ist noch immer da und macht das, was er immer gemacht hat: Er bohrt, hammert, er kriegt seine Tobsuchtsanfälle, er leitet Strom und giftige Chemikalien in die Wohnung von Else Schumann, die unter ihm wohnt. Manchmal bricht er bei ihr ein, zerknüllt eine ihrer Blusen und legt sie auf die Waschmaschine, damit sie merkt, dass er da war, und sich fürchtet.

Und Else Schumann fürchtet sich. Seit zehn Jahren.

Sie ist hierher gezogen, als ihr Mann starb. Die alte Wohnung war zu groß geworden, und im Garten tauchten immer häufiger düstere Gestalten auf, die bis in die Morgenstunden tranken, als wären sie dort zu Hause.

Ihr Mann war tot, aber sie war noch einigermaßen jung, keine 60. Also hat sie erst einmal die neue Freiheit genossen. Sie ist ausgegangen und hat Reisen unternommen. Ihr Mann hatte ihr ja nicht einmal erlaubt, den Führerschein zu machen, weil er der Auffassung gewesen war, dass Frauen nicht hinters Steuer gehören.

Dann wurde dieses Appartement frei: 60 qm im vierten Stock, Wohnzimmer, Schlafzimmer, Bad, Küche, ein schöner Balkon nach Süden und der Edeka direkt vor der Haustür. Und noch besser: Ihre ein Jahr ältere Schwester Johanna wohnt auch hier, sogar auf dem selben Flur.

Ach ja, die arme Johanna: Neulich lag sie bis auf ein T-Shirt entkleidet vor ihrer Wohnungstür, an der Schläfe klebte Blut. Hagel war in ihre Wohnung eingedrungen, hatte sie überwältigt und betäubt, anschließend auf den Flur geschleppt und ihren Kopf zwischen der Wand und einer Truhe eingeklemmt. Daher das Blut. Weil es sich um ein Gewaltverbrechen handelte, hat Else Schumann an die Hausverwaltung geschrieben: »Wie lange darf sich Hagel das noch erlauben«, hatte sie in ihrem Brief gefragt.

Geboren wurde Else Schumann 1923 in derselben Stadt, in der sie heute noch lebt. Sie hat das Dritte Reich miterlebt, die Aufmärsche der Nazis, die Tage, an denen die Bäckerei ihres Vaters rammelvoll war mit strammen Deutschen. Weil sie keinen Luftschutzkeller hatten, ist ihre Familie vor den Bombenangriffen in die SS-Kaserne gleich gegenüber geflohen.

Eigentlich hat sie den Krieg gut überstanden. Ihr Bruder, der an der Front war, kam heil nach Hause zurück. Die Bäckerei musste schließen, aber wenigstens lebte man. Heute strahlt Else Schumann jene Rüstigkeit aus, die die Kriegsgeneration auszeichnet. Etwas Unverwüstliches geht von dieser kleinen Person aus, von der man den Eindruck hat, dass man sie beugen, aber nicht brechen kann.

Else Schumann kramt in einem kleinen geflochtenen Kasten, in dem sie ihre wichtigen Unterlagen aufbewahrt. Sie tragen die Adressen der Hausverwaltung, von Anwaltskanzleien, einige vom Landgericht. Ihre Briefe, die sie säuberlich kopiert hat, haben keinen Briefkopf. Sie sind bis zur letzten Zeile in akkurater Handschrift verfasst – selbst die, die sechs Seiten lang sind, das Papier vorne und hinten beschrieben. In ihnen stehen Worte, die gar nicht zu einer alten Dame passen: »Perverser Spanner« steht da, »Dreckschwein« und »gerechte Strafe«. Immer geht es um Herrn Hagel.

Er war schon da, als Else Schumann in die Wohnung zog. Vom ersten Tag an war Hagel nicht zu überhören. Sein lautes Stöhnen, die Musik, der ständig laufende Fernseher, sein

Rumpeln. Vielleicht die normalen Geräusche eines lauten Nachbarn. Vielleicht aber auch etwas zu laut. Wer will das heute noch sagen.

Jedenfalls fand Else Schumann keine Ruhe mehr. Wenn sie ins Bett ging, lauschte sie schon bang und natürlich hörte sie wieder was. Erst leise, dann lauter. Sie wälzte sich hin und her, selbst im Morgengrauen war an Ruhe nicht zu denken. »Am 25.8.2003 zwischen 5 und 6 Uhr 30 hörte es sich an, als rolle Hagel große Kugeln durch seine Wohnung«, steht in einem ihrer Beschwerdebriefe an die Hausverwaltung.

Der Lärm war das eine. Dann fielen Else Schumann andere Sachen auf. Als sie unter der Dusche stand, fühlte sie sich plötzlich ganz komisch – als würde ihr jemand zugucken. Sie konnte sich gut vorstellen, dass Hagel sie beobachtete. Wie er das anstellte, das weiß sie bis heute nicht. Auch andere Vorfälle blieben mysteriös. Zum Beispiel die Sache mit dem Gas. Es fing damit an, dass ihr der Boden im Bad glitschig vorkam und einen süßlichen Geruch verströmte. Gas riecht süßlich und legt sich seifig auf die Fliesen. Wochenlang war an Duschen nicht mehr zu denken.

So gibt es fast jeden Tag Überraschungen: Einmal kam Frau Schumann nach

ANGST

25

DESIGN Benjamin Schulte and Bjoern Wolf, *Berlin and Düsseldorf* **ART DIRECTION** Benjamin Schulte and Bjoern Wolf **CREATIVE DIRECTION** Benjamin Schulte and Bjoern Wolf **LETTERING** Benjamin Schulte and Bjoern Wolf **CLIENT** Dummy Verlag **PRINCIPAL TYPE** Akzidenz Grotesk, Amerigo, Arnhem, and handlettering **DIMENSIONS** 7.7 × 10.8 in. (19.5 × 27.5 cm)

```php
<?php
class WebDeveloper extends ThisisRealArt {

    const constant   = 'opportunities';

    public  $company = 'This is Real Art';
    public  $address = '2 Sycamore St, London, EC1Y 0SF';
    public  $phone   = '020 7253 2181';
    private $email   = 'info@thisisrealart.com';

    public function getRecruit(){

        // What do we require?
        $this->db->select('webDeveloper');

        // From where are we selecting?
        $this->db->from('peopleWhoLoveIdeas');

        // Select criteria
        $where = "'PHP OOP & mySQL'  = 'strong'
                  AND 'XHTML & CSS' = 'strict'
                  AND ('jQuery'     = 'bonus'
                      OR 'linux'    = 'bonus'
                      OR 'flash'    = 'bonus') ";
        $this->db->where($where);

        // How should we prioritize?
        $orderBy = array(
                        'ability'=>'DESC',
                        'hardWorking'=>'DESC',
                        'sociable'=>'DESC',
                        'davidBowieFan'=>'DESC',
                        'ManUtdSupporter'=>'ASC'
        );
        $this->db->orderBy($orderBy);

        // How many results do we need?
        $this->db->limit(1);

        // Run the search
        $this->db->get();
    }

    protected function _setBenefits(){
        $this->daysHoliday = 28;
        $this->fun         = 'guaranteed';
        $this->salary      = 'negotiable';

    }
}
?>
```


DESIGN Paul Belford, *London* WRITER Andy Mathieson DESIGN OFFICE This is Real Art PRINCIPAL TYPE OCR-B
DIMENSIONS 16.5 × 23.4 in. (42 × 59.4 cm)

ART DIRECTION Christian Doering, Hamburg CREATIVE DIRECTION Katrin Oeding COPYWRITER Till Grabsch GRAPHIC DESIGNER Ana Magalhaes AGENCY Kolle Rebbe/KOREFE CLIENT T.D.G. Vertriebs UG (haftungsbeschraenkt) & Co. KG PRINCIPAL TYPE ANA DIMENSIONS various

ART DIRECTION Flo Gaertner, *Karlsruhe, Germany* DESIGN OFFICE MAGMA Brand Design GmbH & Co. KG CLIENT Vitra Design Museum
PRINCIPAL TYPE Akkurat DIMENSIONS 23.4 × 33.1 in. (59.4 × 84.1 cm)

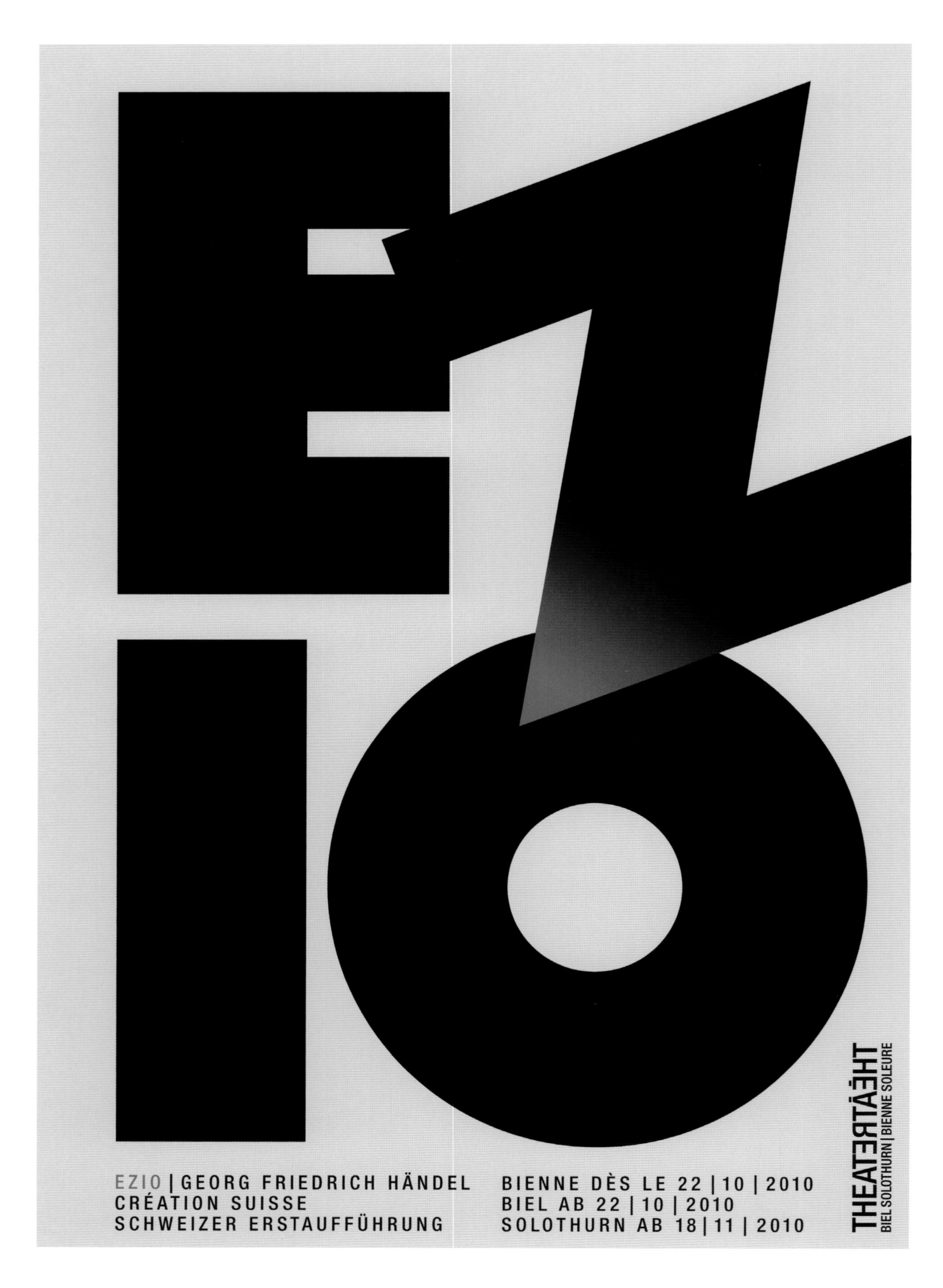

 Poster

DESIGN Stephan Bundi, *Berne, Switzerland* STUDIO Atelier Bundi AG CLIENT Theater Biel Solothurn PRINCIPAL TYPE Helvetica Neue and custom
DIMENSIONS 35.2 × 50.4 in. (89.5 × 128 cm)

Unpublished

DESIGN Tomoya Kaishi, *Tokyo* ART DIRECTION Tomoya Kaishi DESIGN OFFICE room-composite PRINCIPAL TYPE Chu Gothic BBB and Yokobuto Mincho
DIMENSIONS 28.7 × 40.6 in. (72.8 × 103 cm)

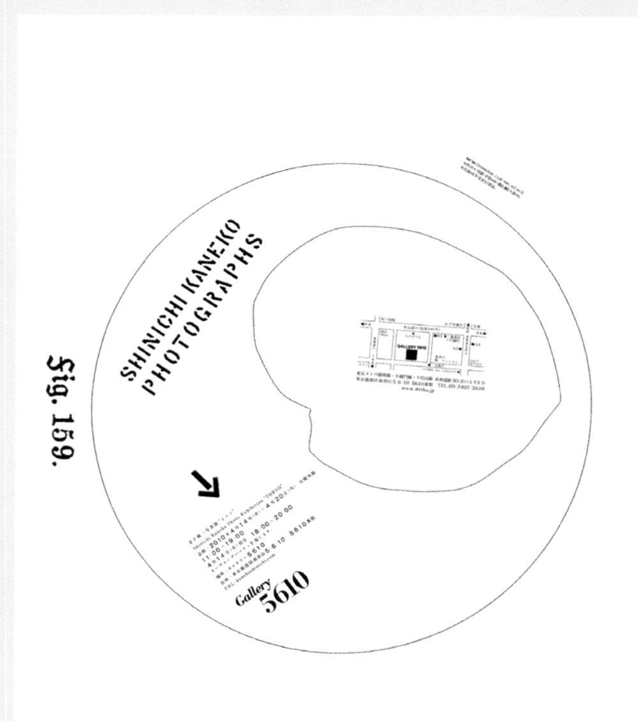

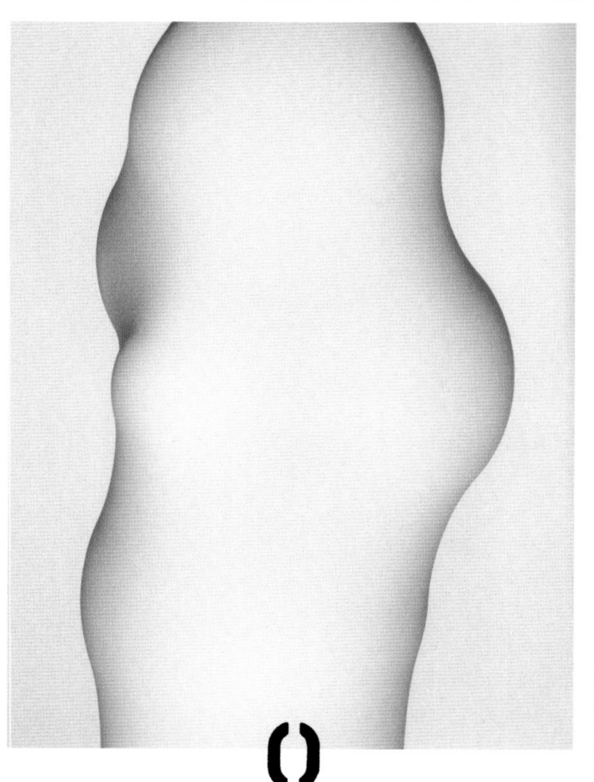

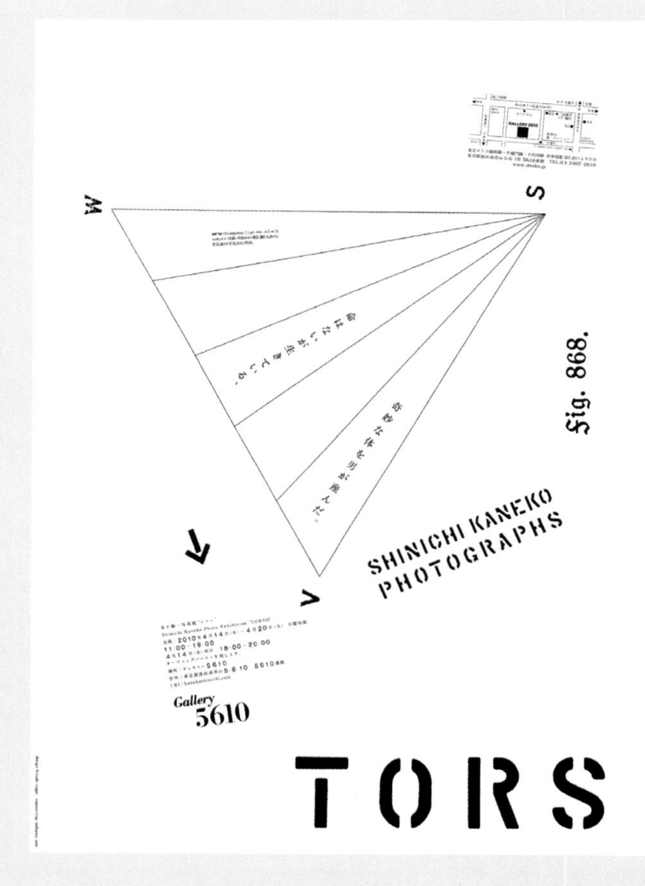

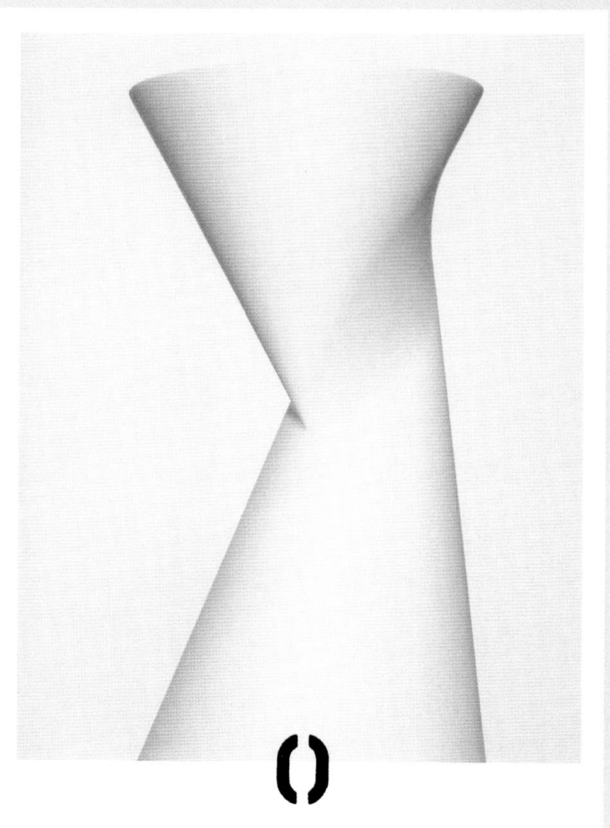

DESIGN Hiroaki Nagai and Akiko Wake, *Tokyo* **ART DIRECTION** Hiroaki Nagai **PHOTOGRAPHY** Shinichi Kaneko **COPYWRITER** Tadayasu Seto
DESIGN OFFICE N.G.Inc. **CLIENT** Shinich Kaneko **PRINCIPAL TYPE** custom **DIMENSIONS** 40.6 × 57.3 in. (103 × 145.6 cm)

T-shirt

DESIGN Oliver Carver and Mark Denton, *London* CONCEPT Fern Berresford TYPOGRAPHER Andy Dymock PRODUCTION COMPANY Coy! Communications
CLIENT A Large Evil Corporation PRINCIPAL TYPE Franklin Gothic Wide

DESIGN Andrew Byrom, Joe Shouldice, and Stephan Walter, *New York* ART DIRECTION Stefan Sagmeister AGENCY CREATIVE DIRECTION John Merrifield AGENCY PRODUCER Shareen Thumbo PRODUCTION COMPANY Passion Pictures AGENCY TBWA Asia Pacific STUDIO Sagmeister Inc. CLIENT Standard Chartered PRINCIPAL TYPE custom

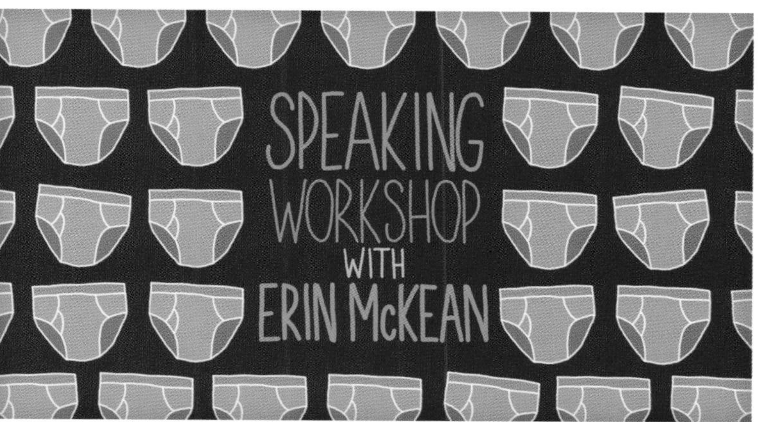

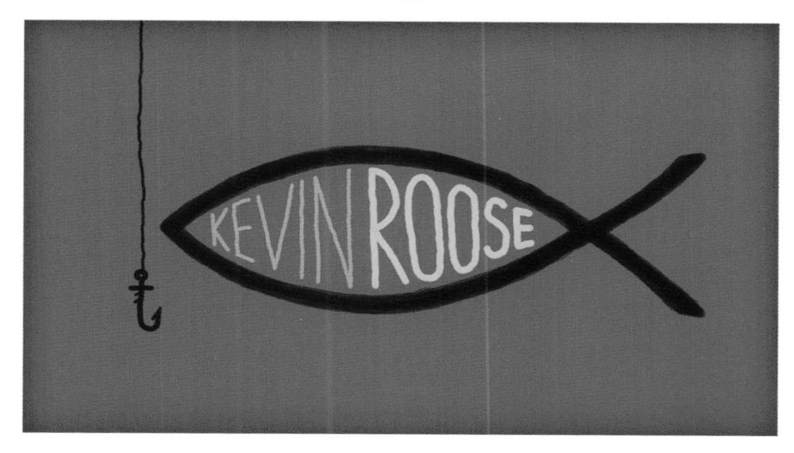

DESIGN Guillaume Alix and Kyle Miller, *New York* ART DIRECTION Kyle Miller CREATIVE DIRECTION Scott Matz, Justin Meredith LETTERING Kyle Miller ANIMATION Ken Krueger and Kyle Miller MUSIC AND SOUND DESIGN Michael Montes DESIGN OFFICE Thornberg & Forester CLIENT GEL Conference 2010 PRINCIPAL TYPE handlettering

DESIGN Samuel Jacques, *Montréal* CREATIVE DIRECTION Philippe Lamarre LETTERING Samuel Jacques AGENCY TOXA
CLIENT Nouveau Théâtre Expérimental PRINCIPAL TYPE handlettering

/Volumes/Intel Server/Jobs/11463-Typography 32/Supplied/031611/typo.swf

EDIT PRINT

Web Editor for CF font

/Volumes/Intel Server/Jobs/11463-Typography 32/Supplied/031611/typo.swf

EDIT PRINT

/Volumes/Intel Server/Jobs/11463-Typography 32/Supplied/031611/typo.swf

EDIT PRINT

/Volumes/Intel Server/Jobs/11463-Typography 32/Supplied/031611/typo.swf

EDIT PRINT

/Volumes/Intel Server/Jobs/11463-Typography 32/Supplied/031611/typo.swf

EDIT PRINT

/Volumes/Intel Server/Jobs/11463-Typography 32/Supplied/031611/typo.swf

COMPLETE

Web Editor for CF font

DESIGN Young Soon Lee, *Seoul* CREATIVE DIRECTION Jae Woo Lee AGENCY Markers
PRINCIPAL TYPE custom

 Student Project

DESIGN Elisa Bates, *Brooklyn, New York* **SCHOOL** School of Visual Arts, *New York* **INSTRUCTOR** Gail Anderson
PRINCIPAL TYPE various scanned wood type

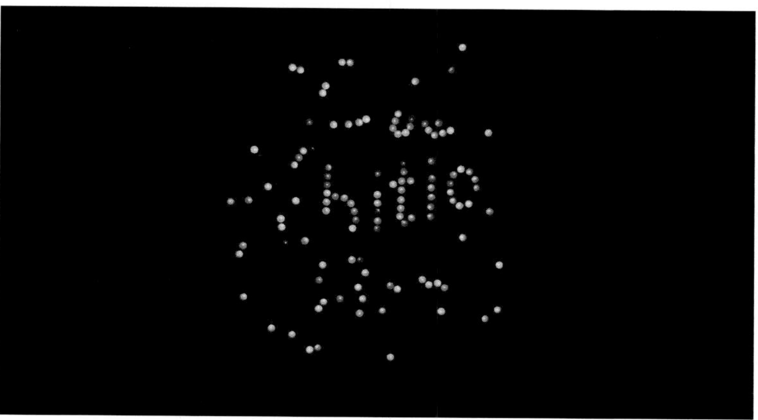

DESIGN Elisa Bates, *Brooklyn, New York* SCHOOL School of Visual Arts, *New York* INSTRUCTOR Stefan Sagmeister
PRINCIPAL TYPE various scanned wood type

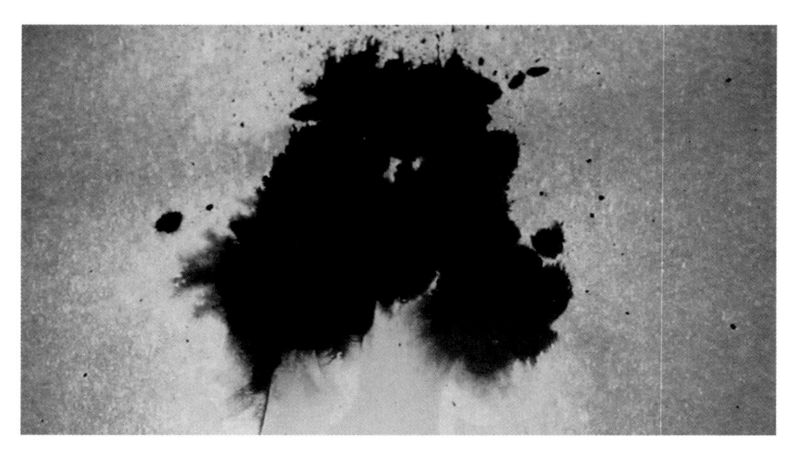

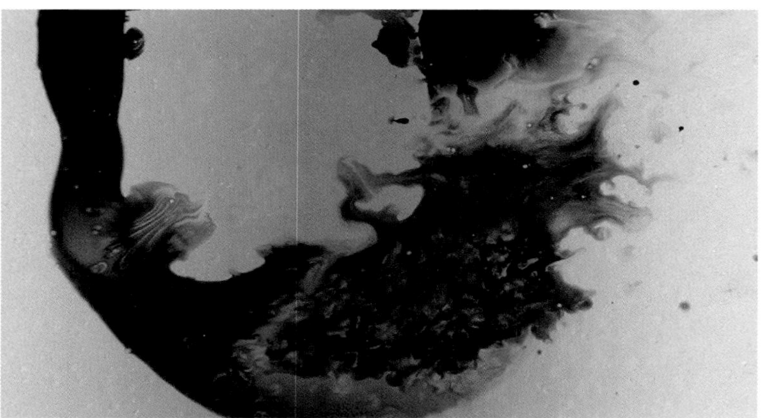

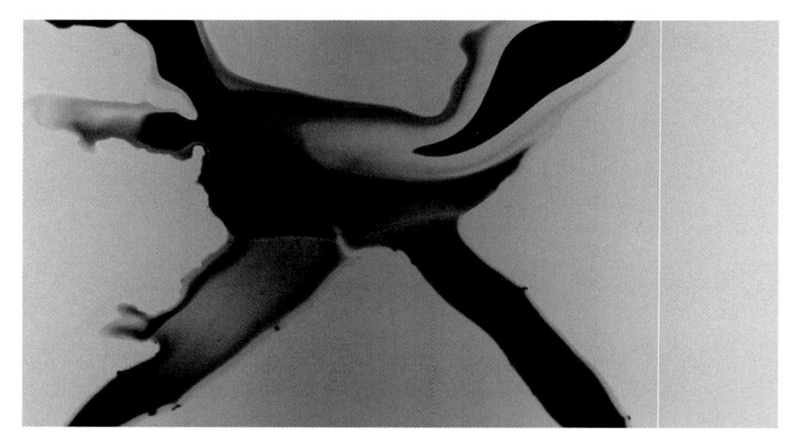

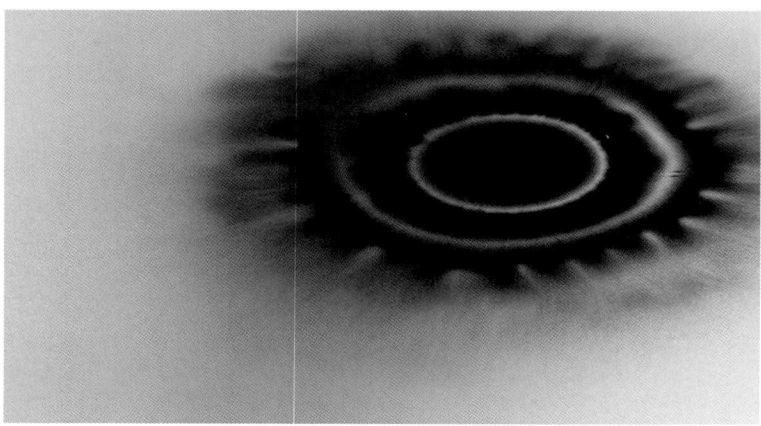

 Student Project

DESIGN Tim Hucklesby SCHOOL School of Visual Arts, *New York* INSTRUCTORS Gail Anderson and Stefan Sagmeister
PRINCIPAL TYPE custom

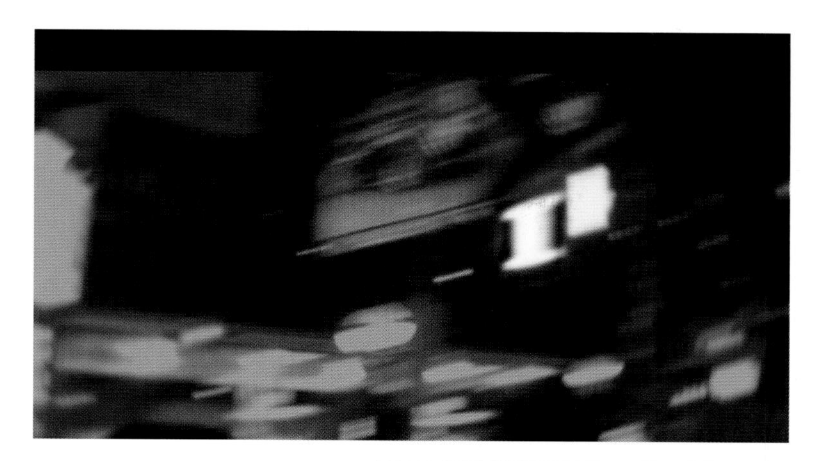

DESIGN Tim Hucklesby SCHOOL School of Visual Arts, *New York* INSTRUCTORS Gail Anderson and Stefan Sagmeister
PRINCIPAL TYPE Clearview, Geometric Slabserif 712, and Helvetica

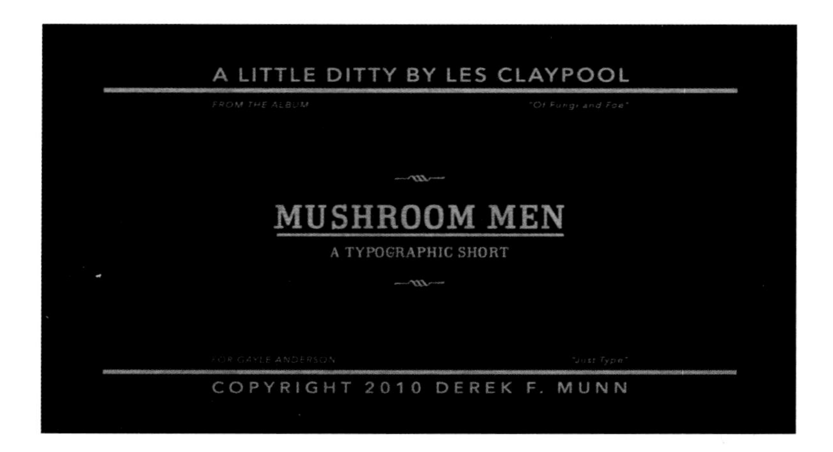

 Student Project

DESIGN Derek Munn, *Brooklyn, New York* **SCHOOL** School of Visual Arts, *New York* **INSTRUCTOR** Gail Anderson
PRINCIPAL TYPE various

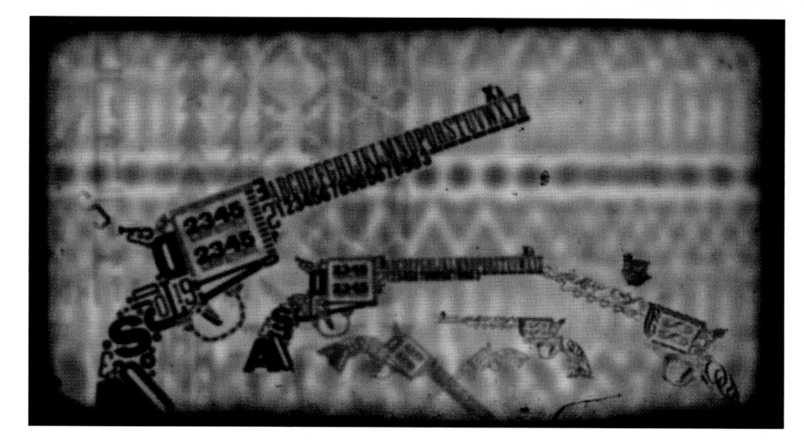

DESIGN Sebastian Ebarb, *Brooklyn, New York* SCHOOL School of Visual Arts, *New York* INSTRUCTOR Gail Anderson
PRINCIPAL TYPE Baskerville, Futura, Gold Rush Regular, and Ivy League

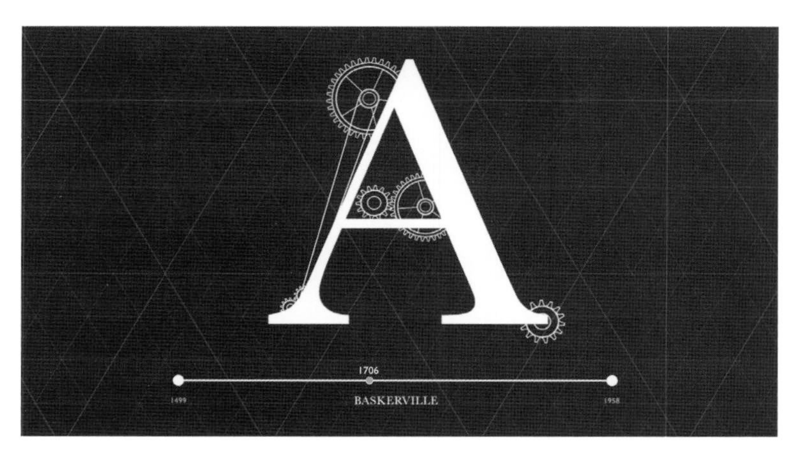

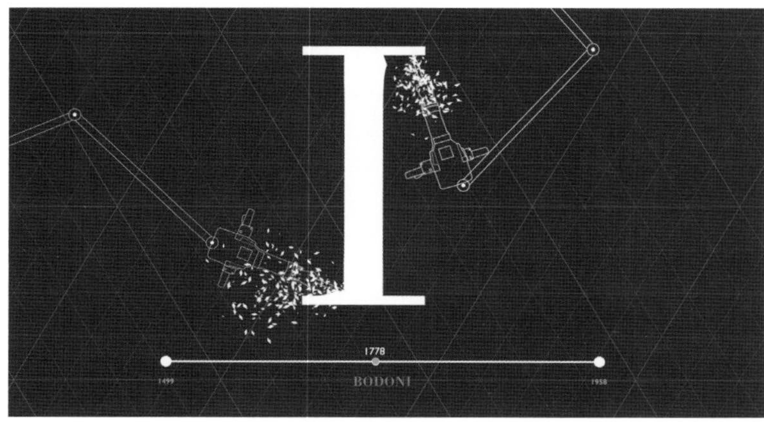

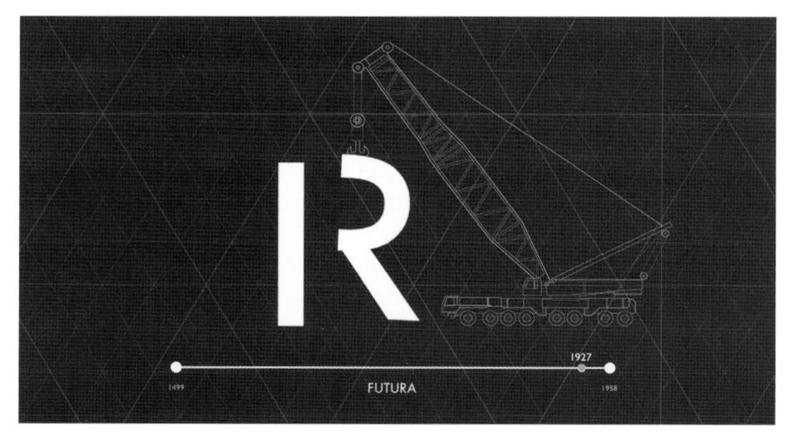

DESIGN Jihwan Kim, *New York* SCHOOL School of Visual Arts, *New York* INSTRUCTOR Ori Kleiner
PRINCIPAL TYPE Baskerville, Bodoni, Futura, Adobe Garamond, and Optima

VOL.

49

January 2010

Archives

For volumes older than September 2010 visit the old Quipsologies.

A DIVISION OF

UNDERCONSIDERATION

Chronicling the most curious, creative, and notable projects, stories, and events of the graphic design industry on a daily basis.

More about Quipsologies

CONTRIBUTING QUIPSOLOGISTS

- Plamen
- Doug Bartow
- Josh Berta
- Niki Blaker
- James I Bowie
- Ricardo Cordoba
- Jason Dean
- Joe Marianek
- Paul Soulellis
- Diane Zerr

CSS TYPOGRAPHIC CONTROL

Fancy type
Same ol' HTML type

BACKGROUND COLOR CODE

Quip'd by a representative of UnderConsideration

Quip'd by a contributing Quipsologist

Submitted by our readers and Quip'd by UnderConsideration

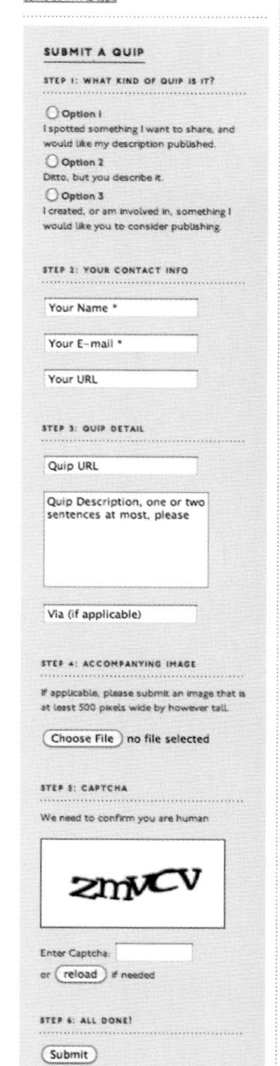

ADV @ UNDERCONSIDERATION

Peek here for details

NO.

179

BY RICARDO CORDOBA

Some great book covers designed by Barcelona studio Hey for Edicions 62.

Link

01.30.2011

VIA

We Just Like It

NO.

178

BY ARMIN

One of the most useless pieces of graphic design is being retired, thank goodness: The Department of Homeland Security's color-coded threat level system will no longer be used.

Link

01.28.2011

SUBMITTED BY

Debbie Millman

Attacks happened more often when the level was yellow ("significant risk") than when it was orange ("high risk"). And the one time it was red ("severe risk"), nothing happened. It's never been blue or green, the two least dangerous levels. [...] Were there plane trips you delayed when the level was orange that you made when it was yellow? Did any company base business decisions on it? Do we think the president consulted the level every morning?

NO.

177

BY NIKI BLAKER

Nancy Duarte breaks down Martin Luther King Jr.'s "I Have a Dream" speech into a visual graphic to show how the speech follows masterful form.

Link

01.28.2011

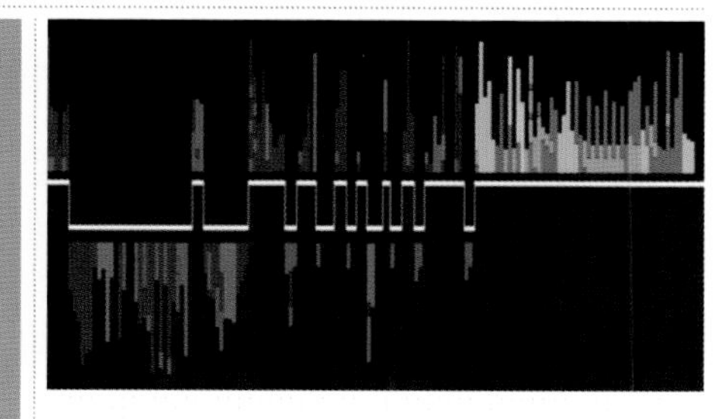

ABOUT

- Quipsologies, is a division of UnderConsideration, chronicling the most curious, creative, and notable projects, stories, and events of the graphic design industry on a daily basis.
- Quipsologies uses TypeKit to render P22 Underground, Skolar Web by TypeTogether, and Coquette by Mark Simonson.
- Quipsologies is run with Six Apart's MovableType 4.32-en
- Syndicate / RSS Feed
- All comments, ideas and thoughts on Quipsologies are property of their authors; reproduction without the author's or Quipsologies's permission is strictly prohibited
- Contact us by e-mail
- Search through our archives (starting with Vol. 45 September 2010)

Search

Go

NO.

176

BY JOSH BERTA

The Contemporary Art Center of Virginia is raffling off five artist-modified Eames rocking chairs.

If you like putting your butt on art, then go buy a raffle ticket and help them out.

Link

01.28.2011

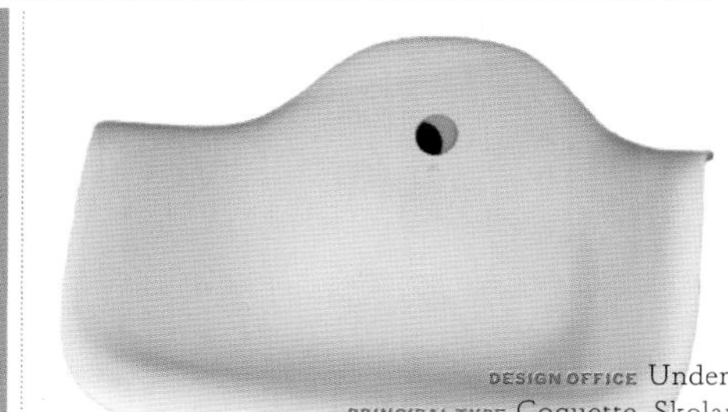

ALSO BY UNDERCONSIDERATION

UnderConsideration is a graphic design enterprise that runs a network of blogs, publishes books, organizes live events, and designs for clients.

DESIGN OFFICE UnderConsideration, *Austin, Texas*
PRINCIPAL TYPE Coquette, Skolar Web, and P22 Underground

 Student Project

DESIGN Jesse Senje Yuan, *Rego Park, New York* SONG Ibuki by the Yoshida Brothers SCHOOL School of Visual Arts, *New York*
INSTRUCTOR Gail Anderson PRINCIPAL TYPE Li Song Pro

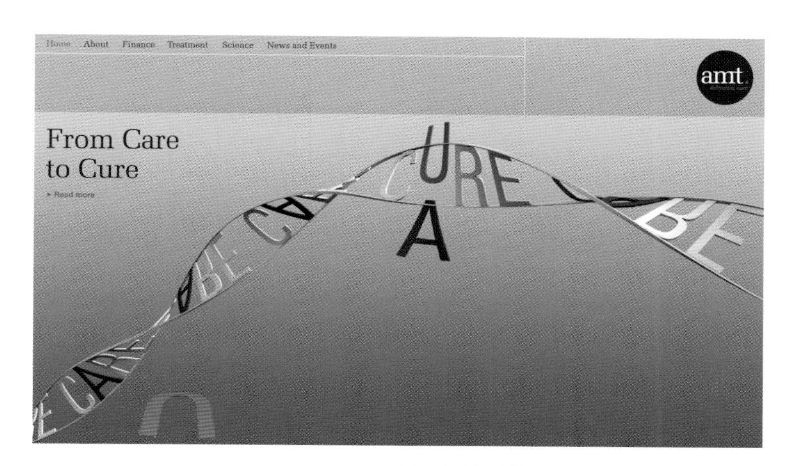

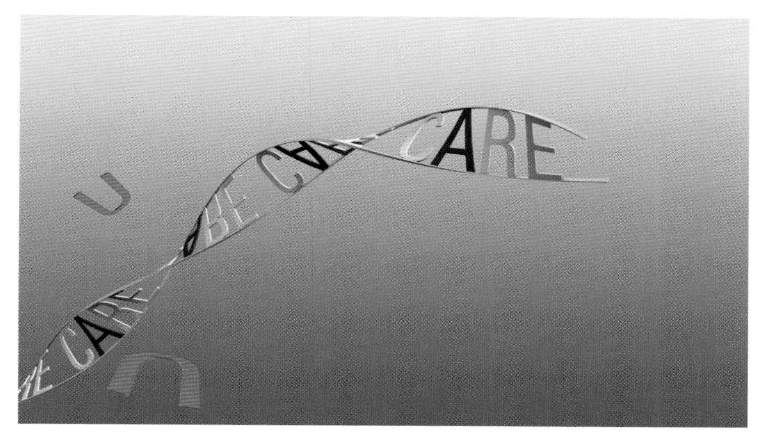

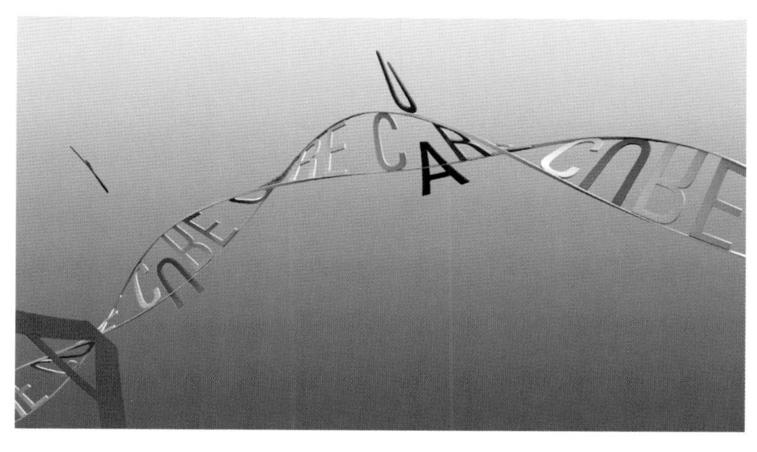

DESIGN Knut Maierhofer, *Munich* MOTION DESIGN Gabriel Weiss EXPERT MOTION DESIGN Cecil Rustemeyer MUSIC Christian Ring CLIENT MANAGER Nadine Vicentini BRAND COMPANY KMS TEAM GmbH CLIENT Amsterdam Molecular Therapeutics (AMT) PRINCIPAL TYPE Univers

a perfect day

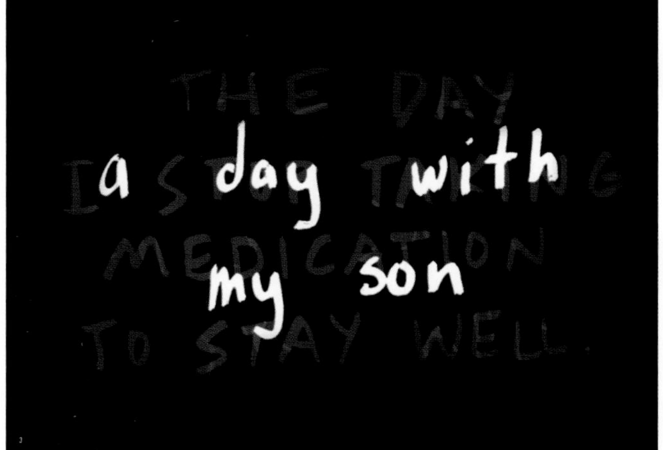

DESIGN Elliott Walker, *Brooklyn, New York* SCHOOL School of Visual Arts, *New York* INSTRUCTOR Gail Anderson
PRINCIPAL TYPE handlettering

DESIGN Matt Luckhurst, *Brooklyn, New York* **SCHOOL** School of Visual Arts, *New York*
PRINCIPAL TYPE handlettering

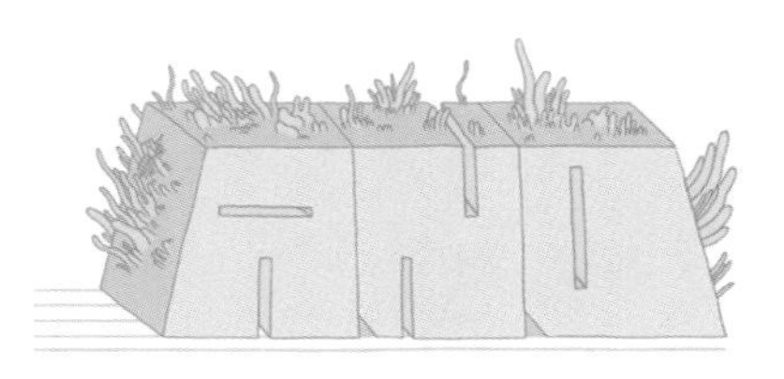

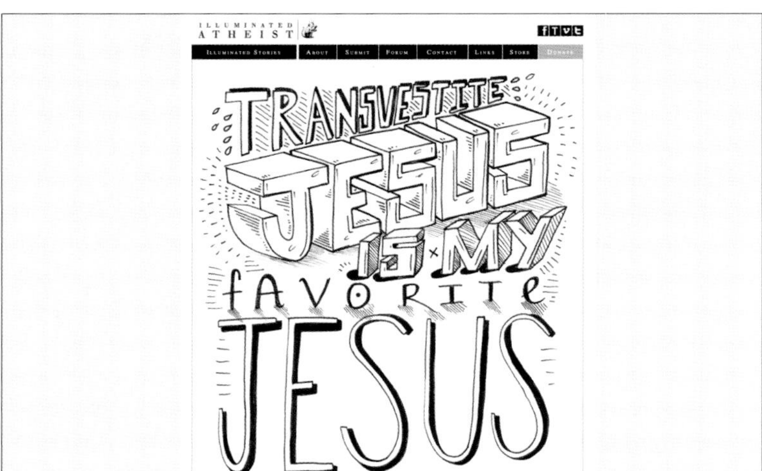

 Student Project

DESIGN Matt Luckhurst, *Brooklyn, New York* **SCHOOL** School of Visual Arts, *New York* **THESIS ADVISOR** Paula Scher
PRINCIPAL TYPE ITC Cheltenham and Walbaum

DEAR COLLEAGUE,
I AM
TONE
CHECK
ON

DEAR COLLEAGUE,
I AM ANGRY
TONE
CHECK
ON

DEAR COLLEAGUE,
I AM SORRY
WE EVER MET
TONE
CHECK
ON

DEAR COLLEAGUE,
I AM SORRY.
TONE
CHECK
ON

DESIGN Michael Bierut and Christina Nizar, *New York* DESIGN OFFICE Pentagram Design New York CLIENT *The New York Times Magazine*
PRINCIPAL TYPE National Regular

DESIGN Daniel Chang, Lynn Cho, Matthew Encina, Vanessa Marzaroli, Chris ONeill, Michael Relth, and Lawrence Wyatt, *Santa Monica, California*
CREATIVE DIRECTION Vanessa Marzaroli CREATIVES Tom Phillips and Jason Swinscoe, *New York* CALLIGRAPHY Bill Kemp ILLUSTRATION Daniel Chang, Lynn Cho, Vanessa Marzaroli, Chris ONeill, and Michael Relth EXECUTIVE PRODUCER Dave Kleinman PRODUCER Carrie Schupper POST PRODUCER Dana Vaden
2D ANIMATION Daniel Chang, Jiaren Hui, Vanessa Marzaroli, Chris ONeill, Michael Relth, Maithy Tran, and Lawrence Wyatt STORYBOARD ARTIST Vincent Lucido
MUSIC The Cinematic Orchestra: Jason Swinscoe PRODUCTION COMPANY Blind, Inc. AGENCY Exposure USA CLIENT Bill Kemp PRINCIPAL TYPE handlettering

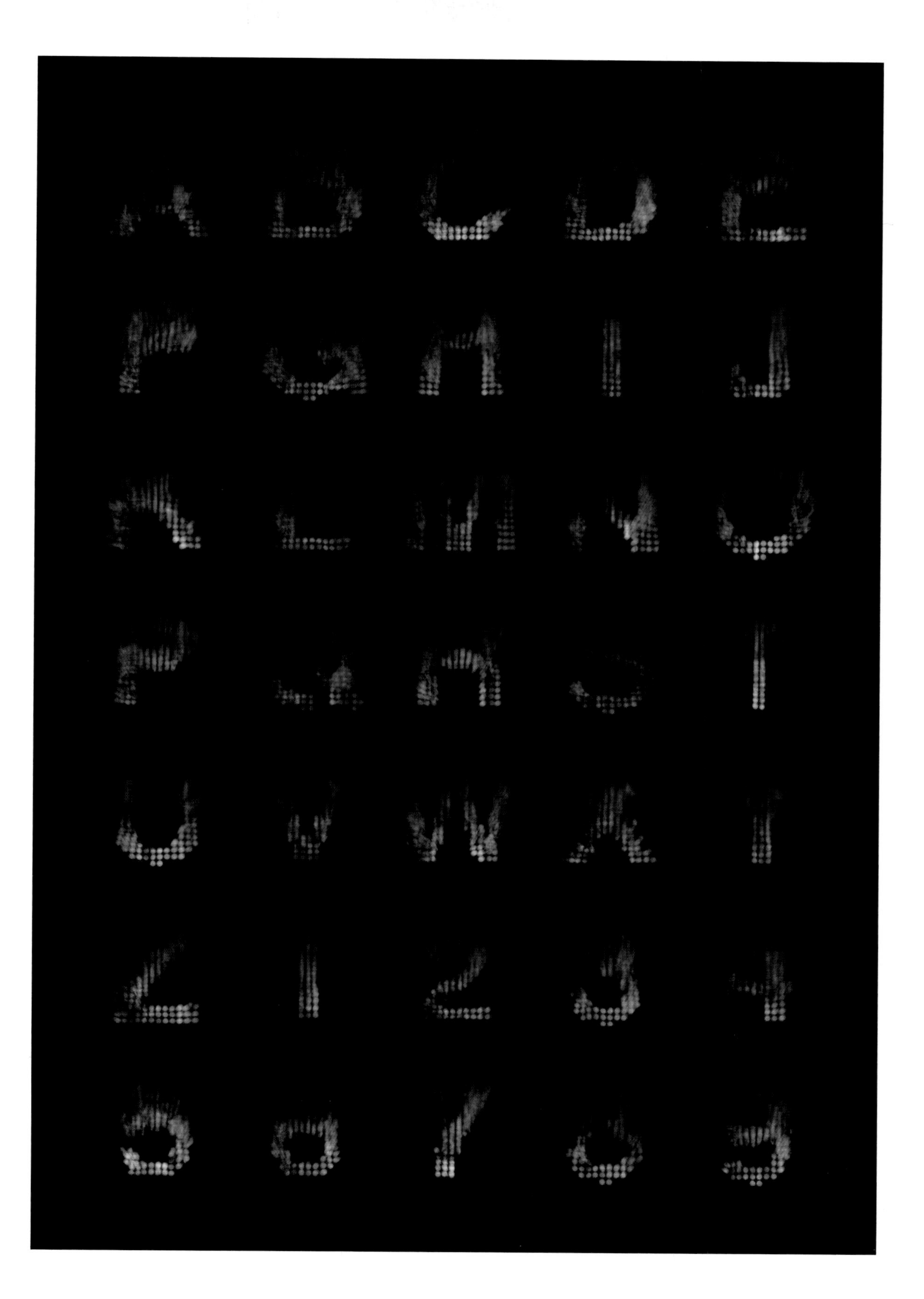

DESIGN Cameron Zotter, *Baltimore* **SCHOOL** Maryland Institute College of Art
INSTRUCTOR Brockett Horne **PRINCIPAL TYPE** custom

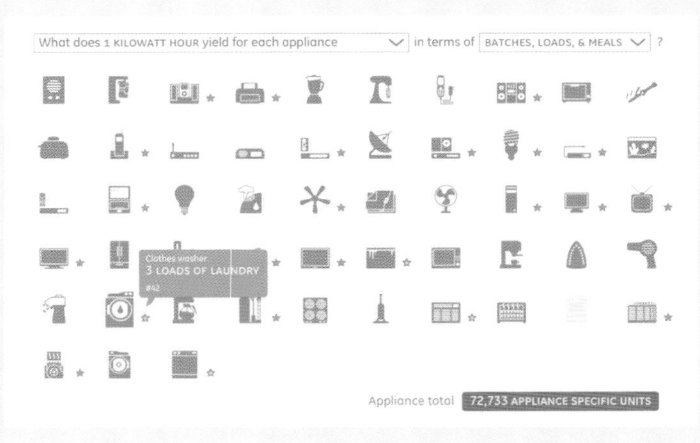

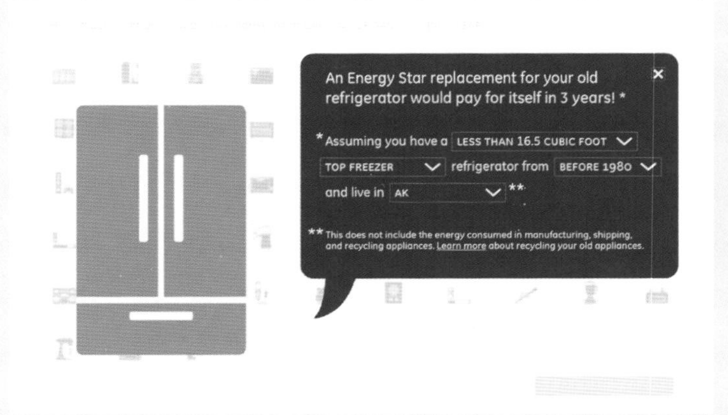

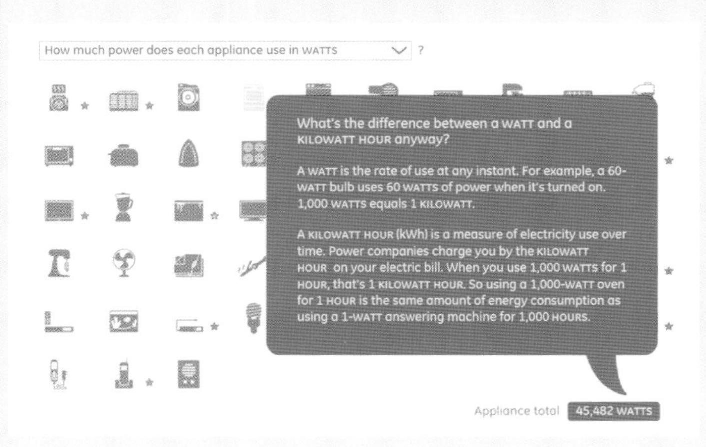

DESIGN Michael Deal, Hilla Katki, Lisa Strausfeld, and Adam Suharjah, *New York* CREATIVE DIRECTION Lisa Strausfeld DESIGNER/DEVELOPER Adam Suharja DESIGN OFFICE Pentagram Design New York CLIENT GE PRINCIPAL TYPE GE Inspira

Book Jacket *245*

DESIGN Ariane Spanier, *Berlin* DESIGN OFFICE Ariane Spanier Design CLIENT Fukt Magazine, Björn Hegardt
PRINCIPAL TYPE handlettering DIMENSIONS 6 × 9 in. (15.2 × 22.9 cm)

CHAIRMAN'S STATEMENT

I find myself in the unique position of having been involved with this competition from its beginning. Paul Shaw and I started it, we served as co-chairs for the first two competitions, and since then I have been a judge once and a chairman twice. When I have not been directly involved, I have helped out during the days of judging and I have observed or been involved with eleven or twelve of the fourteen TDC^2 competitions.

During this period I have seen an exponential increase in the quality of the submissions. This year we received the most entries ever for a single year of eligibility. The number of non-Latin designs continues to grow, and the demands on the expertise of the judges are now greater than ever. The judges are a wonderfully thoughtful and cooperative bunch. Listening to the intense discussion surrounding their choices was an education that anyone involved in type design would value. Besides the expertise of the judges the competition could not have been successfully concluded without the hard work of Maxim Zhukov, who coordinated the examination and commentary of all of the non-Latin submissions with our Non-Latin Review Board. I thank everyone for their hard work and good humor.

—James Montalbano

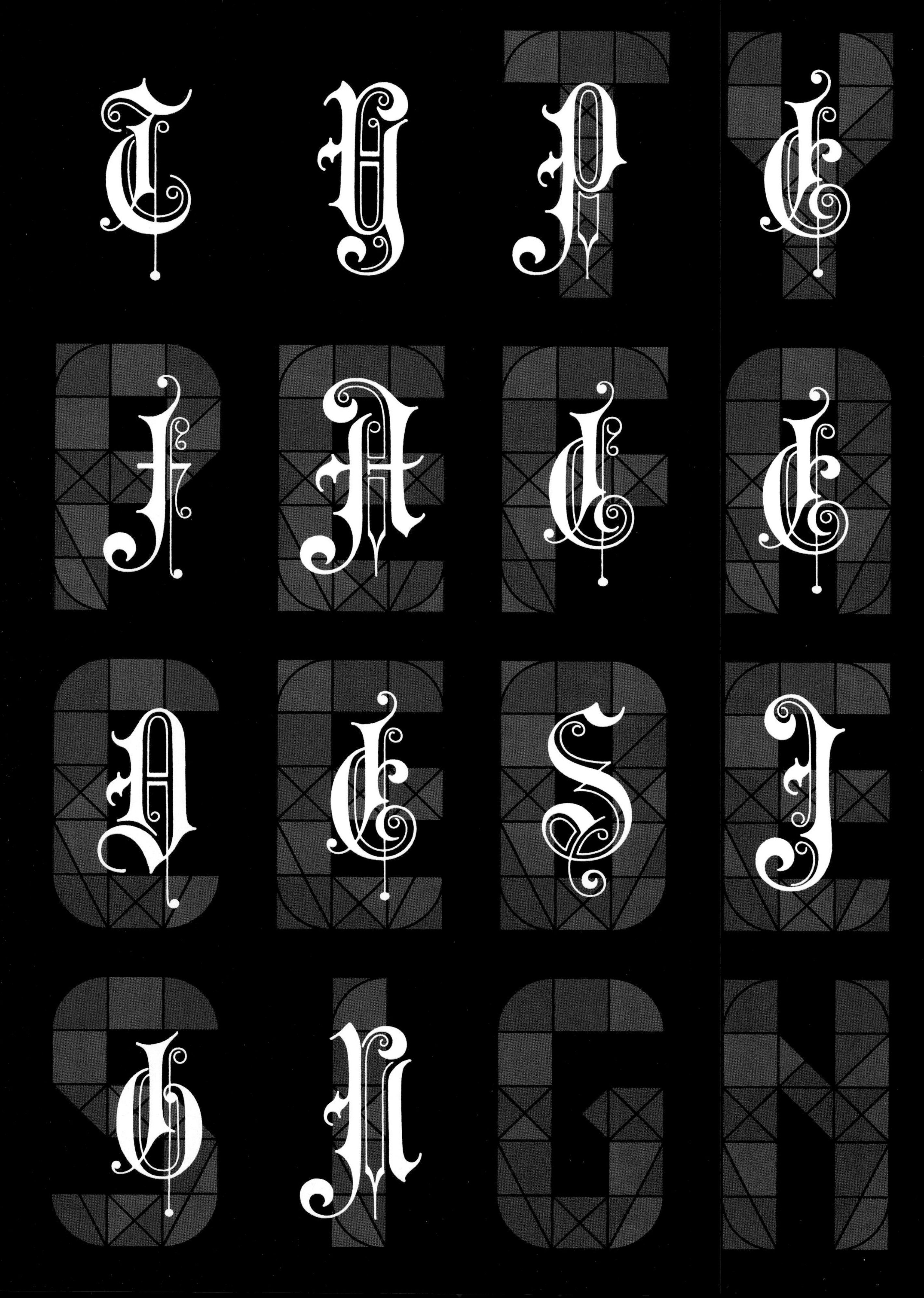
TYPE
FACE
DESI
GN

TDC^{2} CHAIR

JAMES MONTALBANO

James Montalbano began his professional career as a public school industrial arts teacher. After receiving an M.Ed in Technology Education, he studied lettering with Ed Benguiat, began drawing type, and working in the wild world of New York City type shops and magazine art departments. He continued his career as a magazine art director, moving on to become a design director responsible for twenty trade magazines whose subject matter no one should be required to remember. He tried his hand at designing pharmaceutical packaging, but that only made him ill.

Since 1990, Montalbano has been principal of Terminal Design Inc. (www.terminaldesign.com). His Brooklyn firm specializes in typeface design, font development, and digital lettering. He has designed custom fonts and lettering for editorial, corporate, government, and publishing clients. Over the last fifteen years he has been working on the Clearview™ type system for text, display, roadway, and interior guide signage. In 2004 the ClearviewHwy typefaces were granted interim approval by the Federal Highway Administration for use on all U.S. roads. In 2011 the ClearviewHwy typefaces were included in the Cooper-Hewitt National Design Triennial "Why Design Now?" His work has been featured in *The New York Times, Print, Creative Review, ID,* and *Wired*. He is a past president of the TDC, and teaches at Parsons The New School for Design and the School of Visual Arts.

JUDGES, JUDGES' CHOICES, AND DESIGNERS' STATEMENTS

JUDGES, JUDGES' CHOICES, AND DESIGNERS' STATEMENTS

TDC² JUDGE

JOS BUIVENGA

can be passionate about a lot of things. He loves to paint, listen to music, brew an almost perfect espresso... but nothing challenges and rewards him more than designing type. If ever he were stranded on a desert island he would still draw alphabets in the sand, even if there was no one else to see them.

He is the founder of exljbris, the one-man Dutch font foundry through which he releases and offers his typefaces. For fifteen years, his online friends and fans were able to follow the development of his typefaces and download the results at no cost. In 2008, while still working as an art director at an advertising agency, he released his first commercial typeface, Museo, with several weights offered for free. The strategy paid off and Museo became a huge bestseller. Partly thanks to that success he now calls himself a full-time type designer. Recent projects include a custom version of Museo and Museo Sans for Dell, and the Questa project, a collaboration with the well-known type designer Martin Majoor.

CALLUNA
Norwegian **noon**
typography
Is also the name of a so-called heather plant.
€645.000.000
A (*quadruped's*) HOCK!
HAMSTRING

JOS BUIVENGA'S SELECTION

t was at the art academy in Arnhem, where I studied graphic design, that I first came into contact with type featuring a reversed contrast. The late Evert Bloemsma, who was working on his Balance typeface at that time, introduced me to a related typeface designed by Roger Excoffon: Antique Olive. It completely blew me away and opened my eyes to some—for me—unknown areas of type design. Most striking of all was the weight distribution, which is so much more heavy at the top of the characters.

So it's not that strange that this newly designed typeface, Aero, immediately caught my eye because of its resemblance to the so-called Nord weight of Excoffon's masterpiece.

Aero clearly takes inspiration from Antique Olive, but it does that in a clever and subtle way. The reversed contrast is most apparent not in the weight but in the shape of the characters; the inverted stress is only really present in the heavier weights, resulting in an attractive and well balanced typeface.

If Quentin Tarantino were a type designer he could have designed this.

DESIGNER'S STATEMENT

ero takes inspiration from Roger Excoffon's landmark design Antique Olive, particularly the heavy "Nord" weight. Instead of revisiting the original, Aero was drawn from memories of Antique Olive, its high waist and reversed contrast. And that wonderful scooped lowercase *i*. The result is a contemporary reflection of a sixties-era classic, with the volume turned up and applied to a wider weight range.

FORWARD MOTION

Contrails

Heavier-than-air flying machines

Supersonic

343.2 MPS OR (1,126 FT/S)

Horizon

Aerodynamics

TYPEFACE Aero TYPEFACE DESIGNERS Chester Jenkins and Jeremy Mickel, *Brooklyn, New York, and Providence, Rhode Island* FOUNDRY Village Type and Design
MEMBERS OF TYPEFACE FAMILY/SYSTEM Fine, Fine Italic, Thin, Thin Italic, Extralight, Extralight Italic, Light, Light Italic, Book, Book Italic, Medium, Medium Italic, Bold, Bold Italic, Heavy, Heavy Italic, Super, and Super Italic

TDC² JUDGE

JESSICA HISCHE

Jessica Hische is a letterer and illustrator based in Brooklyn, New York. After graduating from Tyler School of Art in Philadelphia with a BFA in graphic design, she was hired by Louise Fili Ltd., where she served as senior designer for two years. While working for Louise Fili, she was simultaneously developing her freelance illustration and lettering career, working for clients such as Tiffany & Co., Target, Samsung, and Penguin Books. Jessica and her work have been featured in numerous design and illustration publications, and she has been named an ADC Young Gun, one of *Print* magazine's New Visual Artists (20 under 30), one of *Step*'s 25 Emerging Artists, and a GD USA "Person to Watch." She is well known for her personal projects such as Daily Drop Cap and the "Should I Work for Free?" flowchart.

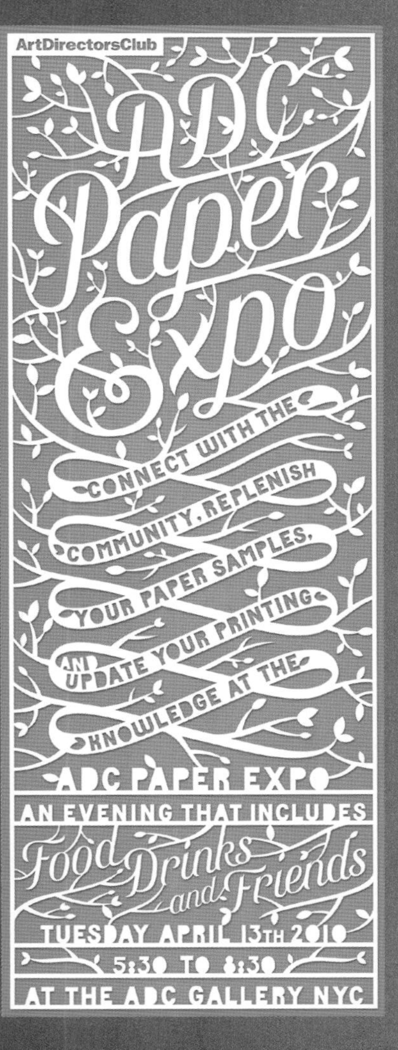

JESSICA HISCHE'S SELECTION

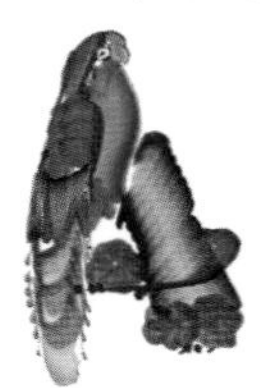

s someone with a graphic design background, I was looking forward to judging the TDC show immensely, if only to mentally catalogue all of the awesome typefaces I needed to have this year. The process was wonderful and I was thoroughly impressed with the quality of work across the board—but while going through the show, few pieces gave me as immediate and visceral a reaction as Brandon Grotesque. As soon as I saw the typeface, all I wanted to do was run to the studio and brainstorm new projects to use it for! As someone who is primarily a letterer, the typefaces that really make my heart flutter are what I would consider to be "best-supporting actor" typefaces—useful type that still has a good amount of character and personality, something that could hold its own as headline text (or subhead text) but also play second fiddle to lettering work. Brandon Grotesque is such a wonderfully warm typeface and it's confident without being showy. I love the subtle rounded corners that whisper "I'm printed," rather than screaming it like textured typefaces do. Brandon would definitely fill a niche in any designer's library—it's like the Futura that you dream about when you dream about Futura.

DESIGNER'S STATEMENT

y father gave me some magazines from the 1920s and 1930s, which he had found at my grandfather's. I was fascinated by the surface feel and by the general atmosphere of these magazines; the way the body type was set and by the various combinations of typefaces. I absolutely wanted to create a typeface with that kind of feel: a geometric face that nonetheless would possess a certain softness and warmth. Because of "bad" printing, the text faces in those magazines had slightly rounded corners, lending them an emotionality that today's clean-cut type lacks. So I decided to give Brandon slightly rounded-off corners to allow it to radiate warmth in spite of its geometric clarity. A real italic was designed to provide additional individuality and to distinguish the font from most other geometric sans faces, making it even more "human."

FOR *the* LOVE OF

PRINTED TYPE

BRANDON GROTESQUE

Supplément Régulier

TYPOGRAPHIE

Handsetzerei

Italienische Automobilwerke

Meisterklasse

Junger Laufbursche

Zirkuszelt

Nachrichten aus Presse und Rundfunk

Upplysningsbyrå

OZEANDAMPFER

TYPEFACE Brandon Grotesque TYPEFACE DESIGNER Hannes von Döhren, *Berlin* FOUNDRY HVD Fonts

MEMBERS OF TYPEFACE FAMILY/SYSTEM Thin, Thin Italic, Light, Light Italic, Regular, Regular Italic, Medium, Medium Italic, Bold, Bold Italic, Black, Black Italic

HISTORIC REVIVAL — Bertham Pro™

There is something wonderfully attractive in this king *tree, even when beheld from afar, that draws us to it* with INDESCRIBABLE ENTHUSIASM

HISTORIC REVIVAL — Friar Pro™

Its superior height & massive smoothly rounded outlines proclaiming its character in any company & when one of the oldest attains full stature on

CUSTOM — Droid™ Sans

some commanding ridge it seems the very god of the woods. I ran back *to camp, packed Brownie, steered over the divide and down into the heart* of the Fresno Grove. Then choosing a camp on the side of a brook *where the grass was good, I made a cup of tea, and set off free among* **the brown giants, glorying in the abundance of new work about me** *One of the first special things that caught my attention was an ext-* **ensive landslip. The ground on the side of a stream had given** ***way to a depth of about fifty feet and with all its trees had been*** **launched into the bottom of the stream ravine.** — JOHN MUIR

TDC^2 JUDGE

STEVE MATTESON

is the Director of Type Design for Ascender Corporation and has created fonts for both screen-display environments and print publishing since 1987. A graduate of Rochester Institute of Technology, Steve has an extensive background in typography, design, and printing, which he has applied to his development of high quality typefaces.

His work can be found in user interface designs such as that for the Xbox 360, Zune, and Google's Android mobile products. He has produced several revivals of the work of Frederic Goudy, including Bertham Pro and Friar. His experience includes extensive work with non-Latin scripts including Greek, Cyrillic, Hebrew, and Thai. Most recently Steve worked with Matthew Carter to create extensions to the Georgia family.

Steve lectures frequently about the legacy of the Goudys, type design for branding, and the issues surrounding type for screen displays. He lives in Louisville, Colorado, where the altitude and UV index fuel his creativity and active lifestyle.

STEVE MATTESON'S SELECTION

was truly amazed by the number of very high quality type designs submitted to the competition. The outstanding craftsmanship exhibited in so many of the typefaces made the selection process very difficult.

As a designer of mostly custom designs I often am faced with solving a particular typographic problem or filling a specific niche for a client. On several occasions my projects have called for matching various non-Latin scripts with a Latin designed for a corporate brand or operating system. One of the most challenging scenarios is pairing Arabic with Latin.

I can very much appreciate the difficult balancing act the designer has performed in creating a Naskh style that is appropriate for extended reading while being stylistically relevant to the Latin sans serif. Nadine's approach to Palatino Sans Arabic fills a previously empty space in the range of Arabic type designs much as Zapf's Optima did for Latin in 1958, or Goudy's Kennerly did in 1912.

An appreciation of the difficulty of the task and a recognition of the need for this style of typeface is what drew me to select the design as my judge's choice.

DESIGNER'S STATEMENT

he Palatino® Sans Arabic typeface family is a collaboration between Lebanese designer Nadine Chahine and Professor Hermann Zapf. The design is based on classical Naskh structures and proportions, with a hint of Thuluth. The forms, though, are treated as if written with a pen, rather than a reed. This results in curves that are soft, round, and friendly. It is designed for use in print, and brings into Arabic the informal and friendly appearance of Palatino Sans. The counters are wide open to allow for better readability in small sizes as well as to maintain an open and friendly appearance. Because of its classical reference, Palatino Sans Arabic is also well suited for setting spoken Arabic as well as children's books.

ا ا أ أ إ إ آ آ ب ببب ت تتت

ث ثثث ج ججج ح ححح خ

خخخ چ چچچ د ـد ذ ـذ ڈ ـڈ

ر ـر ز ـز ژ ـژ ڑ ـڑ س سسس

ش ششش ص صصص ض

ضضض ط ططط ظ ظظظ

ع ععع غ غغغ ف ففف ڤ

ڤڤڤ ق ققق ك ككك ککک

ک گ گگگ ل للل م ممم

ن ننن ه ههه ھ ہ ۂ ۃ

ة ـة و ـو ؤ ـؤ ی ئ ئئئ ي ييي

١٢٣٤٥٦٧٨٩٠

خط لحكايات الكبار والصغار

Palatino Sans Arabic

Nadine Chahine and Prof. Hermann Zapf

من ما غنّى زكي ناصيف...

حيران أينتظر؟ والقلب به ضجر

ما التلة ما القمر ما النشوة ما السهر

ان عدت الى القلق هائمة في الافق

سابحة في الشفق فهيامك لن يجدي

يا عاشقة الورد ان كنت على وعدي

فحبيبك منتظر يا عاشقة الورد

TYPEFACE Palatino Sans Arabic TYPEFACE DESIGNER Nadine Chahine and Hermann Zapf, *Bad Homburg, Germany*
FOUNDRY Linotype GmbH LANGUAGE Arabic

MATCHING
THE HATCH

NEW ENGLAND WILD FLOWER SOCIETY'S
FLORA
NOVAE
ANGLIAE
A MANUAL FOR THE IDENTIFICATION OF NATIVE AND
NATURALIZED HIGHER VASCULAR PLANTS OF NEW ENGLAND
ARTHUR HAINES
ILLUSTRATED BY ELIZABETH FARNSWORTH
AND GORDON MORRISON

DINO-RAMA
ILLUSTRATIONS BY JOHN SIBBICK
TEXT BY GEORGE SCOTT
DESIGN BY CHARLES NIX
BARNES & NOBLE · NEW YORK

PART 2
ORNITHISCHIANS
STEGOSAURS
ANKYLOSAURS
PACHYCEPHALOSAURS
ORNITHOPODS
CERATOPSIANS
PART 3
SAURISCHIANS
SAUROPODS
THEROPODS
PART 4
PTEROSAURS
PTERANODON

TDC² JUDGE

CHARLES NIX

is a partner in the publishing firm Scott & Nix Inc. and the president of the TDC. He has taught design and typography for more than fifteen years, and was Chair of Communication Design at the Parsons School of Design from 2002 until 2005, and at the Center for Advanced Design in Kuala Lumpur, Malaysia, from 1997 until 1998.

He has lectured and exhibited throughout the world, and his work is included in the permanent collection of the Smithsonian Cooper-Hewitt, National Design Museum. He has won awards from the American Association of Museums, the Art Libraries Society of North America, the Association of American University Presses, the American Institute of Graphic Arts, and the Type Directors Club. In 2005, he chaired TDC 51, an annual typography competition, and in 2004 chaired the TDC² type-design competition.

His company Scott & Nix brings detailed information to readers who want to learn about science and nature. Scott & Nix works with established publishers and also publishes projects on its own. Their clients include Alfred A. Knopf, Barnes & Noble, Bulfinch Press, HarperCollins, Johns Hopkins University Press, Lyons Press, University of California Press, Workman Publishing, and Yale University Press. Recent projects from Scott & Nix include *The Sibley Guide to Trees* by David Sibley; *The Smithsonian Field Guide to the Birds of North America* by Ted Floyd; and *Cutthroat: Native Trout of the West* by Patrick Trotter.

CHARLES NIX'S SELECTION

ames Century Modern captures the warmth and vitality of the classic metal Clarendons—Consort, Egizio, Fortune, and the outstanding Craw Clarendon. It's pleasantly soft in its serif brackets and thin-to-thick transitions, and assuredly snappy in the corners and ball-serif exits. The bowls of the roman characters are slightly squarish, but not flat, and are cleverly torqued in the italics.

In a clever twist on the idea of display styles, the designers have included alternate forms for the *c*, *g*, and *s*, with sharper serif notches for use in display settings. There are nine figure styles and support for setting in over two dozen languages, as is expected now of professional-grade OpenType fonts.

The Thin and Thin Italic are lively and charming with just enough skin on their bones to dance on the colorful side of the mono-weight line. Like all good Clarendons, its Black weight is a spirited argument between form and counter. But unlike other Clarendons, the argument goes further with form winning out in the Stencil variant (and then, to celebrate the triumph, a Stencil Cameo).

From Thin Italic to Stencil Cameo (and their cousins, Eames Poster Numbers, Ornaments, and Frames), this extended-extended family displays a curatorial inclusiveness that's truly contemporary.

But most of all, the family looks fun. It's full of verve. And in that respect, its name is quite appropriate. Like Charles and Ray Eames's work, it's modern and full of joy.

DESIGNER'S STATEMENT

harles and Ray Eames did not design a typeface, and this project was not about creating fonts that they would have drawn had they felt the need or inspiration to do so. It was about creating a tool that had the same universal appeal as monuments to the Eames aesthetic, many of which have been so ingrained in our visual landscape that we barely notice them. Eames Century Modern is crafted in this vein; its dignified legibility effectively transmits the message without overpowering the medium, while devilishly intoxicating details in words, letters, serifs, spaces, stems, and tapers find their way into the subconscious of even the most casual observer. Much like waiting in a departure lounge on Eames system airport seating, you don't know why you're comfortable; you just are.

EAMES

GÊNIO? QUE NADA!

the little toy

1932

artifacts

Naugahyde

901 Washington Blvd.

JUDGE'S CHOICE

TYPEFACE Eames Century Modern TYPEFACE DESIGNER Erik van Blokland, *The Hague* FOUNDRY House Industries, *Yorklyn, Delaware*
MEMBERS OF TYPEFACE FAMILY/SYSTEM Regular, Regular Italic, Book, Book Italic, Light, Light Italic, Thin, Thin Italic, Medium, Medium Italic, Bold, Bold Italic, Extra Bold, Extra Bold Italic, Black, Black Italic, Stencil, and Stencil Cameo

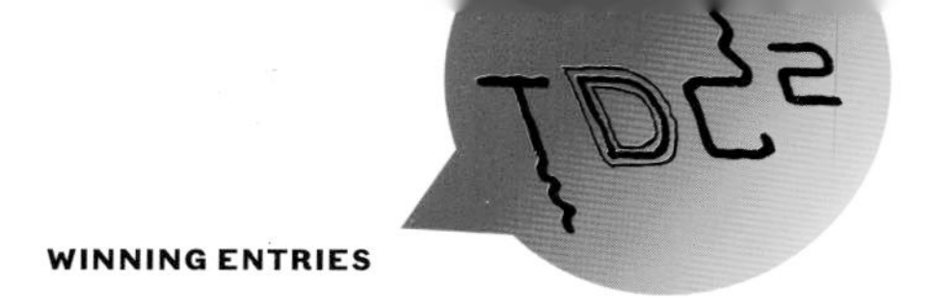

TUNDRA

By LUDWIG ÜBELE, Letter-Founder, WWW.LUDWIGUEBELE.DE

Quousque tandem abutere, Catilina, patientia nostra? Nihilne te nocturnum praesidium Palati, nihil urbis vigiliae, *nihil timor populi, nihil concur sus bonorum omnium, nihil hic munitissimus haben*

Quousque tandem abutere, Catilina, pati entia nostra? Nihilne te nocturnum prae sidium Palati, nihil urbis vigiliae, nihil ti mor populi, *nihil concursus bonorum omni um, nihil hic munitissimus habendi senatus locus, nihil horum ora voltusque move runt?*

Quousque tandem abutere, Catilina, patientia nostra? Nihilne te nocturnum praesidium Pala ti, nihil urbis vigiliae, *nihil timor populi, nihil con cursus bonorum omnium, nihil hic munitissimus ha*

Quousque tandem abutere, Catilina, pat ientia nostra? Nihilne te nocturnum pra esidium Palati, nihil urbis vigiliae, nihil timor populi, *nihil concursus bonorum om nium, nihil hic munitissimus habendi senat us locus, nihil horum ora voltusque move ru*

Quousque tandem abutere, Catilina, patientia nostra? Nihilne te nocturnum praesidium Pala ti, nihil urbis vigiliae, *nihil timor populi, nihil con cursus bonorum omnium, nihil hic munitissimus ha*

Quousque tandem abutere, Catilina, pat ientia nostra? Nihilne te nocturnum pra esidium Palati, nihil urbis vigiliae, nihil timor populi, *nihil concursus bonorum om nium, nihil hic munitissimus habendi senat us locus, nihil horum ora voltusque move ru*

Quousque tandem abutere, Catilina, patientia nostra? Nihilne te nocturnum praesidium Pala ti, nihil urbis vigiliae, *nihil timor populi, nihil con cursus bonorum omnium, nihil hic munitissimus*

Quousque tandem abutere, Catilina, pat ientia nostra? Nihilne te nocturnum pra esidium Palati, nihil urbis vigiliae, nihil timor populi, *nihil concursus bonorum omnium, nihil hic munitissimus habendi senatus locus, nihil horum ora voltusque*

Quousque tandem abutere, Catilina, patientia nostra? Nihilne te nocturnum praesidium Pala ti, nihil urbis vigiliae, *nihil timor populi, nihil co ncursus bonorum omnium, nihil hic munitissim*

Quousque tandem abutere, Catilina, pa tientia nostra? Nihilne te nocturnum praesidium Palati, nihil urbis vigiliae, nihil timor populi, *nihil concursus bono rum omnium, nihil hic munitissimus hab endi senatus locus, nihil horum ora voltu*

Quousque tandem abutere, Catilina, patientia nostra? Nihilne te nocturnum praesidium Pal ati, nihil urbis vigiliae, *nihil timor populi, nihil concursus bonorum omnium, nihil hic munitis*

Quousque tandem abutere, Catilina, patientia nostra? Nihilne te nocturnu praesidium Palati, nihil urbis vigiliae, nihil timor populi, *nihil concursus bon orum omnium, nihil hic munitissimus habendi senatus locus, nihil horum ora*

TYPEFACE Tundra
TYPEFACE DESIGNER Ludwig Übele, *Berlin*
FOUNDRY FontFont
MEMBERS OF TYPEFACE FAMILY/SYSTEM Regular, Regular Italic, Light, Light Italic, Extralight, Extralight Italic, Medium, Medium Italic, Demibold, Demibold Italic, Bold, and Bold Italic

Tundra is a narrow running typeface with warm, curvaceous letterforms. To avoid a fence-effect caused by the narrowness, Tundra emphasizes the horizontal line with strong serifs and flat shoulders. The bold and open terminals help also to guide the eye along the line and therefore ease the reading. Tundra contains a big set of characters and comes in six weights from Extralight to Bold.

Amalta

* *

The quick brown fox jumps over the lazy dog!

чёрный кофе

Съешь этих мягких французских булок, да выпей чаю!

Barbara, Theobald, Eddy

gŕåçhì přilètêlĩ

всего лишь 840 снегирей и 526 синиц

* * * * * * * * * © Vera Evstafieva * * * * * * * * *

Amalta is a display typeface with calligraphic background. It inherits weight and letter constructions from the original brush lettering. Amalta's Latin and Cyrillic sets were designed simultaneously with an equal attention to details and overall pattern. They both include initial and final swash forms, which can be used as a typographer chooses. Amalta is suitable for large size typesetting headlines, few-line texts, etc.

TYPEFACE Amalta
TYPEFACE DESIGNER Vera Evstafieva, *Moscow*
FOUNDRY Infonta
LANGUAGES Latin and Cyrillic

ا آ أ إ ا آ أ إ ب ببب ب ت تتت ت ث ثثث ث ج ججج ج ح ححح ح خ خخخ خ د
ذ ر ز س سسس س ش ششش ش ص صصص ص ض ضضض ض ط ططط
ظ ظظظ ظ ع ععع ع غ غغغ غ ف ففف ف ق ققق ق ك ككك ك ل للل ل م ممم م
ن ننن ن ه ههه ه ة ة و لا لآ لأ لإ لا لآ لأ لإ ي ييي ي ئ ئ ء
١٢٣٤٥٦٧٨٩٠ . ... ! ؟ :

ثريا خط ديواني

يا إلهي!

حكي قرايا وحكي سرايا

انت ملئ الأماني

دعوني أجود على حبيبي الوحيد

الملهى الليلي

كان يا ما كان في قديم الزمان أمير صغير وحيد

حبيب القلب

TYPEFACE Thuraya Regular
TYPEFACE DESIGNER Kristyan Sarkis, *Beirut, Lebanon*
FOUNDRY Typotheque, www.typotheque.com
LANGUAGES Arabic

Thuraya is an Arabic display typeface that explores a contemporary context for the complex Diwani style with maximized calligraphic features. The research focused on the meeting point between calligraphy and type within a digital type environment and questioned the possibility of compromises on one account or the other. The completely curved baseline, the horizontally slanted letters, and the extended character set including ligatures and alternates, which are crucial for a harmonious calligraphic flow, are characteristics that define Thuraya. It is mainly intended for lettering purposes, headlines, logotypes, and short texts.

HORROR STORIES OF DATA LOSS

Exotic Writers

MONUMENTAL STENOGRAPHIC PROCEDURE

Shearling

valley of the kings

Amber Hues

Tinted

QUESTIONS ABOUND

Blickensfer Manufacturing Company

Shift is inspired by American slab-serifs from the late 19th century. In its lighter weights, it takes on the personality of a typewriter face, with flared terminals and prominent serifs. In the heavier weights, it acts as a titling Egyptian, with thin spaces between characters and small counters. Designed as a display face, it also works well for text.

TYPEFACE Shift TYPEFACE DESIGNER Jeremy Mickel, *Providence, Rhode Island* FOUNDRY Mickel Design MEMBERS OF TYPEFACE FAMILY/SYSTEM Extralight, Extralight Italic, Light, Light Italic, Book, Book Italic, Medium, Medium Italic, Bold, Bold Italic, Black, and Black Italic

KUNSTMUSEUM ZÜRICH

Ausstellungseröffnung am 25. November 1963

Leipziger Grotesk

Supria Sans™ is an extended family of 36 fonts. It contains two widths, six weights and three styles, *including the curvy, feminine Italic as well as the more conventional Oblique.* Although it is inspired by the utilitarian clarity of Swiss type design, subtle curves and fine detailing impart a more playful character to the whole Supria Sans family.

OPERNHAUS

5th Architecture Conference

TYPEFACE Supria Sans
TYPEFACE DESIGNER Hannes von Döhren, *Berlin*
FOUNDRY HVD Fonts
MEMBERS OF TYPEFACE FAMILY/SYSTEM Light, Light Italic, Light Oblique, Regular, Regular Italic, Regular Oblique, Medium, Medium Italic, Medium Oblique, Bold, Bold Italic, Bold Oblique, Heavy, Heavy Italic, Heavy Oblique, Black, Black Italic, Black Oblique, Condensed Light, Condensed Light Italic, Condensed Light Oblique, Condensed Regular, Condensed Regular Italic, Condensed Regular Oblique, Condensed Medium, Condensed Medium Italic, Condensed Medium Oblique, Condensed Bold, Condensed Bold Italic, Condensed Bold Oblique, Condensed Heavy, Condensed Heavy Italic, Condensed Heavy Oblique, Condensed Black, Condensed Black Italic, Condensed Black Oblique

Supria Sans™ is an extended family of 36 fonts designed by Hannes von Döhren. It contains two widths, six weights, and three styles, including the curvy, feminine Italic as well as the more conventional Oblique. Although it is inspired by the utilitarian clarity of Swiss type design, subtle curves and fine detailing impart a more playful character to the whole Supria Sans family.

Supria Sans™ Condensed is the second component of the Supria type system. Encompassing the same six weights and three styles as Supria Sans, and characterized by the same approach to the modernist source material, this condensed set of fonts is 20% narrower than the normal version, allowing for significant space saving economies. Used together, Supria Sans and Supria Sans Condensed become much more than just a versatile and functional workhorse—ideal for resolving complex design issues with elegance and sophistication.

Ranking hawaiian sumo wrestler

Asashio

has again been performing brilliantly

In the New Year

GRAND SUMO TOURNAMENT

was named Saturday to be the recipient of the Award for

outstanding

Asashio was promoted to *komusubi* in May 1980 and *sekiwake* in July 1980. In November 1981 he lost a playoff for the tournament championship to new *yokozuna Chiyonofuji*. He was runner-up to *Chiyonofuji* once again in May 1982 and to *Kotokaze* in January 1983.

In the poll of sumo aficionados

TAMANOUMI WAS HONORED FOR HIS COURAGEOUS EFFORTS

JOINING TAKASAGO

Suhmo is inspired by classic Egyptian and typewriter fonts such as Courier and American Typewriter, which feature headline and text use. This impressive duality was a guideline for the concept. At the same time, many formal details were derived from the typical neon lettering you can find on aged Italian restaurants in Germany. Suhmo has short ascenders and descenders and a generous x-height, making it a good choice for editorial design. It combines simplicity and functionality with playfulness, offering interesting details such as loops and swashes and a slight stroke contrast. Its varied details are unobtrusive in text sizes while developing character and sparkle in headlines. Suhmo's extensive character set includes numerous special characters and ligatures, several figure sets, and small caps throughout all styles. The Suhmo family consists of four weights: Light, Regular, Bold, and Black, each with an Italic. The weights were staggered to complement each other within a layout, the Black corresponding to the Regular and the Light corresponding to the Bold weight, allowing words or phrases to be clearly stressed within a text. The Italics are lighter than the Roman and have a relatively slight angle of slope. The forms are derived from a manual writing process and often cross the base-line or the x-height.

TYPEFACE FF Suhmo
TYPEFACE DESIGNER Alex Rütten, *Berlin*
FOUNDRY FSI Font Shop International
MEMBERS OF TYPEFACE FAMILY/SYSTEM Regular, Regular Italic, Light, Light Italic, Bold, Bold Italic, Black, and Black Italic

ニュース

迷子の子ネコちゃん、あなたのお家はどこですか。
お家を聞いても分からない。名前を聞いても分からない。

にゃんにゃんにゃにゃーん、泣いてばかりいる子ネコちゃん。
犬のおまわりさん、困ってしまってワンワンワワーン。

迷子の子ネコちゃん、この子のお家はどこですか。
カラスに聞いても分からない。すずめに聞いても分からない。

にゃんにゃんにゃにゃーん、泣いてばかりいる子ネコちゃん。
犬のおまわりさん、困ってしまってワンワンワワーン。

迷子の子ネコちゃん、
あなたのお家はどこですか。
お家を聞いても分からない。
名前を聞いても分からない。

にゃんにゃんにゃにゃーん、
泣いてばかりいる子ネコちゃん。
犬のおまわりさん、
困ってしまってワンワンワワーン。

迷子の子ネコちゃん、
この子のお家はどこですか。
カラスに聞いても分からない。
すずめに聞いても分からない。

にゃんにゃんにゃにゃーん、
泣いてばかりいる子ネコちゃん。
犬のおまわりさん、
困ってしまってワンワンワワーン。

TYPEFACE News
TYPEFACE DESIGNER Aki Toyoshima, *New York*
FOUNDRY FONT1000
LANGUAGE Japanese
MEMBERS OF TYPEFACE FAMILY/SYSTEM Regular, Light, Medium, and Bold

This font conveys a more joyful expression that I really want to tell.

Take my camel, dear

Vaughan died yesterday in his last car-crash.

Spitzbogenfenster

together with his wife and four friends

Towers of Trebizond

curling flower spaces

no doubt of his sex

Quo usque tandem abutere,

Nottinghamshire

For a long time, I went to bed early.

Wolkenkuckucksheim

Daisy started with the lowercase *c*. I liked the idea that the counter consisted only of a thin line, which basically defines the drop shaped terminal. Most extreme heavy typefaces are sans serifs without any contrast. But would it also be possible to create an extreme fat typeface based on classic old face letterforms? Since the counter forms are fixed by the thin line, other factors like line thickness and letter width must be more flexible in order to create a harmonious alphabet. Ligatures and alternates expand the typographic possibilities.

TYPEFACE Daisy

TYPEFACE DESIGNER Ludwig Übele, *Berlin*

FOUNDRY www.ludwiguebele.de

MEMBERS OF TYPEFACE FAMILY/SYSTEM Regular and Italic

matrona
very
black
textures
to fill the space
matrona
black

www.hubertjocham.de matrona

TYPEFACE Matrona
TYPEFACE DESIGNER Hubert Jocham, *Lautrach, Germany*
FOUNDRY Hubert Jocham Type

When letterpress started with the Gutenberg Bible, the typeface was like a texture. Before humanism, type did not really need to be legible. The letters were rather drawn in an ornamental way. It filled a space. My idea for Matrona was to create a similar structure. I wanted it to be very bold and still as legible as possible. The result was a headline typeface that can fill spaces. You can even fill it with a picture. Or you create an ornament with contents. There are three weights to extend the usage to different sizes.

05246
81&93
6!35€
12930
€2874
4513$
6?921

The Eames Poster Numerals are numerological necessities punctuated with a pulchritudinous parade of pachydermic power whose circusized woodcut-inspired shapes were drawn in three stackable weights and boast a broad range of color choices limited only by the imagination, RGB or CMYK spectra, and the availability of custom pigmented emulsions.

TYPEFACE Eames Poster Numerals
TYPEFACE DESIGNER Erik van Blokland, *The Hague*
FOUNDRY House Industries, *Yorklyn, Delaware*

 TYPEFACE Nori
TYPEFACE DESIGNER Neil Summerour, *Jefferson, Georgia*
FOUNDRY Positype

Nori is a hand-lettered typeface that contains over 1,100 glyphs, 250 ligatures, 487 alternate characters, 125 swash and titling alternates, lining, and old style numerals. I do not use digital textures. It is the result of brush and ink on paper. The textures produced in each glyph are real and the imperfections are intentional and add to the sincerity of the letters. To view the words and sentences formed by this typeface is to look at how my hand makes letters. The fluidity, as well as the irregularity, is human, honest, and intentional. To do so lets the brush I am holding breathe life into each letter. Once digital, any number of points and repetitive processes can't mask its influences—and I like that.

0123456789

Tabati started with the story of a little red ball and its escapades in a world populated by circular *sh*, triangular trees, rectangular buses, and square rocks. It is an experiment in abstraction, simplicity, and legibility. Tabati presents an alternative reading of the Arabic alphabet through the basic geometric shapes or masses it defines rather than the lines it traces on paper.

TYPEFACE Tabati
TYPEFACE DESIGNER Lara Assouad Khoury, *Beirut, Lebanon*
CLIENT Dar Onboz Publishing
LANGUAGES Arabic

k
@
2/3
w
x
4

ft
7
v
ä
E
¶

Mehr Obatzda

A GOOD POEM SHOULD BE READ SLOWLY

(As refreshing as that old Biergarten after a long Alpine hike)

Die Macht der Gedanken

Reclaiming Craft: New Blackletter with Small Caps + Italic

Käsekreiner or Fancy Soufflé Restaurant

RIESLING / SCHNAPPS / KÖLSCH / ALTBIER / HELLES / MAIBOCK

Westpark 28, München?

Vítejte v Pivovaru a restauraci u Fleků. Once Upon a Crème Pâtissière

A Contemporary Fraktur with Depth

Schweinsteiger, Özil and Müller during the World Cup. Hours of fondue on New Years. Robert picking mushrooms in the woods near Augsburg in the cold fall rain. Homemade Spätzle from scratch next to a warm wood fire. Growing our first (and only) tomato off our small balcony. Discovering pumpkin seed oil. A first edition of a Luther Bible printed by Hans Lufft. Seeing the Lesesaal in Wien. Lindsay's blaue Augen.

25

"JUST AS ARCHITECTURE REFLECTS THE FULL BREADTH OF A PERIOD AND THE EXTERIOR LIFE OF A PEOPLE, SO DOES SCRIPT REFLECT THEIR INTERIOR VOLITION, DELIVERING THEIR PRIDE AND HUMILITY, SELF-CONFIDENCE AND DOUBT." —PETER BEHRENS

&

Augustiner | Liebe | {Kalligrafie} | Buch

Enzian: Regular | REGULAR SMALL CAP | **Bold** | **BOLD SMALL CAP** | *Italic*

TYPEFACE Enzian
TYPEFACE DESIGNERS Jason Mannix and Lindsay Mannix, *Washington, D.C.*
DESIGN FIRM Polygraph
MEMBERS OF TYPEFACE FAMILY/SYSTEM Regular (with small caps), Bold (with small caps), and Unconventional Italic

Enzian is the product of a German research fellowship sponsored by the Alexander von Humboldt Foundation. We set out with two goals: to better understand the technical nuance and complicated history of German Blackletter and produce an original typeface inspired by our findings. During our research, we discovered the extraordinary collections of the libraries in Munich, Nuremberg, and Vienna, and developed a humble appreciation for the craft of calligraphy. The result is a versatile Blackletter with uncommon depth, hand-influenced letterforms, and, hopefully, a bit of charm.

Photographic

ONE-LINER

decorative

NEW YORK DODGERS

MYSTERY

216 East 45th Street, NYC

BENGUIAT & Co

Que Cerá Cerá

Originally designed by Paul Carlyle in the early 1940s, Eventide was added to the Photo-Lettering, Inc., film library in 1971 as a single-layer caps-only style. House Industries' philosophy for the new Photo-Lettering service is to reinterpret the original designs, making them more useful for contemporary designers. We reimagined the alphabet to work in eight layers that can be combined or used independently, and expanded the character set to include a lowercase, punctuation, symbols, and a full complement of Central European accented characters.

TYPEFACE Eventide
TYPEFACE DESIGNER Jeremy Mickel, *Providence, Rhode Island*
ART DIRECTORS Ken Barber and Christian Schwartz
FOUNDRY Photo-Lettering, Inc. / House Industries
CLIENT Photo-Lettering, Inc., www.photolettering.com
MEMBERS OF TYPEFACE FAMILY/SYSTEM Banner, Diagonal, Dots, Fill, Highlight, Horizontal, Vertical, and Stroke

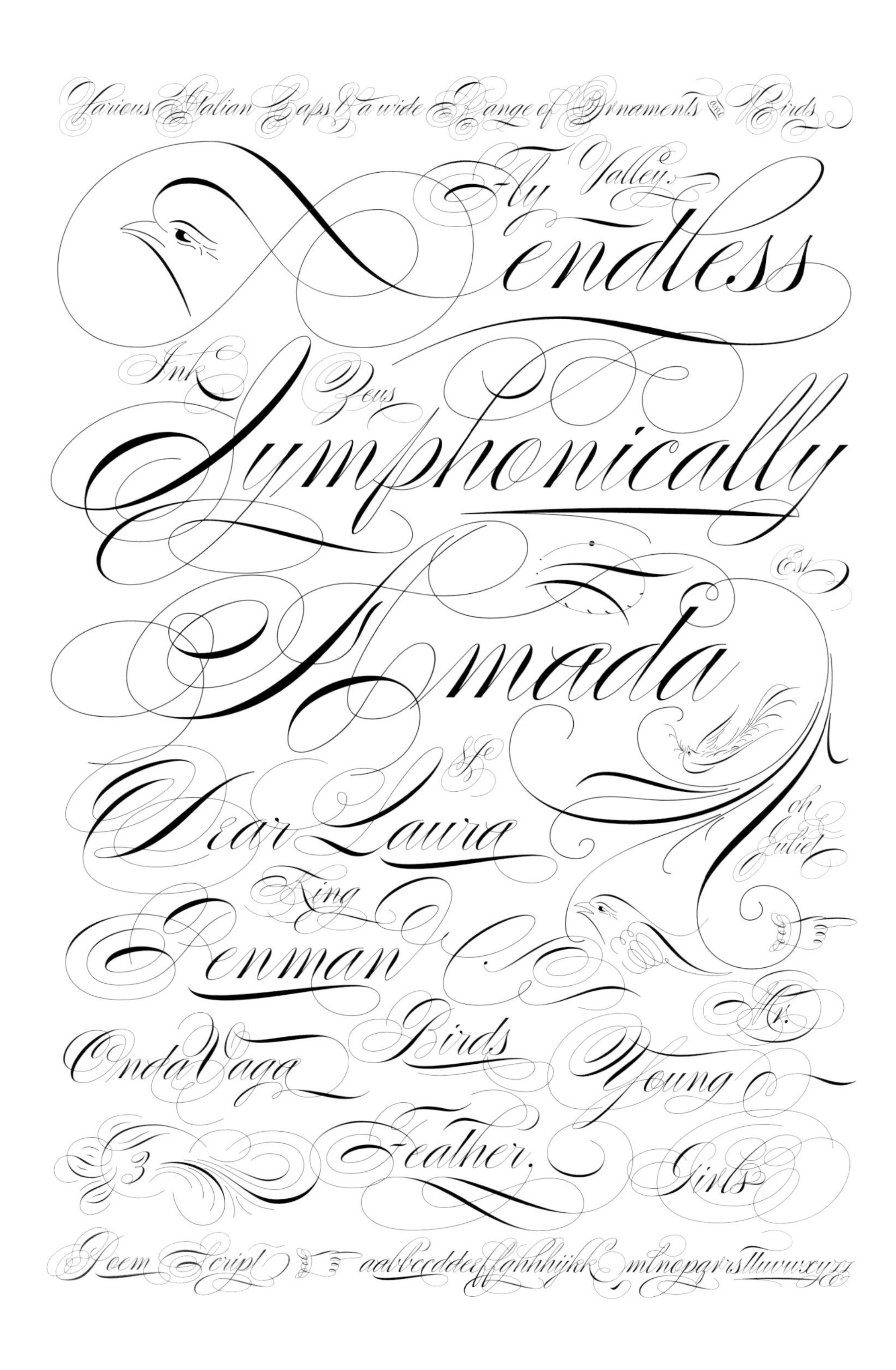

TYPEFACE Poem Script
TYPEFACE DESIGNER Alejandro Paul,
Buenos Aires, Argentina
FOUNDRY Sudtipos

Poem Script is a mixed collection of interpretations conjuring a late nineteenth century American pen script style. Though not an actual Italian letterform, this style was called Italian Alphabet, stemming from an old penman's term for an alphabet where the stress or shades are opposite their normal placement.

The American variant followed from the late eighteenth century British hand also confusingly called Italian Hand, which itself evolved from some seventeenth century French Batarde scripts.

It showcases the phenomenal control and mastery of hand skills required to create such ornamental and lively letters centuries ago. Producing the shaded strokes in these reversed positions required holding the pen in a position horizontal to the baseline, or the letterforms would have to be written backwards or by rotating the paper at peculiar and extreme angles to achieve the effect.

Exotic, elaborate, and very attractive, Poem Script contains plenty of variations on each letter and comes with hundreds of calligraphic ornaments.

Elegy was the most difficult design job I've ever done in my life. Since its release in August 2010, Elegy has been very well received. It is based on the original ITC logo designed by Ed Benguiat in 1970. The typeface is modeled after American Spencerian Script styles of penmanship developed by Platt Rogers Spencer in the early nineteenth century done with a pointed spring steel pen nib. The typeface has a modern look to it utilizing drop caps, flourishes, and details Benguiat incorporated in the original logo. Because of its fine qualities, recommended usage is at display sizes of 24 point and above. The design would be a perfect fit for printed invitations, logotypes, signage, packaging, and any other application where an elegant and unique Round Hand Script is desired. OpenType support has been added for old style figures, arbitrary fractions, proportional numbers, tabular numbers, discretionary ligatures, and contextual alternates. For the features of the typeface to work correctly, Elegy must be used in an OpenType savvy page layout application such as Adobe InDesign.

TYPEFACE Elegy
TYPEFACE DESIGNER Jim Wasco, *Redwood City, California*
FOUNDRY Monotype Imaging, *Woburn, Massachusetts*

MOVIE TITLE DESIGN

CHAIRMAN'S STATEMENT

Consider it. Envision it. Need it. Pick it. Type it. Kern it. Touch it. Analyze it. Change it. Like it. Size it. Move it. Rotate it. Reject it. Restart it. Reinvent it. Feel it. Animate it. Love it. Submit it. Judge it. Admire it. Award it.

This is the second year of TDC Intro and once again we had an amazing amount of fantastic work to look through. The judges worked hard to analyze every aspect of the work, and there were many spirited conversations about the state of titles today. Both the creative expression and the arc of storytelling were in focus, and we are happy to announce this year's winners, who deserve all praise for their excellent work.

—Jakob Trollbäck

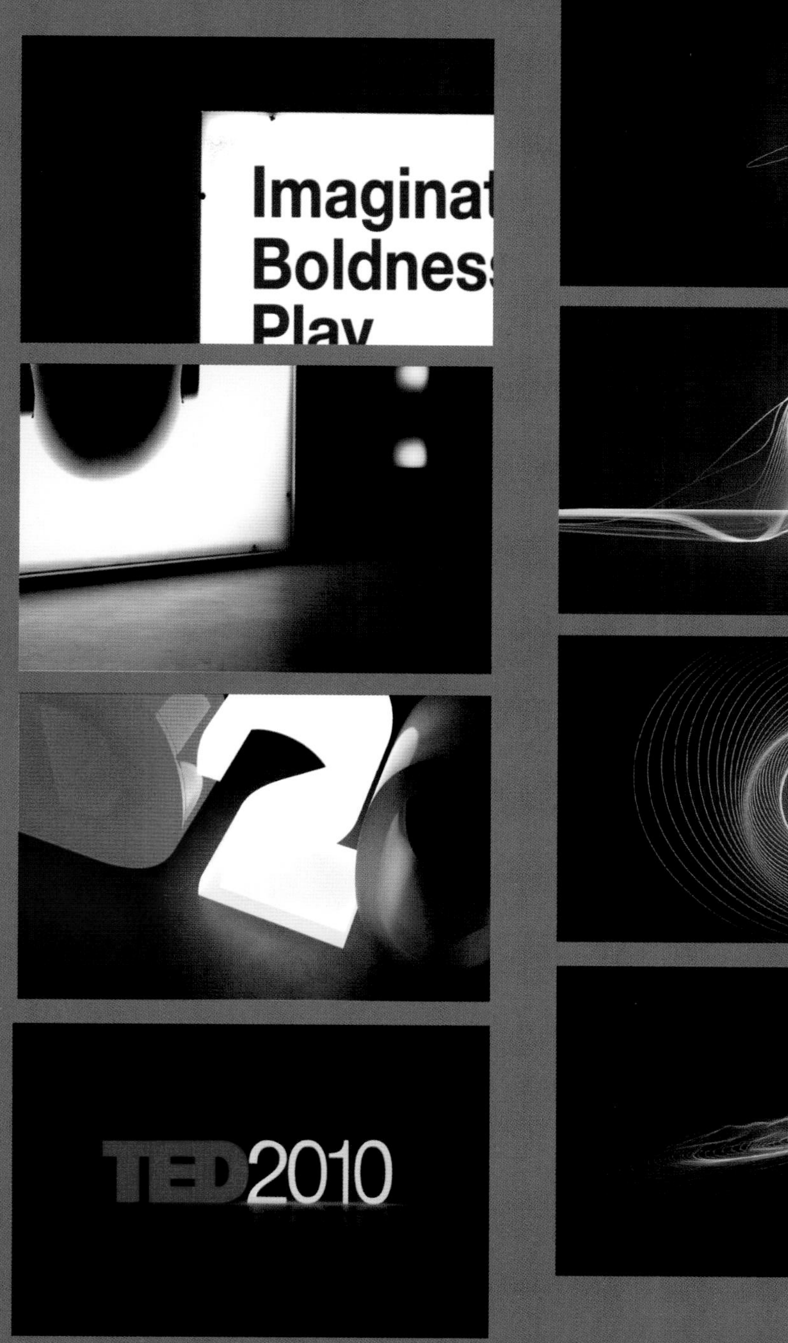

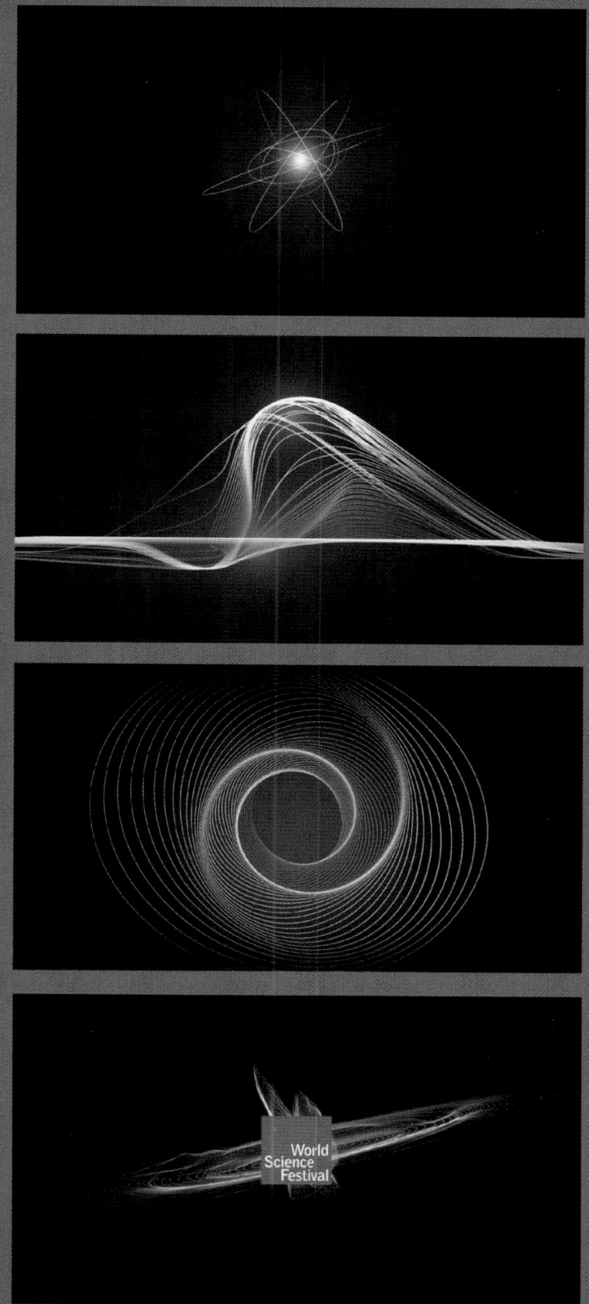

TDC INTRO CHAIR

JAKOB TROLLBÄCK

A self-taught DJ-turned-designer from Sweden, Jabok Trollbäck is an acknowledged leader in branding and motion graphic design. He is the founder and executive director of the New York–based Trollback + Company, a visual and conceptual creative studio producing expressive and purposeful graphics, design, and live action for advertising, broadcast, and entertainment.

30ROCK

TRUE GRIT

TDC INTRO JUDGE

RANDY BALSMEYER

Randy Balsmeyer grew up in southern California and attended college at UC Irvine, the USC School of Architecture, and the CalArts Design School. He began working in animation and title design at Alpha Cine FX in Seattle, winning a regional Emmy for *The Tut Minutes*. He moved to New York and joined R/Greenberg Associates in 1980, designing and directing title sequences for such films as *The World According to Garp* and *Ragtime*. In 1986, he and his wife-to-be, Mimi Everett, started their own design and effects boutique, Balsmeyer & Everett, Inc. They made a name for both their title design work (*Do the Right Thing*) and their innovations in visual effects (the world's first portable motion control camera for *Dead Ringers* and *Ghost*). Their early clients included Spike Lee, Errol Morris, and David Cronenberg. Randy and Mimi were featured in *Premiere* magazine's "It List" and mentioned for "Oscar categories that ought to exist but don't (title design). " They won numerous awards for their work, including a New York Film Festival Award for *M. Butterfly* and a Daytime Emmy for the opening for *Sesame Street* (1992), in which Randy directed both children and Muppets. Along the way, Mimi and Randy added two daughters to their family.

Mimi left the company in 2000 to become a full-time mom. Randy transformed the company from a traditional animation and opticals operation to an all-digital post-production house. Big Film Design (BFD!) was born and the tradition of innovation continued. Randy won more Daytime Emmys for directing title sequences for *Sesame Street* (2002) and *Between the Lions* (2001). In 2003 he won a Gold Medal in the Creativity 33 Show for the main title sequence for *Chicago*, and in 2004 his title design work was featured in a full-page retrospective in the Sunday *New York Times* and he won an Art Directors Club Silver Cube for designing the title sequence for *Intolerable Cruelty*. He was also nominated for an Emmy for creating the opening to Mike Nichols's *Angels in America*. He continues to design and direct title sequences for feature films (*True Grit*) and television (*30 Rock*). He also supervises and produces visual effects for films, such as *Burn After Reading*, *Revolutionary Road*, and *The Adjustment Bureau*, and he has done second unit directing and shooting for films such as *Factory Girl* and *Dear John*. He continues to partner with the most amazing filmmakers in the world, including Woody Allen, Joel and Ethan Coen, Jim Jarmusch, Spike Lee, Sam Mendes, and Mike Nichols. As Director of Transitions for *New York, I Love You*, he combined all his design, storytelling. and filmmaking talents to create a common thread to link and cross-pollinate the separate-but-connected segments.

In short, Randy loves filmmaking in all its forms: designing, directing, shooting, and post-production.

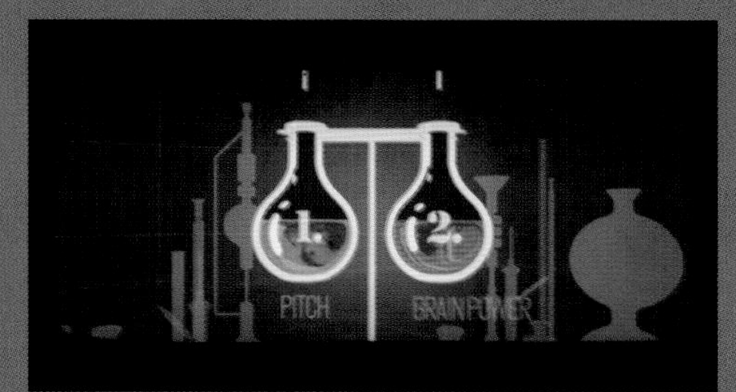

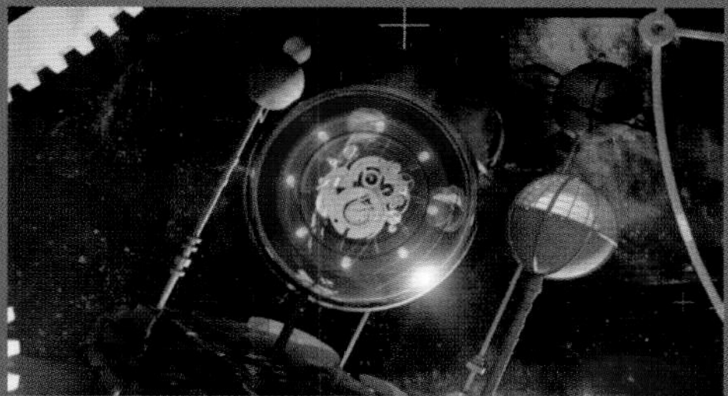

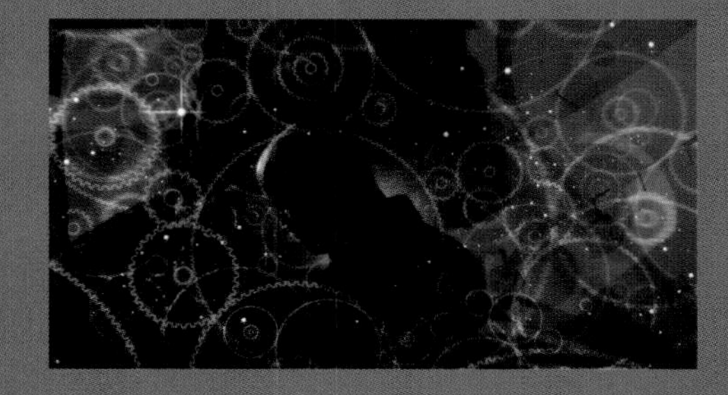

TDC INTRO JUDGE

TIMMY FISHER

Timmy Fisher is a co-founder of MK12, a design and filmmaking collective acclaimed in both commercial and artistic arenas. Founded in 2000, MK12 constantly challenges the boundaries between narrative structure and experimental storytelling via juxtapositions of live action, graphic design, nostalgic influence, and new technologies. MK12 has been sought after to direct numerous commercial and network-based projects, and has also provided graphic design, animation, and film titles for feature films such as *Stranger than Fiction*, *The Kite Runner*, and *Quantum of Solace*. Their latest short film, *TELEPHONEME*, screened at many film festivals, including The Atlantic Film Festival, OneDotZero Film Festival, and AFI Fest.

TDC INTRO JUDGE

MARK KUDSI

As a director and creative director at Motion Theory, Mark Kudsi's impressively wide-ranging experience in different media has helped him to create an inspired array of work—from live-action and integrated VFX commercials to full animation and design-oriented projects.

Mark has directed award-winning projects and campaigns for clients including Microsoft, Google, Reebok, Sears, and John Hancock, all of which stand as testaments to Mark's distinct ability to augment live action material by putting design principles in motion.

Mark is a Grammy winner, and his work has been recognized by numerous publications and organizations including the AICP, Art Directors Club, Clios, and AIGA.

For more information, please visit http://www.motiontheory.com.

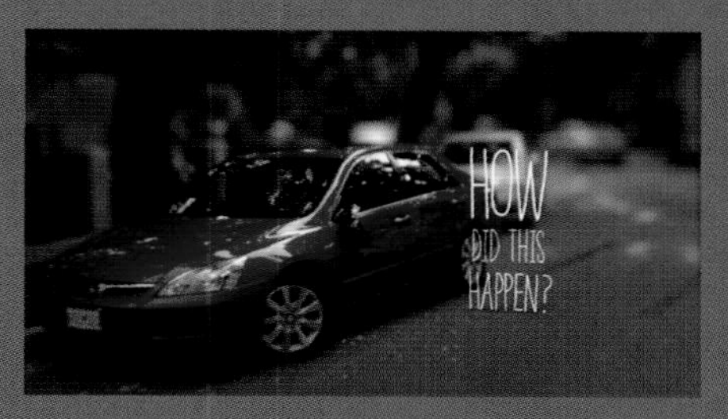

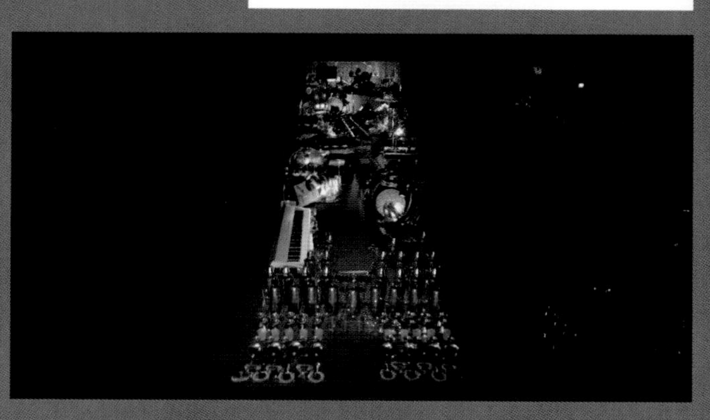

WINNING ENTRIES

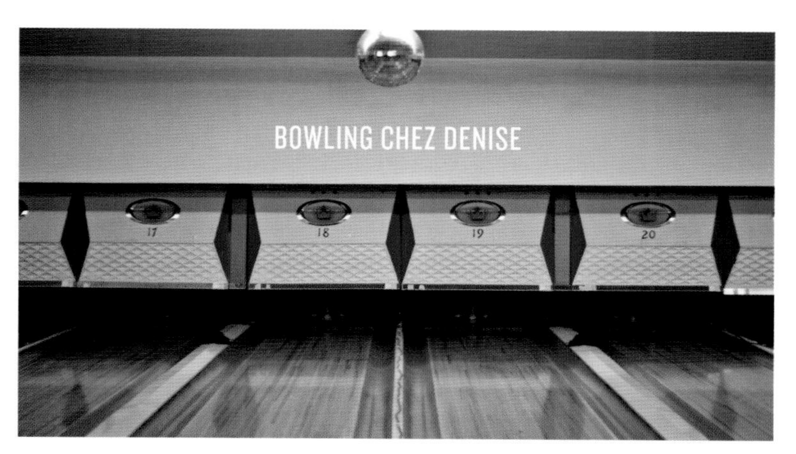

TITLE *Bowling chez Denise* DESIGN Justin Lorie, *Montréal* SCHOOL Université du Québec à Montréal (UQAM) INSTRUCTOR Denis Dulude
PRINCIPAL TYPE Knockout No. 28 Junior Featherweight PRODUCTION TOOLS Adobe After Effects

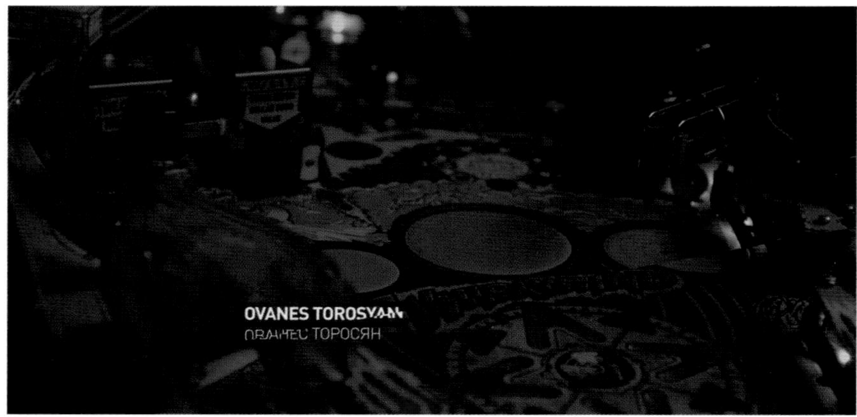

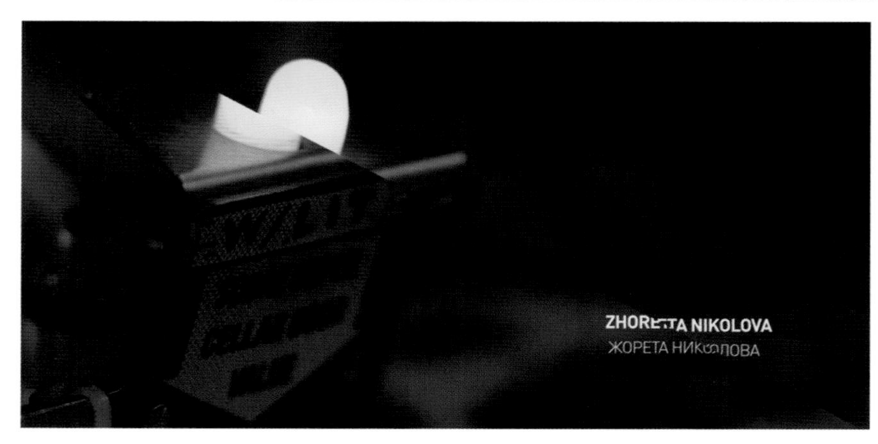

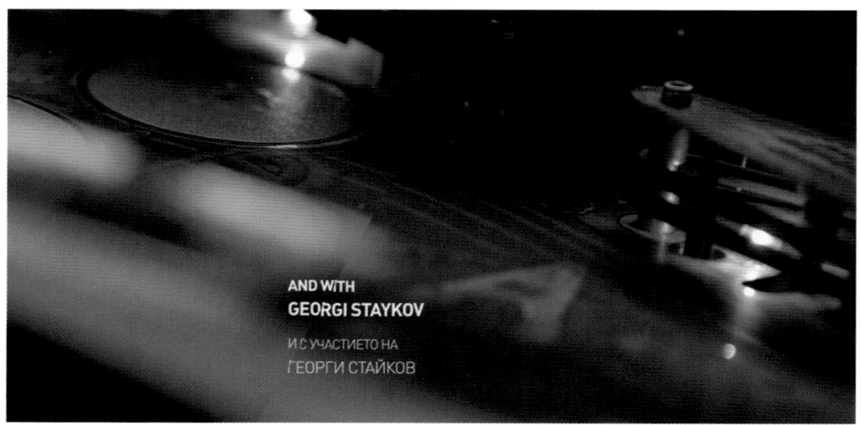

 FEATURE FILM Typography, *Honorable Mention*

TITLE *Tilt* DESIGN Maxim Ivanov, *Sofia, Bulgaria* ART DIRECTION Maxim Ivanov PRODUCER The Chouchkov Brothers
PRINCIPAL TYPE Din Cyrillic Bold and Din Cyrillic Light PRINCIPAL TOOLS Adobe After Effects, Final Cut Pro, and Adobe Illustrator

TITLE *Into the Woods* Motion Graphics ART DIRECTION Britta Johnson and Dave Peacock, *Seattle* ANIMATION Britta Johnson
CLIENT American Institute of Graphic Arts, *Seattle* PRINCIPAL TYPE custom PRODUCTION TOOLS Adobe After Effects, Dragon Stop Motion, and Final Cut Pro

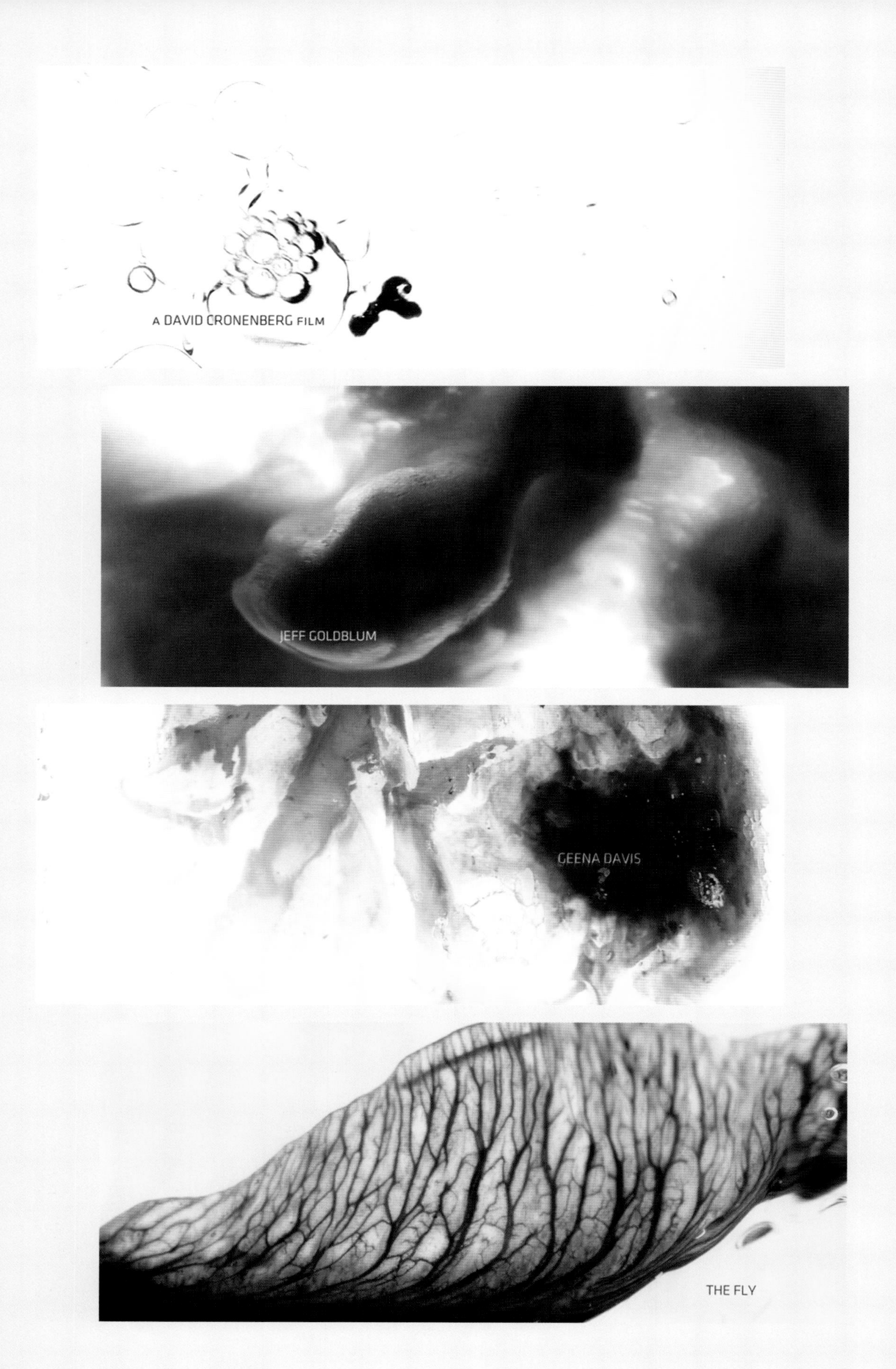

 FEATURE FILM Student, *Honorable Mention*

TITLE *The Fly* DESIGN Doug Chang, *Pasadena, California* SCHOOL Art Center College of Design INSTRUCTOR Kaan Atilla PRINCIPAL TYPE Klavika
PRODUCTION TOOLS Adobe After Effects, Apple Motion, Canon 20D, Canon 5D, Fine Cut Pro, Adobe Illustrator, Photoshop, and 50mm Macro Lens

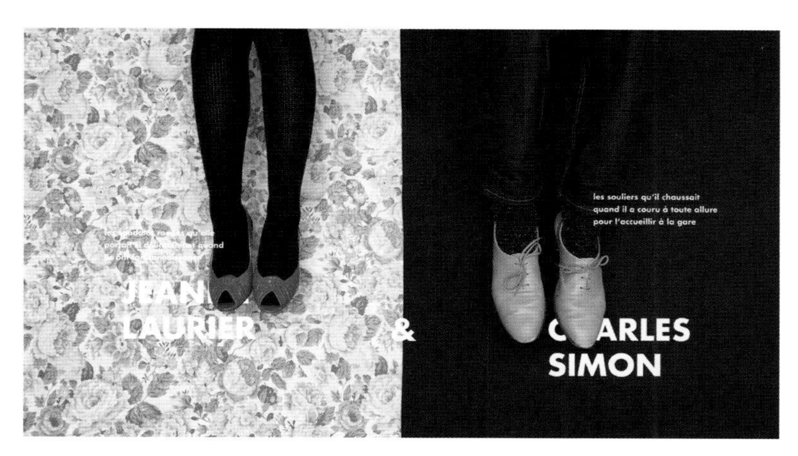

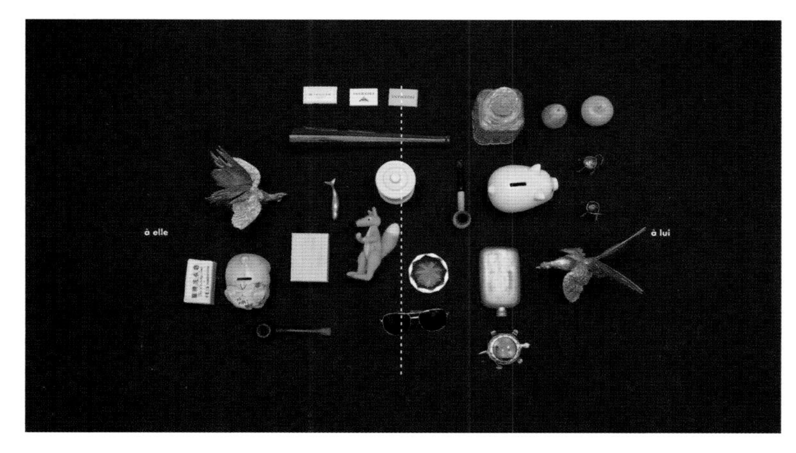

TITLE *Les grands lendemains* DESIGN Nadine Brunet, *Montréal* SCHOOL Université du Québec à Montréal (UQAM) INSTRUCTOR Denis Dulude
PRINCIPAL TYPE Futura PRODUCTION TOOLS stop motion photography

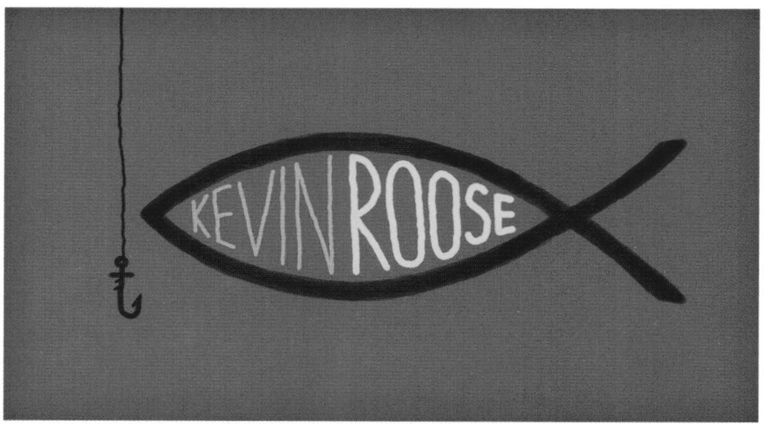

300 EVENTS Animation, *Honorable Mention*

DESIGN Guillaume Alix, *New York* CREATIVE DIRECTION Scott Matz and Justin Meredith LETTERING Kyle Miller MUSIC AND SOUND DESIGN Michael Montes ANIMATION Keith Endow, Ken Krueger, Jaehyuck Lee, Dan Savage, and Rachel Yonda DESIGN OFFICE Thornberg & Forester CLIENT GEL Conference 2010 PRINCIPAL TYPE handlettering PRODUCTION TOOLS Adobe After Effects and Photoshop

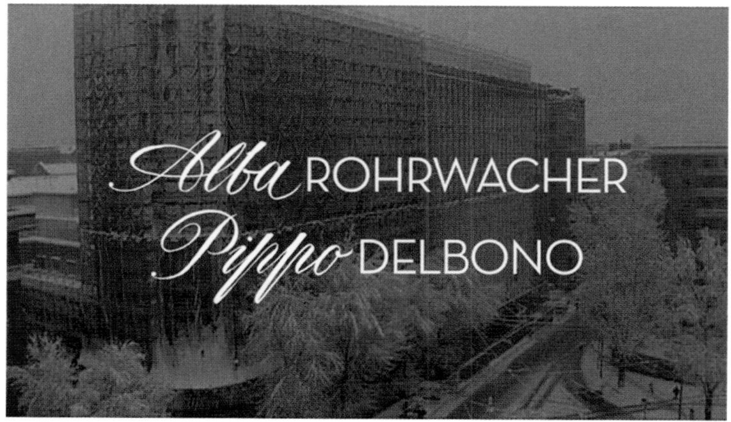

TITLE *Io Sono l'Amore* ART DIRECTION Marco Cendron, *Milan* LETTERING Luca Barcellona ICONOGRAPHIC RESEARCH Alessandro Cavallini
AGENCY POMO CLIENT Firstsun–Mikado PRINCIPAL TYPE Neutraface and handlettering PRODUCTION TOOLS Adobe Creative Suite

 FEATURE FILM Student, *Honorable Mention*

TITLE *The Imaginarium of Doctor Parnassus* DESIGN Eunji Kim, *New York* SCHOOL School of Visual Arts, *New York* INSTRUCTOR Ori Kleiner
PRINCIPAL TYPE Knockout No.47 Bantamweight and Mesquite PRODUCTION TOOLS Adobe After Effects and Corel Painter

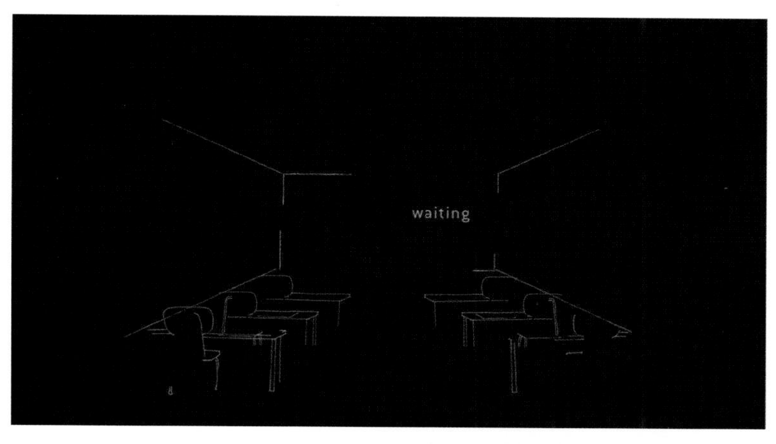

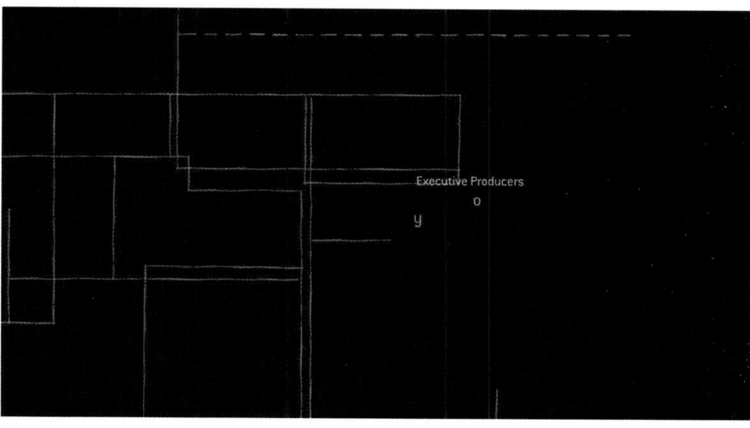

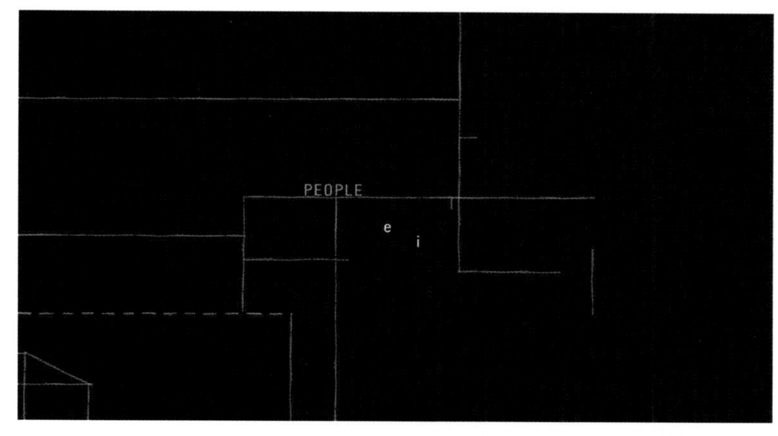

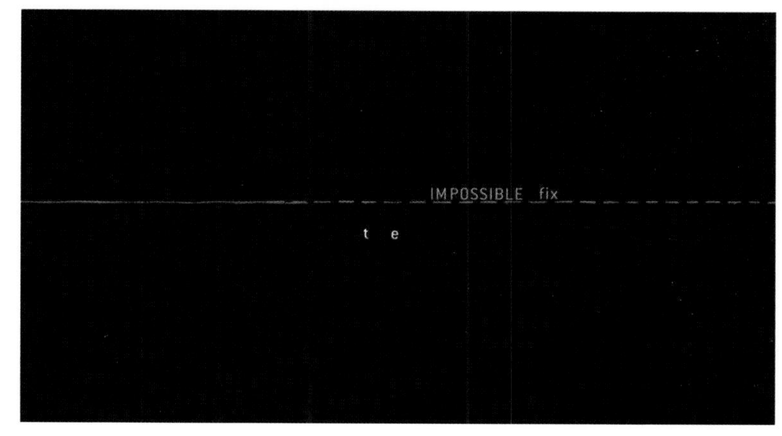

TITLE *Waiting for Superman* DESIGN Edwin Baker, Gary Garza, and Etsuko Uji, *Los Angeles* ART DIRECTION Garson Yu CREATIVE DIRECTION Garson Yu DESIGN OFFICE yU+co CLIENT Public Education Picture PRINCIPAL TYPE ITC Conduit PRODUCTION TOOLS Adobe After Effects, Adobe Illustrator, and Photoshop

nsemble × Braun Tube Project

JUKU

Maki Nomiya

HIFANA × Daito Manabe + Motoi Ishibashi

Takamasa Aoki

Fuyuki Yamakawa

TITLE Harajuku Performance + 2010 DESIGN Masayoshi Kodaira, *Tokyo* ART DIRECTION Masayoshi Kodaira EDITOR Masaaki Takakura PRODUCER Yasuo Ozawa and Japan Performance/Art Institute DESIGN OFFICE FLAME, Inc. CLIENT LAFORET HARAJUKU PRINCIPAL TYPE ITC Century and custom PRODUCTION TOOLS Adobe After Effects, Final Cut, and Adobe Illustarator

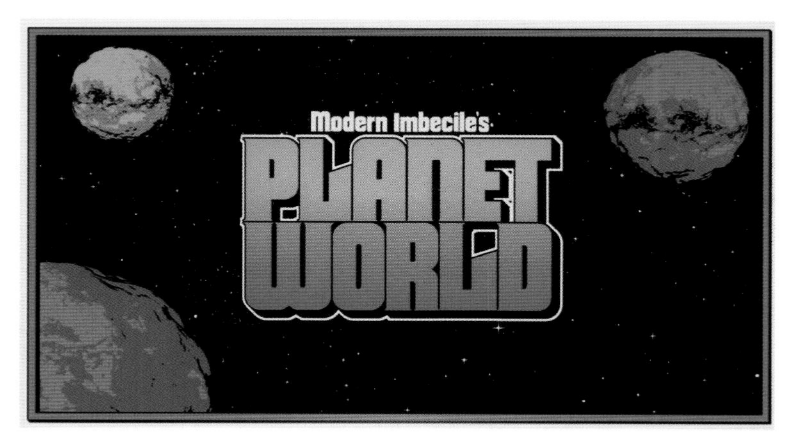

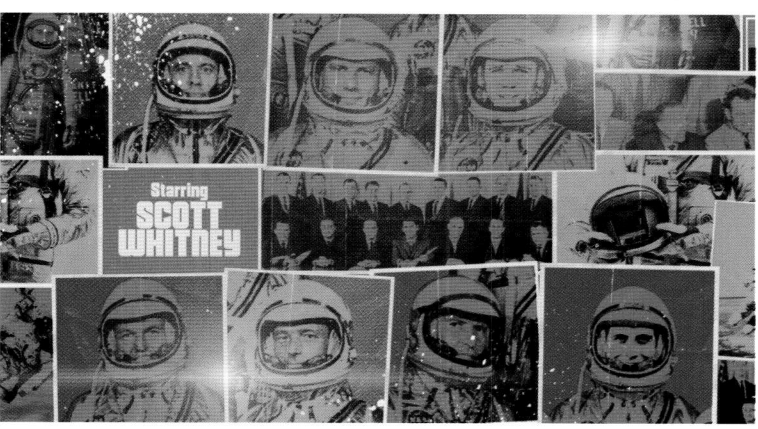

TITLE *Modern Imbecile's Planet World* DESIGN Mark Butchko, *Chicago* STUDIO Lamesville PRINCIPAL TYPE Othello
PRODUCTION TOOLS Adobe After Effects, Cinema 4D, and Adobe Illustrator

ORIGINALLY PUBLISHED IN 1962, DESIGNED BY PAUL RAND

8TH ANNUAL AWARDS : THE NEW YORK TYPE DIRECTORS CLUB

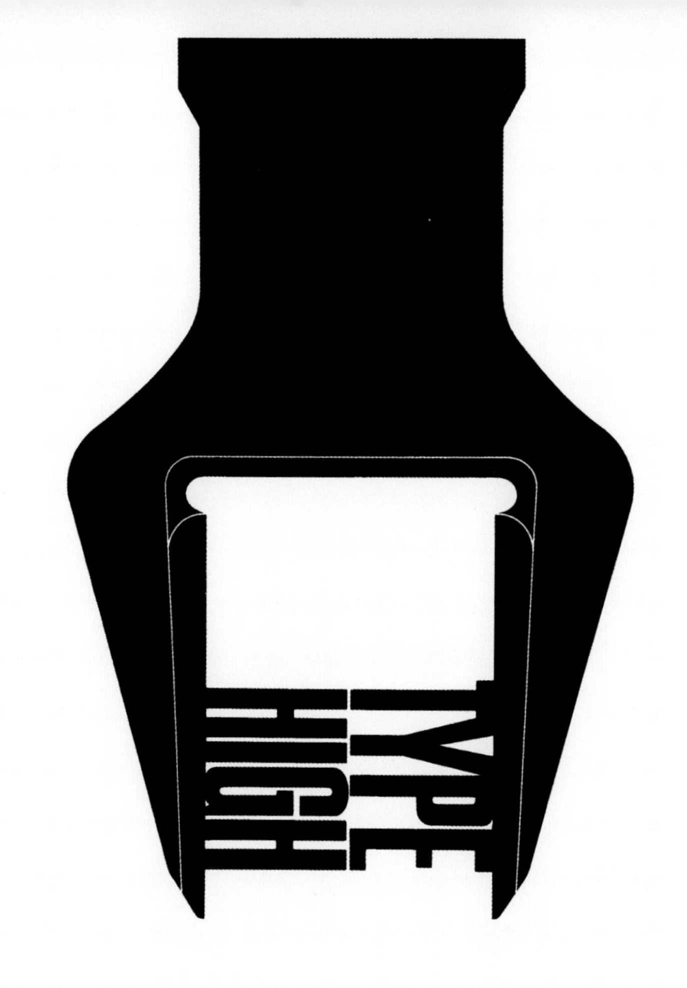

8TH ANNUAL AWARDS : THE NEW YORK TYPE DIRECTORS CLUB

An astute, sensitive and renowned jury selected 214 pieces of the 2300 submitted from the United States and Canada.

THE JURY:

Robert Sutter	Jury Chairman
Milton K. Zudeck	Art Director-Typographer, McCann-Erickson, Inc.
Henry Wolf	Art Director, Show Magazine
Oscar Ogg	Vice President & Art Director, Book-of-the-Month-Club, Inc.
Paul Rand	Designer

Thank You.

The response to our annual call was heartfelt and gratifying.

It has proved that the TDC has an organic "outer" life, as well as a life of its own. All of you who are not members—the contributors and winners—as well as those of you whose work has not been selected for presentation, comprise the "outer" life of our ideology and endeavor.

Thus, we can present to the public the outstanding professional work done throughout the United States and Canada. Our show will travel, and we hope it will come to your city, so that you can point with eagerness and pride to the accomplishments of artisans at work in one of the finest expressions of the art field... typography in design.

We are at a pinnacle. Today we call our level "TYPE-HIGH," tomorrow it will be higher—but we must work and experiment and strive.

In the near future, we would like to show work done by students of typography in design, from the United States, Canada, and from all over the world.

New expressions will appear on the horizon, enabling us to judge the entire, unlimited scope of our medium on a worldwide basis; from the novices and from the experts. Exhibits of this nature will also aid significantly in international relations.

EDGAR J. MALECKI

1
Designer: Abe Seltzer/Howard Menken
Type Director: Tom Carnese
Client / Agency: Abe & Judith Seltzer
Typographer: Composition Service, Inc.

2
Designer: Tony Mandarino
Type Director: Tony Mandarino
Client / Agency: Holiday Magazine
Typographer: Atlas Typographic Services, Inc.

3
Designer: Joe Weston
Type Director: Joe Weston
Client / Agency: Advertising Designers, Inc.
Typographer: Saul Marks, The Plantin Press

4
Designer: Milton Ackoff
Client / Agency: Westinghouse Electric Corp.
Typographer: Kurt H. Volk, Inc.

5
Designer: Joseph A. Watson
Type Director: Joseph A. Watson
Client / Agency: The Carborundum Company
Typographer: The J. W. Ford Company
Cincinnati, Ohio

6
Designer: Robert M. Jones
Type Director: Robert M. Jones
Client / Agency: Robert M. Jones
Typographer: Robert M. Jones

7
Designer: Barry Steinman, Jerry Litofsky
Type Director: Frank Wojcicki Jr.,
Beverly Golbin,
John Matt, Howard Sperber
Client / Agency: Pratt Institute
Typographer: Prattonia

8
Designer: Peter Bradford
Type Director: Peter Bradford
Client / Agency: Museum of Modern Art
Typographer: Clarke & Way, Inc.

9
Designer: Edward Nussbaum
Type Director: Edward Nussbaum
Client / Agency: Nussbaum Family
Typographer: Empire Typographers, Inc.

10
Designer: Joseph Schindelman
Type Director: Joseph Schindelman
Client / Agency: CBS Television Network
Typographer: Typography Place, Inc.

1

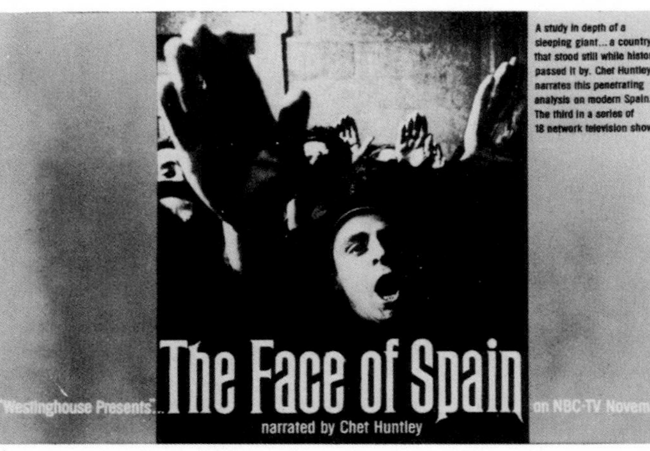

4

1961

7

2

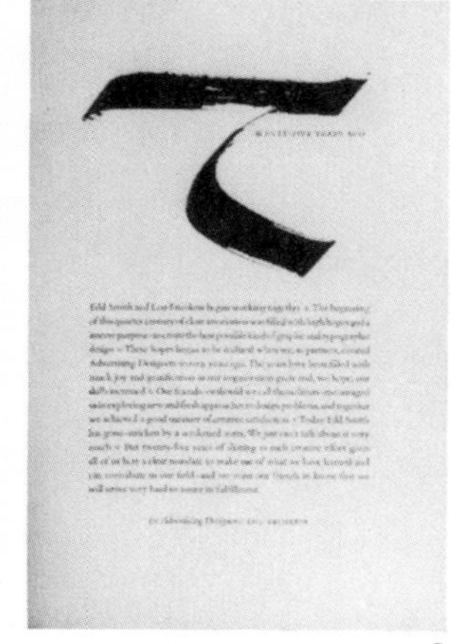

3

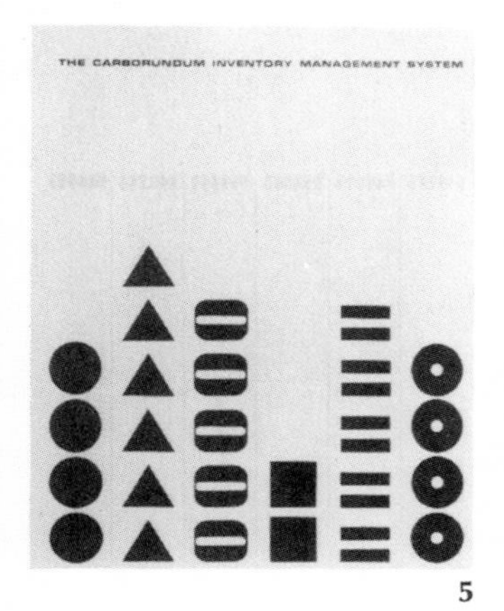

5

PROGRESS

100 YEARS AGO TODAY:
AUGUST 5th, 1861
For the first time in history,
the United States levied a tax
on incomes -- 3 per cent on all
income in excess of $800.00

THE GLAD HAND PRESS
R.M. Jones, prop., An Ugly American

6

8

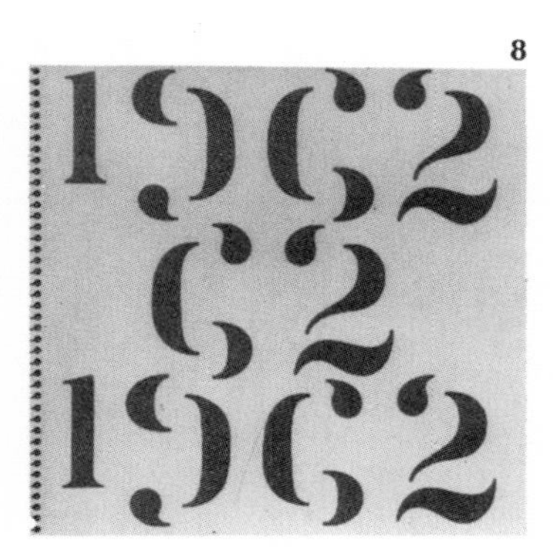

9

10

11

Designer:	Mort Rubenstein
Type Director:	Mort Rubenstein
Client/Agency:	WCBS-TV
Typographer:	Typography Place, Inc.

12

Designer:	Mo Lebowitz
Type Director:	Mo Lebowitz
Client/Agency:	The Antique Press
Typographer:	Mo Lebowitz

13

Designer:	Rene H. Bittel
Type Director:	Rene H. Bittel
Client/Agency:	Rover Motor Co./ Sudler & Hennessey Inc.

14

Designer:	Mike Parker
Type Director:	Jackson Burke
Client/Agency:	Mergenthaler Linotype Co.
Typographer:	Mergenthaler Linotype Co.

15

Designer:	Alan J. Klawans
Type Director:	J. C. Caldwell
Client/Agency:	Smith Kline & French
Typographer:	W. T. Armstrong, Inc.

16

Designer:	Carl Brett
Type Director:	Carl Brett
Client/Agency:	Howarth & Smith
Typographer:	Howarth & Smith Monotype Limited

17

Designer:	Andrew Ross
Type Director:	Andrew Ross
Client/Agency:	Metro Typographers Inc.
Typographer:	Metro Typographers Inc.

18

Designer:	Allan R. Fleming
Type Director:	Allan R. Fleming
Client/Agency:	Cooper & Beatty, Limited
Typographer:	Allan R. Fleming

19

Designer:	James P. Camperos
Type Director:	James P. Camperos
Client/Agency:	Mr. & Mrs. J. Camperos
Typographer:	Advertising Composition Inc.

20

Designer:	Peter Bradford
Type Director:	Peter Bradford
Client/Agency:	Whitney Publications
Typographer:	The Composing Room, Inc.

21

Designer:	Seymour Chwast/Milton Glaser
Type Director:	Seymour Chwast/Milton Glaser
Client/Agency:	Push Pin Studios Inc.
Typographer:	Weltz Ad Service

11

14

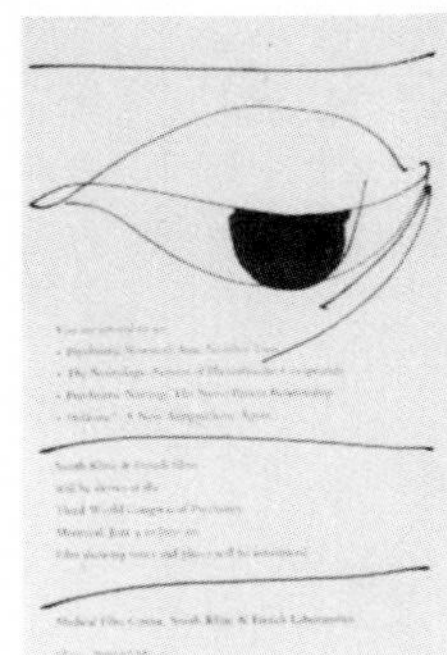

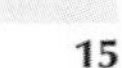

15

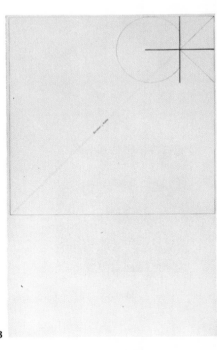

18

12

13

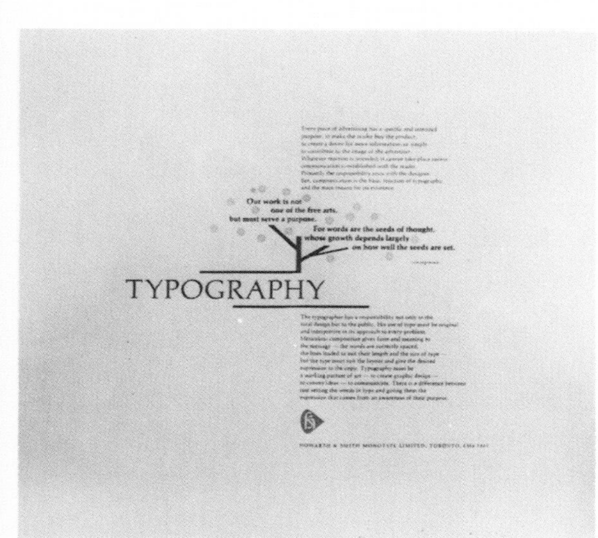

16

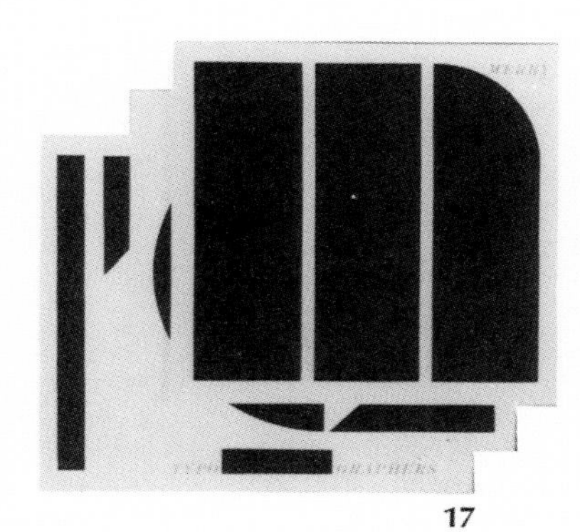

17

19

PRODUCTS &
PACKAGES:
A YEAR OF
INDUSTRIAL
DESIGN

20

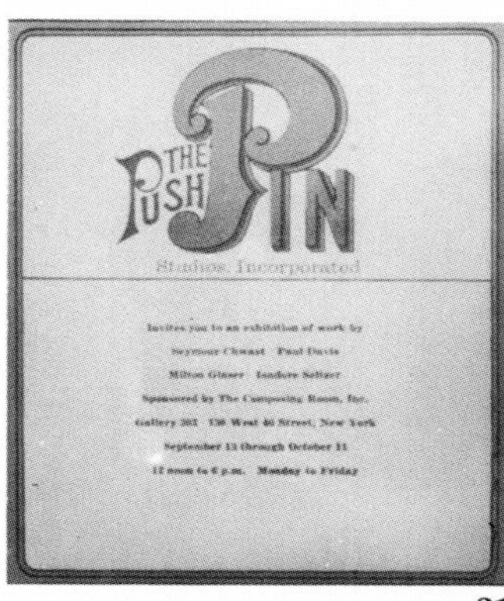

21

22

Designer: Chermayeff & Geismar/Ivan Chermayeff/Gene Sercander
Type Director: Gene Sercander
Client/Agency: Chermayeff & Geismar Associates
Typographer: Haber Typographers, Inc.

23

Designer: Jacqueline S. Casey and Ralph M. Coburn
Type Director: Jacqueline S. Casey and Ralph M. Coburn
Client/Agency: M.I.T. Centennial Committee M.I.T. Office of Publications
Typographer: Machine Composition Company

24

Designer: Chermayeff & Geismar Associates/Ivan Chermayeff
Type Director: Ivan Chermayeff
Client/Agency: Howard Wise Gallery

25

Designer: Kurt Lowey Malcolm Mansfield
Type Director: Malcolm Mansfield
Client/Agency: Vogue Magazine-Condé Nast Publications
Typographer: Typographic Service Co.

26

Designer: Robert M. Jones
Type Director: Robert M. Jones
Client/Agency: Robert M. Jones
Typographer: Robert M. Jones

27

Designer: William Cadge
Type Director: Verdun P. Cook
Client/Agency: Redbook Magazine
Typographer: The Composing Room, Inc.

28

Designer: Gennaro Andreozzi
Type Director: Burt Purmell
Client/Agency: Bernhard Altmann/Gilbert Advertising Agency Inc.
Typographer: Provident Typographers, Inc.

29

Designer: Herb Reade
Type Director: Herb Reade
Client/Agency: Glamour Magazine-Business Image
Typographer: Master Typo, Inc.

30

Designer: Bevans, Marks & Barrow
Type Director: Bevans, Marks & Barrow
Client/Agency: Mr. Boston Distiller Inc.
Typographer: Westcott & Thompson, Inc.

31

Designer: George Giusti
Type Director: R. A. Freiman
Client/Agency: Random House
Typographer: Kurt H. Volk, Inc.

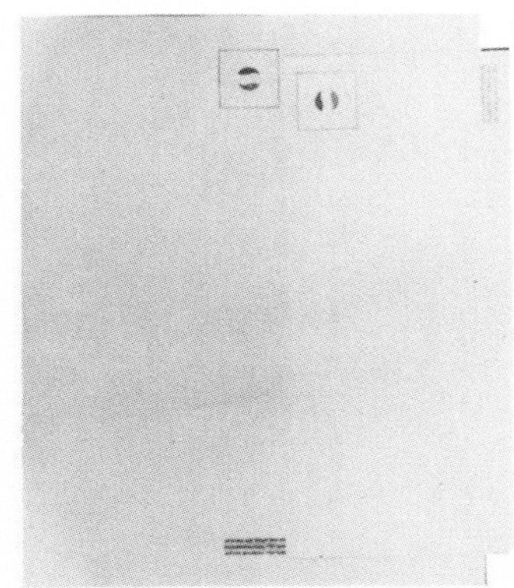

22

23

25

28

24

26

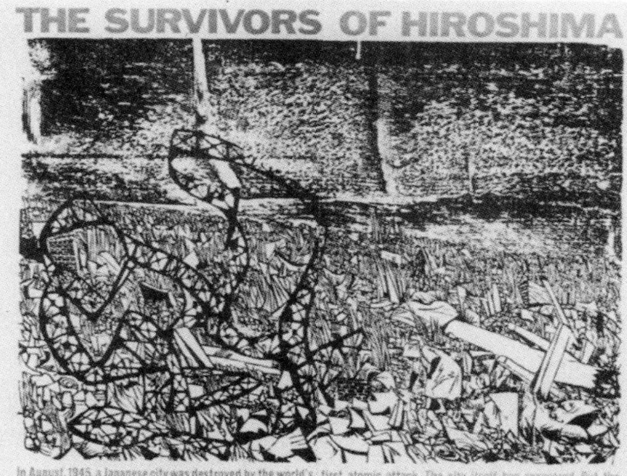

27

29

30

31

32

Designer: Allen F. Hurlburt
Type Director: Allen F. Hurlburt
Typographer: Riegert & Kennedy

33

Designer: Tony Mandarino
Type Director: Tony Mandarino
Client / Agency: Cunard Eagle Airways
Keyes Madden & Jones
Typographer: Graphic Arts Typographers, Inc.

34

Designer: John J. J. Janos
Type Director: John J. J. Janos
Client / Agency: Everett Hoffman
Typographer: John J. J. Janos

35

Designer: T. R. Stumpf
Type Director: T. R. Stumpf
Client / Agency: Standard Oil Company (N. J.)
Typographer: Huxley House, Ltd.

36

Designer: Dan Cromer
Type Director: William Sekuler
Client / Agency: Western Union
Typographer: Frederick W. Schmidt, Inc.

37

Designer: Ed and Jane Bedno
Type Director: Ed and Jane Bedno
Client / Agency: Ed and Jane Bedno
Typographer: Runkle, Thompson & Kovats

38

Designer: Jim Comperas
Type Director: Jim Comperas
Client / Agency: Lithographix, Inc.
Typographer: Lithographix, Inc.

39

Designer: Philip Gips
Type Director: Philip Gips
Client / Agency: Life En Espanol
Typographer: Haber Typographers, Inc.

40

Designer: Bernie Zlotnick/Rene Bittel
Type Director: Bernie Zlotnick
Client / Agency: Holiday Magazine/
Sudler & Hennessey, Inc.

41

Designer: Cristos Gianakos
Type Director: Cristos Gianakos
Client / Agency: Associated Design
Typographer: Linocraft Typographers, Inc.

32

35

36

39

40

33

CUNARD
EAGLE
SUNSET
FLIGHTS
NEW YORK
$85*
round trip
BERMUDA
CUNARD EAGLE AIRWAYS

34

37

Oh
tidings
of
Comfort

38

LITHOGRAPHIX, INC.
LITHOGRAPHIX, INC.

41

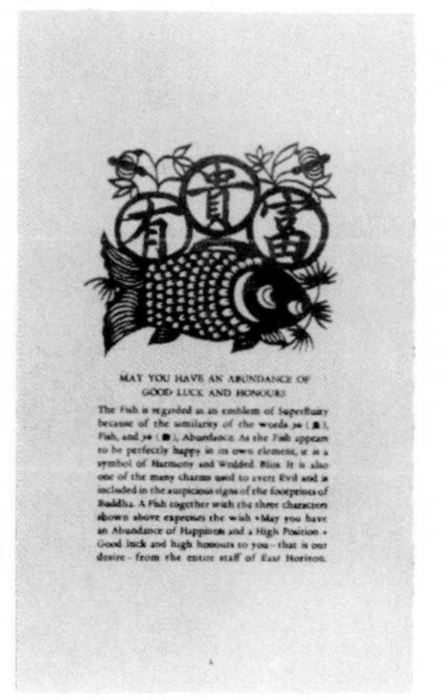
有
貴
富
MAY YOU HAVE AN ABUNDANCE OF
GOOD LUCK AND HONOURS
The Fish is regarded as an emblem of Superfluity because of the similarity of the words yu ( ), Fish, and yu ( ), Abundance. As the Fish appears to be perfectly happy in its own element, it is a symbol of Harmony and Wedded Bliss. It is also one of the many charms used to avert Evil and is included in the auspicious signs of the footprints of Buddha. A Fish together with the three characters shown above expresses the wish »May you have an Abundance of Happiness and a High Position.« Good luck and high honours to you – that is our desire – from the entire staff of East Horizon.

42

Designer:	Mo Lebowitz
Type Director:	Mo Lebowitz
Client /Agency:	The Antique Press
Typographer:	Mo Lebowitz

43

Designer:	Herbert Lubalin
Type Director:	W. J. Bailey
Client /Agency:	The Saturday Evening Post
Typographer:	Curtis Publishing Co.

44

Designer:	Clarence Lee
Type Director:	Clarence Lee
Client /Agency:	IBM
Typographer:	Diamant Typographic Service, Inc.

45

Designer:	Giovanni Pintori
Type Director:	Florence Bezrutczyk
Client /Agency:	Underwood Corp.
Typographer:	Harry Silverstein, Inc.

46

Designer:	Richard F. Lopez
Type Director:	Richard F. Lopez
Client /Agency:	M. Velazquez, Inc./R. F. Lopez
Typographer:	Graphic Arts Typographers, Inc.

47

Designer:	Aaron Burns
Type Director:	Aaron Burns
Client /Agency:	Graphic Arts Typographers, Inc.
Typographer:	Graphic Arts Typographers, Inc.

48

Designer:	Bill Weber/Franz F. H. Wagner
Type Director:	Franz F. H. Wagner
Client /Agency:	General Dynamics/ D'Arcy Advertising Co.
Typographer:	The Composing Room, Inc./ Advertising Agencies' Service Co., Inc.

49

Designer:	Felix Beltran
Type Director:	Felix Beltran
Client /Agency:	Puerto Rican Fair
Typographer:	Photo-Lettering, Inc.

50

Designer:	James Cross
Type Director:	James Cross
Client /Agency:	Northrop Corporation
Typographer:	Nicholas-Preston Co.

42

45

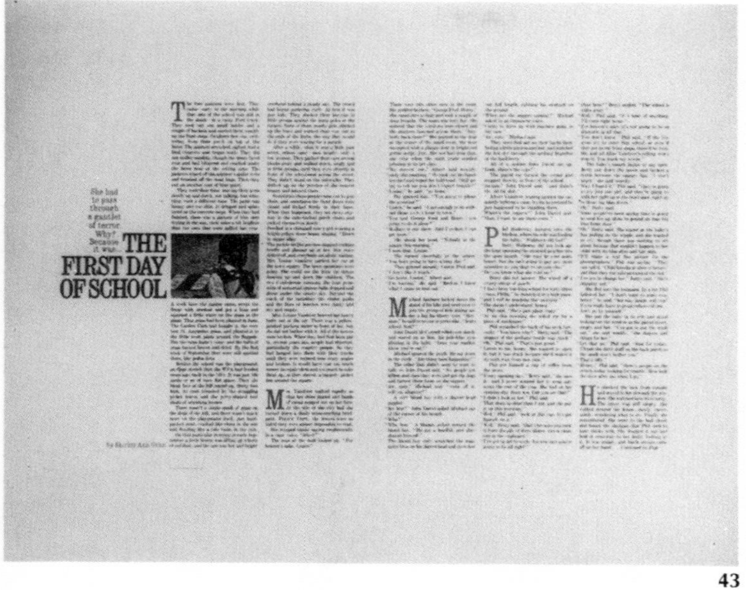

43

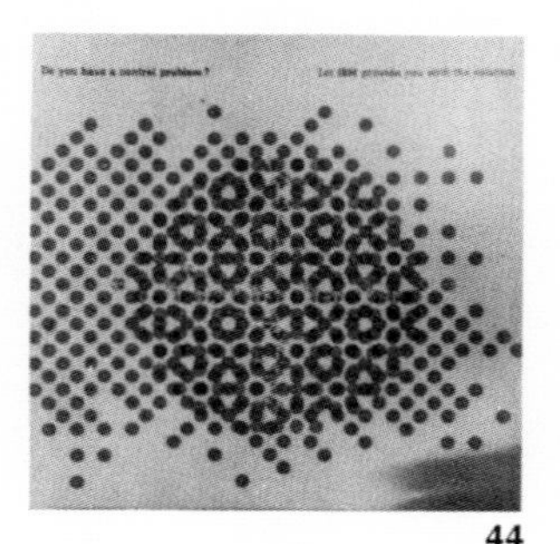

44

M. Velazquez Guitars, Inc.

46

47

48

49

50

51

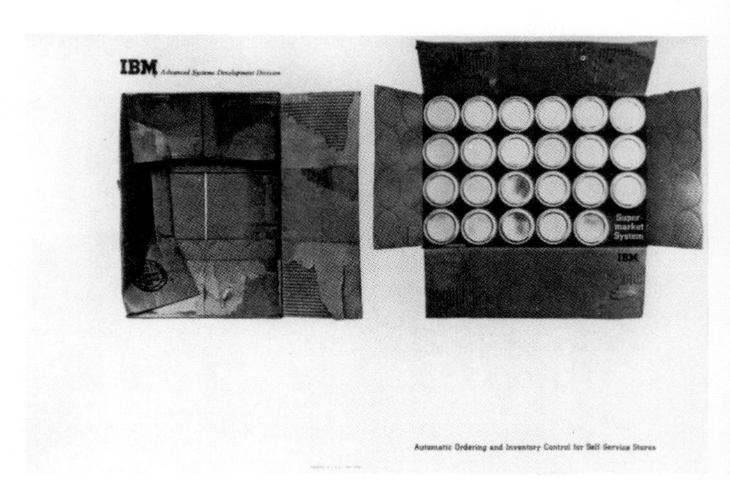

54

57
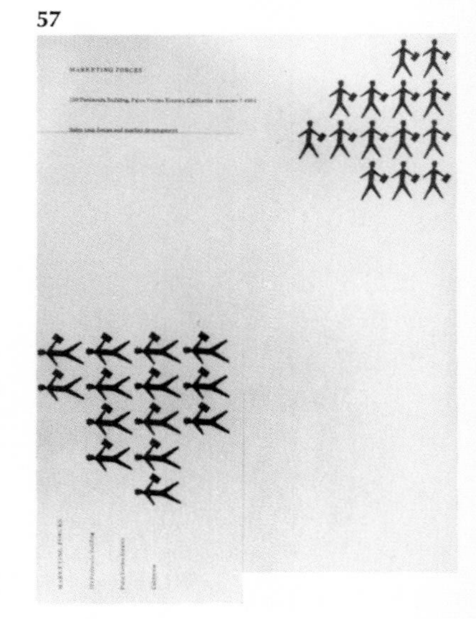

51
Designer: Brad Thompson
Type Director: Brad Thompson
Client / Agency: Keuka College
Typographer: The Typographic Service, Inc.

52
Designer: Seymour Chwast
Type Director: Otto Storch
Client / Agency: McCall's Magazine
Typographer: Metro Typographers, Inc.

53
Designer: John Evans
Type Director: Carl Brett
Client / Agency: Howarth & Smith
Typographer: Howarth & Smith Monotype Limited

54
Designer: James Begany
Type Director: James Begany
Client / Agency: IBM Staff
Typographer: Huxley House, Ltd.

55
Designer: Mo Lebowitz
Type Director: Mo Lebowitz
Client / Agency: American Machine & Foundry Co.
Typographer: Rapid Typographers, Inc.
Hand Lettering– John Costa

56
Designer: Amil Gargano
Type Director: Amil Gargano
Client / Agency: Pratt & Whitney Aircraft
Campbell-Ewald Co.
Typographer: Kurt H. Volk, Inc.

57
Designer: Joe Weston
Type Director: Joe Weston
Client / Agency: Marketing Forces
Typographer: Advertising Designers, Inc.

58
Designer: Arthur Paul
Type Director: Arthur Paul
Client / Agency: Playboy Magazine/
HMH Publishing
Typographer: M&L Typesetting

59
Designer: Frank Mayo
Type Director: John S. Marmaras
Client / Agency: Ciba Pharmaceutical Co.
Typographer: Kurt H. Volk, Inc.

52

APR1L

53

55

E. 39 ST.

FIFTH AVE.

Santa has come to Fifth Avenue and 39th Street...

and he has a free gift for you! You may be the lucky person to get one of the AMF Pleasure Products displayed in the windows. Just fill out entry blank at the AMF desk inside the store. Pick up a FREE colorful copy of the AMF Holiday Guide... packed with helpful hints on Leisure time fun and fitness, with many suggestions for your Christmas gift list. ■ Incidentally, these windows are a 3-D representation of the multi-page ad which has just appeared in LIFE Magazine and also as a special Sunday supplement in the NEW YORK TIMES. ■ So... a Merry Christmas to all from your neighbors at AMERICAN MACHINE & FOUNDRY COMPANY.

56

How to make a seven-day vacation exactly that:

59

This arthritic
patient felt
much better
on Dianabol

58

stravinsky

the world's greatest contemporary composer as revealed by his masterworks

article by ROLAND GELATT

60

Designer:	Florence Bezrutczyk
Type Director:	Florence Bezrutczyk
Client /Agency:	Underwood Corp.
Typographer:	Harry Silverstein, Inc.

61

Designer:	Ed Gold
Type Director:	Ed Gold
Client /Agency:	Bryn Mawr/Barton-Gillet
Typographer:	Progessive/Duvall

62

Designer:	Samuel Maitin
Type Director:	Samuel Maitin
Client /Agency:	DuPont
Typographer:	Typographic Service Inc.

63

Designer:	Arnold Varga
Type Director:	Arnold Varga
Client /Agency:	Cox's Inc., BBDO
Typographer:	T. J. Lyons

64

Designer:	James H. McWilliams
Type Director:	James H. McWilliams
Client /Agency:	The Curtis Publishing Co.
Typographer:	The Curtis Publishing Co.

65

Designer:	Gollin, Bright & Zolotow
Type Director:	Gollin, Bright & Zolotow
Client /Agency:	Gollin, Bright & Zolotow
Typographer:	Vernon Simpson

66

Designer:	M. Ahern, A. Burkhardt, A. Steinberg
Type Director:	George Salter & Leo Manso
Client /Agency:	The Cooper Union School of Art & Architecture
Typographer:	Clarke & Way

67

Designer:	Samuel Maitin
Type Director:	Samuel Maitin
Client /Agency:	YM/YWHA Arts Council Handlettering: Samuel Maitin
Typographer:	Typographic Service Inc.

68

Designer:	Bill Tobias
Type Director:	Robert M. Runyan
Client /Agency:	Journal of Commercial Art
Typographer:	Adtype Service Co.

69

Designer:	Ira Barkoff
Type Director:	Ira Barkoff
Client /Agency:	Golo Footwear Corp./ Ehrlich, Neuwirth & Sobo
Typographer:	Royal Typographers Inc.

70

Designer:	Robert Fabian, Janet Lico
Type Director:	Robert Fabian, Janet Lico
Client /Agency:	I. Miller Salons
Typographer:	Graphic Arts Typographers, Inc.

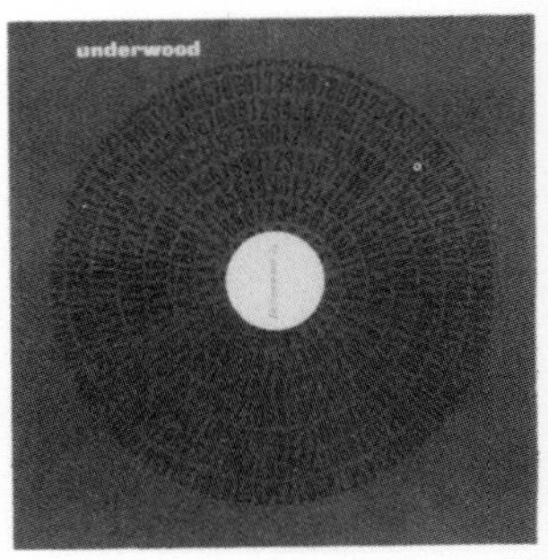

60

63

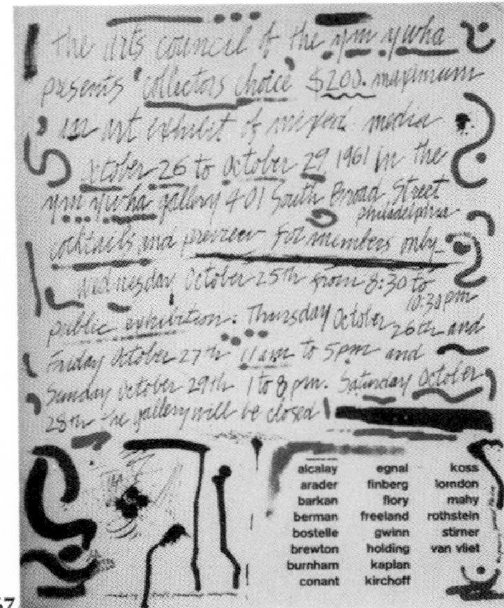

67

61

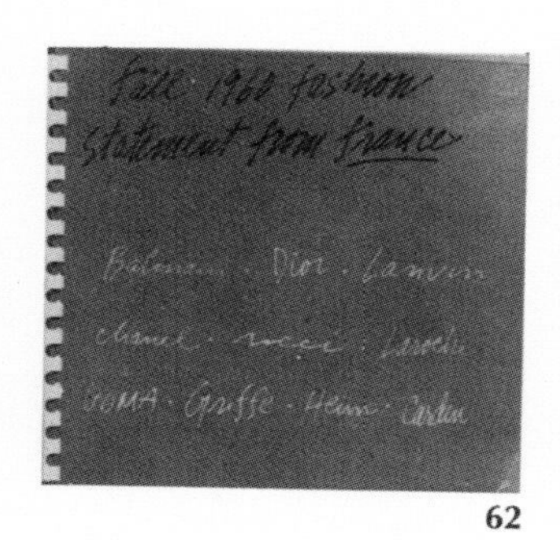

62

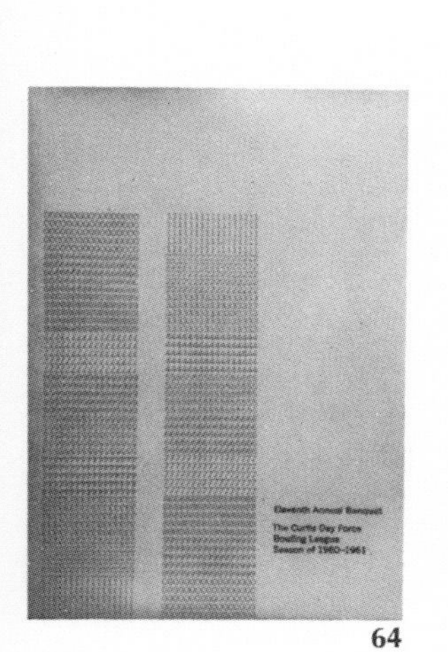

64

65

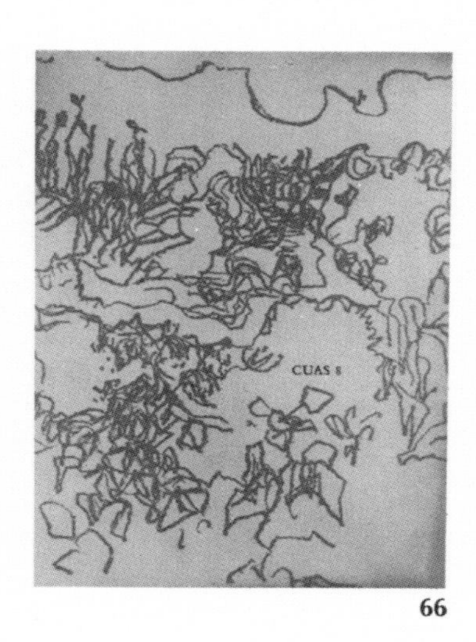

66

68

69

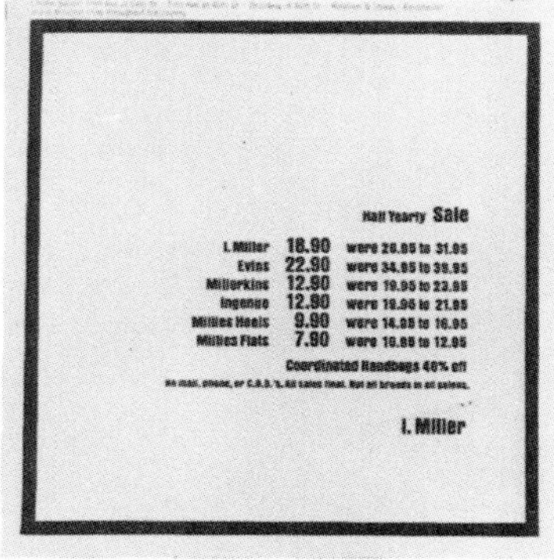

70

shop rules:

the antique press (1)

71

71

Designer: Mo Lebowitz
Type Director: Mo Lebowitz
Client / Agency: The Antique Press
Typographer: Mo Lebowitz

72

Designer: Mort Rubenstein
Type Director: Mort Rubenstein
Client / Agency: CBS
Typographer: Typography Place, Inc.

73

Designer: Joe Police
Type Director: Joe Police
Client / Agency: Ramo-Wooldridge (STRWEA)
Typographer: Joe Police

74

Designer: Seymour Chwast/Milton Glaser
Type Director: Seymour Chwast/Milton Glaser
Client / Agency: Push Pin/Weaver/Weltz
Typographer: Morgan Press/
Weltz Typographer

75

Designer: Eileen Broser
Type Director: Eileen Broser
Client / Agency: Amphenol-Borg Electronics Corp.
Typographer: The Composing Room, Inc.

76

Designer: Albert Storz
Type Director: Albert Storz
Client / Agency: Graphic Directions, Inc.
Typographer: Hand Lettering–William Yaris

77

Designer: Robert O'Dell
Type Director: Robert O'Dell
Client / Agency: House & Garden Magazine
Typographer: The Composing Room, Inc.

78

Designer: Chermayeff & Geismar Associates
Type Director: Ivan Chermayeff
Client / Agency: The Chrysler Art Museum
Typographer: Clarke & Way

79

Designer: Peter Hirsch
Type Director: Peter Hirsch
Client / Agency: Douglas D. Simon Adv., Inc.
Typographer: The Composing Room, Inc.

80

Designer: Gollin, Bright & Zolotow
Type Director: Gollin, Bright & Zolotow
Client / Agency: Pasadena Art Museum
Typographer: Advertisers Composition Co.

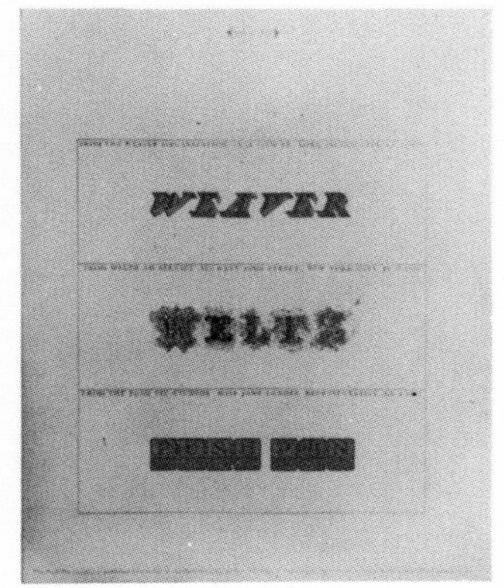

74

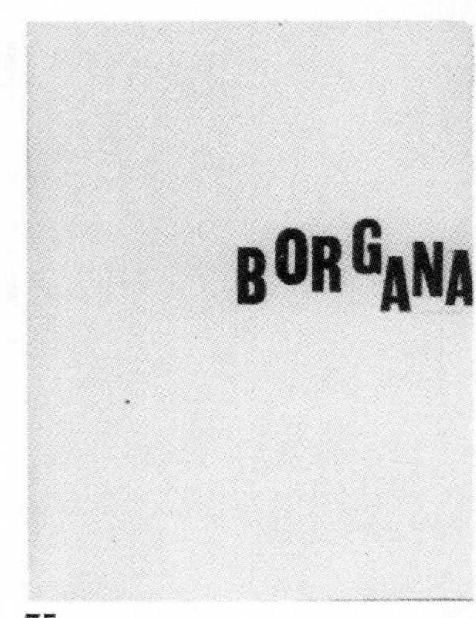

75

76

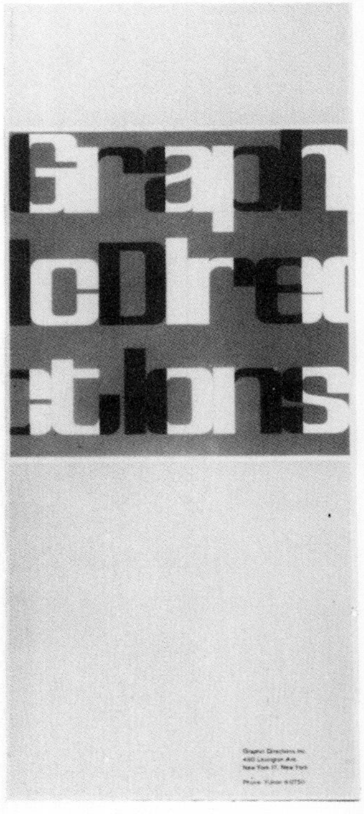

72

73

77

78

79

80

APRIL 23 THROUGH JUNE 4, 1961 ■ THE PASADENA ART MUSEUM ■ PASADENA, CALIFORNIA

GERMAN EXPRESSIONISM

81

Designer:	Michael Wollman
Type Director:	Michael Wollman
Client/Agency:	Grey Advertising Agency, Inc.
Typographer:	Adset Service, Inc.

82

Designer:	Arnold Varga
Type Director:	Arnold Varga
Client/Agency:	Cox's, Inc. (BBDO)
Typographer:	Arnold Varga

83

Designer:	Kurt Lowey Malcolm Mansfield
Type Director:	Malcolm Mansfield
Client/Agency:	Vogue Magazine-Condé Nast Publications
Typographer:	Typographic Service Co.

84

Designer:	A. R. DeNatale
Type Director:	A. R. DeNatale
Client/Agency:	Virginia Museum of Fine Arts
Typographer:	J. W. Ford Company Cincinnati, Ohio

85

Designer:	Saul Bass
Type Director:	Saul Bass
Client/Agency:	Hunt Foods & Industries, Inc.
Typographer:	Advertisers' Composition Co.

86

Designer:	S. Neil Fujita
Type Director:	W. J. Bailey
Client/Agency:	The Saturday Evening Post
Typographer:	Curtis Publishing Co.

87

Designer:	Robertson-Montgomery
Type Director:	Robertson-Montgomery
Client/Agency:	Wilsey Ham & Blair
Typographer:	Spartan Typographers

88

Designer:	Aron & Falcone/Phil Swift
Type Director:	Aron & Falcone/Phil Swift
Client/Agency:	CIBA Pharmaceutical Company
Typographer:	Alex G. Highton, Inc.

89

Designer:	Freeman Craw
Type Director:	Freeman Craw
Client/Agency:	College Entrance Examination Board
Typographer:	Tri-Arts Press, Inc.

90

Designer:	Marilyn Hoffner-Al Greenberg
Type Director:	Marilyn Hoffner-Al Greenberg
Client/Agency:	Print Magazine

81

84

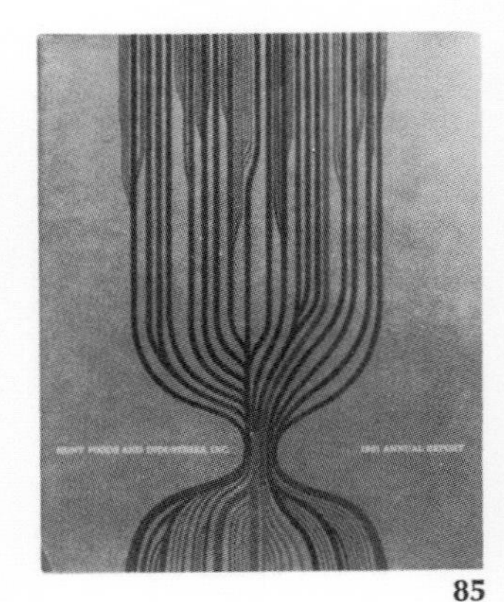

85

88

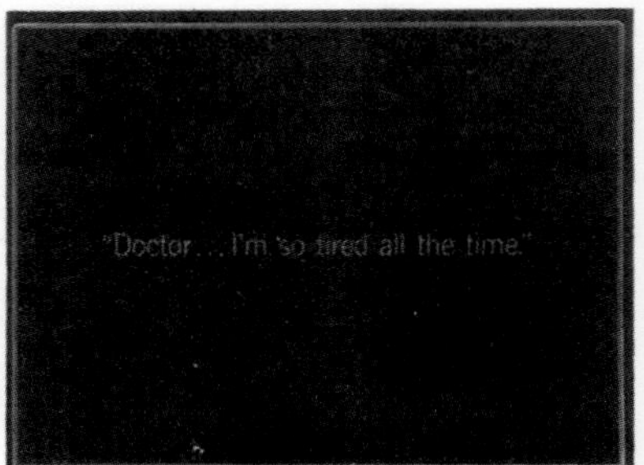

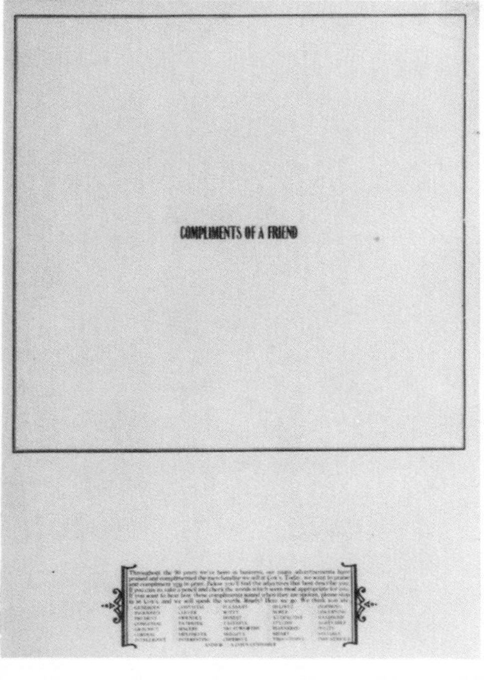

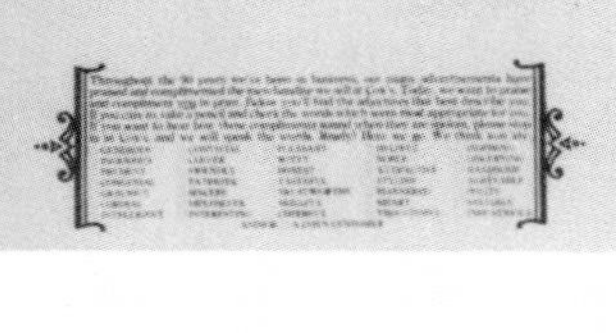

82

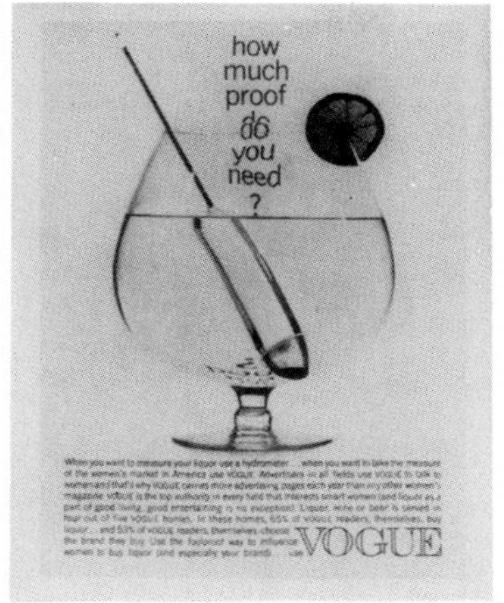

83

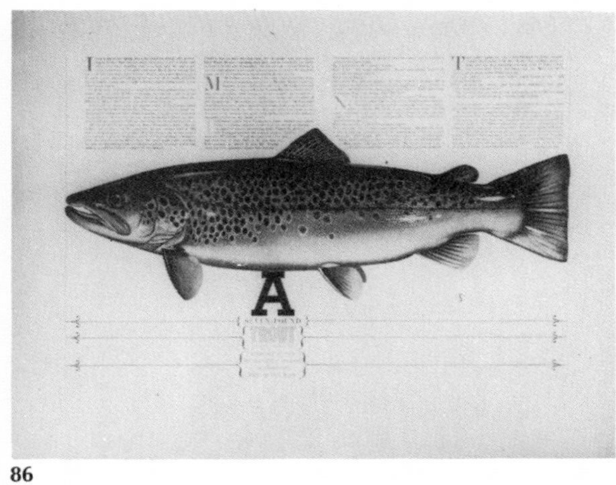

86

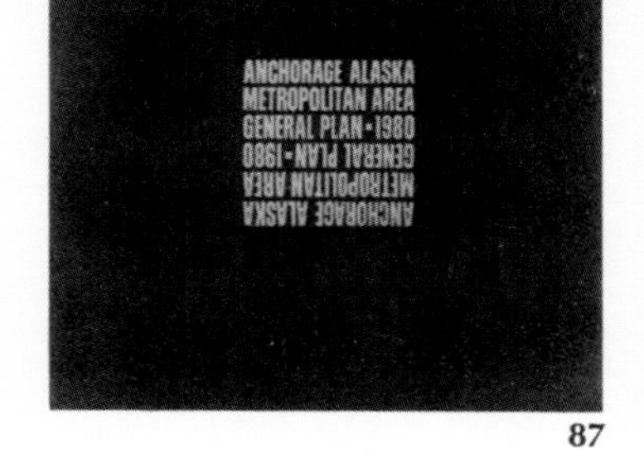

87

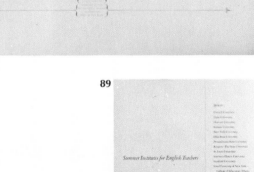

89

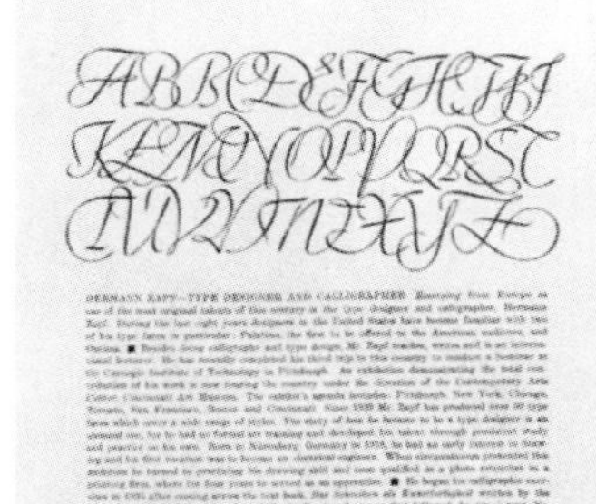

90

91

Designer:	Nick Kornaza
Type Director:	Nick Kornaza
Client /Agency:	Merrill, Lynch, Pierce, Fenner & Smith, Inc.
Typographer:	Kurt H. Volk, Inc.

92

Designer:	Blake Hampton
Type Director:	Robert Benton
Client /Agency:	Esquire
Typographer:	Hand Lettering

93

Designer:	Amil Gargano
Type Director:	Amil Gargano
Client /Agency:	Swissair/ Campbell-Ewald Co., Inc.
Typographer:	Kurt H. Volk, Inc.

94

Designer:	Jerry C. Demoney
Type Director:	Robert O'Dell
Client /Agency:	House & Garden Magazine
Typographer:	The Composing Room, Inc.

95

Designer:	James Valkus Inc.
Type Director:	George Klauber
Client /Agency:	Canadian National/ James Valkus Inc.

96

Designer:	Milton Ackoff
Client /Agency:	Westinghouse Electric Corp.
Typographer:	Kurt H. Volk, Inc.

97

Designer:	Irwin Sarason
Type Director:	Irwin Sarason
Client /Agency:	CBS Television Network
Typographer:	Typography Place, Inc.

98

Designer:	Gollin, Bright & Zolotow
Type Director:	Gollin, Bright & Zolotow
Client /Agency:	Jerry Wald Productions
Typographer:	Vern Simpson

99

Designer:	Robert Flynn
Type Director:	Robert Flynn
Client /Agency:	Robert Flynn
Typographer:	Empire Typographers, Inc.

100

Designer:	Jerry Soling
Type Director:	Jerry Soling
Client /Agency:	Jerry Soling
Typographer:	Jerry Soling

91

92

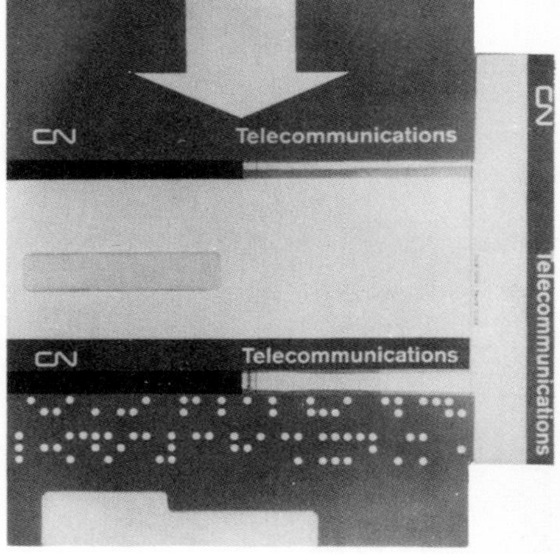

95

99

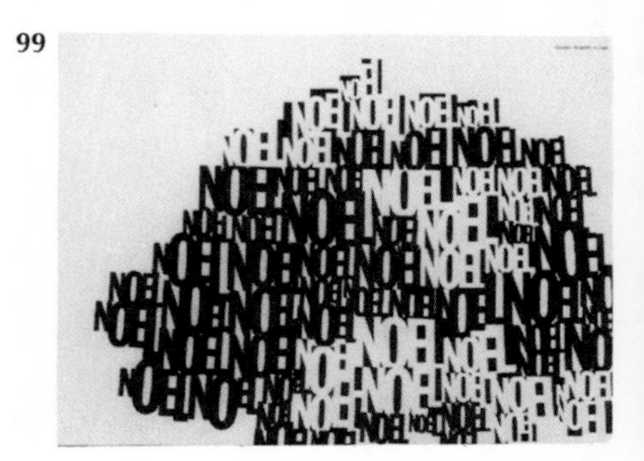

This country talks your language.

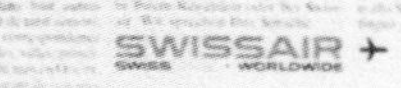

93

94

96

TELL
IT
TO
GROUCHO

97

98

from the bold pen of Ernest Hemingway comes the Jerry Wald production beginning in Michigan Sept. 18 Hemingway's "Young Man"
DIRECTED BY MARTY RITT FROM THE SCREENPLAY BY A.E. HOTCHNER RELEASED BY TWENTIETH CENTURY FOX

100

Wishing you
merry christmas &
happy new year...

101
Designer: Lenny Sirowitz
Type Director: Klaus Schmidt
Client /Agency: Rainier Peer/Doyle, Dane, Bernbach, Inc.
Typographer: ProvidentTypographers

102
Designer: Kurt Lowey Malcolm Mansfield
Type Director: Malcolm Mansfield
Client /Agency: Vogue Magazine-Condé Nast Publications
Typographer: Typographic Service Co.

103
Designer: Malcolm Mansfield, Victor Orsatz
Type Director: Malcolm Mansfield
Client /Agency: Vogue Magazine Condé-Nast
Typographer: The Typographic Service Co.

104
Designer: John Massey-Virginia Kemper
Type Director: John Massey
Client /Agency: Miehle-Goss-Dexter
Typographer: Frederic Ryder Co.

105
Designer: Alphonso Amato
Type Director: Alphonso Amato
Client /Agency: CBS Television Network
Typographer: Typography Place, Inc.

106
Designer: Bill Tobias
Type Director: Robert M. Runyan
Client /Agency: Metro Goldwyn Mayer
Typographer: Adtype Service Co.

107
Designer: George Tscherny
Client /Agency: Campbell-Ewald Co., Inc.
Typographer: The Composing Room, Inc.

108
Designer: Irwin Sarason
Type Director: Irwin Sarason
Client /Agency: CBS Television Network
Typographer: Typography Place, Inc.

109
Designer: Bernie Zlotnick
Type Director: Bernie Zlotnick
Client /Agency: CBS Radio/ Sudler & Hennessey Inc.
Typographer: The Composing Room, Inc.

110
Designer: Gennaro Andreozzi
Type Director: Burt Purmell
Client /Agency: Gamins/Gilbert Adv. Agency
Typographer: Provident Typographers, Inc.

101

105

106

107

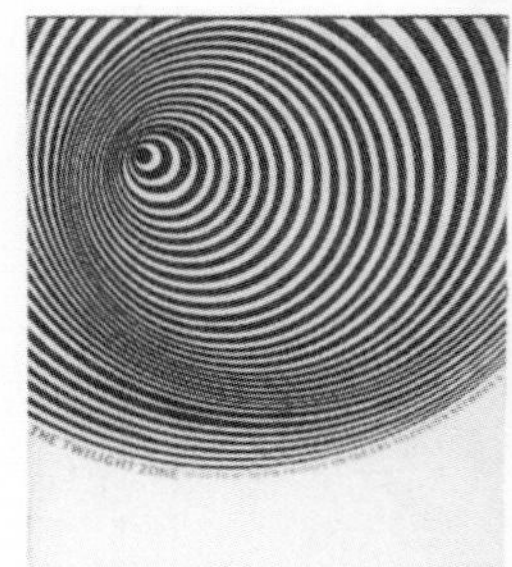

108

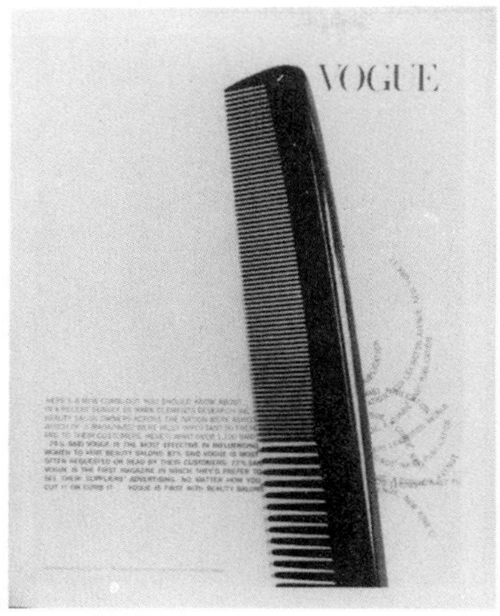

103

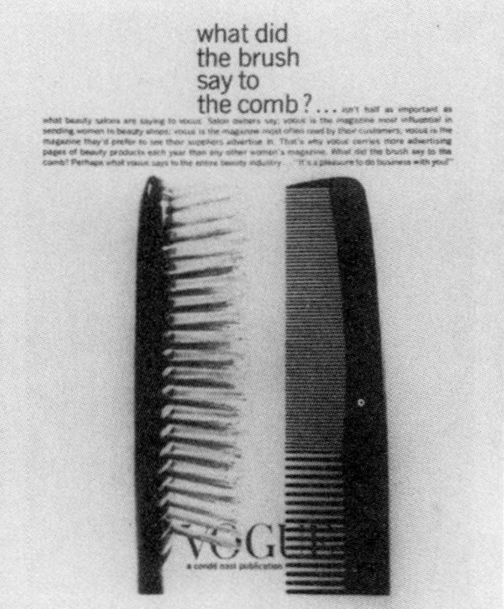

102

104

109

WHO'S first with the best people in network radio? Listen: Carol Burnett, Eric Sevareid, Allan Jackson, Daniel Schorr, Bing Crosby, Howard K. Smith, Art Linkletter, Alexander Kendrick, Richard Hayes, Arthur Godfrey, Larry LeSueur, Leonard Bernstein, Walter Cronkite, Bill Downs, David Schoenbrun, Jerry Coleman, Peter Kalischer, Phil Rizzuto, Paul Niven, Charles Collingwood, Marvin Kalb, Robert Trout, Kenneth Banghart, Ned Calmer, Garry Moore, Winston Burdett, Nancy Hanschman, Harry Reasoner, Rosemary Clooney, Douglas Edwards, Bill Leonard, Richard C. Hottelet, Charles von Fremd, Dallas Townsend, George Herman, Lowell Thomas, Stuart Novins, Durward Kirby, Ralph Story and more. That's **WHO!**

THE CBS RADIO NETWORK

110

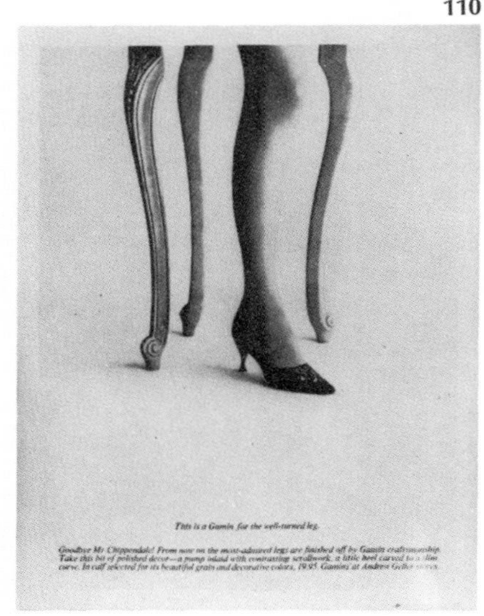

111
Designer: L. Dorfsman, J. Schindelman, Alphonso Amato
Type Director: L. Dorfsman, J. Schindelman
Client/Agency: CBS Television Network
Typographer: The Composing Room, Inc.

112
Designer: Joe Weston
Type Director: Joe Weston
Client/Agency: Joe Weston
Typographer: Joe Weston

113
Designer: Allan R. Fleming
Type Director: Allan R. Fleming
Client/Agency: Typographic Designers of Canada
Typographer: Allan R. Fleming

114
Designer: Hermann Zapf
Type Director: Hermann Zapf
Client/Agency: D. Stempel A. G.
Typographer: D. Stempel A. G.

115
Designer: Frank Mayo & Edward G. Infurna
Type Director: Frank Mayo
Client/Agency: Frank Mayo Design Studio
Typographer: Linocraft Typographers, Inc.

116
Designer: Robert Fabian
Type Director: Robert Fabian
Client/Agency: I. Miller Salons
Typographer: The Composing Room, Inc.

117
Designer: Everett S. Aison
Type Director: Everett S. Aison
Client/Agency: Film Pathways, Inc.
Typographer: Maurice Skeehan

118
Designer: A. R. DeNatale
Type Director: A. R. DeNatale
Client/Agency: The Carborundum Company
Typographer: The J. W. Ford Company

119
Designer: James Cross
Type Director: James Cross
Client/Agency: Northrop Corporation
Typographer: Monsen Typographers, Inc.

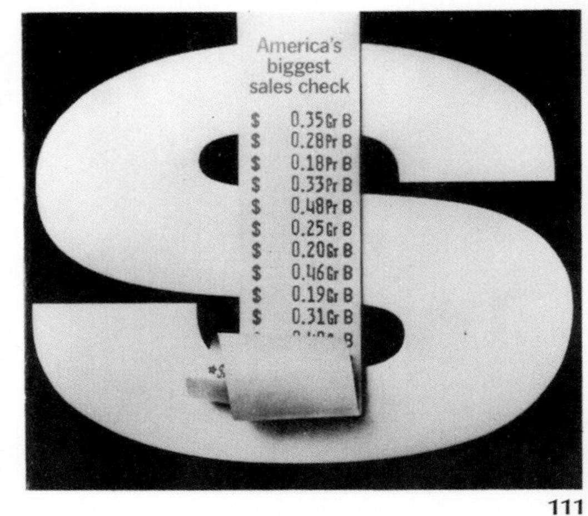

111

PALATINO
EINE
WEITVERZWEIGTE
FAMILIE
MIT DER
SIE IMMER
ZUSAMMEN-
ARBEITEN
SOLLTEN
D. STEMPEL AG
FRANKFURT AM MAIN
LINOTYPE GMBH

114

117

112

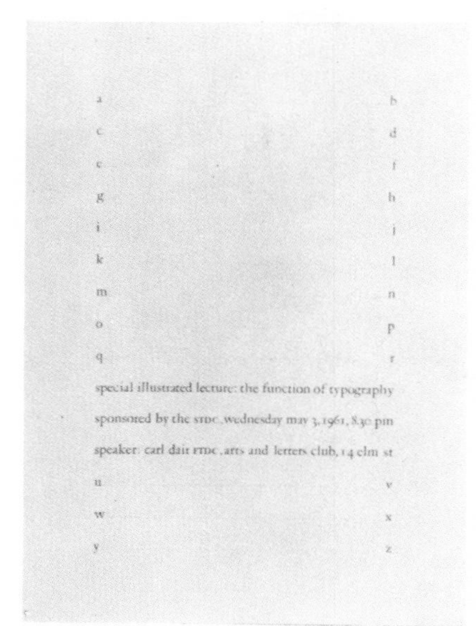

113

O P E N

115

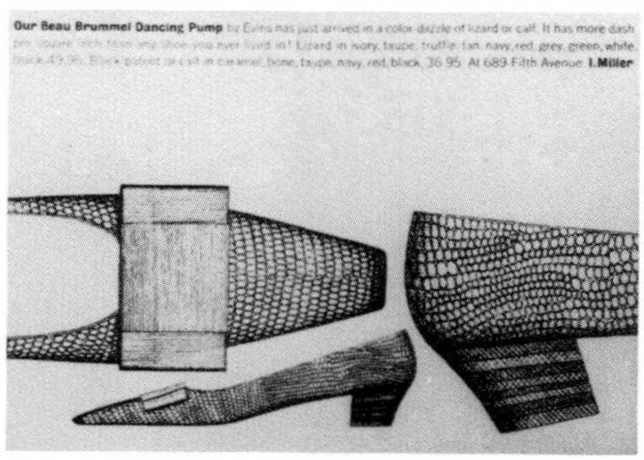

116

118

119

120

Designer: Allen F. Hurlburt
Type Director: Allen F. Hurlburt
Typographer: Riegert & Kennedy

121

Designer: Arne Lewis
Type Director: Mort Rubenstein
Client /Agency: WBBM-TV
Typographer: Rapid Typographers, Inc.

122

Designer: Irwin Sarason
Type Director: Irwin Sarason
Client /Agency: CBS Television Network
Typographer: Typography Place, Inc.

123

Designer: Richard Bergeron
Type Director: Ken Lavey/Richard Bergeron
Client /Agency: Parke-Davis & Co./
L. W. Frohlich & Co., Inc.
Typographer: Empire Typographers, Inc.

124

Designer: Gennaro Andreozzi
Type Director: Burt Purmell
Client /Agency: Gamins/Gilbert Adv. Agency
Typographer: Provident Typographers, Inc.

125

Designer: F. Newfeld
Type Director: F. Newfeld
Client /Agency: McClelland & Stewart Ltd.
Typographer: F. Newfeld

126

Designer: Robert M. Jones
Type Director: Robert M. Jones
Client /Agency: Robert M. Jones
Typographer: Robert M. Jones

127

Designer: Robertson-Montgomery
Type Director: Robertson-Montgomery
Client /Agency: Gorin & Holmes
Typographer: Spartan Typographers

128

Designer: Robert O'Dell
Type Director: Robert O'Dell
Client /Agency: House & Garden Magazine
Typographer: The Composing Room, Inc.

129

Designer: Suren Ermoyan
Type Director: Joseph Armellino
Client /Agency: Austin Briggs & Famous Artists
School/BBDO
Typographer: Morgan Press &
Frederick Nelson Phillips

120

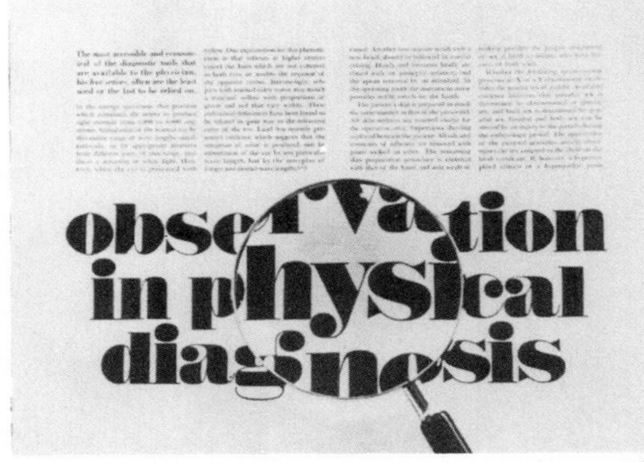

123

127

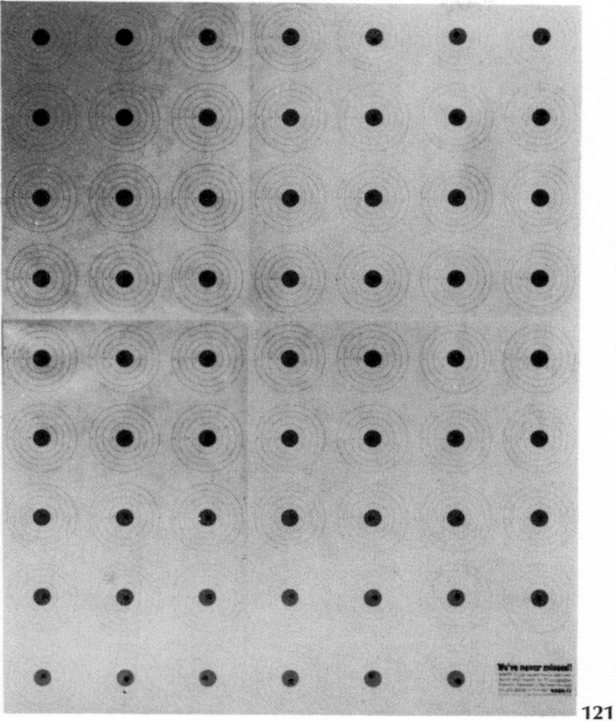

121

122

126

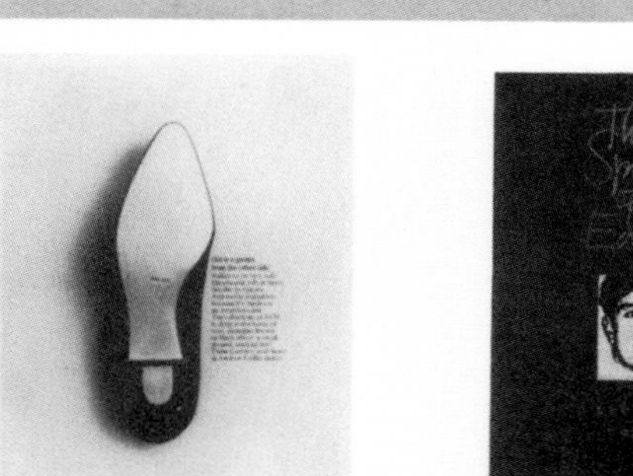

124

125

129

130

Designer: Herb Lubalin
Type Director: Herb Lubalin
Client /Agency: Callaway Mills/
Sudler & Hennessey, Inc.

131

Designer: Sid Myers
Type Director: Al Robinson
Client /Agency: Eversweet/DDB
Typographer: Provident Typographers, Inc.

132

Designer: Mary Beresford
Type Director: Mary Beresford
Client /Agency: IBM
Typographer: Tri-Arts Press, Inc.

133

Designer: Otto Storch, Anthony Olivetto
Type Director: Otto Storch, Anthony Olivetto
Client /Agency: McCall Corp.
Typographer: The Composing Room, Inc.

134

Designer: Gilbert Lesser
Type Director: Gilbert Lesser
Client /Agency: Fortune Magazine
Typographer: The Composing Room, Inc.

135

Designer: Robert O'Dell
Type Director: Robert O'Dell
Client /Agency: House & Garden Magazine
Typographer: Hand Lettering/Ed Benguait

136

Designer: Lester Beall
Type Director: Lester Beall
Client /Agency: International Paper Company
Typographer: Southern New England
Typographic Service

137

Designer: A. R. DeNatale
Type Director: A. R. DeNatale
Client /Agency: Virginia Museum of Fine Arts
Typographer: J. W. Ford Company
Cincinnati, Ohio

138

Designer: Ralph Ammirati
Type Director: Joseph Armellino
Client /Agency: Holiday Magazine/BBDO
Typographer: Atlas Typographic Service, Inc.

130

KIDS STILL SAY THE DARNDEST THINGS

133

137

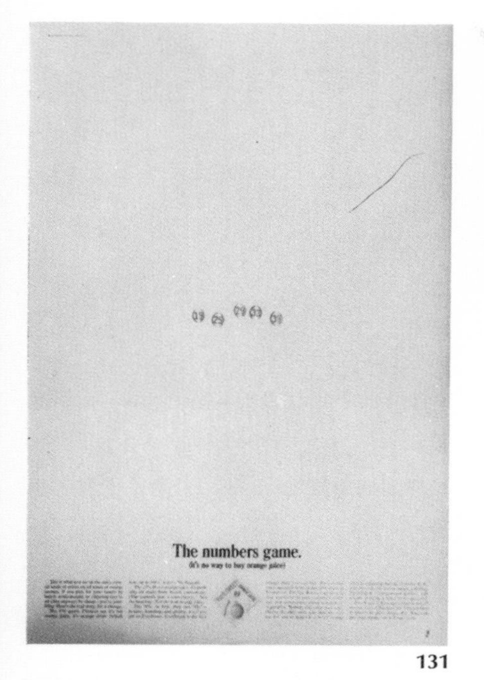
The numbers game.

131

IBM
Second Systems Engineering Symposium
Washington, D.C. October 14-17, 1962

132

FORTUNE'S
PRINTING
PRIMER

134

135

136

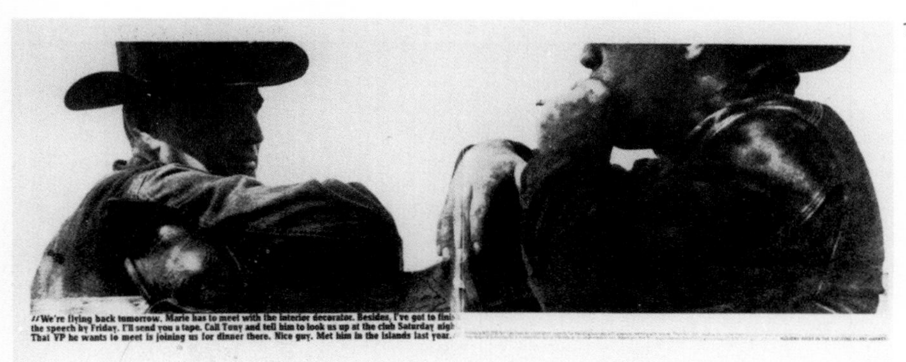
//We're flying back tomorrow. Marie has to meet with the interior decorator. Besides, I've got to fini
the speech by Friday. I'll send you a tape. Call Tony and tell him to look us up at the club Saturday nigh
That VP he wants to meet is joining us for dinner there. Nice guy. Met him in the islands last year./

138

139
Designer: Gene Federico
Type Director: Gene Federico
Client / Agency: Saturday Evening Post
Typographer: The Composing Room, Inc.

140
Designer: Fred Witzig
Type Director: Fred Witzig
Client / Agency: Art Center of Northern New Jersey
Typographer: Empire Typographers, Inc.

141
Designer: Sol Myers
Type Director: Ann Brown
Client / Agency: Eversweet/DDB
Typographer: Provident Typographers, Inc.

142
Designer: Irwin Sarason
Type Director: Irwin Sarason
Client / Agency: CBS Television
Typographer: Typography Place, Inc.

143
Designer: Alphonso Amato
Type Director: Alphonso Amato
Client / Agency: CBS Television Network
Typographer: Typography Place, Inc.

144
Designer: John Griffin
Type Director: John Griffin
Client / Agency: Coats & Clark, Inc. Fuller & Smith & Ross, Inc.
Typographer: Advertising Agencies' Service Co., Inc.

145
Designer: Joseph Schindelman
Type Director: Joseph Schindelman
Client / Agency: CBS Television Network
Typographer: Typography Place, Inc.

146
Designer: Bebe Gershenzon
Type Director: Bebe Gershenzon
Client / Agency: Cooper Union/ Sudler & Hennessey, Inc.

147
Designer: Art Glazer
Type Director: Art Glazer
Client / Agency: Redbook Magazine
Typographer: Provident Typographers, Inc.

148
Designer: Carl Zahn
Type Director: Carl Zahn
Client / Agency: AIGA
Typographer: Typographic House, Inc.

149
Designer: Lester Beall/Cliff Stead
Type Director: Lester Beall/Cliff Stead
Client / Agency: Standard Oil Co. of N.J.
Typographer: Huxley House, Ltd.

139

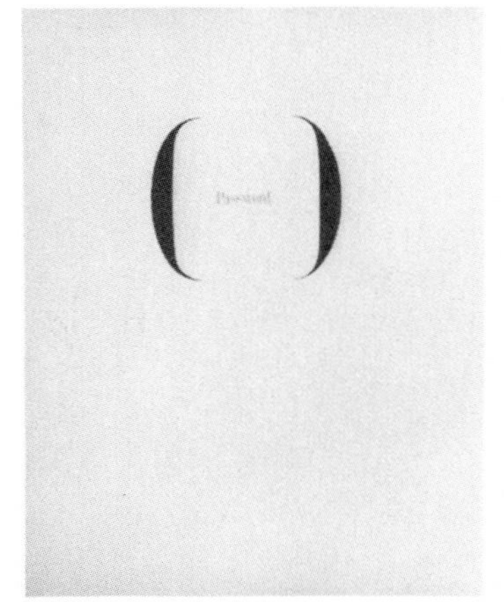
142

143

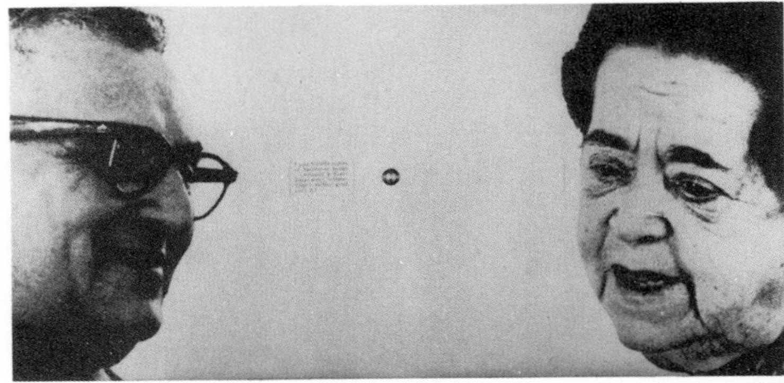
147

Contemporary House Tour
October 8, 1.30-5pm
sponsored by the Art Center of Northern New Jersey
tickets now available 2 dollars LO.7-3293
59 Engle Street Englewood

140

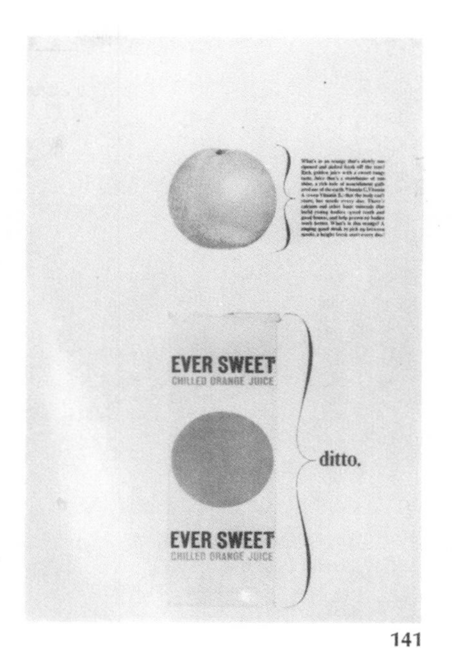
EVER SWEET
CHILLED ORANGE JUICE
ditto.
EVER SWEET
CHILLED ORANGE JUICE

141

YES

144

'WAY
OUT

145

146

148

call
fifty
books
1961
aiga
fifty books 1961
entry form

149

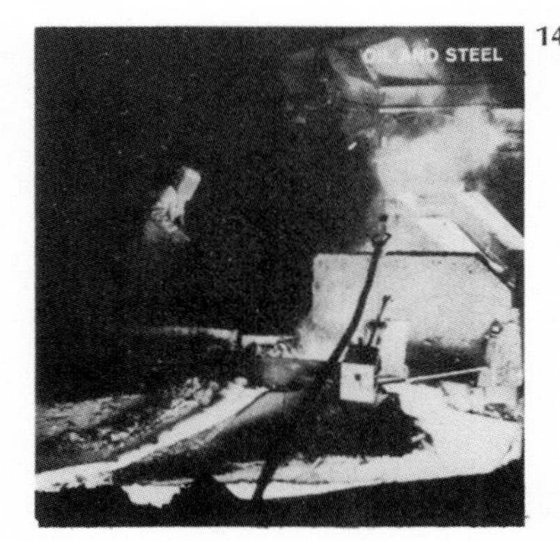
OIL AND STEEL

150

Designer:	Barry Steinman, Jerry Litofsky
Type Director:	Frank Wojcicki Jr., Beverly Golbin, John Matt, Howard Sperber
Client/Agency:	Pratt Institute
Typographer:	Prattonia

151

Designer:	Werner Pfeiffer
Type Director:	Werner Pfeiffer
Client/Agency:	Dept. Advertising Design School of Art, Pratt Institute
Typographer:	Werner Pfeiffer

152

Designer:	Lou Silverstein
Type Director:	Lou Silverstein
Client/Agency:	Gallery 303
Typographer:	The Composing Room, Inc.

153

Designer:	F. Newfeld
Type Director:	F. Newfeld
Client/Agency:	McClelland & Stewart Ltd.
Typographer:	F. Newfeld

154

Designer:	James Cross
Type Director:	James Cross
Client/Agency:	Northrop Corporation
Typographer:	Monsen Typographers, Inc.

155

Designer:	Louis Dorfsman
Type Director:	J. Schindelman
Client/Agency:	CBS Television Network
Typographer:	Typography Place, Inc.

156

Designer:	George Tscherny
Client/Agency:	American Federation of Arts Handlettering

157

Designer:	Herb Lubalin
Type Director:	Herb Lubalin
Client/Agency:	Lightolier/ Sudler & Hennessey, Inc.

158

Designer:	Bruce Blackburn
Type Director:	Bruce Blackburn/Guy Salvato
Client/Agency:	University of Cincinnati
Typographer:	J. W. Ford Co.

159

Designer:	Art Boden
Type Director:	Art Boden
Client/Agency:	Franklin Typographers, Inc.
Typographer:	Franklin Typographers, Inc.

160

Designer:	Ralph M. Coburn
Type Director:	Ralph M. Coburn
Client/Agency:	M.I.T. Admissions Office/ M.I.T. Office of Publications
Typographer:	Machine Composition Co.

150

design in brazil
aloisio megalhaes
lecture memorial hall
monday feb 5th 2pm
department advertising design

151

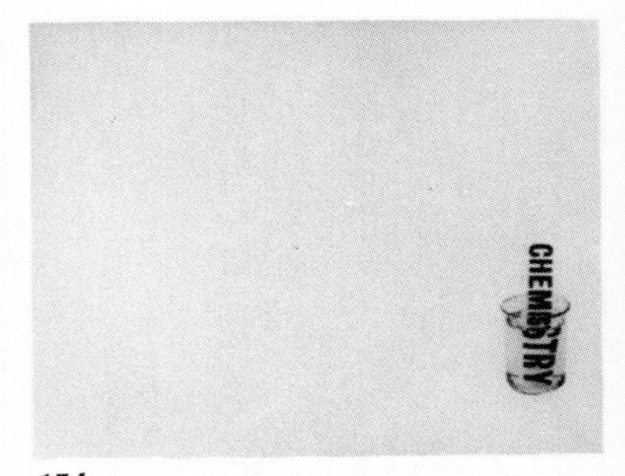

154

157

158

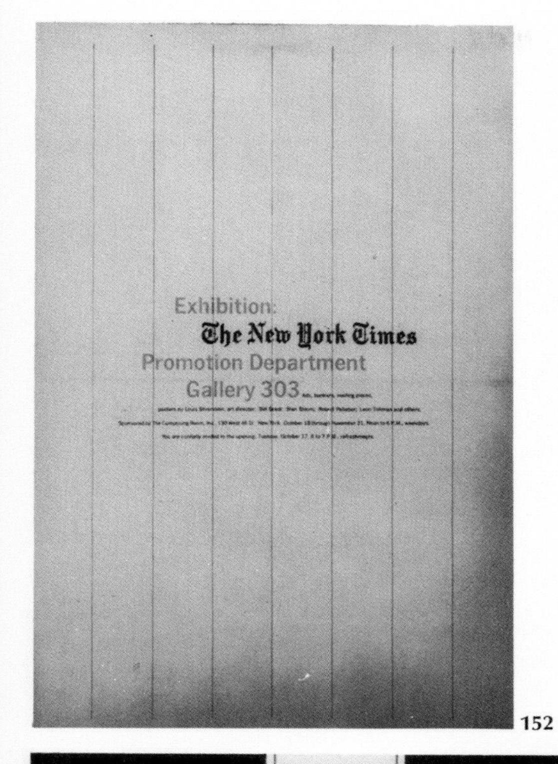

152

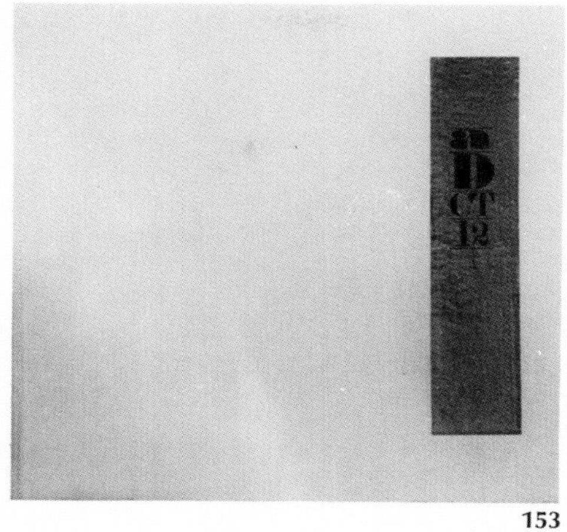
153

156

155

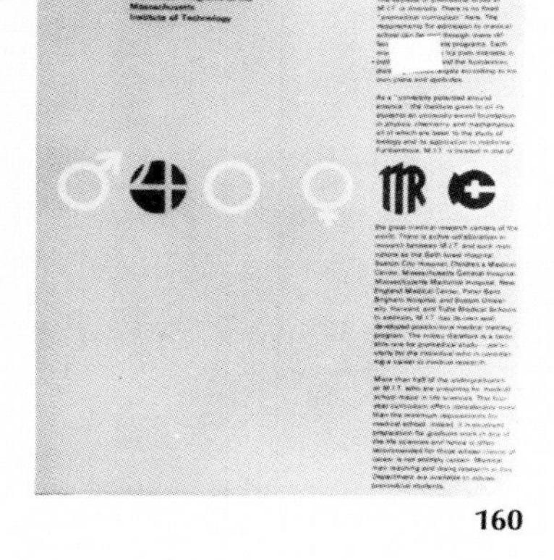

160

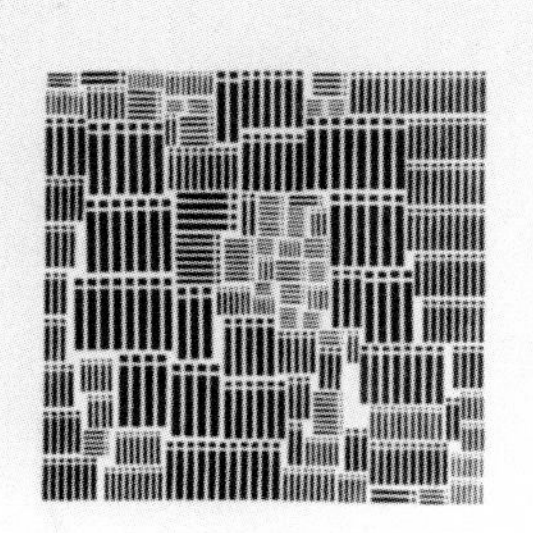
159

161

161

Designer: Mel Richman Design Associates
Type Director: Sam Ciccone/Mel Richman
Client/Agency: Hershey Chocolate Co.
Typographer: Typographic Service Inc.

162

Designer: Tor Winstrup
Type Director: Tor Winstrup
Client/Agency: Adv. Agencys Production Managers of Los Angeles
Typographer: ACC, Adtype, Bisch Type Inc.

163

Designer: Barry Steinman, Jerry Litofsky
Type Director: Frank Wojcicki Jr., Beverly Golbin, John Matt, Howard Sperber
Client/Agency: Pratt Institute
Typographer: Prattonia

164

Designer: Fred Witzig
Type Director: Fred Witzig
Client/Agency: Fred Witzig
Typographer: Empire Typographers, Inc.

165

Designer: John J. Reiss
Type Director: John J. Reiss
Client/Agency: Milwaukee Art Center
Typographer: Zahn Klicka Hill

166

Designer: James Valkus Inc.
Type Director: Jim McElheron
Client/Agency: Canadian National/ James Valkus Inc.

167

Designer: Sheldon Cotler/Walter Lefman
Type Director: Sheldon Cotler
Client/Agency: Time Inc.
Typographer: The Typographic Service Co.

168

Designer: Greg Bruno
Type Director: Greg Bruno
Typographer: Advertising Agencies' Service Co., Inc.

163

166

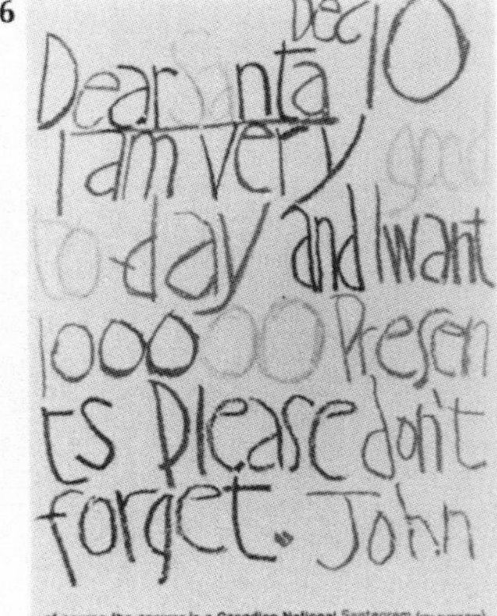

aapm certificate, 1960-1961: this, our new membership certificate, is presented to the ninety members of aapm for furthering the club's principle—advancement of production standards. fourteen suppliers, who are representative of the local graphic arts industry's high standards, made this project possible. their enthusiasm and cooperation is gratefully acknowledged.
ROBERT L. ONEACRE
PRESIDENT
SECRETARY

162

164

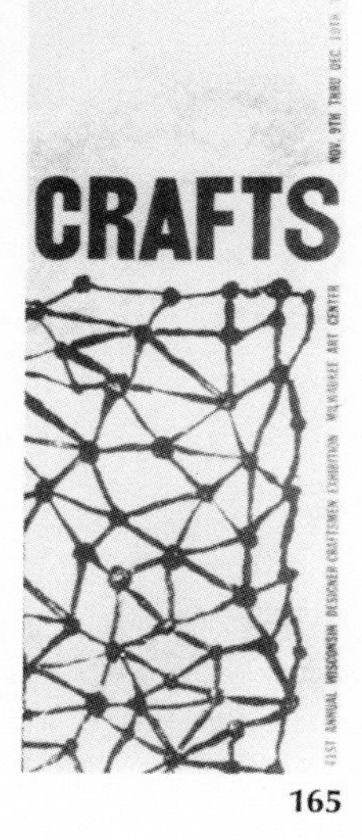
NOV. 9TH THRU DEC.
CRAFTS
ANNUAL WISCONSIN DESIGNER CRAFTSMEN EXHIBITION MILWAUKEE ART CENTER

165

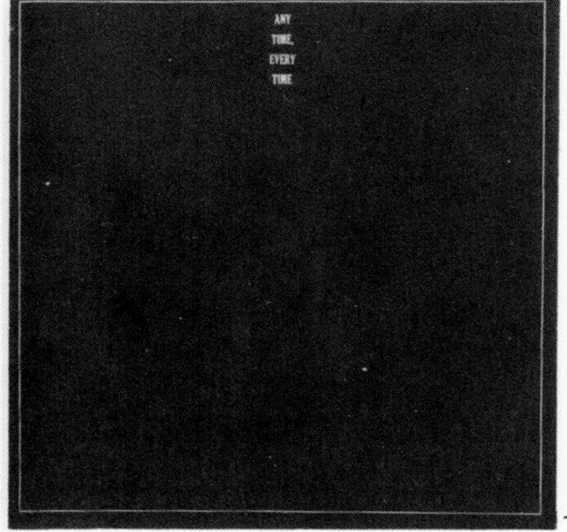
ANY
TIME,
EVERY
TIME

167

168

169
Designer: Louis Dorfsman & Alphonso Amato
Type Director: Louis Dorfsman & Alphonso Amato
Client/Agency: CBS Television Network
Typographer: Typography Place, Inc.

170
Designer: Louis Dorfsman
Type Director: Louis Dorfsman
Client/Agency: CBS Television Network
Typographer: Typography Place, Inc.

171
Designer: John Massey
Type Director: John Massey
Client/Agency: Sefton Division/C.C.A.
Typographer: Frederic Ryder Co.

172
Designer: Richard Walukanis
Type Director: Richard Walukanis
Client/Agency: Fortune Magazine
Typographer: Franklin Typographers, Inc.

173
Designer: Ralph Ammirati
Type Director: Joseph Armellino
Client/Agency: N.Y. Racing Assoc./BBDO
Typographer: Advertising Agencies' Service Co., Inc.

174
Designer: Jon Aron
Type Director: Jon Aron
Client/Agency: Ferro, Mogubgub & Schwartz/ Trinkaus, Aron & Wayman
Typographer: Southern New England Typographic Service

175
Designer: Suren Ermoyan
Type Director: Joseph Armellino
Client/Agency: U.S. Steel/BBDO
Typographer: Atlas Typographic Service, Inc.

176
Designer: Morton Goldsholl
Type Director: Morton Goldsholl
Client/Agency: International Minerals & Chemical Corp.
Typographer: Lettering, Inc.

177
Designer: Ralph M. Coburn
Type Director: Ralph M. Coburn
Client/Agency: M.I.T. Centennial Committee M.I.T. Office of Publications
Typographer: Machine Composition Co.

178
Designer: Ciemen Drimer
Type Director: Ciemen Drimer
Client/Agency: American Management Association
Typographer: Empire Typographers, Inc.

169

172

Be at the Big A Saturday when racing's finest thoroughbreds battle in the $100,000 Brooklyn. Will 1960's Horse of the Year, Kelso, become the third horse ever to sweep the Handicap Triple Crown? Don't miss the exciting answer! See 9 big races. 1st race 1:30. Aqueduct is easy to reach by car, bus or IND subway. Go! Go! Go!

173

176

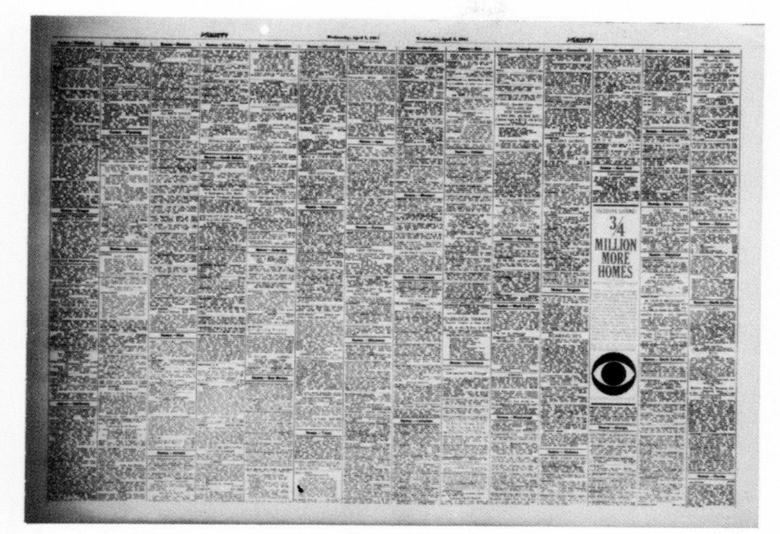

170

171

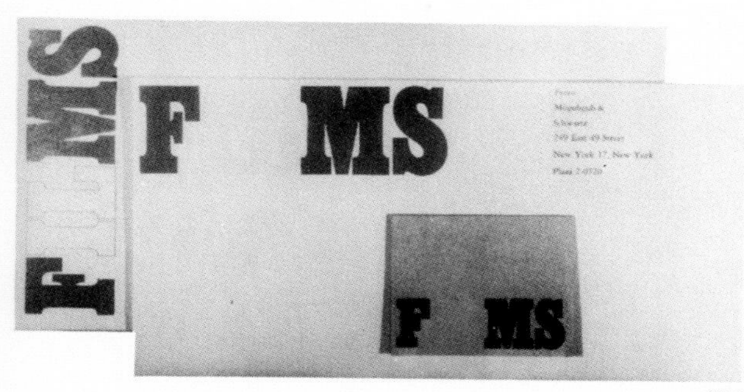

174

175

177

178

179
Designer: Albert Greenberg/ Robt. P. Smith
Type Director: A/D Albert Greenberg
Client/Agency: Gentlemen's Quarterly Magazine
Typographer: Haber Typographers, Inc.

180
Designer: Joe Weston
Type Director: Joe Weston
Client/Agency: Institute for Defense Analyses
Typographer: Advertising Designers, Inc.

181
Designer: Philip Sykes
Type Director: Philip Sykes
Typographer: Riegert & Kennedy and Photo-Lettering Inc.

182
Designer: Theo Dimson
Type Director: Arnold Rockman
Client/Agency: Bryant Press
Typographer: Cooper & Beatty, Ltd.

183
Designer: Gollin, Bright & Zolotow
Type Director: Gollin, Bright & Zolotow
Client/Agency: Los Angeles Litho Club
Typographer: Vernon Simpson

184
Designer: Seymour Chwast/Milton Glaser
Type Director: Seymour Chwast/Milton Glaser
Client/Agency: Push Pin Studios Inc.
Typographer: Weltz Ad Service

185
Designer: Samuel Maitin
Type Director: Samuel Maitin
Client/Agency: The Print Club
Typographer: Leon Segal Co.

186
Designer: Albert Greenberg
Type Director: Albert Greenberg
Client/Agency: Gentlemen's Quarterly Magazine
Typographer: Haber Typographers, Inc.

187
Designer: Louis Dorfsman & J. Schindelman
Type Director: J. Schindelman
Client/Agency: CBS Television Network
Typographer: Typography Place, Inc.

188
Designer: Frank Mayo
Type Director: Frank Mayo
Client/Agency: Stendig Inc.
Typographer: Gould Co.

179

182

186

187

IDA
Annual Report
Number Five
Institute for
Defense Analyses

180

181

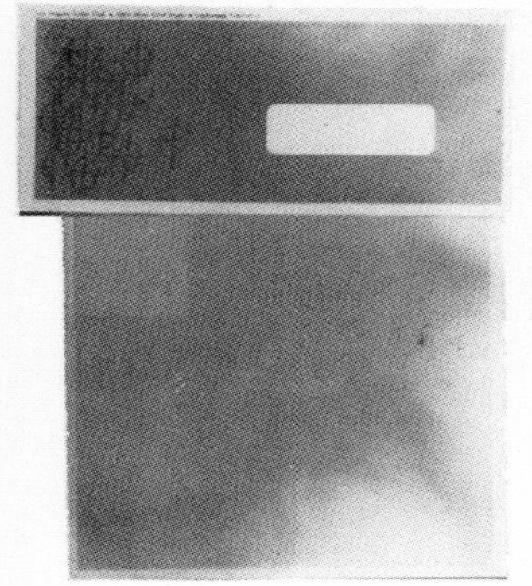

183

184

PRINTS IN PROGRESS — Last year, The Print Club embarked on a unique plan to introduce students in local schools to the graphic arts.
To implement the program, a transportable press adaptable to printing etchings and lithographs was purchased and the service of several well-known local printmakers enlisted. To date, fifty-four demonstrations have been given for some 2,500 students. This year, thanks to generous gifts from interested people and foundations and to the continued cooperation of Jack Bookbinder of the Philadelphia Board of Education, the schedule promises to be even busier, particularly in elementary schools, where woodcut and serigraph sessions are especially successful.
The program, in short, has been a marked success. Besides introducing students to the print media and enabling them to watch accomplished artists at work, it has given these artists an added source of income and stimulated them to do new prints. Wherever possible students assist the artist and, when the medium permits, actually make their own print collectively. To further arouse their interest in the graphics, a collection of prints of all media is displayed at the demonstrations. With Prints in Progress, The Print Club has taken on an important new dimension that, frankly, already justifies the support and active participation of club members. Specifically, volunteer aides to transport artists to and assist them at school demonstrations are always needed, a few words about the program to art teachers and principals known to members will also be appreciated. All inquiries should be addressed to John Borton, Executive Director, Prints in Progress, The Print Club, 1614 Latimer Street, Philadelphia 3. The telephone number to call is PE 5-6090.

185

188

189

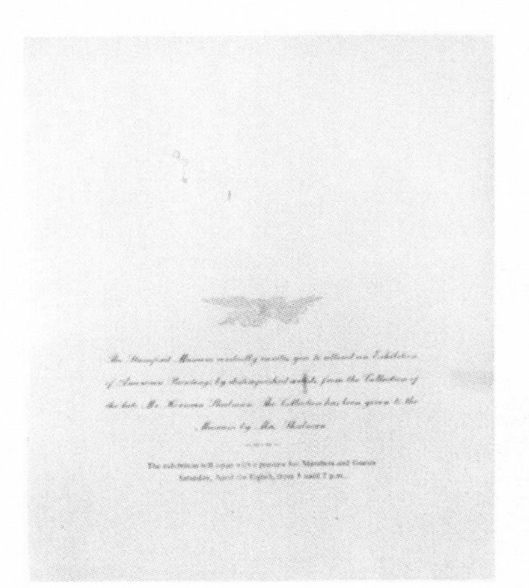

192

The figures change, but the story is the same all year 'round: in St. Louis, audiences prefer KMOX-TV. These reprints from the past twelve issues of Spot Television Rates & Data (SRDS) will give you a number of reasons why.

GENE WILKEY

193

196

189
Designer: Philip Gips
Type Director: Philip Gips
Client/Agency: Life International
Typographer: Typographic Service Co.

190
Designer: Philip Gips
Type Director: Philip Gips
Client/Agency: Bruce Friedlich Advertising
Typographer: Empire Typographers, Inc.

191
Designer: Mort Rubenstein
Type Director: Mort Rubenstein
Client/Agency: CBS
Typographer: Typography Place, Inc.

192
Designer: Robert M. Jones
Type Director: Robert M. Jones
Client/Agency: Stamford Museum
Typographer: Robert M. Jones

193
Designer: Arne Lewis
Type Director: Mort Rubenstein
Client/Agency: KMOX-TV (St. Louis)
Typographer: Rapid Typographers, Inc.
Typography Place, Inc.

194
Designer: Chuck Blas
Type Director: Al Robinson
Client/Agency: Chemstrand Corp./
Doyle, Dane, Bernbach, Inc.
Typographer: Atlas Typographic Service, Inc.

195
Designer: Robert Flynn
Type Director: Robert Flynn
Client/Agency: Doubleday & Co., Inc.
Typographer: Empire Typographers, Inc.

196
Designer: Florence Bezrutczyk
Type Director: Florence Bezrutczyk
Client/Agency: Underwood Corporation
Typographer: Harry Silverstein, Inc.

197
Designer: Gennaro Andreozzi
Type Director: Burt Purmell
Client/Agency: Andrew Geller/
Gilbert Adv. Agency Inc.
Typographer: Provident Typographers, Inc.

190

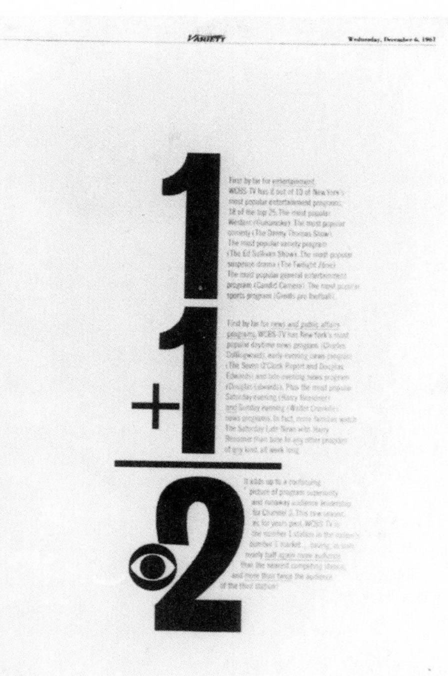

191

194

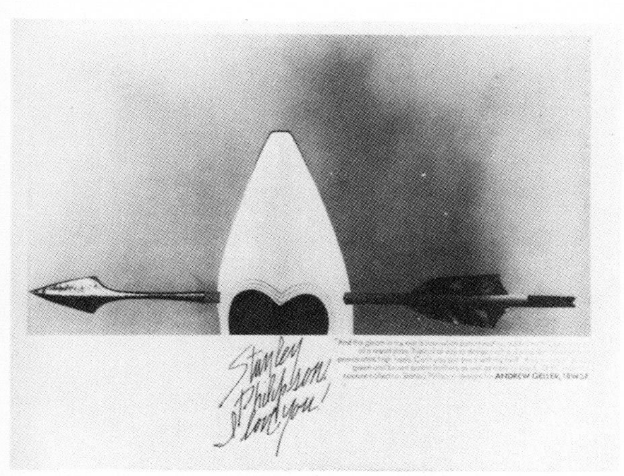

197

198
Designer: Philip Gips
Type Director: Philip Gips
Client/Agency: The International Editions of Time
Typographer: Haber Typographers, Inc.

199
Designer: James Cross
Type Director: James Cross
Client/Agency: Northrop Corporation
Typographer: J. F. Mawson Co.

200
Designer: Herb Reade
Type Director: Herb Reade
Client/Agency: Glamour Magazine-Business Image
Typographer: Master Typo Co.

201
Designer: Sylvia Winter
Type Director: William R. Stone
Client/Agency: Lee Paper Company
Typographer: Sequoia Press

202
Designer: Ivan Chermayeff/Tony Palladino
Type Director: Ivan Chermayeff/Tony Palladino
Client/Agency: School of Visual Arts
Typographer:

203
Designer: Gollin, Bright & Zolotow
Type Director: Gollin, Bright & Zolotow
Client/Agency: Economy Lithograph
Typographer: Vern Simpson

204
Designer: Tom Courtos & J. Schindelman
Type Director: Tom Courtos
Client/Agency: CBS Television Network
Typographer: Typography Place, Inc.

205
Designer: Helen Siegl
Type Director: Claire Van Vliet
Client/Agency: The Print Club of Philadelphia
Typographer: Janus Press

206
Designer: Arthur Boden
Type Director: Arthur Boden
Client/Agency: IBM
Typographer: A. Colish, Inc.

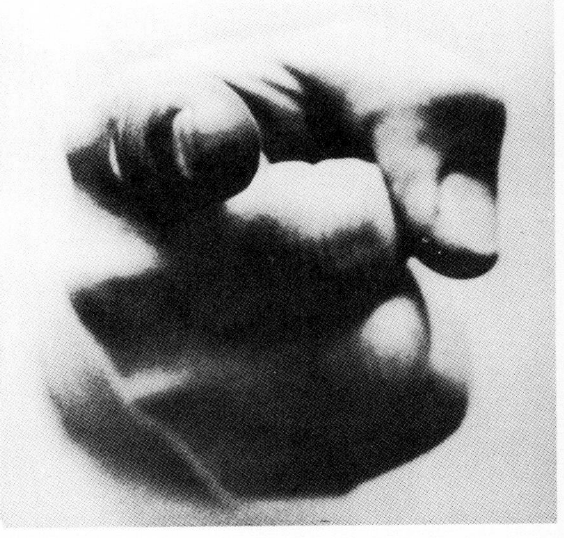

198

202

204

199

Women
are
wonderful
!
but some are more wonderful than others—none more deserving of commendation and documentation than the one million, one-in-a-million young women who see themselves in Glamour. To know them is to sell them! To understand what makes them buy, consider Glamour's word portrait of The Twenties market. This folio of ads projects fifteen reader reasons why The Twenties market leads with strength and the magazine for The Soaring Twenties, Glamour, leads the field.
*

200

201

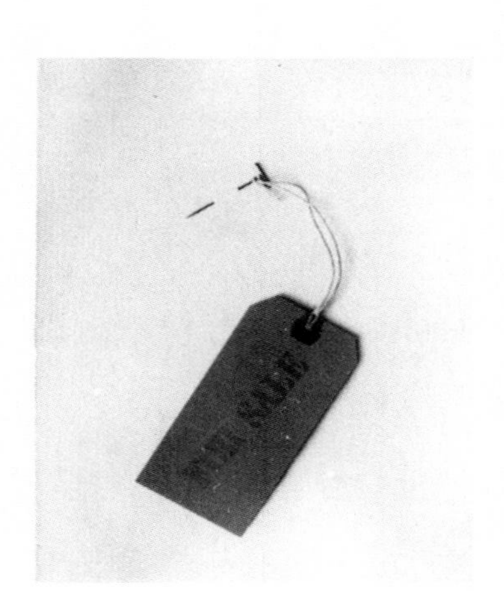

203

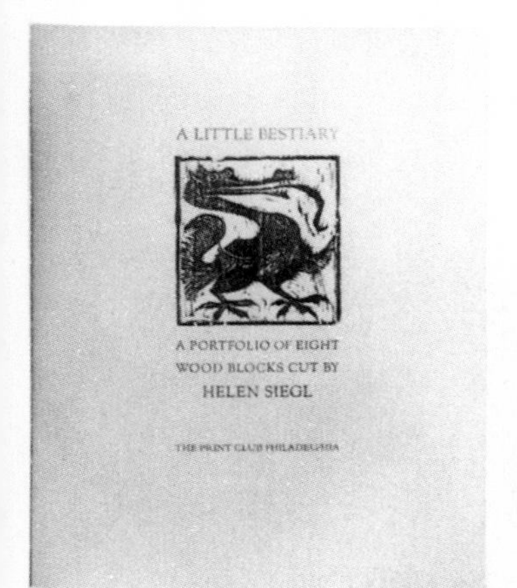

A LITTLE BESTIARY
A PORTFOLIO OF EIGHT
WOOD BLOCKS CUT BY
HELEN SIEGL
THE PRINT CLUB PHILADELPHIA

205

IBM

You can be ahead of time with Inventory Management Simulation

206

208

207
Designer: Morton Goldsholl
Type Director: Morton Goldsholl
Client / Agency: Carolton Envelope Div. Kimberly Clark Corp.
Typographer: Monsen, Inc.

208
Designer: Joe Weston
Type Director: Joe Weston
Client / Agency: Marketing Forces
Typographer: Advertising Designers, Inc.

209
Designer: Sutter & Wartik, Inc.
Type Director: Sutter & Wartik, Inc.
Client / Agency: Theological Seminary
Typographer: Herbick & Held Printing Co.

210
Designer: Carl Brett
Type Director: Carl Brett
Client / Agency: Howarth & Smith
Typographer: Howarth & Smith Monotype Limited

211
Designer: James Cross
Type Director: James Cross
Client / Agency: Northrop Corporation
Typographer: J. F. Mawson Co.

212
Designer: Richard Boland
Type Director: Sheldon Cotler
Client / Agency: Time Inc.
Typographer: The Typographic Service Co.

213
Designer: Milton Ackoff
Client / Agency: Westinghouse Electric Corp.
Typographer: Kurt H. Volk, Inc.

214
Designer: Louis Dorfsman & J. Schindelman
Type Director: J. Schindelman
Client / Agency: CBS Television Network
Typographer: Typography Place, Inc.

207

210

SIGHT

SOUND

THE FACULTY

PRINCETON THEOLOGICAL SEMINARY

Vm huic operi manũ primum admouerem, nihil minus cogitabã, Rex clarissime, quàm scribere quæ Maiestati tuæ offerrentur. Tantum erat animus, rudimenta quædã tradere, quibus formarentur ad ueram pietatẽ, qui aliquo religionis studio tanguntur. Atq; hunc laborem Gallis nostris potissimũ desudabam, quorũ permultos esurire & sitire Christũ uidebã; paucissimos, qui uel modica eius cogni

CHRIST. RELIG. INSTIT. 43

be strong in the grace that is in Christ Jesus. And the things that thou hast heard of me among many witnesses, the same commit thou to faithful men, who shall be able to teach others also. Thou therefore endure

209

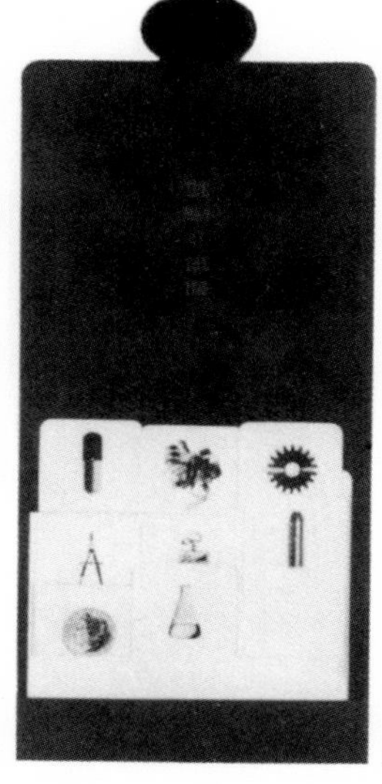

212

211

214

The Path to Leadership

WILLIAM S. PALEY

"Westinghouse Presents"...
Come Again to Carthage
The dramatic story
of a nun
torn between
devotion
to God and
devotion
to her family
Starring Piper Laurie
Ina Balin
Arthur Hill
Joan Hackett
Ann Harding and
special guest star
Maurice Evans
CBS-TV Dec. 8

213

TYPE DIRECTORS CLUB

ACTIVE MEMBERS:

Kelvin J. Arden
Joseph S. Armellino
Arnold Bank
Paul Bennett
Ted Bergman
Amos G. Bethke
Pieter Brattinga
Bernard Brussel-Smith
Aaron Burns
Will Burtin
Burton Cherry
Travis Cliett
Mahlon A. Cline
Martin Connell
Freeman Craw
James A. Cross
Thomas L. Dartnell
Eugene De Lopatecki
O. Alfred Dickman
Louis Dorfsman
Gene Dunn
Eugene M. Ettenberg
Bob Farber
Sidney Feinberg
Charles J. Felten
Bruce Fitzgerald
Glenn Foss
Vincent Giannone
Louis L. Glassheim
William P. Gleason
Edward M. Gottschall, *V. Pres.*
Austin Grandjean
James Halpin
Kurt Hintermann
Hollis W. Holland
Jack Hough
Robert M. Jones
R. Randolph Karch
Wilber King
Zoltan Kiss
Emil J. Klumpp
Edwin B. Kolsby
Ray Komai
Ray Konrad
Richard A. Kroll
Morris Lebowitz
Arthur B. Lee, *Treasurer*
Acy R. Lehman
Clifton Line
Wally Littman
Gillis L. Long
Melvin Loos
John H. Lord
Herb Lubalin
Edgar J. Malecki
Egon Merker
Frank Merriman
Lawrence J. Meyer
Herbert M. Meyers
Francis Monaco
Tobias Moss
Louis A. Musto
Alexander Nesbitt
Martin S. O'Connor
Oscar Ogg
Gerard J. O'Neill
Dr. G. W. Ovink
Eugene P. Pattberg
Jan van der Ploeg
George A. Podorson
Frank E. Powers, *President*
John A. Pfriender
Ernst Reichl
Andrew Roberts
Robert Roche
Edward Rondthaler
Herbert M. Rosenthal
Frank Rossi
Gustave L. Saelens
Lou Sardella
Klaus F. Schmidt
James M. Secrest
William L. Sekuler
Edwin W. Shaar
Martin Solomon
Walter Stanton, *Corres. Sec.*
Herbert Stoltz
Otto Storch
Herb Strasser
William A. Streever
Robert Sutter
David B. Tasler
William Taubin
Anthony Teano
Bradbury Thompson
M. Joseph Trautwein
Abraham A. Versh
Meyer Wagman
Beatrice Warde
Herschel Wartik, *Record. Sec.*
Stevens L. Watts
Joseph F. Weiler
Irving Werbin
Howard Wilcox
Hal Zamboni
Hermann Zapf
Zeke Ziner
Milton K. Zudeck

SUSTAINING MEMBERS:

Advertising Agencies' Service Co., Inc.
American Type Founders
Amsterdam-Continental Types
& Graphic Equipment, Inc.
The Composing Room, Inc.
Cooper & Beatty Ltd.
Craftsman Type Inc.
A. T. Edwards Typography, Inc.
Electrographic Corporation
Empire Typographers, Inc.
Graphic Arts Typographers, Inc.
The Highton Company
Huxley House, Ltd.
King Typographic Service Corp.
Lanston Monotype Company
Oscar Leventhal, Inc.
Linocraft Typographers
Ludlow Typograph Company
Mead Corporation
William Patrick Company, Inc.
Philmac Typographers Inc.
Progressive Composition Company
Rapid Typographers, Inc.
Frederick W. Schmidt, Inc.
Skillset Typographers
Societa Nebiolo
Superior Typographers, Inc.
Tudor Typographers
The Typographic House, Inc.
The Typographic Service Company
Typography Place, Inc.
Kurt H. Volk, Inc.
Westcott & Thompson Inc.

TYPE-HIGH COMMITTEE
Edgar J. Malecki, *Chairman*
Mo Lebowitz, *Design, direct-mail, catalog*
Zeke Ziner, *Design, execution of exhibit*
Arthur Lee, *Financial, tour of exhibit*
Robert Sutter
Edward Gottschall
Frank Orser
James Halpin
Robert Prestyly
Herbert Stoltz
William Griffin
Freeman Craw
George Podorson
Tobias Moss
Richard Beasley
O. Alfred Dickman
Joe Chase

Grateful acknowledgements are made to the following people for their contributions to the success of the exhibition: Edward Rondthaler and his staff at Photo-Lettering, Inc. Robert Jones and RCA Victor Records Division. Dwight Rockwell and his staff of the Mead Gallery of Ideas, Mead Corporation.

CATALOG
Production: John Costa
Photography: Art Green
Typography: Graphic Arts Typographers, Inc.
Printing: Publication Press
Papers: Mead Black & White Dull text, cover

OBJECTIVES OF THE TYPE DIRECTORS CLUB:

To raise the standards of typography and related fields of the graphic arts.

To provide the means for inspiration, stimulation, and research in typography and related graphic arts fields.

To aid in the compilation and dissemination of knowledge concerning the use of type and related materials.

To cooperate with other organizations having similar aims and purposes.

TDC OFFICERS

BOARD OF DIRECTORS 2010–2011

OFFICERS

PRESIDENT

Diego Vainesman, *40N47 Design, Inc.*

VICE PRESIDENT

Graham Clifford, *Graham Clifford Design*

SECRETARY/TREASURER

Matteo Bologna, *Mucca Design*

DIRECTORS-AT-LARGE

Scott Citron, *Scott Citron Design*
Roberto de Vicq de Cumptich, *de Vicq design*
Sean King, *Landor Associates*
Brian Miller, *Brian Miller Design*
Ina Saltz
Jakob Trollbäck, *Trollbäck+Company*
Scott Valins, *Valins + Co.*

CHAIRMAN OF THE BOARD

Charles Nix, *Scott & Nix, Inc.*

EXECUTIVE DIRECTOR

Carol Wahler

BOARD OF DIRECTORS 2011–2012

OFFICERS

PRESIDENT

Diego Vainesman, *40N47 Design, Inc.*

VICE PRESIDENT

Graham Clifford, *Graham Clifford Design*

SECRETARY/TREASURER

Matteo Bologna, *Mucca Design*

DIRECTORS-AT-LARGE

Scott Citron, *Scott Citron Design*
Roberto de Vicq de Cumptich, *de Vicq design*
Jessica Hische
Sean King, *Landor Associates*
Brian Miller, *Brian Miller Design*
Ina Saltz, *Saltz Design*
Scott Valins, *Valins + Co.*

CHAIRMAN OF THE BOARD

Charles Nix, *Scott & Nix, Inc.*

EXECUTIVE DIRECTOR

Carol Wahler

COMMITTEE FOR TDC 57

CHAIRMAN

Roberto de Vicq de Cumptich

CALL POSTER DESIGN (ELECTRONIC)

Mucca Design

COORDINATOR

Carol Wahler

ASSISTANTS TO JUDGES

Victoria A. Bellavia
Graham Clifford
Deborah Gonet
Nana Kobayashi
Juan Marin
Brian Miller
Alexa Nosal
Daniel Pelavin
Diego Vainesman
Nina Vo
Allan R. Wahler
Alex W. White

COMMITTEE FOR TDC² 2011

CHAIRMAN

James Montalbano

CALL CARD DESIGNER

Charles Nix

ASSISTANTS TO THE JUDGES

Chris Andreola
Gary Munch
Maxim Zhukov

NON-LATIN ADVISORY BOARD (NLAB)

NLAB is an informal group of experts that provides guidance and advice to the judges of the TDC type design competitions in assessing typeface designs developed for non-Latin scripts (Arabic, Cyrillic, Greek, Indic, and others).

TDC NON-LATIN ADVISORY BOARD

Gayaneh Bagdasaryan
Misha Beletsky
Martin J. Heijdra
John Hudson
Gerry Leonidas
Ken Lunde
Klimis Mastoridis
Fiona Ross
Hyunguk Ryu
Mamoun Sakkal
Taro Yamamoto
Vladimir Yefimov

COORDINATOR

Maxim Zhukov

TYPE DIRECTORS CLUB PRESIDENTS

Frank Powers, *1946, 1947*
Milton Zudeck, *1948*
Alfred Dickman, *1949*
Joseph Weiler, *1950*
James Secrest, *1951, 1952, 1953*
Gustave Saelens, *1954, 1955*
Arthur Lee, *1956, 1957*
Martin Connell, *1958*
James Secrest, *1959, 1960*
Frank Powers, *1961, 1962*
Milton Zudeck, *1963, 1964*
Gene Ettenberg, *1965, 1966*
Edward Gottschall, *1967, 1968*
Saadyah Maximon, *1969*
Louis Lepis, *1970, 1971*
Gerard O'Neill, *1972, 1973*
Zoltan Kiss, *1974, 1975*
Roy Zucca, *1976, 1977*
William Streever, *1978, 1979*
Bonnie Hazelton, *1980, 1981*
Jack George Tauss, *1982, 1983*
Klaus F. Schmidt, *1984, 1985*
John Luke, *1986, 1987*
Jack Odette, *1988, 1989*
Ed Benguiat, *1990, 1991*
Allan Haley, *1992, 1993*
B. Martin Pedersen, *1994, 1995*
Mara Kurtz, *1996, 1997*
Mark Solsburg, *1998, 1999*
Daniel Pelavin, *2000, 2001*
James Montalbano, *2002, 2003*
Gary Munch, *2004, 2005*
Alex W. White, *2006, 2007*
Charles Nix, *2008, 2009*
Diego Vainesman, *2010, 2011*

TDC MEDAL RECIPIENTS

Hermann Zapf, *1967*
R. Hunter Middleton, *1968*
Frank Powers, *1971*
Dr. Robert Leslie, *1972*
Edward Rondthaler, *1975*
Arnold Bank, *1979*
Georg Trump, *1982*
Paul Standard, *1983*
Herb Lubalin, *1984* (posthumously)
Paul Rand, *1984*
Aaron Burns, *1985*
Bradbury Thompson, *1986*
Adrian Frutiger, *1987*
Freeman Craw, *1988*
Ed Benguiat, *1989*
Gene Federico, *1991*
Lou Dorfsman, *1995*
Matthew Carter, *1997*
Rolling Stone magazine, *1997*
Colin Brignall, *2000*
Günter Gerhard Lange, *2000*
Martin Solomon, *2003*
Paula Scher, *2006*
Mike Parker, *2011*
Erik Spiekermann, *2011*

SPECIAL CITATIONS TO TDC MEMBERS

Edward Gottschall, *1955*
Freeman Craw, *1968*
James Secrest, *1974*
Olaf Leu, *1984, 1990*
William Streever, *1984*
Klaus F. Schmidt, *1985*
John Luke, *1987*
Jack Odette, *1989*

2011 TDC SCHOLARSHIP RECIPIENTS

Mary Anne Di Lillo, *School of Visual Arts, New York*
Sarah Hawkless, *Whanganui School of Design*
Anne Reutinger, *UCLA Design Media Arts*
Walter Shock, *Pratt Institute, New York*
Gregory Skiano, *The Cooper Union School of Art*

2011 STUDENT AWARD WINNERS

STUDENT BEST IN SHOW ($1,000)

Niko Skourtis,
California College of the Arts, San Francisco

SECOND PLACE ($500)

Min Hee Lee, *University of Pennsylvania*

THIRD PLACE ($300)

Cristina Vasquez, *School of Visual Arts, New York*

INTERNATIONAL LIAISON CHAIRPERSONS

UNITED KINGDOM

John Bateson
Bateson Studio
5 Astrop Mews
London W6 7HR

FRANCE

Bastien Hermand
ECV—Ecole de Communication Visuelle
1, rue du Dahomey
75011 Paris

GERMANY

Bertram Schmidt-Friderichs
Verlag Hermann Schmidt Mainz GmbH & Co.
Robert Koch Strasse 8
Postfach 42 07 28
55129 Mainz Hechtsheim

JAPAN

Zempaku Suzuki
Japan Typography Association
Sanukin Bldg., 5th Floor
1-7-10 Nihonbashi-honcho
Chuo-ku, Toyko 104-0041

MEXICO

Prof. Felix Beltran
Apartado de Correos
M 10733 Mexico 06000

SOUTH AMERICA

Diego Vainesman
181 East 93 Street, Apt. 4E
New York, NY 10128

SPAIN

Christian Giribets
Bau, Escola Superior de Disseny
Pujades 118
08005 Barcelona

VIETNAM

Richard Moore
21 Bond Street
New York, NY 10012

TYPE DIRECTORS CLUB

347 West 36 Street
Suite 603
New York, NY 10018
tel: 212-633-8943
fax: 212-633-8944
email: director@tdc.org
www.tdc.org

DESIGN CREDITS

BOOK DESIGN

Christine Celic Strohl, *Mucca Design*
Matteo Bologna, *Mucca Design*

TYPEFACE DESIGN

One Atlantic
Joshua Darden, *Darden Studio*
Mucca Athenian
Matteo Bologna, *Mucca Design*
Jesse Ragan
Mucca Zhanna
Matteo Bologna, *Mucca Design*
Luke Wilhelmi
and OT programming by Georg Seifert

PORTRAITS

Wei Chen

CAROL WAHLER

TDC MEMBERSHIP

LEGEND:

- C CHARTER MEMBER
- H HONORARY MEMBER
- L LIFE MEMBER
- S STUDENT MEMBER
- A ASSOCIATE MEMBER

Huda Smitshuijzen AbiFarès, *2010*
Christopher Abrams, *2009* S
Marcella Accardi-Sanders, *1998* S
Linda Adamo, *2010* S
Jillian Adel, *2010*
Ana Aguilar-Hauke, *2007* S
Anastasia Aizman, *2010* S
Shigeto Akiyama, *2011*
Seth Akkerman, *2008*
Najeebah Al-Ghadban, *2010* S
Zahra Al-Harazi, *2009*
Chris Anderson, *2008*
Gail Anderson, *2011*
Jack Anderson, *1996*
Matthew Anderson, *2011*
Lück Andreas, *2006*
Christopher Andreola, *2003*
Patrick Andresen, *2010*
J. R. Arebalo, Jr., *2003*
Carlos Arriaga, *2010*
Robyn Attaway, *2002*
Bob Aufuldish, *2006*
Eran Bacharach, *2011*
Gayaneh Bagdasaryan, *2007*
Dave Bailey, *2011*
Peter Bain, *1986*
Sanjit Fernandes Bakshi, *2008*
Joshua Bankes, *2006*
Giorgio Baravalle, *2007*
Mark Batty, *2003*
Dawn Beard, *2010*
Katja Becker, *2008*
Misha Beletsky, *2007*
Paul Belford, *2005*
Felix Beltran, *1988*
Ed Benguiat, *1964* L
Kirk Benshoff, *2011*
Jerome Berard, *2010*
Anna Berkenbusch, *1989*
Sam Berlow, *2009*
Ana Gomez Bernaus, *2011*
John D. Berry, *1996*
Peter Bertolami, *1969* L
William Bevington, *2010*
Michael Bierut, *2010*
Klaus Bietz, *1993*
Henrik Birkvig, *1996*
Heribert Birnbach, *2007*
Debra Bishop, *2008*
R. P. Bissland, *2004*
Roger Black, *1980*
Marc Blaustein, *2001*
Anders Bodebeck, *2004*
Matteo Bologna, *2003*
Jason Booher, *2011*
Joao Borges, *2010*
Maury Botton, *2008*
Chris Bowden, *2010*
John Breakey, *2006*
Ed Brodsky, *1980* L
Craig Brown, *2004*
Paul Buckley, *2007*
Michael Bundscherer, *2007*
Bill Bundzak, *1964* L
Christina Burton, *2010* S
Steve Byers, *2010*
Raymond Byrom, *2011* S
Ronn Campisi, *1988*
Christopher Cannon, *2006*
Francesco Canovaro, *2009*
Amid Capeci, *2009*
Wilson Capellan, *2007*
Tomaso Capuano, *2008*
Aaron Carambula, *2005*
Andrea Cardenas, *2011*
Mauro Carichini, *2011*
Paul Carlos, *2008*
Scott Carslake, *2001*
Michael Carsten, *2008*
Matthew Carter, *1988* L
Veronica Caruso, *2011*
James Castanzo, *2008*
Marta Castrosin, *2010*
Ken Cato, *1988*
Jackson Cavanaugh, *2010*
Eduard Cehovin, *2003*
Caitlin Chandler, *2010* S
Yai-Jung Chang, *2008*
Karen Charatan, *2010*
Len Cheeseman, *1993*
Jessie Chiuhui Chen, *2010*
Joshua Chen, *2008*
Pingbo Chen, *2010*
David Cheung, Jr., *1998*
Todd Childers, *2011*
Alexandra Ching, *2009*
Jessica Cho, *2010* S
Eun-Jeong Choi, *2010*
Meagan Choi, *2011* S
Steve Choi, *2011* S
YonJoo Choi, *2010*
Siu Chong, *2010*
Stanley Church, *1997*
Nicholas Cintron, *2003* S
Scott Citron, *2007*
Georgina Clarke, *2011*
John Clarke, *2011*
Graham Clifford, *1998*
Doug Clouse, *2009*
Daniele Codega, *2010*
Emanuel Cohen, *2010* S
Robert Cohen, *2011*
Christopher Çolak, *2010* S
Lynn Cole, *2011*
Angelo Colella, *1990*
Sarah J. Coleman, *2009*
Ed Colker, *1983* L
Nancy Sharon Collins, *2006*
John Connolly, *2010*
Cherise Conrick, *2009*
Jon Contino, *2011*
Nick Cooke, *2001*
Jordan Cooperman, *2011* S
Ricardo Cordoba, *2009*
Madeleine Corson, *1996*
Susan Cotler-Block, *1989*
James Craig, *2004*
Freeman Craw, *1947* C
Kathleen Creighton, *2008*
Benjamin Critton, *2008* S
Andreas Croonenbroeck, *2006*
Ray Cruz, *1999*
Noble Cumming, *2010* S
Micah Currier, *2010*
John Curry, *2009* S
Rick Cusick, *1989*
Scott Dadich, *2008*
Si Daniels, *2009*
Susan Darbyshire, *1987*
Joseph D'Armiento, *2010* S
Kathryn Davenel, *2009* S
Jo Davison, *2007*
Claudia de Almeida, *2010*
Filip de Baudringhien, *2008*
Josanne De Natale, *1986*
Roberto de Vicq de Cumptich, *2005*
Meaghan Dee, *2011* S
Ken DeLago, *2008*
Olivier Delhaye, *2006*
Liz DeLuna, *2005*
Richard R. Dendy, *2000*
Thomas Dennerlein, *2010*
David Dennis, *2010*
Jenna DeNoyelles, *2010* S
Mark Denton, *2001*
Stewart Devlin, *2010*
James DeVries, *2005*
Cara Di Edwardo, *2009*
Tony Di Spigna, *2010*
Chank Diesel, *2005*
Claude A. Dieterich, *1984*
Kirsten Dietz, *2000*
Rachel Digerness, *2011* S
Joseph DiGioia, *1999*
Elisabetta DiStefano, *2007* S
Katie Dominguez, *2011*
Jeremy Dooley, *2011*
Dino Dos Santos, *2004*
Lauren Draper, *2011*
Christian Drury, *2007*
Christopher Dubber, *1985* L
Joseph P. Duffy III, *2003*
Denis Dulude, *2004*
Christopher Dunn, *2010*
Christoph Dunst, *2007*
Andrea Duquette, *2009*
Simon Dwelly, *1998*
Lasko Dzurovski, *2000*
Amanda Elder, *2011* S
Nicholas Eldridge, *2009*
Adly Elewa, *2010* S
Colleen Ellis, *2010*
Garry Emery, *1993*
Marc Engenhart, *2006*
Jan Erasmus, *2008*
Joseph Michael Essex, *1978*
Knut Ettling, *2007*
Florence Everett, *1989* L
John Fairley, *2010*
David Farey, *1993*
Matt Ferranto, *2004*
Vicente Gil Filho, *2002*
Louise Fili, *2004*
Kristine Fitzgerald, *1990*
Julie Flahiff, *2004*
Linda Florio, *2009*
Louise Fortin, *2007*
Dirk Fowler, *2003*
Alessandro Franchini, *1996*
Carol Freed, *1987*
Dinah Fried, *2009* S
Anina Frischknecht, *2011*
Ryan Pescatore Frisk, *2004*
Adrian Frutiger, *1967* H
Dirk Fütterer, *2008*
Evan Gaffney, *2009*

Louis Gagnon, *2002*
Christina Galbiati, *2010* S
Peter Garceau, *2008*
Jeffrey Garofalo, *2006* S
Christof Gassner, *1990*
David Gatti, *1981* L
Alex George, *2010*
Pepe Gimeno, *2001*
Sean Gladden, *2010* S
Lou Glassheim, *1947* C
Howard Glener, *1977* L
Mario Godbout, *2002*
Jamie Godfrey, *2011*
Abby Goldstein, *2010*
Juan Pablo Gomez, *2010* S
Giuliano Cesar Gonçalves, *2001*
Deborah Gonet, *2005*
Hope Miller Goodell, *2008*
Eber Gordon, *2010*
Wesley Gott, *2010* S
Edward Gottschall, *1952* L
Jonathan Gouthier, *2009*
Mark Gowing, *2006*
Norman Graber, *1969* L
Friedrich-Wilhelm Graf, *2008*
Diana Graham, *1984*
Tino Grass, *2007*
Renata Graw, *2011*
Katheryne Gray, *2004*
Pamela Green, *2010*
Joan Greenfield, *2006*
Tim Greenzweig, *2009*
James Grieshaber, *1996*
Robson Grieve, *2010*
Catherine Griffiths, *2006*
Amelia Grohman, *2009*
Katarzna Gruda, *2009*
Rosanne Guararra, *1992*
Nora Gummert-Hauser, *2005*
Shandele Gumucio, *2011*
Raymond Guzman, *2010*
Peter Gyllan, *1997*
Andy Hadel, *2010*
Brock Haldeman, *2002*
Allan Haley, *1978*
Debra Hall, *1996*
Dawn Hancock, *2003*
Sascha Hanke, *2008*
Egil Haraldsen, *2000*
Chantal Harding, *2010*
Lamis Harib, *2011* S
Rob Harrigan, *2009*
Knut Hartmann, *1985*

Lukas Hartmann, *2003*
Lynn Hasday, *2010* S
Katie Hatz, *2010* S
Luke Hayman, *2006*
Oliver Haynold, *2009*
Bonnie Hazelton, *1975* L
Amy Hecht, *2001*
Eric Heiman, *2002*
Karl Heine, *2010*
Anja Patricia Helm, *2008*
Hayes Henderson, *2003*
Michael Hendrix, *2011*
Cristobal Henestrosa, *2010*
Oliver Henn, *2009*
Nitzan Hermon, *2011*
Berto Herrera, *2009*
Luis Herrera, *2011* S
Klaus Hesse, *1995*
Jason Heuer, *2011*
Paul Heys, *2010*
Fons M. Hickmann, *1996*
Jay Higgins, *1988*
Clemens Hilger, *2008*
Bill Hilson, *2007*
Kit Hinrichs, *2002*
Norihiko Hirata, *1996*
Laura Hirschman, *2010* S
Jessica Hische, *2010*
Genevieve Hitchings, *2010*
Michael Hochleitner, *2010*
Michael Hodgson, *1989*
Julia Hoffmann, *2010*
Fritz Hofrichter, *1980* L
Jack Hogg, *2011* S
Michael Hoinkes, *2006*
Janet Holmes, *2011*
Derick Holt, *2011*
Simon Hong, *2011*
Karen Horton, *2007*
Kevin Horvath, *1987*
Kiyomi Hoshikawa, *2009* S
Fabian Hotz, *2001*
Paul Howell, *2010*
Christian Hruschka, *2005*
Anton Huber, *2001*
John Hudson, *2004*
Aimee Hughes, *2008*
Keith C. Humphrey, *2008*
Christine Hunt, *2010* S
Jane Huschka, *2011* S
Grant Hutchison, *2011*
Hyun-Jung Hwang, *2010*
Ryu Hyunguk, *2011*

Luca Ionescu, *2010*
Yuko Ishizaki, *2009*
Donald Jackson, *1978* H
Peter Jacobson, *2010* S
Jessica Jaffe, *2010* S
Torsten Jahnke, *2002*
Mark Jamra, *1999*
Etienne Jardel, *2006*
Alin Camara Jardim, *2011*
Darshan Jasani, *2010* S
Yi-Chieh Jen, *2011* S
Thomas Jockin, *2010*
Helen Joe, *2011*
Becky Johnson, *2010* S
Robert Johnson, *2009*
Giovanni Jubert, *2004*
William Jurewicz, *2004*
Edward Kahler, *2010*
John Kallio, *1996*
Alexandra Kalouta, *2010* S
Simone Kalt, *2010*
I-Ching Kao, *2002*
Milt Kass, *2009*
Diti Katona, *2006*
Kyoko Katsumoto, *2008*
Shigeru Katsumoto, *2008*
Kenna Kay, *2011*
Russell Keer, *2005*
Paula Kelly, *2010*
Ruby Khatcherian, *2011* S
Shirly Khaw, *2010*
Samira Khoshnood, *2011* S
kHyal, *2010*
Elizabeth Kiehner, *2010*
Catherine Kiesler, *2010* S
Shuji Kikuchi, *2008*
Satohiro Kikutake, *2002*
Beom Seok Kim, *2009*
Florence Kim, *2010*
Hoon Kim, *2010*
Hyun Jeong Kim, *2010* S
June Hyung Kim, *2006*
Minah Kim, *2010* S
Sung Joong Kim, *2010*
Yeon Jung Kim, *2005*
Yuna Kim, *2010*
Rick King, *1993*
Sean King, *2007*
Katsuhiro Kinoshita, *2002*
Ian Kirk, *2010* S
Nathalie Kirsheh, *2004*
Susanne Klaar, *2011*
Arne Alexander Klett, *2005*

Brandie Knox, *2008*
Akira Kobayashi, *1999*
Kota Kobayashi, *2010*
Nana Kobayashi, *1994*
Claus Koch, *1996*
Boris Kochan, *2002*
Masayoshi Kodaira, *2002*
Alice Koh, *2009* A
Marcus Koll, *2011*
Linda Kosarin, *2009*
Lauren Kosteski, *2009* S
Thomas Kowallik, *2010*
Rosemary Kracke, *2009*
Dmitry Krasny, *2009*
Markus Kraus, *1997*
Stephanie Kreber, *2001*
Bernhard J. Kress, *1963* L
Gregor Krisztian, *2005*
Jan Kruse, *2006*
Hao In Kuan, *2010* S
Henrik Kubel, *2010*
John Kudos, *2010*
Christian Kunnert, *1997*
Hsin-Ting Kuo, *2010* S
Diana Kusnati, *2011*
Dominik Kyeck, *2002*
Raymond F. Laccetti, *1987* L
Caspar Lam, *2010* S
Melchior Lamy, *2001*
Mindy Lang, *2008*
Bernd Langanke, *2010*
John Langdon, *1993*
Cory Lasser, *2009*
Louis Lavalle, *2010*
Amanda Lawrence, *2006*
Anna Laytham, *2011* S
Erika Lee, *2011*
Julianna Lee, *2011*
Kwangyong Lee, *2010* S
Lillian Lee, *2006* S
Liz Lee, *2010* S
Luis Lee, *2010* S
Yujin Lee, *2011* S
Pum Lefebure, *2006*
Leftloft, *2008*
Taylor Leishman, *2010*
David Lemon, *1995*
Gerry Leonidas, *2007*
Ludovic Leroy, *2009*
Mat Letellier, *2010*
Olaf Leu, *1966* L
Sherry Leung, *2009* S
Joshua Levi, *2010*

Edward Levine, *2011*
Aura Lewis, *2010* S
Grzegorz Lewkowicz, *2011* S
Kevin Ley, *2009*
Gilbert Li, *2010*
Armin Lindauer, *2007*
Domenic Lippa, *2004*
Caren Litherland, *2009*
Jason Little, *2009*
Wally Littman, *1960* L
Alicia Lo, *2010* S
Sascha Lobe, *2007*
Ralf Lobeck, *2007*
Uwe Loesch, *1996*
Oliver Lohrengel, *2004*
Gerry L'Orange, *1991*
John Howland Lord, *1947* H
Chercy Lott, *2008*
Arline Lowe, *2009*
Christopher Lozos, *2005*
Michael Luboa, *2010* S
Alexander Luckow, *1994*
Gregg Lukasiewicz, *1990*
Annica Lydenberg, *2010*
Kathleen Lynch, *2011*
Peter Lytwyniuk, *2011*
Callum MacGregor, *2009*
Stephen MacKley, *2011*
Danusch Mahmoudi, *2001*
Avril Makula, *2010*
Raymond Mancini, *2011* S
Donna Meadow Manier, *1999*
Andrew Mapes, *2010*
Dasha Marcial, *2010* S
Marilyn Marcus, *1979* L
Bernardo Margulis, *2010*
Erik Marinovich, *2010*
Nicolas Markwald, *2002*
Bobby Martin, *2011*
Zoa Martinez, *2009*
Laurel Marx, *2010*
Shigeru Masaki, *2006*
Jakob Maser, *2006*
Klimis Mastoridis, *2010*
Mary Mathieux, *2010*
David Matt, *2010*
Steve Matteson, *2006*
Ted Mauseth 2001
Andreas Maxbauer, *1995*
Loie Maxwell, *2004*
Cheryl McBride, *2009*
Lara McCormick, *2011*
Mark McCormick, *2010*
Rod McDonald, *1995*
Camille McMorrow, *2011* S
Alexa McNae, *2011*
Marc A. Meadows, *1996*
Gabriel Martinez Meave, *2011*
Roland Mehler, *1992*
Niyati Mehta, *2009* S
Cristina Mele, *2010* S
Uwe Melichar, *2000*
Peter Mendelsund, *2010*
Oswaldo Mendes, *2010*
Gretchen Mergenthaler, *2011*
Frédéric Metz, *1985* L
Liz Meyer, *2011*
JD Michaels, *2003*
Jeremy Mickel, *2009*
Natasha Mileshina, *2011*
Abbott Miller, *2010*
Brian Miller, *2006*
John Milligan, *1978* L
Michael Miranda, *1984*
Ralf Mischnick, *1998*
Can Misirlioglu, *2007*
Susan L. Mitchell, *1998*
Derek Moates, *2011* S
Bernd Moellenstaedt, *2001*
Amanda Molnar, *2010* S
Geoffrey Monaghan, *2011*
Sakol Mongkolkasetarin, *1995*
James Montalbano, *1993*
Aoife Mooney, *2010* S
Richard Earl Moore, *1982*
Kevin Moran, *2010*
Minoru Morita, *1975* L
Lars Müller, *1997*
Joachim Müller-Lancé, *1995*
Gary Munch, *1997*
Kara Murphy, *2006*
Jerry King Musser, *1988*
Louis A. Musto, *1965* L
Steven Mykolyn, *2003*
Ed Nacional, *2010*
Miki Nagao, *2009* S
Marc Nahas, *2011*
Norikazu Nakamura, *2009*
Andrea Nalerio, *2008* S
Eduardo Nemeth, *2011*
Titus Nemeth, *2010* S
Cristiana Neri-Downey, *1997*
Helmut Ness, *1999*
Nina Neusitzer, *2003* S
Ulli Neutzling, *2009*
Joe Newton, *2009*
Vincent Ng, *2004*
Lauren Nichols, *2010*
Stefan Nitzsche, *2009*
Charles Nix, *2000*
Michelle Nix, *2008*
Gertrud Nolte, *2001* S
Adam Norbury, *2011* S
Alexa Nosal, *1987*
Thomas Notarangelo, *2010*
Yves Nottebrock, *2011*
Bekah Nutt, *2010* S
Niall O'Kelly, *2010*
Francesa O'Malley, *2008*
Emily Oberman, *2007*
Gaku Ohsugi, *2003*
Akari Oka, *2010* S
Akio Okumara, *1996*
Jeffrey Oley, *2010*
Robson Oliveira, *2002*
Alfred Orla, *2010*
Santiago Orozco, *2010*
Petra Cerne Oven, *2010*
Robert Overholtzer, *1994*
Michael Pacey, *2001*
Michael Padgett, *2009* S
Juan Carlos Pagan, *2010*
Lauren Panepinto, *2010*
Michael Paone, *2010*
Amy Papaelias, *2008*
Enrique Pardo, *1999*
Christine Park, *2010* S
Doon Yoon Park, *2010* S
Philip Park, *2010*
Jonathan Parker, *2009*
Jim Parkinson, *1994*
Karen Parry, *2008*
Donald Partyka, *2009*
Guy Pask, *1997*
John Passfiume, *2010*
Dennis Pasternak, *2006*
Mauro Pastore, *2006*
Neil Patel, *2011*
Gudrun Pawelke, *1996*
Alan Peckolick, *2007*
Daniel Pelavin, *1992*
Taylor Pemberton, *2010* S
Andre Pennycooke, *2008*
Tamaye Perry, *2010*
Giorgio Pesce, *2008*
Steve Peter, *2004*
Max Phillips, *2000*
Stefano Picco, *2010*
Clive Piercy, *1996*
Ian Pilbeam, *1999*
Melissa Pilon, *2010* S
Ebru Pinar, *2010*
Cory Pitzer, *2011* S
Beth Player-DiCicco, *2011*
J. H. M. Pohlen, *2006*
Niberca Polo, *2009* S
Donna Marie Ponferrada, *2011*
Albert-Jan Pool, *2000*
Aleksandar Popovic, *2009* S
Dara Pottruck, *2011*
Neil Powell, *2010*
Alenka Prah, *2008* S
Vittorio Prina, *1988*
James Propp, *1997*
Lars Pryds, *2006*
James Puckett, *2010*
Richard Puder, *2009*
Martin James Pyper, *2007*
Chuck Queener, *2010*
Vitor Quelhas, *2011* S
Marc Rabinowitz, *2011*
Mirna Raduka, *2009* S
Jochen Raedeker, *2000*
Jesse Ragan, *2009*
Erwin Raith, *1967* L
Stephanie Rajalingam, *2010* S
Rathna Ramanathan, *2009*
Sal Randazzo, *2000*
Steven Rank, *2011*
Laetitia Raoust, *2011* S
Susan Raymond, *2011*
Peggy Re, *2011*
Mark Reilly, *2011*
Heather L. Reitze, *2001*
James Reyman, *2005*
Douglas Riccardi, *2010*
Andre Rieberger, *2008*
Claudia Riedel, *2004*
Helge Dirk Rieder, *2003*
Tobias Rink, *2002*
Phillip Ritzenberg, *1997*
Chad Roberts, *2001*
Phoebe Robinson, *2009* S
Claudia Roeschmann, *2007*
Stuart Rogers, *2010*
Camilo Rojas-Lavado, *2011*
Kurt Roscoe, *1993*
Nancy Harris Rouemy, *2007*
Maija Rozenfelde, *2011* S
John Rutner, *2010* A
Erkki Ruuhinen, *1986*
Carol-Anne Ryce-Paul, *2001* S

Michael Rylander, *1993*
Jerald Saddle, *2010* S
Jonathan Sainsbury, *2005*
Mamoun Sakkal, *2004*
Ilja Sallacz, *1999*
Ina Saltz, *1996*
Rodrigo Sanchez, *1996*
Sarah Sansom, *2010*
Michihito Sasaki, *2003*
Nathan Savage, *2001*
Nina Scerbo, *2006*
Hartmut Schaarschmidt, *2001*
Hanno Schabacker, *2008*
H. D. Schellnack, *2009*
Paula Scher, *2010*
Peter Schlief, *2000*
Hermann J. Schlieper, *1987* L
Holger Schmidhuber, *1999*
Hermann Schmidt, *1983* L
Klaus Schmidt, *1959* L
Bertram Schmidt-Friderichs, *1989*
Thomas Schmitz, *2009*
Guido Schneider, *2003*
Werner Schneider, *1987*
Markus Schroeppel, *2003*
Holger Schubert, *2006*
Eileen Hedy Schultz, *1985*
Eckehart Schumacher-Gebler, *1985* L
Robert Schumann, *2007*
Annie Schussler, *2009* S
Peter Scott, *2002*
Leslie Segal, *2003*
Jonathan Selikoff, *2010*
Chris Sergio, *2011*
Thomas Serres, *2004*
Patrick Seymour, *2006*
Graham Shaw, *2010*
Paul Shaw, *1987*
Lisa Sheirer, *2009*
Nick Sherman, *2009*
David Shields, *2007*
Emily Shields, *2010* S
Jeemin Shim, *2010* S
Kyuha Shim, *2011* S
Sangmin Shim, *2010* S
Inessa Shkolnikov, *2008*
Manvel Shmavonyan, *2007*
Philip Shore, Jr., *1992*
Greg Shutters, *2011*
Bonnie Siegler, *2007*
Robert Siegmund, *2001*
Scott Simmons, *1994*
Danni Sinisi, *2010* S

Alanna Siviero, *2011*
Pat Sloan, *2005*
Elizabeth Carey Smith, *2010*
Kevin Smith, *2008*
Laura Smith, *2011*
Steve Snider, *2004*
Jan Solpera, *1985* L
Mark Solsburg, *2004*
Brian Sooy, *1998*
Erik Spiekermann, *1988*
Aymie Spitzer, *2010*
Brooke Sprickman, *2010* S
Frank Stahlberg, *2000*
Adriane Stark, *2011* S
Rolf Staudt, *1984* L
Olaf Stein, *1996*
Adi Stern, *2011*
Alice Stevens, *2011*
Charles Stewart, *1992*
Roland Stieger, *2009* S
Michael Stinson, *2005*
Clifford Stoltze, *2003*
DJ Stout, *2010*
Charlotte Strick, *2010*
Ilene Strizver, *1988*
Hansjorg Stulle, *1987* L
Angela Sucar, *2010* S
Mine Suda, *2008*
Neil Summerour, *2008*
Matt Sung, *2011*
Yun Gui Sung, *2010* S
Monica Susantio, *2010* S
Derek Sussner, *2005*
Zempaku Suzuki, *1992*
Don Swanson, *2007*
Paul Sych, *2009*
Lila Symons, *2010*
Yukichi Takada, *1995*
Yoshimaru Takahashi, *1996*
Kei Takimoto, *2011*
Katsumi Tamura, *2003*
Ai Lin Eida Tan, *2010* S
Chiharu Tanaka, *2010* S
Judy Tashji, *2011* S
Jack Tauss, *1975* L
Pat Taylor, *1985*
Anthony J. Teano, *1962* L
Marcel Teine, *2003*
Nicole Tenbieg, *2010* S
Mitzie Testani, *2007*
Paul Tew, *2009*
Eric Thoelke, *2010*
Anne Thomas, *2007*

Charles Thomas, *2009*
Simone Tieber, *2010*
Eric Tilley, *1995*
Colin Tillyer, *1997*
James Timmins, *2010*
William Tobias, *2010*
Alexander Tochilovsky, *2010*
Laura Tolkow, *1996*
Alessandro Tramontana, *2009* S
Jakob Trollbäck, *2004*
Heidi Trost, *2010*
Niklaus Troxler, *2000*
Minao Tsukada, *2000*
Korissa Tsuyuki, *2009*
Richard Tucker, *2011*
Manfred Tuerk, *2000*
Natascha Tümpel, *2002*
François Turcotte, *1999*
Richard Turley, *2011*
Anne Twomey, *2005*
Andreas Uebele, *2002*
Katsuhiro Ueno, *2011*
Diego Vainesman, *1991*
Elizabeth Ackerman Valins, *2008*
Scott Valins, *2009*
Patrick Vallée, *1999*
Jeffrey Vanlerberghe, *2005*
Darlene VanUden, *2011*
Soren Varming, *2011*
Leonardo Vasquez, *2010*
Panos Vassiliou, *2007*
Rozina Vavetsi, *2011*
Meryl Vedros, *2010* S
Adriana Viaduca, *2009*
Sarah Vinas, *2010*
Patricia Vining, *2009*
Dominique Vitali, *2011*
Frank Viva, *2010*
Nina Vo, *2010*
Nici von Alvensleben, *2010*
Mark Von Ulrich, *2009*
Angela Voulangas, *2009*
Frank Wagner, *1994*
Oliver Wagner, *2001*
Paul Wagner, *2011*
Allan R. Wahler, *1998*
Jurek Wajdowicz, *1980*
Sergio Waksman, *1996*
Elliott Walker, *2011* S
Garth Walker, *1992*
Payton Wallace, *2010* S
Garret Walter, *2010*
Angie Wang, *2010*

Katsunori Watanabe, *2001*
Cardon Webb, *2009*
Harald Weber, *1999*
John Wegner, *2011* S
Amy Weibel, *2011*
Claus F. Weidmueller, *1997*
Sylvia Weimer, *2001*
Craig Welsh, *2010*
Amit Werber, *2010* S
Sharon Werner, *2004*
Alex W. White, *1993*
Bambang Widodo, *2009*
Christopher Wiehl, *2003*
Richard Wilde, *1993*
James Williams, *1988*
Marian Williams, *2010*
Steve Williams, *2005*
Steven Williams, *2011* S
Grant Windridge, *2000*
Conny J. Winter, *1985*
Delve Withrington, *1997*
Burkhard Wittemeier, *2003*
Peter Wong, *1996*
Phillip Wong, *2011* S
Fred Woodward, *1995*
Mary Maru Wright, *2011*
Erni Xavier, *2011*
Wendy Xu, *2011*
Oscar Yañez, *2006*
James Yang, *2008* S
Neal Yang, *2010* S
Carmen Yazejian, *2010*
Henry Sene Yee, *2006*
Vladmir Yefimov, *2007*
Garson Yu, *2005*
Eugene Yukechev, *2011*
Carmile Zaino, *2010*
Hermann Zapf, *1952* H
David Zauhar, *2001*
Zipeng Zhu, *2010* S
Maxim Zhukov, *1996*
Natalie Ziamalova, *2011* S
Roy Zucca, *1969* L

CORPORATE MEMBERS

Diwan Software Limited, *2003*
Grand Central Publishing, *2005*
School of Visual Arts, NY, *2007*

Membership as of May 6, 2011

TYPE INDEX

TYPE, CONT.

INDEX, TDC 32

NEW YORK, NY 10022. FIRST EDITION FIRS
IMPRINT OF HARPERCOLLINSPUBLISHERS
(212) 207-7000 FAX: (212) 207-7654 HARPERDES
LINS.COM DISTRIBUTED THROUGHOUT TH
EAST 53RD STREET NEW YORK, NY 10022 FA
OF CONGRESS CONTROL NUMBER: 2011927198
POSITION OF TYPOGRAPHY 32 ARE MUCCA A
BOOK DESIGN BY CHRISTINE CELIC STRO
CAROL WAHLER EXECUTIVE DIRECTOR TY
SUITE 603 NEW YORK, NEW YORK 10018 TEL
ORG WEBSITE: TDC.ORG PRODUCED BY CR
CRESCENTHILLBOOKS.COM PRINTED IN CHI
CLUB GRATEFULLY ACKNOWLEDGES THE
TRIBUTIONS TO THE SUCCESS OF TDC57, T
DESIGN EDITING: MARTIN COLEMAN JUDGI
CAMPUS EXHIBITION FACILITIES: THE CO
PHOTOS: CATALINA KULCZAR-MARIN TDC5
MUCCA DESIGN TDC² 2011 COMPETITIO
NIX, SCOTT & NIX ON-LINE SUBMISSION